THE MAKING OF THE EUROPEAN MONETARY SYSTEM

DISPOSED OF
BY LIBRARY
HOUSE OF LORDS

Butterworths European Studies is a series of monographs providing authoritative treatments of major issues in modern European political economy.

General Editor

François Duchêne   Director, Sussex European Research Centre, University of Sussex, England

Consultant Editors

David Allen   Department of European Studies, University of Loughborough, England

Hedley Bull   Montague Burton Professor of International Relations, University of Oxford, England

Wolfgang Hager   Visiting Professor, European University Institute, Florence, Italy

Stanley Hoffmann   Professor of Government and Director, Center for European Studies, Harvard University, USA

Hanns Maull   Journalist, Bavarian Radio, Munich. Formerly European Secretary, Trilateral Commission, Paris

Roger Morgan   Head of European Centre for Political Studies, Policy Studies Institute, London, England

Donald Puchala   Professor of Government and Dean, School of International Affairs, Columbia University, USA

Susan Strange   Professor of International Relations, London School of Economics, England

William Wallace   Director of Studies, Royal Institute of International Affairs, London, England

Already Published

An Electoral Atlas of Europe 1968–81 by John Sallnow and Anna John
Europe and World Energy by Hanns Maull
European Environmental Policy: East and West by Josef Füllenbach
European Political Cooperation by D. Allen, R. Rummel and W. Wessels
Monetary Integration in Western Europe: EMU, EMS and Beyond by D. C. Kruse
Europe Under Stress by Yao-su Hu
The Mediterranean Basin: Its Political Economy and Changing International Relations by Glenda G. Rosenthal
Pay Inequalities in the European Community by Christopher Saunders and David Marsden

Forthcoming Titles

The Defence of Western Europe
The EEC and the Developing Countries
European Integration and the Common Fisheries Policy
Political Forces in Spain, Greece and Portugal
Britain in the European Community

The Making of the European Monetary System

A case study of the politics of the European Community

Peter Ludlow

Butterworth Scientific

London   Boston   Sydney   Wellington   Durban   Toronto

All rights reserved. No part of this publication may be reproduced or transmitted in any form or by any means, including photocopying and recording, without the written permission of the copyright holder, application for which should be addressed to the Publishers. Such written permission must also be obtained before any part of this publication is stored in a retrieval system of any nature.

This book is sold subject to the Standard Conditions of Sale of Net Books and may not be re-sold in the UK below the net price given by the Publishers in their current price list.

First published 1982

© Peter Ludlow 1982

British Library Cataloguing in Publication Data

Ludlow, Peter
   The making of the European Monetary System.–
(Butterworths European studies)
   1. Monetary unions   2. Monetary policy – European
Economic Community countries
   332.4′566094   HG221

ISBN 0-408-10728-6

Photoset by Butterworths Litho Preparation Department
Printed by Butler & Tanner Ltd, Frome, Somerset

To JRL and RNL
with respect and gratitude

List of Abbreviations

BIS	Bank for International Settlements
CAP	Common Agricultural Policy
CDU/CSU	German Christian Democratic and Christian Social Parties
CET	Common External Tariff
COREPER	Committee of Permanent Representatives
ECOFIN	Council of Economics and Finance Ministers of the EEC
ECU	European Currency Unit
EIB	European Investment Bank
EMCF	European Monetary Cooperation Fund
EMF	European Monetary Fund
EMS	European Monetary System
EMU	Economic and Monetary Union
EPC	Economic Policy Committee
EUA	European unit of account
EUI	European University Institute
FDP	German Free Democratic Party
FNSEA	Fédération Nationale des Syndicats des Exploitants Agricoles (National Federation of Agricultural Producers' Organisations)
GDP	Gross National Product
GNP	Gross Domestic Product
IDA	Irish Development Agency
IMF	International Monetary Fund
MCAs	Monetary Compensatory Amounts
MTFA	Medium-term financial assistance
NATO	North Atlantic Treaty Organization
NEC	National Executive Committee
OECD	Organisation for Economic Cooperation and Development
PCI	Italian Communist Party
PLP	Parliamentary Labour Party
PSDI	Italian Socialist Democratic Party
PSI	Italian Socialist Party
RPR	Rassemblement pour la République
SDR	Special drawing rights
SPD	German Social Democrats
STMS	Short-term monetary support
TUC	Trades Union Council
UDF	Union pour la Démocratie Française

Preface

Like several of the events it describes, this book is in a certain sense the product of a diplomatic timetable, though in this case the timetable was not the work of governments, so much as of two institutions, the Johns Hopkins Center at Bologna and the European University Institute (EUI) at Florence, which agreed sometime before I arrived on the scene to hold a joint conference on a theme of common concern to North America and Western Europe at Bologna in November 1978. Saddled with the responsibility of proposing a subject, the small steering committee settled for the European Monetary System (EMS); pushed to find an EUI contributor, my colleagues plumped for me. The paper was duly produced and has now appeared in the Johns Hopkins series of Occasional Papers. Discussion both at and after the conference, however, encouraged me to build on this rather modest essay in contemporary history and turn it into a book.

Viewed in a slightly longer perspective, the book is the result of at least two other factors: fascination with the EMS negotiations as they developed in 1978 and a long-standing involvement with the history of European integration and cooperation, which the EUI not only indulged, but encouraged and extended. So important has this latter preoccupation been in shaping my approach and influencing my judgements that I feel I ought to begin by acknowledging the help of those, particularly the British Academy, the German Academic Exchange Service, the Leverhulme Trust, the Nuffield Foundation and, through the European University Institute, the European Commission, who have enabled me to travel as widely and stay as long in all the countries concerned as any historian of western European integration must, and who thus ensured that I had a network of contacts throughout Western Europe and North America that I could put to good advantage when I set about writing this book. Research for the book itself was financed by the EUI, firstly from a small fund set aside for the EUI–Bologna conference referred to above, and latterly by a grant given for the Integration Project by the European Commission.

For reasons that are explained in the Note on Sources, I cannot list the majority of those, inside and outside governments, who have spared me their time and recollections or given or lent me their documentary materials. Without their help, needless to say, this book could not have been written, and I trust that I have respected the confidence that they so generously placed in me. Of those whom I can name, one – Sir Andrew Shonfield – was in a category all on his own. His interest fuelled mine in almost daily conversations in the latter part of 1978; his expertise and scepticism spared me from elementary blunders when I began to prepare the paper and then the book; his knowledge of how Arnold Toynbee and others had prepared the Chatham House Surveys guided me on a venture into history more contemporary than anything I had written before, and, it might be added, encouraged me to develop the idea of producing other, similar volumes at and through the new Centre for European Policy Studies at Louvain-la-Neuve and Brussels, the plans for which he also influenced greatly. In addition to Andrew Shonfield, several other professional economists have, sometimes without knowing it perhaps, given me the crash course in international economics and finance that I so desperately needed. I would particularly like to thank Luigi Spaventa, Niels Thygesen and Robert Triffin, all of whom read the book in typescript. I am also extremely grateful to Tom de Vries of the International Monetary Fund and Bob Solomon of Brookings, who discussed some of the issues raised by the EMS with me, and who enabled me to meet several key figures on both sides of the Atlantic. The typescript was also read by two of the editors of the series, William Wallace and François Duchêne, and partly as a result of their help, but also it must be said because of the understanding and patience of Peter Richardson of Butterworths, I have not been forced into the savage cutting of a longer than expected text that seemed probable at one point.

Several other persons have given me invaluable help of other sorts. Kate Hobbs of Chatham House photocopied the more important press cuttings on the EMS, while Beatrijs de Hartogh, Maureen Lechleitner and Bonnie Bonis transformed interminable tapes, amateurish typing and wretched handwriting into a respectable typescript. Finally, my family merit both thanks and sympathy. My wife was all that the wives of authors are supposed to be only more so, while Piers, Rachel and Ivan forwent a family holiday and a great deal else without complaining – well only a little.

Blackheath Park

Villa Montemecolli
Impruneta
May 1981

Note on Sources

The primary sources on which this book is based fall into three principal categories:

(1) newspapers, journals and other printed primary materials;
(2) interviews;
(3) documentary evidence provided by participants in the events.

As far as these last two types of material are concerned, I have usually not quoted directly, but even when I have, I have been careful not to attribute quotations, except where, as in the case of a document like the final report of the Economic Policy Committee, circulation was so wide that it would be impossible for anybody to pin down the donor of the material with any degree of certainty. Several of my informants were willing to be referred to by name, but the great majority wished both the oral and documentary information with which they provided me to remain unattributed. Rather than introduce two categories of informant into the text, I have therefore avoided attributions altogether. Suffice it to say that information gleaned from these sources has come from all over the geographical area covered by this book, from Washington to Bonn, from Oslo to Rome.

Most if not all the printed sources can be deduced from the notes. The material can, however, be conveniently divided into five main types:

(1) *Press cuttings*. The writing of this book would have been incomparably harder had it not been for the systematic work carried out by two libraries: the Press Library of the Royal Institute of International Affairs, London, and the Library of the Italian Senate. The cuttings collected by the former, which are systematically arranged under subject headings, were taken from a significant cross-section of the British, Western European and American press. Not the least of the merits of this collection is that it enables the scholar to compare different versions of the same story in newspapers published on the same day throughout the Community and the United States. The three-volume collection of press cuttings on the EMS put together by the 'l'Ufficio documentazione e ricerca del Servizio studi' of the Italian Senate contains verbatim records of speeches by the Italian prime minister, the minister of the treasury, the governor of the central bank and others, as well as a large

number of newspaper articles in the Italian press on the EMS in the second half of 1978 and the early months of 1979. Although it would be dangerous to rely entirely on press cuttings of the kind assembled by both Chatham House and the Italian Senate, the work carried out by these institutions, the quality of which can be deduced if in addition one makes a systematic survey of certain journals, is invaluable to the researcher into contemporary history.

(2) *Systematic readings of certain newspapers.* As a control on and supplement to the press cuttings referred to above, I have also attempted to carry out a systematic reading of certain key newspapers: the *Financial Times*, *Frankfurter Allgemeine Zeitung*, *Le Monde*, *Il Corriere della Sera*, *Wall Street Journal*, the *New York Times*, and *The Economist*. I have also used the twice-weekly press agency publication, *European Report*, throughout the period covered by this book.

(3) *Parliamentary proceedings.* For details see notes.

(4) *Reports by international organizations, central banks, etc.* For present purposes, the most important reports in this category have been the *Annual Survey* of the IMF, the six-monthly *Economic Outlook* of the OECD, the *European Economy*, published by the Directorate-General for Economic and Financial Affairs of the Commission of the European Communities, the *Monthly Bulletin of the Bundesbank*, the *Federal Reserve Bulletin*, and the publications of the other central banks in the North Atlantic area.

(5) *Press releases, speeches, etc.* Government departments, international organizations, etc. also make available the texts of speeches by ministers and officials. Amongst those that have provided material useful for the present book are the European Commission, the United States Treasury and the Bundesbank. For the student of contemporary European Community affairs, *Europa-Archiv* is an invaluable source for documents of this type, since the majority of the issues include a documentary section reproducing material provided by government and other agencies.

Contents

Actors and Issues

The aim of this book is to analyse the origins of the European Monetary System (EMS), which came into existence in March 1979. Given the nature of the subject, technical discussions between experts about the advantages and disadvantages of different approaches to monetary integration inevitably occupy an important place in the narrative. The principal concern of the book is, however, not with these technical issues, some of the most prominent of which have in the event scarcely justified the investment in time and energy that was made in them in the summer of 1978, but with the political considerations that constantly intruded into even the most expert discussions and the political consequences that flowed from the development and outcome of the negotiations.

Taken as an episode in the long history of attempts to forge a Western European monetary union, the negotiations that preceded the creation of the EMS are undoubtedly interesting, but it is still too early to assess how long these particular arrangements will last, or what influence this one chapter may have on those that follow. Even if the EMS were to fail, however, the events that preceded its creation would remain relevant and important, because of the political issues that the proposal raised and the political forces that helped to turn it into a reality. David Calleo recently remarked that the international monetary system is in some measure a metaphor of the international system in general[1]. Whether or not this maxim is universally applicable, it can certainly be used in relation to the making of the EMS. For a year or more the latter became the central question in the politics of the European Community. The motives and conduct of those who sponsored the idea provide a clue to what they wanted to make of the Community in general and how they envisaged it in the international system. The reactions of those who were obliged to decide on the merits of a scheme, the timing of which many of them found surprising, and the details of which they had not helped to formulate, throw light on their understanding of the nature and purposes of the Community, their assessment of their national or sectional interests and their order of priorities in domestic and international affairs. A study of the origins of the EMS should, in other words, provide a vantage point for the study of the Community as a whole in the years 1977 and 1978.

The particular reasons that prompted first Roy Jenkins, then Helmut Schmidt to put monetary integration once again in the forefront of

Community politics will be discussed in detail in chapters 2 and 3. The purpose of this chapter is to set the scene in a more general sense by describing previous attempts to advance European monetary integration, by providing a brief sketch of the institutional framework within which the negotiations were to develop, and by discussing some of the more important weaknesses of the Community on the eve of the period with which this book deals and for which the EMS was intended to be at least a partial palliative.

1.1   The search for EMU before 1977

The history of the discussions about economic and monetary union (EMU) prior to 1976 has recently been written at some length and with considerable skill by Dr Tsoukalis, and there is therefore no need to give more than the briefest recapitulation here[2]. If, like Dr Tsoukalis, we take as our starting point the formation of the Community in 1958, the story can be divided into four principal phases. The first, stretching from 1958 until 1969, consisted essentially of prolegomena: ideas that were floated around more or less seriously, but that were not given any practical outlet. The period is not without its significance, because, as subsequent chapters will show, the enthusiasm for monetary integration of several of those who played a leading role in the EMS negotiations was first kindled during these years and, in the case of Robert Triffin at least, still earlier, but in a western world in which the monetary system established at Bretton Woods in 1944 continued to operate relatively well, those who saw the system's defects and felt that reform was needed remained a minority.

The second period, inaugurated by the meeting of Community heads of government and state at The Hague in December 1969 and terminated by the international monetary crisis in the summer of 1971, was the period in which the first serious efforts were made to achieve EMU. However, for reasons that will be analysed more systematically shortly, the task proved beyond the abilities of the Werner Committee, which was charged to give substance to the broad plan for monetary union sketched out at The Hague summit itself. Despite continuing declarations of intent, the venture so enthusiastically embarked upon in 1969 shuddered to a halt in the international monetary crisis of 1971.

The stoppage proved only temporary, however, and in December 1971, following the Smithsonian Agreement, which restored the semblance if not the reality of order to international monetary affairs, the Community set out once again on a third phase, which lasted until January 1974. The principal achievement of these years was the creation of the Snake, an exchange rate regime that was agreed at the beginning of 1972, and that was intended to keep Community currencies more closely linked with one another than they would have been had each moved separately within the relatively broad 'tunnel' established during the meetings at the Smithsonian Institute in Washington at the end of 1971. Countries participating in the Snake were obliged to keep their currencies within margins determined by a parity/grid, an arrangement under which each was assigned a bilateral central rate with every other currency involved and allowed to fluctuate around this rate within margins fixed at 2.25% either way. If and when a pair of currencies reached the outer limits of their bilateral margins, the central bank in each country was required to intervene to correct the situation. The system was inaugurated by the original six members states in April 1972, and they were joined almost immediately by the United Kingdom (and Ireland), Denmark and Norway, the latter still being at this stage a candidate for admission into the Community itself in 1973. The new arrangements ran into immediate trouble however. A wave of currency speculation built up against the dollar and sterling, and the pound left the Snake within eight weeks of joining. Shortly afterwards, in February 1973, the lira was forced to leave, while in March of that year the DM was revalued by 3%. A fresh revaluation of the DM took place in June 1973 and this was followed by revaluations of the Dutch guilder in September and the Norwegian krone in November of that year. (Like the Swedish krone, the Norwegian currency was allowed to participate in the exchange rate regime, despite the negative vote in the referendum on Community membership in 1972). Finally, in January 1974, the French franc left the system and M. Giscard d'Estaing, who was still finance minister at the time, pronounced the Snake 'un animal de la préhistoire monétaire européenne'[3].

Despite these defeats and disappointments, which were openly acknow-ledged at the meeting of heads of state and government in Paris in December 1974, and which prompted them to abandon the official target of EMU by 1980, hopes of increased monetary integration persisted into a fourth phase. Thus in 1974 itself, the French government outlined a new approach in the Fourcade plan[4]. In March 1975, a group set up by the Commission and chaired by M. Marjolin produced a report that, though extremely pessimis-tic about the prospects of complete union, proposed several short-term measures that might eventually pave the way for more ambitious initiatives[5]. Later in the same year, the French attempted once again to link their currency to the prehistoric monster, while in December 1975 the Belgian prime minister, M. Tindemans, in his report on European Union, developed a series of proposals that would, he hoped, strengthen the Snake and help those countries that were still outside to rejoin it in due course[6]. There were fresh reminders of the difficulties – many would have said the impossibility – of the task in March 1976, when the French opted out of the Snake yet again, and in the autumn when there were further realignments of the currencies that remained within. But the hope that something might still be done to bridge the gap between the Snake and the weaker currencies surfaced once again in the latter half of 1976 in a Dutch proposal, devised very largely by

Conrad Oort but dubbed with the name of the Dutch minister of finance Dr Duisenberg, that envisaged the gradual association of non-Snake countries with the DM and its partners through a system of target zones, within which the central banks in the weaker countries would attempt to keep their currencies, but which they would not be obliged to hold to if the cost in interventions threatened to become too heavy[7]. In December 1976, however, this plan too was consigned to the limbo of good, but unfulfilled intentions in which so many of its predecessors mouldered.

The reasons for the failures and disappointments of previous attempts to push Western Europe towards monetary union are numerous and complex. Four factors seem particularly significant however. First was the scepticism of many of those charged with devising plans, and still more of those in central banks and elsewhere who would have been responsible for implementing them, about the feasibility or relevance of a strategy that aimed to unite Europe through what seemed to be in their eyes a premature and unnatural coupling of disparate currencies. The second factor was political, namely the unwillingness of some of the leading actors to accept the political and institutional consequences of monetary union. The third factor was the impact of the international monetary crisis, which made efforts to create a regional zone of stability difficult if not impossible, and the fourth was the divisive effect of global inflation and recession on the European economy.

Scepticism about the strategy chosen by the heads of state and government at their meeting at The Hague in December 1969 surfaced quickly in the discussions that the summit meeting initiated and was to become ever more marked as the 1970s progressed. The critics, loosely and somewhat inappropriately described as 'economists' in order to distinguish them from the 'monetarists' (who argued that monetary integration could act as the catalyst of economic and political union), were not and are not confined to one particular school or country. Both Keynesians and market economists could and did argue in different ways and with different priorities in view that the exchange rate road to economic union was impracticable and undesirable. There is no need here to enter into a detailed discussion of the criticisms that were advanced against the monetarist strategy, but a brief review of two contrasting and mutually exclusive approaches can serve as an introduction to issues and debates that will re-emerge frequently in the main body of the book. The first is to be found in the policies and statements of the Bundesbank, which were conveniently chronicled and expounded in an essay by its president, Dr Emminger, that appeared only weeks before Mr Jenkins relaunched the debate about monetary union in 1977[8]. The second can be seen, *inter alia*, in a 'counter-report' that John Pinder and Dr Tsoukalis submitted to a conference in Brussels in June 1977, the same month in which Dr Emminger's essay was published[9].

As Dr Emminger's essay shows, the antipathy of the Bundesbank towards a fixed exchange rate regime antedated the Hague summit of 1969. It had its roots in the absolute priority that the German authorities gave to internal stability. Exchange rate policy was a means to further or safeguard this objective rather than an end in itself. Faced therefore by the dilemma, which first became apparent in the mid-1950s, that under a fixed exchange rate regime Germany tended to accumulate substantial balance of payment surpluses, which in turn threatened internal monetary stability, the authorities had come increasingly to the conclusion that revaluations were preferable to imported inflation and, in the end, that floating was best of all. When, therefore, the Werner Committee was set up to prepare a programme implementing the strategy outlined at the Hague summit in 1969, the Bundesbank representatives were amongst the more prominent exponents of the 'economists' critique. The events that followed soon afterwards in the real world only served to strengthen their hostility and when, eventually, in March 1973 the Bretton Woods system finally collapsed, few tears were shed in Frankfurt. On the contrary, the authorities' control over money supply could now, it seemed, be regained and 'Germany was able to cut itself loose from the international inflation convoy, after having been inexorably tugged along for three years'[10]. Even the Snake seemed an unwelcome encumbrance: 'membership of the Snake limits Germany's protection against external monetary disturbances, because the members of this regional system are still obliged to intervene within fixed margins'[11]. Short, therefore, of a dramatic, Damascus-type conversion of the governments – and people – in the other member states to the precepts and practice of the German economic gospel, the Bundesbank did not believe that a fresh move towards linking Community currencies was either feasible or desirable.

Nor was this simply the Bundesbank's view. There were those in Bonn who were prepared on occasions to argue that the need for political solidarity with Germany's partners should take precedence over the efforts to seal the German economy off from the contagious diseases to which its neighbours were vulnerable. Mr Schmidt himself, for example, had been consistently better disposed towards the Snake than Dr Emminger and his colleagues, and when the French franc had come under severe and in the end fatal pressure in 1973–74 and 1976, he had gone to considerable lengths to pledge his support for the French authorities' efforts to keep the franc within the system[12]. But neither Mr Schmidt nor the Foreign Ministry nor German exporters, who might have been expected to complain about their loss of competitiveness, questioned the fundamentals of the Bundesbank's arguments. There were, after all, sound historical reasons for regarding inflation as the principal threat to German political stability, and there was no less impressive evidence in the more recent history of the Federal Republic that the pursuit of internal stability, even at the cost of a steady upward movement of the DM, did not damage German prosperity. There was little inclination or need therefore to tamper with policies that had served the country so well, and that if altered might disturb so many ghosts from the past.

The assumptions underlying the second, critical approach to proposals for monetary union referred to above, namely the paper by John Pinder and Dr Tsoukalis, were also widely shared, particularly but, as chapter 3 will confirm, by no means exclusively in Britain. The preoccupation of this group was not in the first instance with the preservation of internal stability, but with the wasteful under-utilization of human and material resources that seemed bound to result from excessive concentration on exchange rate stability. To be fair to both the authors and their allies, the criticisms that they advanced in 1977 were considerably more restrained in their advocacy of Keynesian-type remedies than some of the contributions from those who had assumed a similar order of priorities earlier in the decade. The experiences of the British and the Italians between 1974 and 1976 precluded any facile advocacy of reflation and currency depreciation as remedies for recession and inflation. As John Pinder himself noted elsewhere: 'Britain, Italy and perhaps France must accept their share of the blame for their excessive inflation and deficits and for becoming points of weakness in the Western economic system'[13]. That said, the monetarist approach, both in the narrow sense of the term used in the context of the debate about EMU and in the broader and more usual sense employed to cover the views of the Bundesbank, Milton Friedman and sundry others, was 'an economic strategy unsuited to the modern economy'[14]. Its fundamental weakness stemmed from the failure of its proponents to recognize that 'price stability and economic growth depend, not just on policy preferences in relation to global demand, but on the behaviour of individuals and groups and on the rigidities of economic structure which can be managed and adjusted only by intervention of a more detailed kind'. The details of the alternative strategy that they outlined in this paper, which anticipated, and may even have influenced, some of the political and institutional ideas that Mr Jenkins was to advance in his Florence and Bonn speeches later in the same year, need not detain us at this point. Suffice it to say that, despite the authors' recognition of the unlikelihood or impossibility of a collective Community leap into federalism, a significant transfer of functions and powers to Community level, as well as a substantial transfer of resources, would be necessary before the 'permanent locking of parities' could become a reality.

The lack of a consensus about the wisdom of the monetarist strategy was already a major handicap in the implementation of the Hague summit's intentions. The task was made still more difficult, however, by the evident unwillingness of the French to accept the political and institutional implications of a commitment to monetary union[15]. The French problem, less than two years after the resignation of General de Gaulle and at a time when his supporters were anyway having to come to terms with M. Pompidou's change of front on the British question, was predictable. In the terms in which it was defined in 1971, it was also transient, since with the reorganization of the institutional structure of the Community, which was more or less completed by the end of 1974, it was no longer inevitable or even likely that a Community monetary authority would be a supranational body beyond the control of the member states.

Even in 1971, the importance of French resistance on this front was quickly eclipsed by the third of the factors referred to above, the eruption of a series of international monetary explosions that made talk of a long-term future of currency stability seem remote and Utopian to politicians and officials, whose principal concern was more than ever to erect defences against short-term threats[16]. The significance of these monetary disturbances was not, however, limited to the immediate havoc that they wrought. Cumulatively they destroyed the Bretton Woods system and, in most quarters at any rate, the assumptions and priorities that had underpinned it. The dollar was dethroned and floating exchange rates became respectable. In a system that depended so heavily on the confidence and expectations of those who held funds, it became increasingly unrealistic to believe that the authorities would possess either the resources or the conviction to intervene in sufficient strength to defend a particular exchange rate. The Snake, in the reduced form that it eventually assumed between and after the successive French departures, might be kept more or less intact, but, as the events of 1972, 1973, 1974 and 1976 showed, the larger European currencies on the borders of the DM zone – the pound, the French franc and the Italian lira – became targets of speculation on such a scale that the will to resist of the central banks concerned was progressively undermined. There were always some who argued alternative strategies, but the change in international fashion that the monetary disturbances of the decade induced and that was formally registered in the revised Articles of Agreement of the International Monetary Fund in the spring of 1976[17] could only reinforce the scepticism or despair of European officials anxious or instructed to prepare plans for EMU.

Even the monetary disorders of the late 1960s and early 1970s pale into insignificance, however, by comparison with the fourth factor, namely the impact of global inflation and recession on the European economy. The causes of the world economic crisis of the 1970s lie outside the scope of this introductory chapter. But its consequences are of central significance for the book as a whole. It affected every economy, and even the performance of 'the strong' was weak by comparison with what they had achieved in the previous decade. Growth rates and investment dropped and unemployment increased throughout the Community. The principal significance of the crisis is, however, to be found in its brutal exposure of differences in the capacity of individual economies to adapt to the challenge that it presented. The extent of the divergence between the member states has been richly documented in a recent publication by the Directorate-General for Economic and Financial Affairs in the Commission entitled *Changes in Industrial Structure in the European Economies since the Oil Crisis, 1973–78*.[18]. There is clearly no space in this book to do justice to the wide range of evidence that this report presents, but a brief summary of some of its principal conclusions is apposite.

The most obvious indications of divergence are to be found in balance of payments trends, prices and incomes movements and exchange rates. It is one of the virtues of this report however that this macroeconomic evidence is included primarily as background information to a remarkably thorough and detailed sectoral analysis, which amongst other things serves as a salutary antidote to total despair on the part of the weak, some of whose industries managed to perform well by Community standards as a whole, or to overconfidence on the part of the strong, all of whom had suspect points in their armoury. When every allowance is made for exceptions to the general rule, however, the picture that emerges in both the macroeconomic chapter and the chapters devoted to discussion of the different sectors bears more resemblance to the final classification in a Western European subgroup in the World Cup qualifying competition, with Germany firmly at the top and the United Kingdom and Italy no less securely at the bottom, than to an association of more or less equal states progressing harmoniously and happily towards union.

By the mid-1970s, Germany had begun to move out of the European league into a group of world economic powers of which the only other members were the United States and Japan. The foundations of German power were numerous and complicated. As the Commission report suggests, they included greater productivity in the sectors most threatened by international competition (steels, textiles, clothing, etc.), a high proportion of the most dynamic industries (equipment goods, chemicals and agri-food industries), capacity to specialize and in particular to concentrate on products with a high technology input and, more generally, the ability to preserve sufficient social cohesion to contain internal production costs within reasonable limits, and the good fortune of a favourable geographical position and trade networks that were firmly established before the recession began. The strength of the German economy as a whole was mirrored by the performance of the DM on the foreign exchange markets. As the table in Appendix 2A shows, the mark rose by over 30% against the currencies of the Federal Republic's 23 major trading partners between the end of 1972 and the first half of 1977. The appreciation against the dollar, the French franc and still more the pound and the lira was well above this average. The confidence in the DM and the German economy that these figures imply had also found expression in increasing pressure on the German authorities to allow the mark to be used as an international reserve currency. The authorities, who had come to accept and even to prefer a strong upward movement of their currency to inflationary stability, resisted this particular tendency with great vigour. The cautionary tales of what had happened to sterling and the dollar were too vivid for any central bank to want to embark on the same road from responsibility to ruin. As *Figure 1.1* shows, however, protestations of indifference or hostility were not enough, and by 1977 the DM, though not in any way a rival to the dollar, had taken over the position in the international monetary system that sterling had occupied at the beginning of the decade[19].

Figure 1.1 *Composition of the foreign exchange reserves of selected central banks (end of year)**

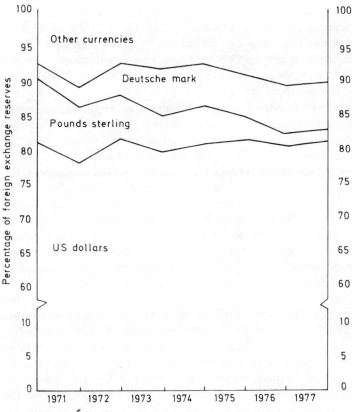

* Figures from 76 central banks, accounting for over two-thirds of the world's foreign exchange reserves at end-1977.
Source: International Monetary Fund. *Monthly Report of the Deutsche Bundesbank*, **31** (11) p. 34

The only economies that had more or less kept up with West Germany's, but that were disqualified from joining the big league on the grounds of size, were the three Benelux states. Productivity gains at about 4.5% on average between 1973 and 1977 were on a par with Germany's but inflation was higher, and the cost of keeping up in terms of unemployment was particularly heavy in Belgium. The other small Community member of the Snake, Denmark, was still *per capita* the richest country in the Nine, but its performance during the recession was in several important respects markedly inferior to that of its Snake partners, with higher than average inflation rates, a deteriorating balance of payments and an increase in the percentage of the active population unemployed – less than Belgium's, but a good deal more than either Germany's or the Netherlands'. In fact, despite its strong and growing dependence on Germany, Denmark still seemed to belong more to Scandinavia than to Western Europe, in terms of its economic performance and the political and social priorities that underlay it. As the crisis of the Scandinavian welfare model deepened, the currencies of all three northern members of the Snake – Sweden, Norway and Denmark – came under increasing pressure, leading to a series of devaluations from the summer of 1976 onwards and, eventually, in August 1977, to the departure of the Swedish krone from the Snake[20].

The difficulties of Denmark and her Scandinavian neighbours notwithstanding, the problems of the four remaining Community states that remained outside the Snake were of quite a different order from those of any of the Snake economies. They were a heterogeneous bunch. In the case of Ireland, for example, the world economic crisis only served to transform the race to catch up into a not entirely successful attempt to avoid falling further behind. The other three – France, Britain and Italy – were of roughly comparable size, but this was almost all that they had in common other than their inferiority to Germany and her Benelux partners. France, whose economy had by most conventional measures outstripped the United Kingdom's in the late 1960s, continued to fare significantly better than either Britain or Italy. It was even in some respects a match for Germany. GDP, for example, grew faster in every year save one between 1973 and 1977 and the rise in industrial production almost kept pace in percentage terms during the same period. As in every other country, investment dropped, particularly in the private sector, but it remained relatively high and was concentrated furthermore on modernization and rationalization. These encouraging features of the French experience between 1973 and 1977 must however be considered alongside other developments that were less cheerful and that suggested that France was still by no means a strong economy. Inflation, for example, was almost twice as high as Germany's for the whole of the period, and the balance of payments was constantly in deficit. Particular sectors too were conspicuously vulnerable by comparison with Germany or the Benelux countries: chemicals, steel, textiles and the agri-food industries being the most obvious examples. The Commission report described the French condition as 'uncertain' and 'fragile' and, to judge by the performance of the French franc on the foreign exchange markets during this period, it was an opinion that was widely shared.

If the French economy was fragile, the British and Italian economies were in a much worse condition for the whole of the mid-1970s. The failure of the United Kingdom to keep up with the rest of the Community economies had long been apparent. In certain respects, therefore, the recession only highlighted trends that were already well known. The extent of the deterioration that occurred during the critical years was nonetheless dramatic and disturbing. On almost every calculation, the United Kingdom came bottom of the list – or top, where being top was the opposite of what was desired, as for example in the rate of inflation. The latter provides a particularly graphic indication of the way in which the world crisis accelerated the United Kingdom's relative decline. Britain, it should be recalled, had not been particularly inflationprone during the 1960s[21]. Over the period 1958–67, consumer prices in the United Kingdom had risen at a significantly lower rate than the Community average, and the French, the Danes and even the Dutch had done much worse. In the 1970s, by contrast, and more particularly between 1974 and 1977, the British figures reached heights that had no postwar precedents and that were totally out of line with any other member states except Italy and Ireland. The contrast with Germany is needless to say particularly striking, but even the French figures were of quite another order. Inflation was, however, only part of the problem and one that was shared with both the Italians and the Irish. More worrying still in many ways was the declining importance of industry in total production and the failure of existing or new industries to move 'up market', as the more successful branches of German industry did in the same period.

Despite certain similarities – in inflation rates, balance of payments and exchange rates – the Italians were in several important respects in a different category from the British even in the worst years of the economic crisis. There is neither space nor need to enter into a discussion at this point of why Italy, which until 1970/71 belonged to the strong currency group in the Community, and which throughout the 1960s had experienced faster growth, both of GDP and industrial production, than any other Western European country, not to mention no more than average inflation rates and almost uninterrupted balance of payments surpluses, should have suffered so many setbacks in the mid-1970s. As in the case of the British, the explanation is to be found as much if not more in the political and social system as in the development of the international economy. Unlike Britain, however, there were still some positive signs. The growth rate, for example, was conspicuously high. The importance of manufacturing industry continued to increase, and Italy managed to develop certain branches, such as steel, where formerly it had lagged behind. There was disturbing evidence to suggest that Italian industry was likely to prove much more vulnerable to competition from the newly industrialized nations, but the Italian position, though bad, was much less preoccupying than the United Kingdom's.

The issues raised by this wide divergence in economic performance and prospects between the member states were to be at the centre of the debate about the EMS. Even before the debate began however, the divisive impact that the world economic crisis had had on the European Community had been perhaps the single most important factor in consolidating a consensus amongst officials and experts opposed to any but the most gradualist approach to economic and monetary union. There was, or there seemed to many to be, no way in which for the time being at any rate Humpty Dumpty, whose condition had been delicate enough anyway prior to his great fall, could possibly be put together again. All that could be done was patiently and laboriously to pick up the pieces, isolating the irreparable ones, strengthening the weak and confirming the strong. In an age of unbelief and realism, miracle cures by currency union seemed to belong to the age of magic.

1.2   The institutional framework

The European Community of the mid-1970s was, it need hardly be said, first and foremost a community of nation states in which, despite the existence of certain supranational institutions – the Commission, the Court and the Parliament – and a number of common policies, power to the extent that it was exercised at all in a Community setting lay overwhelmingly in the hands of the member governments. The latter were not of course sovereign states in the sense in which some at least of them had actually been, and all had pretended to be, in the nineteenth and early twentieth centuries. Western Europe's inability to defend itself, economic interdependence and, by no means least, the political will to create common institutions to manage interdependence and assure their security had diminished the authority of each of them. But, contrary to the expectations of many of those who had 'made Europe' in the postwar decade, they remained the principal actors in a Western European diplomatic system that was as much, if not more, a complex variation on a theme first developed at any length at the Congress of Vienna, as a genuine fulfilment of the supranational aspirations of the federalists and functionalists of the 1940s and 1950s.

The institutional structure of the Community had gradually come to terms with the realities of Western European politics over the years and, although zealots on both sides of the great divide could still invest the supranational elements in the European policy with an authority that they did not possess and in most instances never had possessed, most of the

Western European leaders who followed or, like Jean Monnet, survived de Gaulle showed a refreshing readiness to accommodate the decision-making machinery of the Community to the constraints implicit in a 'semi-Gaullist Europe'. The process of institutional rationalization, which had already begun during and indeed before the ravages of the Gaullist years, is a long and complex one, but it reached its climax in the period 1969–74 when, largely as a result of French leadership, first under M. Pompidou, then under M. Giscard d'Estaing, the Community accomplished the enlargement that de Gaulle had twice prevented, and adopted a 'constitution' that legitimized, consolidated and extended practices and tendencies that had been developing in an *ad hoc* and uncoordinated manner over the previous two decades.

The enlargement of the Community in 1973 was at one and the same time an affirmation of the vitality of the new Western European power grouping that had emerged following the diplomatic revolution of 1950 when, with the launching of the Schuman Plan for the European Coal and Steel Community, six Western European states had decided to go ahead without Britain, and the potential utility of the structure that they had created as a basis for Western European union[22]. It was also however an acknowledgement of the damage that the perpetuation of the divisions that it had caused or reflected was inflicting and had inflicted on Western Europe as a whole, and an acceptance of the durability of the nation state, which had been one of the principal matters in dispute in 1950. Coinciding as it did with a period in which West Germany was becoming a major and increasingly self-confident actor on the international scene, it might have provided the occasion for a constructive and realistic reappraisal of the purposes and prospects of the Community in general. As it was, for reasons that will be touched upon later in this chapter, the readjustments were confined almost exclusively to the institutional sphere, and the erosion of the consensus about what the Community existed for, which had prompted many observers both inside the Six and beyond to predict the demise of the venture in the latter half of the 1960s, was accelerated rather than reversed. The institutional changes that accompanied the enlargement, and that were conveniently codified in the communiqué issued after the meeting of heads of state and government in Paris in December 1974, were nonetheless impressive and require some attention here, since they created the framework in which the European Monetary System was to be negotiated[23].

The most important single element in the new institutional structure that was formally approved at the Paris meeting of December 1974 was the European Council[24], composed of the heads of state and government, who agreed to meet three times a year – once in each of the countries holding the presidency of the Council during the twelve months in question, and the third time in Brussels' or Luxembourg. The function of the Council was to provide leadership in a general sense, both in Community matters covered by the original treaties and in areas such as political cooperation for which there was no treaty authority. Because of the complicated constitutional background to its deliberations, preparations for the European Council were to be unusually cumbersome even by the standards of the European Community, but it was clear from the beginning that, as far as the meetings themselves were concerned, the emphasis was to be on informality and 'political' leadership[25]. Thus ambassadors and senior civil servants were not admitted, and membership was limited to the Nine heads of state and government, their foreign ministers and the president of the Commission. Attendance at the working dinner on the evening of the first day, which had been established as an integral part of the Council programme by the French president at the Paris meeting, was even more restricted, the foreign ministers being obliged to dine elsewhere.

The informality and restricted membership of these meetings were not without their drawbacks. If, for example, as increasingly and inevitably happened, the Council was called upon to sort out disputes that lower institutions in the Community's decision-making machinery had failed to settle, the absence of official advisers who understood the technical details, and who could draft decisions that were sufficiently precise and comprehensive to serve as a basis for subsequent action, was bound to limit the capacity of the heads of state and government to discuss the problems at sufficient depth, let alone arrive at useful conclusions. In order to avoid this danger, several members of the Council, and in particular Chancellor Schmidt, stressed that it was not their task to deal with points of detail that could be better left to the bureaucrats[26]. The Council, it was claimed, existed to lay down the broad lines of policy rather than to lose its way in a maze of technical jargon. Understandable and desirable though this definition in many ways was, it could not entirely overcome the problem, since whether they liked it or not the heads of government were bound to become and indeed ought to be the final court of appeal in a political system based on the nation state, and, still more, because there are extremely few 'high political' questions that can be considered for any length of time without some technical knowledge. As subsequent chapters will show, the information that some prime ministers gave to their subordinates about discussions in which they have clearly been well out of their depth could be seriously misleading. These flaws could, however, be remedied – as Mr Jørgensen's initiative in introducing a notetaker at the after-dinner discussion at Copenhagen in April 1978 showed – and should not detract from the utility of the decision taken in Paris in 1974 to make the Council a permanent element in the Community's institutional structure. Its emergence did not of itself guarantee that the Nine would play an adequate role in international affairs; its absence would however have condemned the Community to remain 'a fiasco in "high politics", something like a hydra with one single body but a multitude of heads'[27].

The European Council formed the apex of a broadly based pyramid of a large and increasing number of ministerial councils and official committees[28]. By 1976, councils existed to deal with agriculture, finance, the Community budget, energy, social affairs, transport, research, development and cooperation, environment, education, and tax. In addition, intergovernmental machinery had been created outside the formal treaty structure to encourage the growth of political cooperation[29]. Indeed, with the exception of defence, there was hardly an area of concern to national governments that was not covered by the terms of reference of the councils and committees, and even security questions could and did figure on the agenda of the foreign ministers and their officials when they met to discuss political cooperation, and of the heads of government in the European Council itself.

The most dignified, but not necessarily the most efficient, of the councils was the Council of Ministers, which unlike the others had been allowed for in the original treaties[30]. It met at least once a month and was in theory if not in practice the body that took all the major decisions concerning Community policy. It is, however, a measure of the extent to which it had ceded much of its authority to the European Council and the technical councils that it does not figure once in the pages that follow, even though it met at least twenty times during the period covered by the book. Of the technical councils that undermined its authority, the most important for present purposes was the ECOFIN, composed of the economic and finance ministers of the Nine and members of the Commission, including on occasions the president himself[31]. Like the Council of Ministers, ECOFIN met formally or informally at least once a month.

Ministers were, of course, accompanied to these meetings by their senior officials, and the latter could deputize for them or, when they were of the calibre of Manfred Lahnstein or Otmar Emminger, play a more important role in the proceedings than the ministers themselves. In most cases, however, officials confined themselves to an advisory role, and limited their active contributions to Community decision-making to the official committees.

As far as monetary and economic affairs were concerned, three official committees were particularly important: the Committee of Central Bank Governors, the Monetary Committee and the Economic Policy Committee. All three had certain features that distinguished them from the general run of official committees servicing the technical councils, but, like their counterparts dealing with agriculture, transport and sundry other matters, they had successfully syphoned off much of the power that still officially lay with the Committee of Permanent Representatives (COREPER), which stood to them in much the same relationship as the Council of Ministers stood to the more specialist ministerial councils[32]. Together, in fact, they dominated the field of financial and economic affairs, reporting directly to ECOFIN, whose agenda and discussions, as this book will show again and again, they frequently determined.

Of the three, the *Committee of Central Bank Governors* was perhaps the oddest, since it did not usually meet within the European Community at all, but at the headquarters of the Bank for International Settlements at Basle. Its identity as a Community body was in fact blurred, and some if not all of its members tended to think of it as no more than a useful appendage to the Group of Ten whose meetings usually preceded its own[33]. It had other peculiarities too. Unlike other Community committees, the Commission was not represented on it as of right, while non-Community bank governors could be and were co-opted, when for example developments within the Snake were on the agenda. Finally, like the Monetary Committee, it elected its chairman in its own way and at the time of its choosing.

The *Monetary Committee*, which like the Committee of Central Bank Governors had been established in 1964, was much more of a Community institution, composed of senior representatives from each of the nine finance ministries, the deputy governors of the central banks or their equivalents or nominees, and two representatives of the Commission. Where it differed from other Community bodies, though not as we have seen from the Central Bank committee, was in the arrangements concerning its chairmanship, which did not, as on other Community committees, change every six months in conjunction with the change in the presidency of the Council of Ministers. Chairmen of the Monetary Committee were elected, and stayed in office for periods of two years or more. The result was not only a series of chairmen of remarkable distinction – Mr van Lennep, Bernard Clappier, Conrad Oort, Karl-Otto Poehl and Jacques van Ypersele held the position between 1964 and 1978 – but a sense of continuity and an esprit de corps that, as we shall see in the following chapters, were to show through in the committee's contributions to the debate about the EMS[34].

The *Economic Policy Committee* (EPC), by contrast, was a much more shadowy and elusive body, which had taken over the functions of three previous committees – the Short-term Economic Policy Committee, the Medium-Term Policy Committee and the Budgetary Policy Committee – in 1974. Unlike the other two major committees, its membership tended to fluctuate according to the subject under discussion. Thus in the story of the EMS, many of those who met in the EPC to discuss the concurrent studies in the summer and autumn of 1978 had not previously been involved in the committee's work, and this lack of shared experience and collective wisdom is probably one of the factors that helps to explain why they, in marked contrast to their colleagues in the two other economic committees, could not overcome their scepticism and mutual antagonisms enough to arrive at any more than an agreement to define their disagreements[35].

There is one other feature of this intergovernmental decision-making machinery that deserves particular attention, namely the presidency of the

European Council[36]. The special arrangements for the chairmanship of the Monetary Committee and the Committee of Central Bank Governors have already been mentioned. In almost every other council or committee, however, the chairmanship changed every six months, with ministers and officials of each member country presiding in turn. In the period covered by this book, for example, the British held the presidency for the first six months of 1977, the Belgians for the second half, the Danes for the first half of 1978, the Germans for the remainder, and the French for the first part of 1979. A recent study singled out five functions that the holders of the presidency are required to perform[37]:

(1) The management of Community business (i.e. the chairmanship of committees, the preparation of the agenda, the imposition of timetables for Community discussions and where necessary the convening of special meetings).

(2) The sponsorship of political initiatives. A good example can be found in the Dutch decision to launch the Duisenberg plan in the second half of 1976, or the Belgians' attempt to revive the debate about monetary questions in the second half of 1977.

(3) Package brokerage in negotiations. In terms of the subject matter of this book, the most notable instance of a successful mediation, namely the Belgian compromise[37a], was the work of the chairmen of the Monetary Committee and the Committee of Central Bank Governors, whose terms of office, as we have seen, did not follow the normal rules. The Germans were, however, extremely active behind the scenes during the later stages of their presidency, and some at least of the credit for removing the principal obstacles to agreement must go to them in their capacity as chairmen, though still more, as will be seen in chapter 6, was due to the personal involvement of the chancellor.

(4) Liaison with other Community institutions and in particular with the Parliament, which ministers and officials from the country holding the presidency addressed in the name of the Nine governments as a whole. Dr Lahnstein's speeches during the budget dispute provide a good example[38].

(5) Representation of the Community in its external relations. Dr Matthöfer, for example, spoke for the Community at the IMF meetings in September 1978, just as a few months earlier Mr Schmidt had had the chief responsibility for explaining what the Community hoped to achieve through the EMS to non-Community leaders at the summit meeting of the Seven in Bonn in July[39].

Subsequent chapters will confirm that the identity of the presidency could exercise an important influence on the development of Community affairs, and it is a matter for speculation whether the EMS could have been launched at all if it had not been for the fact that the Germans held the presidency during the crucial six months in which most of the detailed negotiations were carried out. Even that might not have been enough had they not been preceded by the Belgians and the Danes, both of whom helped to create a momentum that would almost certainly not have developed if the initiative had lain with the British or the French, whose handling of their presidencies in 1977 and 1979 respectively provided striking examples of how not to preside over Community business[40].

Even though the member states were the principal actors in Community affairs, it would nonetheless be misleading to describe the Community system as simply intergovernmental, since national governments operated within a context in which, despite the frustration of the supranational ambitions of the founding generation, the European interest was undoubtedly a presence at the feast. It was assured in at least three ways: through the emergence over the years of transgovernmental European elites, accustomed to approaching the issues within their competence from more than merely a single nation standpoint, through the existence of certain supranational institutions – the Commission, the Parliament and the Court – and through the survival and extension of at least some Community policy instruments.

The decision-making machinery that has been sketched out in the previous paragraphs was underpinned by a complex array of formal and informal networks that helped to blur the differences between national representatives over issues both great and small. A major catalyst of this process was the Community machinery itself, which regularly exposed national policy makers to their counterparts in other member states and encouraged a greater awareness of, if not an automatic sympathy for, the special problems faced by ministers and officials elsewhere in the Community. However, the process also worked itself out in settings and developments far removed from the regular multilateral meetings of ministers and officials described above. Amongst these other settings were the increasingly frequent bilateral meetings between heads of government, their ministers and officials, which had been a feature of the Franco–German relationship since 1963 but which had begun to extend in other directions as well by the mid-1970s[41]. This process was to be given a major boost by the EMS negotiations themselves but, even before these began, arrangements existed for the French president, the German chancellor and the British and Italian prime ministers to meet each other regularly for bilateral discussions. In most of these cases, the meetings were not as elaborate as the six-monthly French–German summits, to which a large number of Cabinet members and camp followers tended to come, but the extension of the practice undoubtedly encouraged the emergence of common positions outside the formal negotiating framework and as a result contributed to the efficiency of the Community system as a whole.

There were also less formal means of contact, the most famous examples of which are to be found in the burgeoning relationship between Chancellor Schmidt and President Giscard d'Estaing, which was advanced through telephone conversations, unscheduled meetings and private dinners at which few if any officials were present. The significance of this friendship in the history of the EMS will become apparent in the pages that follow. So too, however, will the relevance of other informal groupings, which had emerged in many cases in the first place because those concerned were brought together by official business, but which developed a momentum and logic of their own that had little to do with the official machinery. One of the most striking features of the EMS episode is, in fact, the way in which, quite apart from the impulse provided by the French president, the German chancellor and the president of the Commission, the negotiations were advanced by a small group of officials from several countries whose involvement in European affairs and with each other went beyond regular attendance at intergovernmental meetings. On the German side, for example, the chancellor's preferred agents, Dr Schulmann and Dr Lahnstein, were both ex-Brussels men[42]. So too were at least two of the men closest to the French president during the affair, M. Barre and Jean-Claude Payet. And as for M. Clappier, governor of the Banque de France, his experience of the politics of European integration went back at the very least to May 1950, when he had been one of the few people to know about and contribute to the drafting of the Schuman Plan[43]. He had also, as we have seen, been chairman of the Monetary Committee, the inner circle of which at any rate had acquired a 'club spirit' and in some cases a community of purpose that had been and was in the EMS episode to be again a dynamic force, perpetuating an interest in the possibility of monetary integration long after more detached observers had declared it an impossible target.

Looking at the history of the debate about EMU since the late 1960s and the evidence that emerges in the pages that follow it is remarkable how the same names appear again and again: Bernard Clappier, Jacques van Ypersele, Conrad Oort, Raymond Barre, Robert Triffin, Robert Marjolin and Giovanni Magnifico. They did not constitute either a 'school' or a 'club', but it is nonetheless possible to detect a number of links between them. One, which most if not all of them would have acknowledged readily enough, was an intellectual debt to Robert Triffin, the doyen of European monetary experts, who had been at the forefront of discussions about currency reform in Western Europe since the days of the European Payments Union[44]. Another was cultural: the majority of those listed were French or Belgian. The EMS negotiations were to provide further proof of the importance of this particular axis. Yet another was their membership of certain formal and informal committees. Of the official groups, the most important by far was the Monetary Committee. The first three men on the list were all in their time chairmen of the committee. There were also links outside these official settings, however. At an earlier stage, the Monnet Committee had in this as in so many other spheres engineered meetings or informal study groups[45]. More recently a similar role had been played by the Pamphilii Group[46], which was set up in 1976 on the initiative of Giovanni Magnifico, and which included several of the individuals listed above, as well as others, like Niels Thygesen of Copenhagen, who had signed the All Saints Day manifesto in 1975 – a plea for the issue of a new European currency by EEC central banks which was made by nine prominent European economists[47]. None of these bodies was a pressure group in the conventional sense of the term; the presence of so many university economists and therefore of a multiplicity of views guaranteed that. But they were nonetheless of some importance in the politics of monetary integration, ensuring that the issue was mulled over again and again and providing a continuing flow of ideas and proposals that those amongst their number who, like Jacques van Ypersele or Conrad Oort, were in a position to do so could feed to committees or prime ministers as and when they thought fit.

This monetary elite was, of course, not necessarily a typical phenomenon, in either its views or its cohesiveness or durability, nor needless to say was a Brussels experience an essential episode in the career of a rising star in the national bureacracies of every country in the Six, let alone the Nine. Before we can generalize safely, we need an updated and expanded version of the book that Daniel Lerner and Morton Gorden produced on the changing perspectives of the European elites in the 1960s[48]. But even without the support of a systematic survey of this kind, it seems clear that cooperation between the Nine was considerably enhanced in many spheres by the emergence of groups whose loyalties and interests cut across national lines.

The role of both the treaty institutions – the Commission, the Parliament and the Court – and the common policies, such as the CET and the Common Agricultural Policy (CAP), that had emerged over the course of the years, in creating a European factor in Community politics, distinct from and more than the aggregate of nine governments' wills and ambitions, has been so frequently described elsewhere that little needs to be said here. Needless to say, none of the institutions was as formidable a force as devout federalists would have hoped or anti-marketeers in Britain, France or Denmark liked to pretend, nor was the scope of the policies that were implemented through the Community machinery particularly ambitious, expensive or comprehensive. Many British or French higher civil servants had much more opportunity to improve or damage the lives of their fellow countrymen than the oft-abused bureaucrats in Brussels. The excess of overzealous harmonizers notwithstanding, the highest ambition that European civil servants could reasonably aspire to in the mid-1970s was that 'Europe' should be allowed to become a 'tenth member of the Community'[49], with Community policies supplementing rather than replacing national policies, and Community personnel assisting rather than governing their national counterparts. Within these more limited horizons of the post-Luxembourg era[50], however, strong commissioners had been able to make their mark on Community affairs, some at least of the policy instruments, most notably the CET, had performed real functions that were manifestly better carried out at Community rather than national level and, with direct elections in the offing, there seemed every reason to believe that the Parliament, like the Court had already done, would exercise a useful if somewhat unsensational role in limiting the excessive or unnecessary ambitions of both the member states and the Commission, and in developing a public awareness of Community concerns.

1.3   The Community crisis: some general themes

The institutional structure that has been sketched out in the previous section was by no means perfect. Community decision-making was often slow and cumbersome, Community officials were on occasions insufficiently aware of the proper interests and preferences of national or regional societies and, despite the obvious relevance and success of policy instruments such as the CET and the regime that had emerged to implement the Lomé Agreement, there were others, notably the CAP, that were manifestly wasteful and inefficient. Even though, however, these specific examples of malfunctioning or misguided priorities undoubtedly contributed to the sense of crisis that was all-pervasive in the Community in 1976–77, it would be misleading to identify the institutional structure itself as the root cause of the Community's malaise. The latter was real enough, but it stemmed not from the retreat from supranationalism that had certainly taken place over the previous 15 years, but from the failure of Western European leaders to match the rationalization of the Community's decision-making processes that they had advanced so energetically between 1969 and 1974 with any comparable overhaul of Community policies and priorities. From 1950, and still more from 1958 onwards, the Six had claimed and increasingly won recognition as the nucleus around which 'Europe' could be reorganized. With the institutional reforms and in particular the emergence of the European Council during the early years of the 1970s, the Community had acquired a machinery that could, if rightly used, transform it into a real Concert of Europe. It was the Community's misfortune, however, that the latter-day successors of Castlereagh and Metternich were obliged for one reason or another to devote a substantial proportion of their time to haggling over the price of cheese, or the levels of German and British contributions to the Community's miniscule and lopsided budget or the problems of French pig farmers rather than to the high political questions with which they might have been expected to concern themselves. Thus the Tindemans report, which the Council itself had commissioned and which sketched out a high road to European union, was rapidly and only 'half decently buried' in a characteristically fruitless meeting at The Hague in December 1976[51]. At best the Community might be said to be 'walking backwards into unity'[52]; at worst it seemed set to disintegrate under the stultifying impact of its own petty-mindedness, frivolity and irrelevance.

Explanations of (and remedies for) the failure of the Community to develop policies and policy instruments commensurate with the variety and dignity of its institutions (not to mention its size, wealth and potential importance in an international system in which the scope for initiatives in high politics was no longer confined, if it ever had been, to Washington and Moscow) tend to fall into two categories: the global and the particular. The latter involve a detailed analysis of why specific policies and strategies have failed, or, if the object is to remedy rather than to diagnose, why certain lines of approach might be more promising than others[53]. The other, more ambitious and inherently riskier approach, relates the day-to-day fumblings of permanent representatives and prime ministers to larger and longer-term developments in the international system, in domestic politics, in society and in culture[54]. In a book devoted to the emergence of a monetary system, it would be tempting to confine oneself to the lower and easier road: to explain the failures of previous efforts to move towards EMU exclusively in terms of developments in the international monetary system or of the prejudices and preferences of central bankers and economic officials. Tempting though it is to stick to the lower road, it cannot lead us sufficiently far towards an understanding of the Community's crisis, which was more than an aggregate of the failure of individual policies and which itself contributed to their downfall. Rather the reverse, since in its extreme form the 'case study' approach accepts exactly those assumptions about the nature and limits of Community politics that, as this book will illustrate at several points, are fundamental obstacles to the recovery from the crisis. It was in fact precisely the insistence on 'taking each case on its merits', on fighting each issue as if it was the only one at stake, and on conducting campaigns with the limited objectives but reckless enthusiasm of first world war generals that lay at the root of the Community's malaise in the mid-1970s. Although, therefore, it is essential to look as we have done at the specific, technical reasons that explain the failure of EMU to emerge in the 1970s, it is equally important to relate this single, albeit central instance of failure to certain larger issues and themes.

The most important feature of the crisis of identity and purpose from which, in the eyes of both activists and observers, the Community appeared to be suffering in the mid-1970s was aptly described by M. Tindemans in his report on European Union[55]:

> Why has the European concept lost a lot of its force and initial impetus? I
> believe that over the years the European public has lost a guiding light [*un*

fil conducteur], namely the political consensus between our countries on our reasons for undertaking the joint task and the characteristics with which we wish to endow it. We must first of all restore this common vision if we wish to have European Union.

For reasons that have already been discussed, it is hard to believe that the explanation of this crisis is to be found in the move away from supra-nationalism or the rationalization of the institutional structure of the Community that had occurred in the early 1970s. Given the deep roots of most if not all the Community's nation states, and the proven utility of many of the services that national governments could perform, acceptance of the fact that Europe could only be built on the basis of the late-twentieth century states was a precondition of the revival of the European venture rather than a guarantee of its failure. A homogeneous Europe was as undesirable as it was impracticable, and only when the rhetoric of standar-dization for the sake of standardization was abandoned could there be a cool and realistic reassessment of the proper role of Europe in the multi-tiered government that the interdependence of the Nine demanded and that in a multiplicity of ways, multilateral and bilateral, formal and *ad hoc*, it was moulding. The failure of the Nine consisted in their inability to agree on or implement any overall strategy for the Community. The march towards institutional realism and reform had in fact been paralleled by a retreat from systematic discussions about what this more rationally based Community should perform together, and what was best left to each member to do on its own. At the beginning of the decade the heads of government and state had talked grandly of EMU by 1980, of the need to build up the Regional and Social Funds, to offset the disproportionate importance of the CAP and even, in the Heath–Pompidou era, of the possibilities of re-examining the case for a European defence community. As the years had passed, however, and the problems of the western world had deepened, gradualism, which was little more than the acceptance of defeat, had become the dominant philosophy, and the most that the Community's leaders seemed to hope for was that a European *Gemeinschaft* would emerge from years of patient tinkering with the detailed problems of the European *Gesellschaft*.

There are doubtless many general explanations of this loss of a '*fil conducteur*'. Three, however, are particularly relevant to the story of the EMS: the first was the continuing failure of the Community as such to define its role and function in the western system; the second was the inability or unwillingness of its leaders to come to terms with the profound divergence in political priorities and potential that, concurrently with and in some measure at any rate as a result of their differing economic performance, had begun to open up between the principal member states; the third was the increasing political instability of several of the member states, notably Britain, France, Italy and Belgium. All three problems deserve extended treatment, but even the brief discussion that is all that will be possible in the present chapter is essential if the debates and negotiations that preceded the formation of the EMS are to be placed in their proper perspective.

The first of the problems, the failure of the Community to define its position in the western system, was in certain respects as old as the Community itself. Ironically indeed, in the light of what will be said later about British policy, it has become increasingly clear that the fear that the European Coal and Steel Community would be little more than an instrument of American hegemony was one of the more important factors influencing the British decision to stand apart from the Six in 1950[56]. Subsequently, as the Community gained in self-confidence, and as part at least of the Gaullist thesis about the dangers of excessive dependence on the United States became the stock in trade of 'good Europeans' (and, it must be said, of good Atlanticists in the United States itself), it seemed possible that a redefinition of the relationship might be feasible or even, if rivalry and neo-isolationism became too strong, necessary. But despite numerous studies, some at least of them very distinguished[57], and a series of initiatives aimed at tidying up the relationship, the last of them being the ill-starred 'Year of Europe' sponsored by the Nixon administration in 1973[58], relations between the Western European states and their North Atlantic partners remained blurred and uneasy.

The most serious source of confusion was still, as it had been since 1940 when the North Atlantic Community first emerged in something like its contemporary form, the need for American military help. Assessments of how fundamental this need was varied between the member states of the European Community and, perhaps, from time to time. The French still clung, officially at least, to the myth of national independence and even though the Schmidt government, after almost a decade of Germany's *Ostpolitik*, had perhaps moved slightly away from the unquestioning acceptance of the 'prerogatives of the Atlantic Alliance' (which had promp- ted Walter Scheel to dismiss out of hand suggestions from Paris and London that the development of a separate European nuclear capability might be feasible and desirable[59]), the possibility of a credible West European defence community seemed as remote as ever.

The complications introduced into the Community's search for a distinc- tive identity by the western connection were not, however, simply a consequence of the asymmetrical military relationship with the United States. For those like, for example, the British and the Italians who were in economic trouble, the IMF was still in the mid-1970s a more important source of aid – and a sterner task-master – than the Community. As for the strong, the United States or Japan were frequently more important partners in the interdependent western community than the small or the weak within Europe. In monetary matters for example, the Washington (New York) – Frankfurt axis was of considerably greater relevance to the Bundesbank than relations with either London or Paris. More generally, the inauguration of the initiative of the French president of regular meetings of the Seven, to which neither the Community as such nor its smaller members were admitted as of right, threatened to divide the Nine into large and small, and looked suspiciously like a revival of western summitry of the 1940s and 1950s, which could only make the task of defining a Community position on major questions all the harder. A similar trend can be detected in the increasing tendency of the Berlin group of western powers – the United States, Britain, France and West Germany – to use the opportunity offered by their joint responsibility for the safety of West Berlin to coordinate their views on international questions beyond the competence of the 'lesser' powers. Of itself, this increasing evidence of the larger western powers' readiness to accept the need for closer cooperation in the face of the multiple demands of interdependence was not discouraging. But an inevitable consequence was that it undermined the chances of the Nine as such grappling with, let alone achieving, common views on the larger questions of trade, money or security, which they needed to tackle collectively if they were ever to lift the Community out of its 'low political' trough. The Community, it seemed, was simply not regarded as a meaningful framework within which to discuss the most important problems of the day, let alone develop joint strategies to meet them.

The Community's failure to achieve a clear profile in the western system had been brought into still sharper relief in the 1970s by the increasing evidence of conflicts of interest between the Nine and the United States. It had, of course, long been apparent that the interests of Western Europe and the United States were likely to diverge sooner or later, but the disparities of power and wealth between the two sides of the Atlantic had usually smoothed over or concealed outbursts of bad temper or misunderstanding during the 1950s and 1960s. In the 1970s, however, a combination of detente, American decline (which, it must be stressed, was relative rather than absolute), world inflation (which could in some measure at least be blamed on the irresponsibility of successive American administrations and the inherent defects of the dollar-based system) and the energy crisis diminished the constraints on conflict and increased the number of issues and areas in which conflict could arise. The third chapter of this book contains a rapid survey of some of the more important clashes of interest in the first year of the Carter administration. It is important to recall, however, that these instances of misunderstanding were only the latest in a series that had punctuated a decade that began with the collapse of the Bretton Woods system and the Mansfield amendment[59a]. The range and variety of combustible issues were daunting, including as they did the problems, as well as the opportunities, posed by Western Europe's, and more particularly Germany's, increasing financial and commercial involvement with the Soviet Union and Eastern Europe, the political, not to mention moral, dilemmas that Western Europe's greater dependence on Middle Eastern oil raised, as well as more conventional and longer standing difficulties over the CAP and other Community policies. There is no space in this book to enter into any discussion of these and other issues, but they should nevertheless be borne in mind as part of the background to the discussions about the EMS, not simply because they reinforced the desire to clarify relations between Western Europe and the United States that is such a prominent feature of the episode, but also, paradoxically enough, because they made the task of clarification that much harder to achieve, since not all member states were equally affected by all of them, and some, notably Britain, were much less inclined to proceed from particular cases of irritation to a fundamental reappraisal of the Atlantic relationship. Both the intensity and the limitations of the passage of arms with the United States that occurred during the EMS episode can, in other words, only be understood against the background of more general problems and divisions within the western system, and in particular in the relationship between Western Europe and the United States of America.

The second and third factors referred to above, namely the failure of the Community to adjust to the growing divergence of power and interest amongst its member states (in particular its three most powerful governments) and the political instability of several countries, are so closely intertwined that they are best taken together. Amongst the developments and problems that they cover, the most important by far was the emergence of West Germany as the most powerful member of the European Community by almost any measure that one might choose to apply. Some idea of its lead over its principal partners has already been given in the previous section, and the information that is set out there could easily be supplemented by statistics comparing its GNP, its official reserves, its status amongst the world's trading nations, and even its military expenditure and capability with those of the other larger European states. In normal circumstances, this predominance might have been expected to result in German leadership of a Community of nation states and there were some, notably but not exclusively in the United States of America, who sought to encourage the Federal Republic's emergence as the privileged partner of the United States and the successor of President Pompidou's France as the Community's natural spokesman in the transatlantic dialogue[60]. The transition from French to German leadership was, however, not such an easy matter as these critics would appear to have imagined, not simply and indeed not mainly because of opposition from Germany's partners, but because the German leaders themselves showed a marked reluctance to assume the role to which their political stability and economic success appeared to entitle them.

The reasons for this diffidence were numerous and profound, including as they did a genuine fear of both the external and internal consequences of what might appear to be a fresh bid for German hegemony in Western Europe, anxiety about the effect that emphasis on Germany's strength might have on the United States' willingness to provide military protection and, by no means least, mounting hostility to bailing Germany's weaker partners out of the consequences of their own bad management. These inhibitions had already been in evidence long before the winter of 1976–77, but they were given renewed strength during it by the results of the Bundestag elections of October 1976[61], which came as near to producing a 'hung parliament' as was comfortable and left neither the 'winners' (the CDU/CSU), who were nevertheless not quite big enough to form a government of their own, nor the 'losers' (the SPD and FDP), who soldiered on with a greatly reduced majority, disposed to take risks or behave magnanimously. Thus, although Germany's success in weathering the recession may have been conspicuous by comparison with what was achieved elsewhere, there seemed little prospect of leadership from this quarter. Conscious of the strong preference of the electorate to hold on to what they had and to shuffle off the burdens of being Europe's paymasters, which, as a well-advertised article in the Bundesbank's monthly bulletin proved, they currently were[62], the German chancellor, whose disapproval of the Brussels bureaucracy was notorious, appeared willing to be no more than the Samuel Smiles of the European Community, a prophet of self-help, whose idea of international leadership amounted to little more than a succession of sermons to others about how to manage their own affairs[63].

The reluctance of the Germans to assume the leadership of the Community in the mid-1970s was bad enough. Still worse, however, was the apparent inability of the British to take even a share of the burden. The United Kingdom had been admitted to the European Community in the first place because the Five hoped that the newcomer would restore life and initiative to a venture that had been brought virtually to a standstill by Gaullist France, while the French looked to the British to correct the balance in the Community that by 1969 was already beginning to be threatened by German predominance[64]. After four years of membership, however, all that British diplomacy appeared to have accomplished was to persuade the French that partnership with an overpowerful Germany was more conducive to their interests than a special relationship with the United Kingdom, and the Five that the French, though still in many respects unregenerate nationalists, were tolerable compared with the British. Community politics was still all too often a case of one against the rest. All that had changed was the identity of the one.

Explanations of this state of affairs, particularly on the Continent, tend to fasten on the historical differences separating the United Kingdom from its partners in the Community: the special relationship with the United States, the mental attitudes, trading patterns and financial interests that had been shaped by centuries of empire, the pride that stemmed from having been the only major Western European power undefeated during the second world war, and so on. De Gaulle, it was sometimes said, outside France as well as inside, had been right after all: the British were simply not Europeans. The historical argument is clearly relevant and important. It seems equally clear, however, that its relevance and importance were rapidly diminishing. Although the British can and probably always will have a special relationship with the Americans, with whom they share not only common language and literature but so much common history, its character no longer was and is never again likely to be remotely comparable to the special relationship, with its overtones of rivalry as well as friendship, that the two countries had had during the 1940s and 1950s. The same is true of empire. The political ties had long since been cut or transformed, and even though the United Kingdom's trading patterns were still markedly different from those of every other member state, they too were changing rapidly[65]. Whether the British liked it or not, the countries of Western Europe already bought over half of the United Kingdom's total exports in 1976 (as compared with 30% in 1958), and supplied them with 44% of their imports (as compared with 34% in 1958). Recession or no recession, there was nothing to suggest that this rapid Europeanization of British trade would slow down, still less go into reverse. Although, therefore, historical differences had undoubtedly been of major significance in shaping British reactions to the efforts of the Six in the 1950s[66], it is difficult to believe that they were anything like as serious by 1976. The principal explanation of the United Kingdom's European policy in the mid-1970s is in fact to be found not in the recollections of former glories so much as in the realities of contemporary weakness: the demoralization that stemmed from a sense of seemingly inexorable decline, the breakdown of consensus politics and the apparent threat of political instability. The decline of British diplomacy was more a consequence than a cause of the politics of decline.

The causal connection between developments in domestic politics and the British debate about Europe has already been discussed and documented at length by Uwe Kitzinger in his studies of the negotiations preceding Britain's entry into the Community in 1973 and of the Referendum on the United Kingdom's continuing membership in 1975[67]. Prior to the Conservative victory of 1970, European policy had been more or less bipartisan, and there seems little doubt that had Mr Wilson won that election, his government would have negotiated and claimed the credit for Britain's entry into the EEC. The polarization of opinion that resulted from Mr Heath's attempt to implement the Selsdon programme (an economic programme that bears a striking resemblance to much that Mrs Thatcher was to try to do ten years later) and the related swing to the left in the Labour Party that it encouraged, brought the hitherto relatively uncontentious issue of Britain's membership of the Community into the centre of partisan conflict. From 1970 onwards, the debate about the merits of British membership was complicated and overshadowed by the logic and outcome of power struggles between the parties and within them. The position was complicated still further in 1974 when Mr Wilson returned to power, first as the leader of a minority government and then, after the second election of the year, with the barest overall majority[68]. Saddled with the responsibilities of power, neither he nor his foreign secretary, Mr Callaghan, would appear to have had any serious doubts about the necessity and utility of Britain's continuing membership of the Community, and the result of the Referendum, which produced an overwhelming majority in favour, was therefore a major relief. It did not, however, alter the realities of parliamentary arithmetic, where the left remained essential to the survival of the Wilson administration. The Labour government was in fact bound more by its dependence on those who had been defeated in the Referendum than by its obligations towards those who had won. It was Mr Jenkins, who had headed the all-party coalition that fought in favour of British membership in the Referendum campaign, who went into political exile in 1976, and not Mr Benn, who had been trounced.

Mr Callaghan's assumption of the prime ministership in 1976, followed almost immediately afterwards by a major sterling crisis and the implementation of an IMF-sponsored package of stabilization measures, suggested that the British government might be ready to play a more constructive role in the Community and western alliance as soon as recovery from the disasters of 1974–6 was at last under way. But although the new prime minister was undoubtedly more respected than his predecessor by most if not all the other members of the European Council, the domestic constraints within which he operated were still essentially those that had hemmed in Mr Wilson. A pact with the Liberals in March 1977 provided a much-needed counterbalance to the left in parliament, and helped to ensure that the government was slightly less negative in its European policy. But outside parliament the left was busy building a house of its own, which raised serious questions about the political identity of the Labour Party in the long term, and posed a continuing threat to its stability in the short term. Thus, although Mr Callaghan reminded his supporters both in private and in public that British membership of the Community was no longer at issue, his most celebrated and extended attempt to define what his government aimed to achieve in the Community – an open letter to the General Secretary of the Labour Party in 1977 – succeeded in satisfying neither the opponents of membership inside the party nor the majority of his partners across the Channel[69]. With Mrs Thatcher almost equally negative and non-committal, for reasons of her own[70], Britain's contribution to the reformulation of Community strategy and policies that the seriousness of the times demanded was virtually nil. Renegotiation of the terms of British membership may have been formally concluded in 1975, but the reflexes and attitudes that it fostered remained as much in evidence as ever, and the possibility of reform, from which a constructive British government stood to gain almost more than any other, precisely because the Community's budget and policy instruments were so underdeveloped and lopsided, was sacrificed in the interests of short-term party peace and immediate popular approval.

British ministers and officials frequently justified their tactics by evoking the example of the French who, they claimed, were still more ruthless than they were themselves in the defence of sectional interests. It was (and is) not a particularly impressive argument, however, for at least two reasons. Firstly, it overlooked the fact that the British had not been welcomed into the Community by the majority of its members on the assumption that they would emulate the French, whose behaviour had almost destroyed the venture in the 1960s. Secondly, and still more important, it ignored the evidence that although the French were still more inclined than any other member state to play both the Community game and the international game in general according to their own rules, both de Gaulle's successors had ensured that the defence of national interests was counterbalanced by major contributions to the redefinition of the Community's internal structure and external role. Under President Pompidou in fact, France had in many ways assumed the leadership role inside and outside the Community to which Gaullist France had aspired but which the bitterness aroused by the General's behaviour had blocked. *Primus inter pares* in the triumvirate with Mr Brandt and Mr Heath, he was accepted by the Nixon administration as the most authoritative exponent of Western European views on global problems and the Americans' privileged partner[71]. He had also been the key figure in formulating and developing the Community's strategy of completion, deepening and enlargement in the months and years following the Hague summit of 1969. Thus in the negotiations with Britain, it was his meeting with Mr Heath in May 1971 that transformed the atmosphere and ensured the success of the enterprise as a whole[72]. Developments in the final year of his presidency were less edifying and more controversial, but part at least of the trouble can be attributed to the deterioration in his own health and still more to the deepening world crisis and the slippage in France's position vis-à-vis the Federal Republic that this both revealed and accelerated.

M. Pompidou's successor, M. Giscard d'Estaing, assumed the presidency in 1974 at a moment and in a manner that were bound to limit his opportunities for grand gestures or significant new departures. There were at least three major constraints. Firstly, the widening gap between French and German power and the serious problems of the French economy were bound to limit the government's room for manoeuvre and threatened to undermine the style that, as much if not more than the content, had distinguished French foreign policy since 1958 from the foreign policy of the Fourth Republic and contributed significantly to many of its successes[73]. Secondly, the return of a weak, divided and apparently anti-European minority Labour government in Britain in February 1974, a few months before M. Giscard D'Estaing became president, had put paid to any hopes that he or his predecessor might have had of offsetting France's weakness in relation to Germany by a special relationship with the British. In the heyday of the Heath–Pompidou era, this had seemed a distinct possibility. With Mr Wilson, however, the chances were negligible both for the general political reasons already discussed and on personal grounds. Two years later, with a new British prime minister, the French president proposed the inauguration of regular, six-monthly summits on the Franco-German model, an action that prompted *The Economist* to observe: 'If Britain-in-Europe did not exist, it would have to be invented'[74]. But although the meetings, which began in November 1976, were undoubtedly useful, the main priorities of the French president's foreign policy were already established by then, and the relationship with Britain did not figure particularly high on the list. The third constraint was the most important of all. Although M. Giscard d'Estaing had beaten the Gaullist candidate in the presidential elections of 1974, he was still dependent on Gaullist support both in the country, where hopes of encouraging the emergence of a 'third France' of the centre were remote, and still more in parliament, where the Gaullists were far and away the largest single party[75]. However much he may have been inclined to alter the foundations of French foreign policy therefore, he was constantly obliged to pander to the myth of 'independence' and to fight to protect the solid material gains that the French had obtained in earlier Common Market battles. It was a balancing act that demanded considerable ingenuity on the part of the president himself and scarcely less understanding on the part of France's Community partners, and on several notable occasions, as the discussion in chapters 3 and 6 will show, both were wanting.

Despite these constraints however, the change of president in 1974 did inaugurate a new era in the foreign policy of the Fifth Republic[76]. In a general sense, it was both more European and more openly interdependence-orientated than either General de Gaulle's or even M. Pompidou's policy had been. The new line on Europe, which M. Pompidou had anticipated in several important respects, but which the interlude of M. Jobert had gone a long way towards obliterating, was evident almost immediately in the package of proposals that the president put to the other eight heads of government and the president of the Commission whom he invited to a conference at the Elysée on 14 September 1974[77]. The principal French concessions in the package were the agreement to direct elections to the European Parliament, the renunciation of the systematic use of the rule of unanimity in Community business, and a softer line on the constitutional division between Community affairs as such and political cooperation, which the French had until then insisted upon, with consequences that were on occasions farcical[78].

The most distinctive features of M. Giscard d'Estaing's foreign policy in its formative phase, however, were his drive to institutionalize summitry, not only within the Community but also in the western industrialized world as a whole, through regular meetings of the Seven, which began at Rambouillet in 1975, and the priority that he accorded to the German connection. The importance of the European Council in the new Community system has already been touched upon in the previous section; its utility to a president who, like his predecessors, insisted that foreign policy was a presidential preserve is no less obvious. Personal preferences were also an important element in the emphasis that was placed on the German connection. The partnership with Mr Schmidt, who succeeded Mr Brandt at almost the same time as M. Giscard d'Estaing became president in 1974, had begun two years earlier when Mr Schmidt had become German finance minister, and its utility had already been apparent in a phase in which the Franco-German partnership in general was not as close at it had been in earlier years.

The priority that the French president gave to the relationship with Germany, which was immediately demonstrated by the arrangement of no less than three bilateral summits with Mr Schmidt in the first six months following the French presidential elections[79], was, however, founded on much more than personal affection or loyalty to the Franco-German Treaty, which had on occasions been observed more in the letter than in the spirit. There were in addition at least three calculations peculiar to the period in which M. Giscard d'Estaing took over or to his perception of where France's interests lay. The first has already been alluded to, namely the demise of the United Kingdom as a viable alternative. The second and third are, however, in many ways still more relevant to the chapters that follow: the belief that precisely because Germany had become the predominant power in the Community, France's best hope of maintaining (or regaining) the political leadership that, at least until 1973, M. Pompidou had exercised lay in a revival of the special relationship with Bonn; and the conviction that in the longer term France's ability to match or even surpass the Federal Republic lay in emulation of Germany's strength. The first of these calculations presumed on the German leaders' continuing reluctance, emphasized no less strongly by Mr Schmidt than by Mr Brandt, to play a solo role in the Community or indeed elsewhere, while the second assumed that the secrets of German success were not peculiar to the German character but could be copied or acquired through precept and contact. The watchword was to be stability and the principal instrument through which German health was to be communicated was the currency link. Hence, despite initial outbursts of sarcasm about the Snake's prehistoric features at the beginning of 1974, the decision to rejoin in 1975 and the repeated emphasis on the need to extend or rebuild monetary integration, which persisted even after the French had had to leave the system once again in March 1976[80].

Thanks to both his personality and his policies, M. Giscard d'Estaing had undoubtedly established a pre-eminent position in the European Council in 1976. Even at a meeting as disappointing in many respects as the Hague summit of December 1976, he alone of the leaders of the three major powers had come near to developing a systematic appraisal of the Community's weaknesses and prospects[81]. It was in many ways a formidable achievement. But it was also flawed. The French economy and, still more, the domestic political base on which the president relied were simply not strong enough for him to sustain the programmes and ambitions that he developed or nursed. Economically, the gap between France and West Germany widened rather than narrowed between 1974 and 1977. Politically, there was simply not enough agreement about the desirability of the end to tolerate the means that the president and his ministers devised to narrow the gap. The second departure from the Snake was a case in point. The French could have remained within the system. With the exception of the Dutch, the finance ministers concerned had been able to reach agreement on a package of measures at the vital meeting in March 1976, and even the Dutch hesitations were removed when the finance minister in question had had a chance to discuss the matter with his colleagues in the Hague. The measures were not implemented, however, because, during the weekend in question, returns in the French departmental elections, the imminence of which had provoked speculation against the franc in the first place, showed convincing gains for the left in general and the Socialists in particular[82]. Good intentions, in other words, outstripped the capacity to realize them. The same was to be true in a more general sense of the Barre government that replaced M. Chirac's administration in the early autumn of 1976. It was aptly described as the most 'European minded' French government since 1958[83]. It was also more deeply committed than its predecessor to a programme of economic stabilization[84]. And yet, as events in the following 18 months were to demonstrate, it was forced repeatedly to restrain its European enthusiasms and temper the rigours of its economic policies in response to domestic political pressures from both the right and the left.

The Community was therefore virtually leaderless as Mr Jenkins took over the presidency of the Commission in January 1977. The Germans would not lead, the French could not and the British neither would nor could. Beyond this group of three, there was little prospect of any other government, let alone the Commission, regalvanizing the Community's sense of purpose. The Italians had never played the role in the Community's inner councils to which the size of their population and the pro-European sentiments of their electorate might have seemed to entitle them. They were even less likely to do so now against the background of grave economic problems and in the aftermath of the June 1976 parliamentary elections in which the Communist vote had jumped from 27% in 1972 to over 34%, only four percentage points less than the Christian Democrats'[85]. It was a recipe for paralysis, which was only partially broken in March 1978 when the Communists were brought into the 'majority' (but not the government) for the first time for more than 30 years[86]. It was some consolation that in Italy, unlike Britain, the advance of the extreme left did not call the country's membership of the European Community or NATO into question. On the contrary, the Communists' acceptance of Italy's western orientation had been an essential factor in winning them broader popular support[87]. But the paralysis remained and, although a bold European initiative was almost bound to meet with sympathy if not enthusiasm in Italy, a bold Italian initiative to regenerate the Community was simply not on the cards.

Elsewhere, opportunities for influence were even more limited, as the sorry story of the Tindemans report proved only too clearly. Indeed, the best that the leaders of the smaller states and the president of the Commission could hope for was to obtain the support of one if not more of the larger Community states for any policy or cause that they favoured. In the context of 1977, with Britain, France and Italy effectively immobilized, this could only mean an alliance between the smaller states and/or the Commission and Germany. The Germans were by no means solely or even mainly responsible for the Community's crisis, but it had become increasingly clear that only if they assumed a major responsibility for its resolution could the Community hope to emerge from its malaise. Against this background, Mr Jenkins' decision at the beginning of August 1977 to formulate the Commission's plans for the coming years with a view above all to attracting the support of the Federal Republic was as shrewd as it was necessary.

1 David P. Calleo, *Money and the Coming World Order*, New York, 1976, p. xii
2 L. Tsoukalis, *The Politics and Economics of European Monetary Integration*, London, 1977
3 ibid., p. 130
4 ibid., p. 156
5 ibid., p. 165
6 *Bulletin of the European Communities*, Supplement 1/76
7 See W. Ethier and A. I. Bloomfield, 'The Reference Rate Proposal and Related Experience', *Banca Nazionale del Lavoro Quarterly*, September – December 1978. For a useful survey of this and other precursors of the EMS, see N. Thygesen, 'The Emerging European Monetary System: Precursors, first steps and policy options', *Bulletin de la Banque Nationale de Belgique*, 1(4), 1979, pp. 89ff
8 O. Emminger, *The D-Mark in the Conflict between Internal and External Equilibrium, 1948–75*, Princeton Essays

in International Finance, No. 122, June 1977
9 J. Pinder and L. Tsoukalis, 'Counter-Report on Economic and Monetary Policy'. In G. Ionescu (ed.), *The European Alternatives*, Sijthoff and Nordhoff, 1979, pp. 477ff
10 Emminger, op. cit. (note 8), p. 38
11 ibid., p. 41
12 On differences between Mr Schmidt and the Bundesbank, see *The Economist*, 23 October 1976
13 John Pinder, 'The Reform of International Economic Policy: Weak and Strong Countries'. In *International Affairs*, 1977, pp. 345ff
14 Pinder and Tsoukalis, op. cit. (note 9), p. 477
15 Tsoukalis, op. cit. (note 2), p. 104ff
16 See Robert Solomon, *The International Monetary System, 1945–1976*, New York 1977, Chapters XI and XII

17 IMF, *Annual Report*, 1976, pp. 43ff

18 *Changes in Industrial Structure in the European Economies since the Oil Crisis, 1973–78*, Brussels, 1979

19 *Monthly Report of the Deutsche Bundesbank*, November 1979

20 The Scandinavian crisis (crises) of 1973 onwards still awaits its historian. For a factual survey, see however the speech by Per Kleppe in *Stortings forhandlinger. Sesjonen 1978–79*, Oslo, pp. 1983ff

21 See *European Economy*, No. 4, 1979, Statistical Annex

22 See P. W. Ludlow, 'The Unwinding of Appeasement'. In Lothar Kettenacker (ed.), *Das 'Andere Deutschland' im Zweiten Weltkrieg*, Stuttgart, 1977

23 *Bulletin of the European Communities*, 12/1974, pp. 6ff

24 On the European Council, see, in general, Annette Morgan, *From Summit to Council: Evolution in the E.E.C.*, London, 1976, also, Emile Noel, 'Some Reflections on the Preparation, Development and Repercussions of the Meetings between Heads of Government 1974–75' *Government and Opposition*, 11/1975, pp. 20ff

25 See, *inter alia*, the article by Sir Harold Wilson in *The Times*, 28 June 1977

26 *The Economist*, 4 December 1976. A report on the December 1976 Hague meeting of the European Council, which reflects the disappointment in the failure of the institution – or the men – to match the occasion

27 S. Hoffmann, 'The Fate of the Nation-State', *Daedalus*, 1966, pp. 186–92

28 For a useful account of the intergovernmental machinery, see G. Edwards and Helen Wallace, *The Council of Ministers of the European Community and the President-in-Office*, London, 1977

29 See R. Rummel and W. Wessels (eds), *Die Europäische Politische Zusammenarbeit*, Bonn, 1978

30 Treaty of Paris, Articles 26ff, Treaty of Rome, Articles 145ff

31 Helen and William Wallace and Carole Webb (eds), *Policy-Making in the European Communities*, London, 1977, Ch. 3

32 On COREPER see esp. Helen Wallace, *National Governments and the European Communities*, London, 1973

33 On the Group of Ten, see Solomon, op. cit. (note 16)

34 See below, pp. 97ff

35 See below, pp. 170ff

36 See Edwards and Wallace, op. cit. (note 28), passim

37 ibid., p. 20

37a See below, pp. 165ff

38 See below, pp. 251ff

39 See below, pp. 129ff and 190

40 See Edwards and Wallace, op. cit. (note 28), Ch. 5

41 On the Franco-German relationship in its early phase, see F. R. Willis, *France, Germany and the New Europe, 1945–67*, Oxford, 1968

42 See *Der Spiegel*, 3 November 1980

43 Jean Monnet, *Mémoires*, Paris, 1976, Ch. 12, esp. pp. 353–360

44 See Robert Triffin, *Europe and the Money Muddle: From Bilateralism to Near-Convertibility, 1947–56*, New Haven, 1957

45 Monnet, op cit. (note 43), Ch. 16

46 *La Stampa*, 25 July 1976

47 *The Economist*, November 1975

48 D. Lerner and M. Gorden, *Euratlantica: Changing Perspectives of the European Elites*, Cambridge, Mass., 1969

49 See John Pinder, 'Europe as a Tenth Member of the Community', *Government and Opposition*, 1975, pp. 387ff

50 For the Common Market crisis of 1965, see John Newhouse, *Collision in Brussels*, London, 1968

51 *The Economist*, 4 December 1976

52 Wallaces and Webb, op. cit. (note 31), Ch. 12

53 ibid., passim

54 See, for example, R. Aron, *Plaidoyer pour l'Europe décadente*, Paris, 1978, and *La République Impériale*, Paris, 1973, and S. Hoffmann, 'Fragments floating in the here and now', *Daedalus*, 1979, pp. 1–26

55 *Bulletin of the European Communities*, Supplement 1/76, p. 11

56 For a lively, iconoclastic and highly welcome account of the events of 1950, see R. Massigli, *La Comédie des Erreurs*, Paris, 1978

57 See, for example, the series sponsored by the Council on Foreign Relations in the mid-1960s, which included, *inter alia*, H. Kissinger's *The Troubled Partnership*, New York, 1965, Stanley Hoffmann's *Gulliver's Troubles*, New York, 1968, and Richard Cooper's *The Economics of Interdependence*, New York, 1968

58 For documents and some commentary, see G. Mally, *The New Europe and the United States*, Lexington, 1974

59 *Frankfurter Rundschau*, 26 January 1972, 'Bonn will keine EWG Soldaten'

59a See H. Kissinger, *The White House Years*, Boston, 1979

60 See, for example, C. Fred Bergsten, 'The United States and Germany: The Imperative of Economic Bigemony'. In Bergsten, *Towards a New International Economic Order*, Lexington, 1975

61 C. Cerny (ed.), *Germany at the Polls, 1976*, Washington, 1978

62 *Monatsbericht der deutschen Bundesbank*, January 1977, 'Die wachsende Bedeutung der Europäischen Gemeinschaften für die öffentlichen Haushalte der Bundesrepublik'

63 On Mr Schmidt and Europe see, *inter alia*, *The Economist*, 26 February 1977

64 See, in general, U. Kitzinger, *Diplomacy and Persuasion. How Britain joined the Common Market*, London, 1973

65 See note 21 above

66 See Miriam Camps, *Britain and the European Community, 1955–63*, London, 1964

67 Kitzinger, op. cit. (note 64). Also David Butler and U. Kitzinger, *The 1975 Referendum*, London, 1976

68 For the elections of 1974 see D. Butler and Dennis Kavanagh *The British General Election of February 1974*, London, 1974, and *The British General Election of October 1974*, London, 1975

69 See, *inter alia*, *The Economist*, 8 October 1977

70 ibid.

71 See Kissinger, op. cit. (note 59a), pp. 419ff

72 See Kitzinger, op. cit. (note 64), Chs 2–5

73 See, *inter alia*, Alfred Grosser, *French Foreign Policy under de Gaulle*, London, 1967

74 *The Economist*, 20 November 1976

75 See Jack Hayward and Vincent Wright, '"Les deux Frances" and the French Presidential Elections of May 1974', *Parliamentary Affairs*, Summer 1974, pp. 222ff

76 See Marie Claude Smouts, 'De Gaullisme au neo-atlantisme'. In *Les politiques extérieures européennes dans la crise*, Fondation Nationale des Sciences Politiques, Paris, 1976, pp. 87–113

77 See Noel, op. cit. (note 24)

78 See, for example, Wallaces and Webb, op. cit. (note 31), p. 231

79 See *L'Année Politique*, 1974

80 See *The Economist*, 4 December 1976 and 12 January 1977

81 ibid., 4 December 1976

82 For a survey of political developments in France prior to the 1978 parliamentary elections see V. Wright, 'The French General Election of 1978'. In V. Wright (ed.), *Conflict and Consensus in France*, London, 1979, pp. 24ff

83 *The Economist*, 9 October 1976

84 See Diana Green, 'Individualism versus Collectivism: Economic Choices in France'. In Wright (ed.) op. cit. (note 82), pp. 81ff

85 H. Penniman (ed.), *Italy at the Polls*, Washington, 1977

86 See below, esp. pp. 205ff

87 See R. D. Putman, 'Italian Foreign Policy: The emergent consensus'. In Penniman, op. cit. (note 85), pp. 287ff

Setting Community Priorities: Mr Jenkins and the Revival of the Debate about European Monetary Union in 1977

The principal architects of the EMS were the German chancellor, Mr Schmidt, and the French president, M. Giscard d'Estaing, each of whom had reasons of his own for sponsoring the plan. The Franco-German initiative was, however, preceded by a campaign by Mr Jenkins, the president of the European Commission, to revive the debate about economic and monetary union. The precise connection between Mr Jenkins' efforts and Mr Schmidt's decision to launch his proposal at Copenhagen in April 1978 is difficult to assess, but, as the German chancellor himself acknowledged, there were links and parallels. It seems appropriate therefore to begin the detailed description of the events that preceded the EMS negotiations with a brief discussion of the Commission president's efforts and the calculations and hopes that lay behind them.

Mr Jenkins' call for a re-examination of the file on economic and monetary union is normally associated with the lecture that he delivered on the subject at the European University Institute in Florence on 27 October 1977. Although this was undoubtedly the most lucid and systematic statement of his theme, it is not often realized that by the time that Mr Jenkins delivered the speech, his campaign had been under way for some time. The Florence speech is an invaluable guide to several of the principal elements in his argument, but an analysis of its contents needs to be prefaced and supplemented by a discussion of the priorities that he set himself during the first six months of office, the problems that he encountered as he tried to implement them and the strategy that he developed in the light of his early failures, still more than his successes, to which the Florence speech gives an important but still only a partial clue.

2.1   Mr Jenkins' first six months

The key to an understanding of Mr Jenkins' approach to the presidency lies in the fact that unlike his predecessor, M. Ortoli, he had been a professional politician for most of his life and a senior Cabinet minister for eight years[1]. He came to Brussels as a potential prime minister whose hopes of the highest office had been thwarted, but perhaps not finally dashed, by developments in British domestic politics, rather than as a fonctionnaire with limited ministerial experience in the republic of fonctionnaires. He had neither the temperament nor the qualifications to fit him for the kind of role that M. Ortoli had preferred. The focal point of most of his working life had been the British parliament, and even his reputation as a good European had been made not so much in office – unlike Mr Heath his ministerial duties had never exposed him to prolonged dealings with the Community – as on public platforms, notably during the 1975 Referendum campaign when he had been the leader of the all-party coalition that fought successfully to keep the United Kingdom within the European Community[2]. Europe had been a cause rather than a complicated network of administrative arrangements, and although his inexperience of the latter was to cause him many difficulties in the first six months and indeed later, it also ensured that he approached his duties unburdened by the rather weary wisdom that was characteristic of many senior Brussels officials, who for good or ill had been turned into gradualists through overexposure to the limitations of the Commission and the Community. Needless to say, the new president acknowledged from the beginning that there was no prospect whatsoever of reviving the hopes and ambitions of Walter Hallstein who had tried to make the Commission the embryonic government of a supranational Community. On the contrary, as he noted in his Florence speech, 'we must build Europe upon the basis of our late twentieth century nation states'. But the dominant role of national governments in Community decision-making processes did not exclude an important contribution from the Commission and its president. Despite the obvious risks in such a course, therefore, Mr Jenkins aimed at a high profile in Community affairs both for himself and for the organization that he led.

His ambitions were apparent from the moment that he was nominated. Appointed at the suggestion of the French president and the German chancellor[3] – the former apparently regarded him as one of the very few credible British politicians left, while the latter was an old friend and associate who like Mr Jenkins stood well to the right of his party – he set out to achieve the maximum influence in the choice of his fellow commissioners[4]. This was in itself an innovation, since his predecessors had had to accept colleagues nominated by the member governments. Once in office, his intentions became still more obvious. His personal interest in improving the Commission's facilities for projecting its image, which resulted amongst other things in the installation of a new television studio supervised by a British journalist hired from London by the president himself[5], and his promises to the European Parliament that even before direct elections his Commission would treat it as if it were a directly elected assembly[6] were characteristic of his political approach to his duties. So, still more, was the sustained campaign through personal lobbying of the heads of government and the mobilization of the resentments of the smaller states to secure a place as of right at the summit meeting of the Seven scheduled to take place in London in May 1977[7].

His aspirations also showed through in his earliest policy statements. When later in the year Mr Jenkins chose to make monetary union the central theme of his presidency, most observers professed surprise. In many respects, however, the new departure in the summer was a perfectly logical development from the arguments and hopes expressed during his first six months of office, as a brief analysis of his first two statements to the European Parliament in January and February 1977 will show[8]. The first occasion was a personal one, when Mr Jenkins presented his Commission; the second a more formal one, when he outlined the Commission's programme. Both speeches, and particularly the second, covered a large number of topics, but his preoccupation with the problem of divergence between the member states is already evident, as too is the belief that only a bold and radical strategy rather than a gradualist one was appropriate to the situation with which the Community was confronted. Paying tribute to his predecessor, Mr Jenkins observed that he had had to operate 'under the pall of the most discouraging economic weather which we have known for a generation'. As a result the Commission over which he had presided had been obliged to withdraw to 'winter quarters'.

> I am bound to tell you that I do not yet feel any benign stirring of the breezes of spring. But what I do feel is that there comes a time when you have to break out of the citadel or wither within it. That time is now very close upon us. Nor are the omens necessarily unpropitious. The member states have recently gone too much their own way.

In the February speech, Mr Jenkins referred to 'three formidable and interlocking obstacles to advance': high unemployment, high though varying rates of inflation throughout the Community and economic divergence. The effort to overcome all three obstacles together would 'provide the central theme of our economic policies in the period ahead'. The ideas that he advanced about how to tackle them were, he stressed, no more than preliminary observations that would have to be worked out more fully and discussed with member states. The first was a further development of the council and committee system in order to improve national policy coordination. This could, however, be no more than a beginning. 'It must be accompanied by the selective intervention by the Community in the European economy as a whole.' The new Commission had already taken a number of steps to reorganize its portfolios with a view to exercising a proper supervision of the existing financial instruments at the Community's disposal. It would also aim to 'devise a *general* policy to concentrate its present and future resources on the central problem of economic divergence, using not only the Funds, but also the existing loan mechanisms'. Both, however, were too small to be sufficient in themselves. What was needed were more diversified and flexible instruments that would bring about a genuine redistribution of wealth. Anticipating the arguments that were shortly to be set out in much more detail in the MacDougall report, Mr Jenkins claimed that although the task of arresting the process of divergence would not be costless, neither would it be impossibly expensive. The gap between the richest and the poorest member states measured in *per capita* income was not outrageously large by comparison with the gaps that existed between regions within states, and assuming that the Community could apply part at least of the massive mechanisms of public finance, rather than the 'relatively puny' funds currently at its disposal, the gap could be narrowed. These measures would not, needless to say, be taken without ensuring that proper disciplines were observed, but 'if economic union is to be more than a phrase, both the richer and the poorer nations of the Community must accept the reality of the Community's role'.

In the weeks that followed, these general declarations of intent were succeeded by a number of detailed proposals, including most notably the request for an extension of the Community's loan facilities, soon to become known as the Ortoli Facility, and a draft Community budget, which, though still small, was substantially larger than the previous year's. The Regional Fund, for example, was increased by 88%, while provision for investment in energy and schemes for structural reform was raised by 78%.[9].

For all his ambitions however, Mr Jenkins' early experiences of office were singularly unhappy. His efforts to recruit a Commission to his own liking had been only partially successful[10]. He had, it is true, made one or two major coups. The renewal of M. Cheysson's appointment, for example, did not at first appear likely, but Mr Jenkins could claim at least some credit for the change in the French government's attitude. His influence over the appointment of the Italian Socialist, Signor Giolitti, was even more direct and obvious. Elsewhere he had been less fortunate. Mr Burke, the Irish commissioner, was not his candidate, nor was Mr Tugendhat his original choice as second British commissioner, while from the Netherlands he would have preferred Dr Brinkhorst to Mr Vredeling. His most humiliating setback, however, was administered by Helmut Schmidt, who insisted that he should recall Mr Haferkamp, whom Mr Jenkins and, it would seem, almost everybody else in a position to know regarded as unfit for the job.

The fact that the president's feelings about one of his senior colleagues were so widely known cannot have helped the new Commission to develop any strong sense of corporate identity. But there were other obstacles too. Linguistically for example, whereas the European Council could cope fairly well in English, the Jenkins' Commission was hampered by the limited skills of several of its members[11]. The nearest to a common language was French, but the president himself and several other colleagues were scarcely fluent in it. With a vast array of translators and interpreters available, this problem could always be overcome in formal meetings, but the effectiveness of the informal sessions to which Mr Jenkins obviously attached considerable

significance was sometimes impaired by elementary difficulties in communication. These linguistic problems were compounded by the unfamiliar-
ity of the new president with the ways of the Commission. He headed a
bureaucracy that functioned quite differently from the civil service to which
he had grown accustomed after ten years as a minister in London, and his
attempt to coax the secretary general into assuming something like the role
of a permanent secretary in the British system was conspicuously unsuccessful. As a result his grasp over the administration seemed at times clumsy and
unsure[12].

His embarrassment was in some senses symbolized by the continuing
presence in the Commission of his predecessor M. Ortoli, with whom he
was inevitably compared. M. Ortoli's presidency had in many ways been far
from successful. He was too much of a fonctionnaire to be able to lead the
Commission in a period when the Community was at last beginning to
acquire an institutional structure appropriate to the political realities of the
1970s rather than the rhetoric of the 1950s. But in the day-to-day conduct of
business in the small town atmosphere of Berlaymont, he had been
reasonably effective. Mr Jenkins' desire to break out of the limitations that
his predecessor had so readily accepted may have been admirable, but after
six months of experience there were many both inside the building and
outside who wondered whether an efficient gradualist was not preferable to
an inefficient politician.

Mr Jenkins' main problems lay beyond the Commission itself, however.
His shortcomings and inexperience in running the machine could have been
offset by successes outside, in settings such as the television studios,
Parliament and summit meetings, on which he himself laid such stress. But
in his first six months he had suffered reverses and humiliations on the
ground of his own choosing. His relations with the media, for example,
were soon in trouble. The *Economist*, which was better informed about the
new Commission and more sympathetic to its president than perhaps any
other leading international journal, reported in the middle of 1977 that Mr
Jenkins was unpopular with the majority of the Brussels press corps[13]. His
first television press conference – the first of its kind at the Berlaymont
building – had been a notable failure[14]. His relations with Parliament,
though better, were not as easy as he had anticipated, while at the summit
level at which he felt a Commission president should aim to operate, he had
had to fight hard and not altogether successfully to get himself established.

The series of bilateral meetings that he arranged with each of the
Community leaders in their respective capitals was, it is true, fruitful and
successful. Mr Schmidt, for example, let it be known following their
meeting in Bonn in March 1977 that he was greatly relieved that the
Commission was at last in the hands of a man of prime ministerial calibre[15].
The first meeting with the French president was also friendly and useful. But
these man-to-man encounters did not raise the question of Mr Jenkins'

status in the same way as the multilateral meetings of heads of government, and it was in these settings that the new president ran into serious trouble. Even in the more intimate framework of the European Council meeting in Rome in March, he received a sharp reminder that he was *not* a head of government when Italian officials had to steer him away from the front row of seats reserved for presidents and prime ministers at the celebrations to mark the twentieth anniversary of the Treaty of Rome[16]. There was some consolation at the same Council meeting, when M. Giscard d'Estaing, under pressure not only from Mr Jenkins, but also from the Dutch and Belgian prime ministers and, to a lesser extent, from Mr Schmidt, agreed that the president of the Commission could attend the summit meeting of the Seven in London in May, when the latter dealt with matters of interest to the Community as a whole. At the London meeting itself, however, both the French and the British went out of their way to humiliate him. The French president refused to attend a dinner given by Mr Callaghan for Mr Carter and the other heads of government because Mr Jenkins was also invited, while the British inflicted innumerable greater and lesser snubs on the erstwhile Cabinet minister, ensuring for example that at the final press conference seats were reserved for all the delegations except the Commission officials and that alone amongst the participants at the summit Mr Jenkins lacked a microphone with which to address the assembled journalists[17].

Mr Jenkins' policy proposals too ran into difficulties. The proposed increases in the Community's Regional and Social Funds were not accepted by the European Council at its London meeting in June 1977, and hopes that alternative ways of redressing regional imbalances and attacking structural problems in the Community economy might be opened up through increases in the amount and types of loan facilities were also dashed at the same meeting, when the Council postponed a decision on the Ortoli Facility until its next meeting in December 1977[18].

Mr Jenkins' early misfortunes mirrored the malaise of the Community as a whole and in particular the inhibitions that affected the leaders of the three most important member states. It was particularly unfortunate perhaps that the new president's first six months in office should have coincided with the first British presidency of the Council of Ministers. Given the political and economic constraints under which Mr Callaghan's government had to operate during the months immediately following the sterling crisis of 1976 and an IMF package that involved measures that, however justified, were scarcely calculated to endear the government to its left wing, let alone the electorate at large, it was hardly surprising that the British foreign secretary, Mr Crosland, began his period of office with a low-key promise of efficient management rather than innovation and reform[19]. Within a very few weeks, however, Mr Crosland died and was replaced by Dr David Owen, who despite the goodwill of his colleagues in the Council of Ministers and the backing of the prime minister, was too young and too lightweight to prevent ministers like Mr Benn or Mr Silkin using the advantages conferred on them by the chairmanship of their own particular councils to advance short-term British interests and score irrelevant, anti-Community propaganda points. In the end, even the foreign secretary seems to have concluded that mini-Gaullism was a substitute for diplomacy and the British presidency ended in a welter of recrimination and bad feeling[20].

The shortcomings of the British government, which were predictable, might have been tolerable had either the German chancellor or the French president been free of domestic political problems. Their difficulties will be discussed in more detail in chapter 3. Suffice it to say that a chancellor who in the view of many observers could only occasionally act with authority inside the Federal Republic was unlikely to give much of a lead outside it, while a president who was a hostage to his Gaullist supporters was even worse placed to help. Mr Jenkins' personal problems were therefore compounded by a general weakness in the Community, which seemed if anything more marked six months on than it had been when he took over the presidency at the beginning of 1977.

2.2   East Hendred, Florence and Bonn: the formulation of a strategy

It was against this background of six months of high ambition but limited success that the idea of making monetary union the central theme of his presidency began to emerge. The first clear hint of the way in which Mr Jenkins' mind was moving was given in the course of a speech to the European Parliament at the beginning of July. The plan took more definite shape a few weeks later when, on 2 August 1977, the president had a long session with a few close advisers at his country home at East Hendred in Berkshire. Following this meeting, Michael Emerson – who as we shall see was the member of Mr Jenkins' Cabinet on whom, during this period at least, he relied most heavily for economic advice – was asked to prepare a paper in advance of a special meeting of the Commission scheduled to take place in the Ardennes in September. A public launch of the initiative was also envisaged, though when plans were first drawn up in August the intention was to wait until December, when the president had an invitation to speak in Bonn. Florence was an afterthought.

Three considerations would appear to have been uppermost in Mr Jenkins' mind as he embarked upon his campaign. The first was the belief, reinforced by the frustrations of his first six months of office, that the only way in which the Community could be jolted back into a serious discussion of what in the post-Luxembourg epoch the nation states could usefully do together lay in a fresh debate about the fundamental problems raised by monetary union. A debate about money would, if properly conducted, lead logically to the formulation of a strategy to overcome the problems of unemployment, high inflation and, most important of all, economic divergence. The second consideration was the feeling that money alone amongst the various options available might appeal to the short-term interests of the most powerful member state, namely the Federal Republic of Germany, without whose leadership the Community as it existed in 1977 was unlikely to advance much further. The third consideration also reflected an assessment of political realities in Western Europe. Although alternative sources of leadership were not yet in evidence, there were a number of signs that some if not all the governments of the member states would be more susceptible than they had been a year earlier to proposals for a Community strategy founded on monetary union and that one at least, namely the Belgians, would be more than willing to offer the president maximum assistance.

This last point is the least important of the three, but it is worth explaining briefly because it was undoubtedly an element influencing the timing, if not the character, of the Jenkins campaign. As Mr Jenkins drew up his plans, it was still too early to know whether the stabilization programmes to which the Barre administration in France and, perforce, the Callaghan and Andreotti governments in Britain and Italy were committed would succeed, but it seemed reasonable to assume that some or all of these governments would be more than usually receptive to proposals for a Community monetary regime that could, if it was introduced, reinforce the domestic policies that out of choice or necessity they were engaged in implementing. The economic divergence of the years between 1973 and 1976 had not simply reflected the differing capacities of the member states' economies, but the policy preferences of their governments. For one reason or another, however, all three governments were by 1977 attempting to implement economic strategies in which the struggle against inflation was given priority over efforts to reduce unemployment.

The attitude of the Belgian government, however, had a still more immediate relevance to the president of the Commission, since on 1 July 1977 they assumed the presidency of the European Council, and it was quickly apparent that they intended on their own initiative to give monetary questions a high priority during their term of office as a central element in an effort to re-open the debate on the Tindemans report, which, understandably and justly, they felt had been treated with less respect than it merited. Their interests were declared by M. Simonet, the foreign minister, in a speech that he made to the European Parliament on 6 July[21]:

> With all their energies taken up by the problems of inflation and unemployment, the countries of Europe are having difficulties in maintaining the *acquis communautaire* and holding down the instinctive

resurgence of nationalist tendencies which still have their poisonous charms. Under such difficult conditions, they have not been able to devote the attention and effort necessary to the forging of a European Union. The progress we have made and hope to make during our Presidency may, taken on its own, seem slight and incoherent: but its true importance emerges when it is seen in the overall perspective of our future activities, as set forth by Mr Tindemans in his report. It is towards this that the Belgian presidency means to work.

The specific steps in the economic and monetary field that the Belgians wished to initiate were sketched out in M. Simonet's speech, but were dealt with in more detail shortly afterwards in the opening statement by the finance minister, M. Geens, to ECOFIN on 18 July. The Community's fundamental aim, the finance minister declared, was to reduce the divergence between member states' economies. To help towards this end, he proposed action on two fronts: first an attempt to improve the coordination of the monetary and budgetary policies of member governments, and secondly a move to increase the amount of credit available to member states in currency or balance of payments difficulties, while at the same time tightening up the conditions on which these credits would be provided. As M. Geens himself observed, his proposals were in some respects a development of part at least of the Duisenberg plan. It was intended not to replace the Snake, which was still, even with its reduced membership, an indispensable instrument encouraging the convergence of the economies of the participant states, but to develop methods of bringing the economies of the non-Snake members back into a close relationship with the others, so that in time some kind of fixed relationship could be re-established. This double approach on the monetary front should, it was suggested, be reinforced by a fresh attempt to improve the financial instruments of the Community in order to foster structural change in the weaker economies. The Jenkins/Ortoli loan facility, so coolly received at the London meeting of the European Council at the end of June, was singled out for special mention as a proposal that deserved serious and prompt consideration.

Mr Jenkins immediately signalled his welcome for and agreement with the Belgian order of priorities in his own contributions to the debate in the European Parliament of 6 July[22]. His remarks are worth quoting, because quite apart from highlighting the convergence between his own and M. Simonet's views, they give an early hint of themes and arguments that he was to develop at greater length and on more widely reported occasions later in the year:

The plain fact is we [the Community] do not advance as fast as we can. I do not understand ... fears that somehow Mr Simonet might launch us too quickly into a full-scale economic and monetary union or into great political developments. My fear always is that we shall go too slow. I welcome the fact that his approach is my approach. We must do two things – we must deal with day-to-day issues, week-to-week, month-to-month issues and try and get some desperately needed decisions on issues which have to be settled, some of which have been hanging about for too long. But at the same time, while dealing with these day-to-day issues, there is no reason why we should not lift up our heads, and look a little further towards the distant horizon. That, I think, is the proper balance. I am entirely in favour therefore of introducing reconsiderations of Tindemans and I am entirely in favour of looking ahead towards economic and monetary union. I do not believe ... that we shall get economic and monetary union overnight. The view that you could proclaim it and it would happen was perhaps a mistake. But I think it is an equal mistake to recoil from that into believing that economic and monetary union is not something which we should seek and seek extremely hard for the future of this Community.

I believe that many of the problems which we face today, many of the pressing problems – problems related to the CAP, to monetary compensatory amounts and other matters of this sort – arise from the lack of an approach to economic and monetary union. It is not something you can achieve by a proclamation, but equally it is not something which you should not regard as a desirable object to move towards at a sensible pace. Therefore, I am entirely in favour of the approach which the President of the Council has made, which is a practical approach, but at the same time an approach with a good element of vision in it.

In the months that followed, cooperation between Mr Jenkins, his Cabinet and Belgian ministers and officials was to be close and fruitful, and the fact that, against all the odds, the president's proposals received 'a fair wind' at the European Council in December 1977 was due in no small measure to the sympathy and support that he received from the Belgian prime minister, M. Tindemans[23]. The campaign that he developed in the latter half of 1977 was nonetheless very much his own. Encouraging though the support of the Belgian government undoubtedly was, not to mention the changing fashions in economic management that were apparent in Britain, France and Italy, the considerations that were most important in the development of the president's strategy were nevertheless the first two referred to above: the need for a 'high political' approach to the Community's structural problems and the hope that it might be able to establish a link between Germany's short-term interests and the long-term interests of the Community as a whole.

Both these points emerged in the course of a special meeting that the president of the Commission convened at East Hendred in Berkshire on 2 August. The meeting was attended by Mr Jenkins himself, his chef de cabinet, Crispin Tickell, Graham Avery, Michael Emerson, Michael Jenkins, David Marquand, Lord Harris and Renato Ruggiero, who had become the Commission's official spokesman following a spell in Lord Thomson's Cabinet. The purpose was to review the first six months of the presidency and to sort out the priorities for the future. With this latter object in view, several of those who were invited had been asked to prepare papers on particular topics, such as the CAP, enlargement, and monetary union. The setting was informal, the discussion wide-ranging and the remedies varied. One adviser, for example, suggested that the president should make enlargement a major theme of his speeches and actions during the coming months, another the direct elections to the European Parliament, and yet another, Renato Ruggiero, industrial policy, as a radical Community antidote to the menace of political instability in France and Italy. None of these suggestions was dismissed out of hand, but it was nevertheless clear well before the end of the meeting that the president himself had already decided to make monetary union the central theme of the following months. This did not exclude a review of industrial policy, or efforts to reform the common agricultural policy. On the contrary, as Michael Emerson emphasized, a strategy focused on the monetary question would almost certainly boost the development of other Community policies. Monetary union was not, in other words, an end in itself but a means by which the debate about the priorities of the Community could be reopened. It was also, Mr Jenkins himself observed, a theme that might appeal to the medium- and short-term interests of the Bonn government, which, against the background of the continuing fall of the dollar, was bound to be concerned by the threat that this posed to its industry and economic stability. There was thus from the very beginning an implicit acknowledgement of the fact that any decisive move forwards towards European political integration would have to command the assent and arouse the support of the West German authorities. The action programme agreed towards the end of the meeting reflects this political judgement. Mr Emerson was asked to prepare a paper, which would in due course be worked up into a speech covering money, enlargement and agriculture at Bonn in December.

The analysis of the considerations underlying Mr Jenkins' campaign for monetary union in 1977–78 can be carried a stage further by an examination of the two most systematic statements of the case: the Jean Monnet lecture at Florence in October 1977[24] and the Bonn lecture in December 1977[25]. To many of those who read or commented on Mr Jenkins' Florence speech at the time, it seemed like a fundamentalist restatement of the monetarist faith. As the latter had in the view of most experts been discredited by the experience of the 1970s, the president's judgement was widely called into question. However, a close examination of the Florence lecture suggests that it cannot simply be assigned to either the monetarist or the economist camp. Mr Jenkins did not reject the economists' argument that monetary union without prior efforts to promote convergence of national economies was bound to fail; on the contrary, his case was that the political will to sustain these detailed policies could not be generated unless they were seen within the context of a coherent conception of what the Community existed for in the long term. The Community would not 'walk backwards into unity'. The debate about means (the economists' argument) had to be accompanied by a debate about ends (the monetarists' creed), just as much as the discussion of ends could not proceed without realistic consideration of the means necessary to obtain them. Mr Jenkins himself had been concerned throughout the first six months of office with piecemeal improvements to the financial instruments available to the Community, but the relatively modest package of proposals that he and his colleagues had put forward at the London meeting of the European Council in June 1977, involving a new loan facility and increased expenditure on regional and social policies, had not progressed. The case for a monetary union did not denote an acceptance of defeat for detailed proposals to create greater convergence amongst the member states; it was intended instead to justify them by relating them to an overall model of European union of which monetary union was the cornerstone, but in the construction of which they too would be indispensable. The fundamental purpose behind the Florence speech and the campaign throughout the winter of 1977–78 as a whole was therefore political. It was intended to reopen the discussion of what the Community existed for in the final analysis, so that the seemingly intractable problem of reaching agreement on relatively modest policy proposals could be placed within a new context.

The heart of Mr Jenkins' argument is to be found in a few sentences towards the end of the Florence speech, in a section concerned with institutional questions. Given the continuing political strength of the nation state and widespread and entirely legitimate dislike of centralized bureaucracies, we had to explore the possibilities for 'multi-tiered government'.

> Some support the federal model; others would prefer something confederal; others like neither. I for my part believe that the Community must devise its own arrangements and that these are unlikely to correspond to any existing prototype. We must build Europe upon the basis of our late twentieth century nation states. We must only give to the Community functions which will, beyond reasonable doubt, deliver significantly better results because they are performed at a Community level. We must fashion a Community which gives to each Member State the benefits of results which they cannot achieve alone. We must equally leave to them functions which they can do equally well or better on their own.

If, Mr Jenkins argued, the implications of monetary union were properly thought through, it would be found to provide a key to a political model of the Community that would allow full scope to the aspirations of individuals and regional and national groups for the fullest autonomy possible, while ensuring them benefits that they could not achieve by themselves. Monetary union he argued, taking the MacDougall report as his authority, could be sustained by public expenditure representing 5% to 7% of GNP. This was, of course, a very large sum of money, but it was quite small 'by the standards of the classic federations where the top tier of government takes 20% to 25% of GNP'. This 'highly decentralised type of monetary union would leave the public procurement of goods and services 'primarily in national, regional or other hands', and would therefore make for 'a quite small central bureaucracy'. The benefits that would flow from this union would, however, be tangible and largely unobtainable by other means. They were both economic and political in character. Economically, the union would favour a more efficient and developed rationalization of industry; it would provide the Community with the advantages that accrue to the 'issuer of a world currency', which in the light of the 'current problems of the dollar' would be no small gain; properly implemented and administered it would contribute to the battle against inflation; it would help to reduce unemployment and, finally, it would reinforce policies designed to even out regional imbalances within the Community. Politically, it could provide the central point of reference for a rational reconstruction of Community institutions and a catalyst to political integration. 'The successful creation of a European monetary union would take Europe over a political threshold.'

The Florence lecture was the most detached and academic statement of the Commission president's ideas on monetary union and, before proceeding to an analysis of the Bonn speech, in which short-term political calculations were much more in evidence, it is worth investigating how and by whom it was drafted. In the final stages of the preparation of the Florence speech, the president had a number of discussions with Robert Triffin who, as well as being a professor at the University of Louvain-La-Neuve, was also employed by the Commission as an economic consultant. There was also some consultation with M. van Ypersele, monetary adviser to the Belgian finance minister. The contributions from both men were undoubtedly important: Professor Triffin had after all been involved in the discussion of plans for European monetary union for over 20 years, while M. van Ypersele was peculiarly well placed to advise the president on the present state of discussions within the Monetary Committee as well as in more informal groups, such as the Pamphilii group with which he was associated. In the preparation of the Florence speech, however, neither Professor Triffin nor M. van Ypersele was as important an influence as Michael Emerson and, through him, the group of economists who had prepared the MacDougall report, *The role of public finance in European integration*, which had been published earlier in 1977[26].

The MacDougall report was the work of an independent group of economists that had been formed on the initiative of the Commission in the spring of 1975 under the chairmanship of Sir Donald MacDougall, chief economic adviser to the Confederation of British Industries. Other members of the group were Dieter Biehl, professor at the Technische Universität, Berlin, Arthur Brown, professor at the University of Leeds, Francesco Forte, professor at the University of Turin, Yves Freville, professor at the University of Rennes, Martin O'Donoghue, professor at Trinity College, Dublin, and Theo Peeters, professor at the University of Leuven. In preparing their report, the group also drew heavily on the services of officials in the European Commission itself, and one in particular, Michael Emerson, played a major part in drafting the final version in the winter of 1976/77. When, therefore, soon after taking up his post, Mr Jenkins complained that he was finding the normal run of Commission papers that he was obliged to read rather dreary and wanted something 'to get his teeth into' at weekends, his attention was drawn to the report. The latter was not, of course, directly concerned with the question of monetary union. On the contrary, its authors assumed that monetary union was 'a long way off and would probably have to await major developments in the political, monetary and fiscal fields'[27]. But the analysis that its authors developed of the potential role of public finance in European economic union prompted them to make observations, on which Mr Jenkins duly fastened, about both the political and economic preconditions of monetary union and the redistributive effect that, if proper financial instruments were developed, might be expected to flow from it.

The group's analysis of what might be achieved through public finance at Community level was prefaced by a detailed discussion of the role of public finance in eight countries: Australia, Canada, France, Germany, Italy, Switzerland, the United Kingdom and the United States[28]. They found that in these countries public finance, in the form of public expenditure, taxation and grants or transfers, reduced regional inequalities in *per capita* income by about 40% on average. It also played a major role in softening the effects of short-term and cyclical fluctuations by, for example, offsetting a fall in the external sales of one region to the rest of the country concerned through lower payments of taxes and insurance contributions to central government and higher receipt of unemployment and other benefits. The relative importance of the different instruments varied between unitary states and federations. In the former, the redistributive effect was achieved primarily through taxation, particularly personal income tax, and public expenditure. In federal countries, though both taxation and public expenditure played a role, grants from central government to the lower levels of government, general purpose equalization grants and transfers and specific-purpose grants tended to assume greater significance. In the second of these categories, the Committee paid particular attention to the equalization system in the Federal Republic of Germany (the *Länderfinanzausgleich*)[29].

In assessing the implications of experience in existing states for the European Community, the group related their findings to four possible degrees of integration. The first was the *status quo*, which, they suggested, was characterized by a largely completed customs union and modest and uneven progress in a number of public sector activities, involving public expenditure at Community level of below 1% of GDP[30]. The second model they defined as pre-federal integration, which would involve the completion of the common market by the elimination of non-tariff trade barriers and other distortions to trade and the free movement of capital and labour, some increased public sector activities and further steps towards economic and monetary policy intervention, falling short however of monetary union. Particular stress was placed on structural and redistribution policies designed to bring about a greater convergence of economic performance, and, although most economic policy instruments would remain in national hands, Community expenditure might increase to 2% to 2.5% of GDP[31]. The third hypothesis was a federation, with a full political and monetary union but a small public sector at Community level requiring no more than 5% to 7% of GDP. If defence were to become a function of this federation, an additional 2.5% to 3% of GDP would have to be allocated for this purpose[32]. The fourth hypothesis, which the group considered merely as an academic model, was a large public sector federation comparable to the United States or the Federal Republic of Germany where federal public expenditure amounted to around 20% to 25% of GDP[33].

The extent to which increases in public expenditure of the orders suggested under the various hypothetical models would have a significant redistributive effect between regions depended not only on the amount of public funds available, but also on the mechanisms that were devised. The Community's present finances, for example, achieved only a very small redistributive effect, since the agricultural policy, which took up the lion's share of the budget, had specific sectoral objectives with only an incidental inter-member state redistributive effect[34]. If, however, an equalization mechanism similar to the *Finanzausgleich* in use in the Federal Republic was applied in the Community, a budget amounting to 2% of Community GDP could level up member state incomes to the extent of 40%, and finance a large part or all of the current account deficits of the beneficiary states. Assuming that the budget was designed to have a 'high powered' redistributive effect, the group believed that a full economic, monetary and political union could function with a Community-level budget amounting to no more than 5% or 7% of GDP.

This was the model that formed the point of departure for the Florence speech: a 'slim-line federation' in which the Community could achieve a 'high political' profile in the eyes of its citizens by fulfilling functions that were both visible and significant without encroaching unduly on the proper (and entrenched) interests of the nation states. Given its importance in the Florence argument, it is worth examining the functions that it implied would best be performed by the Community in a multi-tiered governmental system. By contrast with existing federations, almost all *social and welfare services* would be provided by lower levels of government, and Community expenditure under this heading would be very small indeed, amounting to no more than 1.5% to 2% of GDP. The remaining 21%, which was the average devoted to these purposes in the countries studied, would be raised and spent by national and regional authorities. The largest element in the Community budget under this heading would be a general purpose equalization mechanism, making transfers to the weakest member states for them to top up their own expenditure programmes. There might also be expenditure on unemployment and housing. Community expenditure of the order of 2% to 3% of GDP would be required for *structural and sectoral policies*: agriculture, energy, public infrastructure, industrial, regional and labour market policies. Here again, however, the aim would be to complement the actions of member states and in particular the weaker member states, rather than to transfer complete responsibility to central government. Community expenditure on *public administration* and *law and order* would remain small, but all *foreign aid* would be channelled through the Community, which would also assume responsibility for *external relations* and possibly *defence*. If the latter were included, total public expenditure at Community level would amount to between 7.5% and 10% of GDP.

On the way to this 'slim-line federation', the group contemplated a pre-federal phase in which for little more than twice the existing Community budget significant redistributive effects could be achieved[35]. Although they envisaged some increase in expenditure on advanced technology industries, and declining industries such as textiles and shipbuilding, steel and fisheries, they argued that most of the money needed for these policies could be raised through loans, with the Community acting as a financial intermediary. In this pre-federal phase, the most significant increases of Community expenditure should occur in structural, cyclical, employment and regional policies. On present reckoning, member states were estimated to be spending $15–27 billion on regional policy aids, labour market policies and unemployment compensation, compared with a Community budget of $10 billion. The group argued that if the Community took over approximately one-third of the expenditure currently raised and administered by the member states, major redistributive consequences would result. If these were backed up by a limited budget equalization scheme for extremely weak member states, a system of cyclical grants to local or regional governments that would depend upon regional economic conditions, and a conjunctural convergence facility that would make available grant finance to member states aimed at preventing acute cyclical problems, the result might be an equalization of about 10% of existing income *per capita* differentials between member states for an expenditure of, say, 10 billion units of account (EUA). (In 1977 $1 equalled approximately 1.2 units of account.)

When the MacDougall report was published in May 1977, it received little public attention, and those comments that were made on it tended to be of the kind made by *The Economist*: 'Well, why not dream?'[36] Similar reactions greeted Mr Jenkins' Florence speech. To the president himself, however, the campaign for a new debate about monetary union was not simply a call for Utopia. On the contrary, there were from the beginning several important links between the long-term future to which full monetary union undoubtedly belonged and and the present. One type of connection, the hope that *'today's* discussion of a more ambitious plan for the day after tomorrow might assist tomorrow's act of better coordination'[37], has already been referred to in the discussion of the Florence speech. As the meeting at East Hendred suggested however, there were other, more mundane, considerations that prompted Mr Jenkins to make monetary union the central subject of his speeches and political initiatives from mid-1977 onwards. First and foremost amongst these was the conviction that if there was one point at which the long-term interests of the Community and the short-term interests of the most powerful member state might overlap it was the monetary issue. Bonn was therefore from the beginning the major target of the president's initiative.

As a speech, the paper that Mr Jenkins read to the Deutsche Gesellschaft für Auswärtige Politik on 8 December 1977 is a good deal less impressive and satisfying than the lecture at Florence. However, in order to understand the link that the president made between political ideals and political reality, it is an indispensable source[38]. Some of what Mr Jenkins said was inevitably no more than a repetition of what had been said at Florence six weeks earlier. In the second half of the speech, however, he addressed himself specifically to his German audience, arguing firstly that the leaders of the Federal Republic were peculiarly well placed to contribute to the debate about the Community's future for which he had called, and secondly that a move towards monetary union would be in the interests of the Germans as much as if not more than any other members of the Community. West Germany, Mr Jenkins implied, could in many ways be taken as a political and economic model for the rest of Western Europe.

> You alone among Community countries have a solid grounding in the mechanisms of a federal system ... you have a strong federal structure, one that is tighter in its degree of central harmonisation (for example on taxation matters) than in Switzerland or the federations of the new world. Admittedly some other of our member states are now introducing constitutional reforms ... but the essential point is that you in Germany can contemplate maturely and openmindedly the wide spectrum of arrangements for multi-tiered government that may be compatible with the functioning of a modern, industrialised economy.

In at least two other respects, he continued, German experience was particularly relevant to the subject in hand. Firstly, bold actions in the monetary field had been fundamental to the postwar prosperity of the Federal Republic. Secondly, the Germans had developed institutional arrangements that had been important in their own success story and that could, suitably modified, be adapted for the Community as a whole. Mr Jenkins mentioned specifically the position of the Bundesbank in the Federal Republic and instruments such as the *Finanzausgleich*, to which there was no equivalent in the Community of today but which would clearly have their place in a more 'mature political structure'.

This appeal to national pride was carefully balanced by an appeal to national self-interest. The dangers to German prosperity represented by the fall in the dollar and the growing trend towards protectionism were alluded to, but Mr Jenkins appears to have regarded them as so self-evident that they did not require detailed exposition. He concentrated instead on the international debate about the appropriate strategy to combat recession, in which, as the next chapter will confirm, the Federal Republic found itself under increasing pressure to reflate. 'Germany resists ... the so-called locomotive theory of cyclical leadership by the more powerful economies whose balance of payments position is strong', Mr Jenkins observed.

> I understand your argument. Virtually every German boom since the war has been led in no small measure by strong export demand, leading to a strong consequential tide of private investment ... The attractiveness of pulling further on levers of domestic demand management policy seems limited. You cannot in the conventional international setting have an important effect on foreign demand without risk of domestic instability ...

On the other hand, the arguments of other medium-sized European economies in which the authorities were obliged to adopt cautious demand management policies because of the risk, if they did not, of sharp falls in their exchange rates, which damaged business confidence and increased inflationary pressures, should also be noted. There was in fact 'a sort of economic stalemate'. The countries that were under no external financial constraint were reliant on the weaker countries for the effectiveness of their policies. But the more vulnerable countries were themselves unable to act on the basis of the collective economic and financial strength of the Community as a whole.

To break out of this stalemate, it was in the interests of both strong and weak to devise a more effective system of control and coordination through the Community. There might be a temptation in Germany to rest on the Republic's very considerable laurels, but, Mr Jenkins argued, the present situation with over 6.5 million unemployed in Europe was urgent and could get worse. 'Beyond the 6.5 million unemployed of today there are 9 million more young people who between now and 1985 are going to be added to the Community labour force looking for extra jobs; and the Federal Republic is, because of its population profile, at the top of this list.' Given, in addition, the vulnerability of international trade and the weakness of the dollar, it was difficult to believe, Mr Jenkins claimed, that German interests could be well served by resisting both demands for international economic coordination expressed by supporters of the locomotive theory and proposals for a strong new Community initiative.

Although the options were by no means exclusive, Mr Jenkins clearly hoped that Germans would decide to give top priority to the creation of what he described as 'a hard-core integrated Community economy'. He agreed with the German finance minister, Mr Apel, who had been reported in the previous week as saying that Europe could not be united by money alone. But there could be no full integration 'without a decisive monetary step':

> That is why the platform from which we launched this debate is a broadly based one ... It is monetary of course; it is also clearly economic; but it is also political and institutional.

2.3   The implementation and fate of the strategy

The initial, public reaction to Mr Jenkins' call for a reconsideration of the advantages of monetary union was overwhelmingly negative. Far from being seen as an example of the president's political flair, the initiative was widely regarded as yet another instance of his inability to adapt to the timetables and realities of Community affairs. The British press, which for obvious reasons had a special interest in the new president's fortunes, was almost without exception disposed to dismiss the proposals before they had been fully developed. *The Economist*, it is true, carried a fairly sympathetic story immediately after the East Hendred meeting, and was still prepared, as late as 24 September (following the discussion between Mr Jenkins and his fellow commissioners in the Ardennes, of which more will be said shortly), to give him the benefit of a doubt, though it did feel that it 'was an astonishingly bold idea from Mr Jenkins, himself nursing a thousand political cuts in his new Brussels role ...'[39]. A month later, however, the general feeling amongst British journalists in Brussels would seem to have been that the Jenkins plan was already dead. On 24 October, for example, three days before the Florence speech, *The Times* referred to what it described as 'the nice historical irony' that found Roy Jenkins 'in the blue corner, wearing psychedelic federalist trunks' and 'favouring a bold initiative with little chance of political acceptance', and the 'portly Corsican François Xavier Ortoli, ... wearing the sombre colours of good old British pragmatism'. To *The Guardian*, in a leader on the same day, Mr Callaghan was the realist, Mr Jenkins, for better or for worse, the dreamer. 'Politics is the art of the possible and economic and monetary union in Europe is not now in that realm.' The Florence speech a few days later was seen, at best, as describing 'a distant goal', at worst as sheer folly[40].

These comments by British journalists, though more numerous, were by and large representative of the European press as a whole. It was perhaps only to be expected that the Brussels correspondent of *Le Monde*, whose outstanding merit as a commentator is that he does not attempt to conceal his prejudices, should season his scepticism with a sharp dose of anti-British, as distinct from merely anti-Jenkins, feelings[41]:

> Peu importe que des esprits chagrins y voient la preuve que le vieux lion ... n'envisage une telle opération que pour en prendre la direction et en planner des dividendes.

But at least he could comfort himself over the coming weeks with the thought that the old lion had got it wrong. Other, more balanced observers were, however, no less forthright in dismissing the president's move. The *Neue Zürcher Zeitung*'s Brussels correspondent, for example, spoke of the president's 'astonishing lack of skill as a political technician'[42]. Many others echoed his view.

The belief that Mr Jenkins' plan had little hope of achievement was considerably reinforced, as several of the quotations in previous paragraphs have suggested, by evidence that his enthusiasm was not shared by his vice-president and predecessor, M. Ortoli. Following the East Hendred meeting, Michael Emerson, helped by Robert Triffin, Crispin Tickell and other members of the Jenkins Cabinet, prepared a 15-page summary of the proposal for consideration by the Commission as a whole at a special weekend conference at Roche-en-Ardennes on 17 and 18 September[43]. The reactions of the president's colleagues were mixed. Some of them, notably Gundelach, Cheysson, Davignon and Tugendhat, were enthusiastic. Others were more reserved and M. Ortoli was downright sceptical. So too was Mr Haferkamp.

In normal circumstances, the president could have reckoned on carrying the Commission with him if only one or two of its members were seriously opposed. But M. Ortoli's position was rather special, not simply or even mainly because he was a former president, but still more because he was the commissioner responsible for monetary questions. In this capacity he had developed proposals of his own, and at the Ardennes meeting at which Mr Jenkins had submitted his paper M. Ortoli had circulated some preliminary ideas on a five-year plan designed to pave the way for economic and monetary union. The details of this plan are less important than the underlying philosophy to which it bore witness, since it was essentially a rag-bag, an unsystematic list of jobs both great and small to which the Community might usefully address itself in the vague hope that some day, somehow, the member states would all wake up and find that they had arrived, without knowing quite how they had done it[44].

As the commissioner responsible, however, M. Ortoli clearly had both a right and a duty to develop his plan, and since Mr Jenkins' first and rather tentative attempts to relaunch the debate about monetary union were greeted by near-universal scepticism, the commissioner for monetary affairs exploited this mood and gradually regained the initiative. The onus was, after all, on the president to prove that anything more than a gradualist approach was feasible, and through both individual briefings and still more openly at a major press conference on 20 October, M. Ortoli let it be known that he considered Mr Jenkins' ideas 'politically absurd'[45]. The president might, even so, have asserted his will, had he really felt that a confrontation was necessary or useful. At the Commission meeting that discussed the Ortoli paper in advance of the ECOFIN meeting scheduled for 20 November, however, he seemed to have little appetite for a fight, and the Ortoli paper went forward without any significant modifications as the official statement of the Commission's views. It was to say the least ironical that within little more than three weeks of the Florence speech launching a 'great debate' on the monetary issue, the ECOFIN considered an official Commission paper on the subject that was to all intents and purposes the work of those whose philosophy and approach the president had discreetly but vigorously disowned in his lecture.

At the Council meeting itself however, even this modest Commission proposal was coolly received in the formal session, and warmly and loudly abused by the German ministers in the corridors outside. Mr Apel, the minister of finance, allegedly described the plan as 'Quatsch', while his colleague Count Lambsdorff told journalists that the European Community was not ready for such a radical venture at present, because economic conditions were unsuitable and because of the lack of any political will amongst governments[46]. Against this background it was only to be expected that those commentators, particularly British, who still felt the Jenkins' suggestions worth a comment made observations more appropriate to the obituary columns than the sections of the paper devoted to current affairs.

Irritating though these setbacks and criticisms undoubtedly were however, the evidence suggests that Mr Jenkins himself was chiefly preoccupied with developments elsewhere, and that he did not see his problems with M. Ortoli or Mr Apel as fundamental threats to his strategy. We return in fact to his conception of his office, which was discussed briefly at the beginning of the chapter. The European Community, he believed, was an amalgam of nation states in which power had passed decisively to the European Council composed of the heads of government. It was at this level that the president of the Commission had to make his mark if in the end he was to make his mark at all, and it was in terms of this constituency, where the priorities and conventions were very different from those that obtained even in the councils of ministers, that the president had to choose his themes and define his policies. Mr Jenkins would undoubtedly have preferred to have had the enthusiastic backing of the whole of the Commission, and his case would have been strengthened still further had his views been endorsed by the ECOFIN. But welcome though these additional signs of approval would have been it seems quite clear that Mr Jenkins intended from early on to use the European Council meeting at Brussels in December, rather than the ECOFIN or any other gathering of monetary experts, as the occasion on which to seek collective backing for a new debate about monetary union. It is significant, for example, that before he briefed his fellow commissioners at their weekend conference in the Ardennes he took the opportunity offered by a meeting with M.Tindemans (who as Belgian prime minister was due to chair the European Council meeting) to secure the latter's agreement that further steps towards monetary union should be taken at the December summit 'irrespective of present difficulties'[47]. It was only the first of a series of moves related to the Council.

Given the lack of complete documentation, it is clearly difficult to piece together every development in this diplomatic campaign at the highest level, but the priorities and assumptions that underlay it are obvious. Of the latter, one in particular is worth singling out. However hostile to fresh experiments in the monetary sphere German and French officials might be, Mr Jenkins knew that the French president had been consistently favourable towards proposals for a European zone of monetary stability in the past and that, to some extent out of deference towards his French partner's views on the matter, the German chancellor had never been as negative or as unhelpful as the Bundesbank or the German ministry of finance. M. Giscard d'Estaing's belief in the desirability of European monetary stability had been reaffirmed on several occasions in 1977 itself, both in public and in private. He and M. Barre had stressed the point, for example, when Mr Jenkins paid his first official visit to Paris early in the year. He had also given a more public manifestation still in February when, somewhat to the embarrassment of the German chancellor, he had insisted that EMU should be placed on the agenda of their bilateral summit meeting[48]. Although, therefore, political and economic weakness may have hobbled the French president for the time being, Mr Jenkins was aware that he could count on the support of M. Giscard d'Estaing in principle, if not yet in any more concrete commitment. Thanks too to the persistence of the French leader, the Commission president also had grounds to hope that the German chancellor might be more sensitive to the kind of arguments that he and his advisers had prepared during the summer than other German ministers and officials. Although, therefore, Mr Jenkins did not ignore German public opinion – hence the Bonn speech – he realized that his principal hope of prodding the Federal Republic into action lay through the German chancellor. High-level diplomacy, in other words, offered the promise of a greater return than rhetoric.

It was with this in mind that at the beginning of October, several weeks before the Florence speech, he invited Dr Sigrist, the German permanent representative, to a private lunch without advisers. In the course of this he explained his ideas and why he felt the proposal should be of particular interest and appeal to the German government[49]. A few weeks later, on 18 November, he went to see Mr Schmidt himself in Bonn[50]. The arguments advanced were essentially those that he rehearsed in public a few weeks later in his Bonn speech and, as on that occasion, the Commission president was particularly careful to emphasize his understanding of German resentment against those who urged the Federal Republic to assume a locomotive role in the international economy[51]. Mr Schmidt's initial reaction to the Jenkins' initiative would seem, however, to have been extremely cautious. Shortly after the Florence speech, he had asked one of his aides to prepare a minute on it, and although this was more restrained and polite than the outspoken comments of Mr Apel or Count Lambsdorff, it was by no means enthusiastic. The chancellor did not therefore give any spontaneous indication of support when Mr Jenkins himself defended his views.

It was not, in fact, until the European Council meeting in Brussels on 5 and 6 December 1977 that the president received the first clear evidence that his strategy was beginning to pay off. Shortly before they went into the meeting he is alleged to have said to Mr Schmidt: 'You may not be very keen on the idea, Helmut, but at least do not kill it.' The German chancellor gave Mr Jenkins the assurance he wanted and kept his word. Indeed he went further. Encouraged by the positive opinions expressed by other heads of government, he gave his full approval to the suggestion of M. Tindemans that Mr Jenkins and the Commission should be encouraged to continue their study of monetary union, with a view to a fresh discussion at Copenhagen in April. He also played a constructive role in finding solutions to a number of lesser problems that had soured the previous Council meeting in London in June. For example, the Anglo-German dispute over the interpretation of Article 131 of the Treaty of Accession, which had dragged on for many months, was one of the issues settled. There was also approval for an increase in the Regional Fund and for a strengthening of short- and medium-term credits. Finally, Mr Schmidt withdrew his opposition to the Ortoli Facility.

The most important of the Council's conclusions were, however, summarized in the official communiqué as follows[52]:

The European Council felt that the implementation of this strategy (to combat recession and inflation) should be accompanied by progress towards Economic and Monetary Union.

The European Council noted with satisfaction the Commission communication on the prospect of EMU.

It reaffirmed its attachment to the objective of EMU.

With this in mind it requested the Council (ministers of economic and financial affairs) to make a thorough study of the Commission communication.

It noted the intention of the Commission to raise this question before the European Parliament, the Economic and Social Committee and in future Tripartite conferences.

Commenting on the meeting afterwards at the press conference[53], M. Tindemans recalled that at the beginning there had been some apprehension about how it would work out. There had been newspaper articles suggesting that it would be as sour and as futile as the previous occasion in London in June. 'Contrary to what was foreseen however I can now say that the Council was very fruitful. I do not say that very often but I can express my satisfaction now that it is over.' Mr Jenkins, who shared the platform with M. Tindemans, was no less relieved. The success of the Council had, he suggested, been a 'testimony to its ability to cut through disagreements where necessary, and to give a renewed momentum to the process of integration'. He had, he revealed, outlined the arguments that made him feel that further progress towards monetary union was essential, laying particular stress on unemployment, the difficulties that enlargement of the Community would be bound to entail and, finally, the fact that 'at present we have no world monetary system'. The response had been almost exactly what he was looking for. 'It has been accepted that the idea of a renewed Community initiative in this area will be given a fair wind.'

By the end of 1977, therefore, Mr Jenkins' judgement that it would be worth reviving the discussion of economic and monetary union appeared to have been at least partially vindicated. Expert opinion was, it is true, still overwhelmingly sceptical. But contrary to the expectations of the great majority of observers he had received more than a perfunctory hearing at the European Council at which his predecessor had seemed to become increasingly a secretary[54], and at which he himself had not made particularly impressive showings in his first two meetings. The meeting in Brussels in December enhanced his authority not only in the Council itself, but also beyond. There were signs of a change, for example, within the Commission itself. Towards the end of December the president appointed the first senior non-Englishman to his Cabinet, M. van den Abeele. The significance of this appointment was not simply that M. van den Abeele was not English, or that he was a monetary expert, but still more that he had been until then a senior member of M. Ortoli's Cabinet. The relations between Mr Jenkins and his predecessor in 1978 were to be a good deal more constructive than they had been for the greater part of 1977, confirming perhaps Mr Jenkins' own axiom that 'the idea of an antithesis between gradual evolution and dramatic advance is misconceived'[55]. Whatever else might be said, in fact, neither Mr Jenkins nor his proposals seemed quite so politically 'absurd' as they had appeared to M. Ortoli only a few weeks earlier.

The importance of what might be termed the Jenkins' episode in the overall history of the emergence of the EMS remains difficult to assess. As the next chapter will show, planning for a new European monetary system only became practical politics when the German chancellor decided that the moment was opportune for a new initiative and when the French president was released from political captivity. Both men had reasons of their own for acting as they did and it would be absurd to suggest that they embarked on their course simply because of the promptings of the Commission president. Mr Jenkins was, like any good politician, lucky that events appeared to point in the same direction as his own arguments. But, to his credit, he had acted all along on the assumption that if momentum was to be restored to the European Community Bonn would have to take the lead and that the monetary question was the one issue on which an appeal to the short-term interests of the Federal Republic might serve the longer term interests of the Community as a whole. The arguments that he had advanced in Florence and in Bonn, in public and in private, were, as this chapter has shown, carefully calculated to interest the German government in general and the chancellor in particular, and although Mr Schmidt undoubtedly kept his own counsel, it is nonetheless true, as the next chapter will show, that the considerations that finally prompted him to take the initiative had in several important respects been anticipated during the Commission president's campaign.

As 1978 progressed, at Copenhagen and elsewhere, Mr Jenkins was more than prepared to accept the role of third man, the French president being the chancellor's 'brilliant second'. But this in itself was a formidable achievement and a striking vindication of the original political judgement that had prompted the campaign. The German chancellor acknowledged the president's special position on several occasions. Mr Jenkins was, for example, amongst the first both inside Germany and outside to hear of what Mr Schmidt had in mind. At another meeting, much later in the year, when the EMS was at an advanced stage of preparation and it was already apparent that the British would not join, Mr Schmidt remarked almost casually that both he and the French president, and Mr Jenkins too, had invested so much political capital in the affair that they could not be deterred by British obstructionism. Given Mr Jenkins' nationality and Mr Schmidt's well-advertised views on the Commission, it is hard to imagine a more impressive compliment.

1 See *Official Journal of the European Communities*, European Parliament, Session 1976/77, 11 January 1977, p. 15: 'I come before you as a politician ... I do not think that it is a bad thing. The Commission should be a political rather than a technical body ...'

2 See especially David Butler and Uwe Kitzinger, *The 1975 Referendum*, London, 1976; Philip Goodhart, *Full-Hearted Consent*, London, 1976; Anthony King, *Britain Says Yes*, Washington, DC, 1977

3 *The Economist*, 16 July 1977

4 ibid., 2 October 1976
5 ibid., 26 February 1977
6 European Parliament, op. cit. (note 1), 1976/77
7 See *The Economist*, 12 March, 26 March and 3 April 1977
8 European Parliament, op. cit. (note 1), 1976/77, 11 January and 8 February 1977
9 See, *inter alia, European Report*, 18 and 20 May 1977 and 18 June 1977
10 *The Economist*, 20 November and 4 December 1976
11 ibid., 22 January 1979
12 For a useful and well-informed survey of this and other problems during the first few months of the new Commission, see Paul Lewis in the *New York Times*, November 1977
13 *The Economist*, 16 July 1977
14 ibid., 26 February 1977
15 ibid., 2 April 1977
16 ibid.
17 *Frankfurter Allgemeine Zeitung*, 6 May 1977, etc.; see *The Economist*, 7 and 14 May 1977 and *New York Times*, 6 November 1977
18 *European Report*, 2 July 1977
19 European Parliament, op. cit., (note 1), 1976/77, 12 January 1977, pp. 67–73
20 For an assessment of the British presidency, see G. Edwards and Helen Wallace, *The Council of Ministers of the European Community and the President-in-Office*, London, 1977, Ch. 5. Also Roy Jenkins himself in *The Observer*, 3 July 1977
21 European Parliament, op. cit. (note 1), 1977/78, 6 July 1977, p. 140
22 ibid., pp. 143ff and 176ff
23 *The Economist*, 10 December 1977
24 Roy Jenkins, 'Europe's Present Challenge and Future Opportunity', The First Jean Monnet Lecture, Florence, 27 October 1977
25 Roy Jenkins, 'The Integration of the Community in the Face of Enlargement', speech to the Deutsche Gesellschaft für Auswärtige Politik, Bonn, 8 December 1977; reprinted in *Europa-Archiv*, 1, 1978, pp. 1–10

26 Commission of the European Communities, *Report of the Study Group on the role of public finance in European integration*, 2 vols, Brussels, April 1977
27 ibid., vol. 1, p. 11
28 ibid., see especially vol. 2, pt. A, pp. 9–275. The findings were summarized in vol. 1, pp. 12–13
29 ibid., see, for example, vol. 1, pp. 40–1 and vol. 2, Chs 5 and 6
30 ibid., vol. 1, p. 19
31 ibid., pp. 66ff
32 ibid., p. 69f
33 ibid., p. 20
34 ibid., p. 61
35 ibid., p. 66f
36 *The Economist*, 21 May 1977
37 Jenkins, Monnet lecture, op. cit. (note 24), p. 10
38 Jenkins, Bonn speech, op. cit. (note 25)
39 *The Economist*, 24 September 1977
40 See, inter alia, the *Times* leader of 28 October 1977, 'A Distant Goal'
41 *Le Monde*, 22 September 1977
42 *Neue Zürcher Zeitung* 20 November 1977
43 See *The Economist*, 24 September 1977
44 The full text of the Ortoli paper in its final form is reprinted in *Europa-Archiv*, 1, 1978, pp. 11ff
45 *The Guardian*, 20 October 1977
46 *Die Zeit*, 25 November 1977
47 *European Report*, 17 September 1977
48 *The Economist*, 12 February 1977
49 *Frankfurter Allgemeine Zeitung*, 12 October 1977
50 ibid., 19 November 1977
51 *The Economist*, 2 April 1977
52 See especially *European Report*, 7 and 10 December 1977
53 Transcript of the presidential press conference, 6 December 1977
54 For M. Ortoli's humble role in the European Council, see especially the interesting article by Sir Harold Wilson in *The Times*, 28 June 1977
55 Jenkins, Monnet lecture, op. cit. (note 24), p. 10

The German Chancellor, the French President and the Birth of the EMS

Sometime in January or February 1978 the German chancellor decided that a new initiative on European monetary union was after all opportune. His decision, which seems to have been entirely his own and was kept secret from all but a very few advisers in Bonn, was communicated to Mr Jenkins at a meeting in the German capital on 28 February and either then or shortly afterwards to M. Giscard d'Estaing. The chancellor's decision, which was endorsed and developed in discussions with the French president at Rambouillet on 2 April created an entirely new political situation. From then on, the question was not whether there would be a new European monetary system, but what form it would take and when it would come into existence, since, as subsequent chapters will show, Mr Schmidt's personal commitment to the creation of the new system was such that abandonment of the proposal was virtually unthinkable so long as he remained in office. Before moving on to the negotiations themselves therefore, it is important to assess the factors that prompted Mr Schmidt to take a decision that, in the light of both his own and his government's previous attitudes, was in many respects surprising and, as events were to prove, remained disquieting to many of his fellow countrymen best qualified to judge for many months to come[1].

One influence on the German chancellor has already been referred to in the previous chapter, namely Roy Jenkins. Another, according to Mr Schmidt himself, was Jean Monnet, whose memoirs he read in the weeks immediately preceding the launching of his initiative. In the light of the Monnet-like bypassing of normal channels that (as the next chapter will show) was to be such a marked feature of the first phase of the EMS negotiations, it is not difficult to accept the chancellor's word on this matter. Important though these personal influences may have been however, the primary considerations prompting the move would seem to have been of another order. Whereas Mr Jenkins took the Community as his point of departure, Mr Schmidt turned to the European Community as a framework for action because of the disorders that had emerged in the Atlantic Community and the threat that these disorders represented to his own country. It was his preoccupation with the dollar crisis, his resentment and anxiety about the growing pressure on the Federal Republic to reflate and, more generally, his unease about what seemed to him to be the fallibility and vulnerability of the new Carter administration in Washington that served as the principal motors of his monetary initiative. A secondary influence, which was nonetheless of considerable importance in determining both the character and the timing of the proposal, was the dramatic change for the better in his own and the French president's domestic political fortunes in the months preceding the April meeting of the European Council at Copenhagen.

3.1   Western Europe and the United States in the first year of the Carter administration: human rights and nuclear energy

As the discussion in chapter 1 showed, the American–Western European partnership had been 'troubled' for many years before Mr Carter became president at the beginning of 1977. The crisis that enveloped the Atlantic Community during the first year of his presidency was nevertheless in many respects more sustained, more disquieting and more personalized than any that had gone before. It was also peculiar in that it was to a very large extent a Bonn–Washington crisis, which affected the European Community as a whole but was concentrated in the German and American capitals.

The omens for a stable relationship between Bonn and Washington were good when Mr Carter took office. The note of optimism, which was widespread on both sides of the Atlantic, is well illustrated in a volume of papers by both practitioners and academic experts in international affairs that were written for a conference on American–Western European relations in Germany in November 1976[2]. Hopes ran high, not simply because Dr Kissinger was going – his conduct during his last two years at the State Department had gone a long way to repairing the damage done during the 'year of Europe' and other celebrated episodes. It was much more that, as the editors of the volume noted, 'with the election of president Carter a school of thought has triumphed which sees in the industrial democracies the first and natural concern of American foreign policy and regards them as partners in the coordination of policy'[3]. It is easy to understand why they felt confident. Indeed, one of the paradoxes of the history of the Atlantic Community during the Carter administration is precisely the fact that there could hardly have been an American administration that contained so many people so deeply committed to the regeneration of Atlantic relations. A list of Mr Carter's early appointments reads like a roll call of good Atlanticists. Richard Cooper, author of a major book on the economics of interdependence[4], became under secretary of state for economic affairs and thus the official directly responsible for relations between Washington and Brussels. Junior to him, but entrusted with the formulation of the administration's policy on nuclear matters, was Joseph Nye, the joint author of a book entitled *Power and Interdependence*, which encapsulated the new orthodoxy of the internationally minded elite[5]. The Treasury had Anthony Solomon and Fred Bergsten while at the White House itself Mr Carter could call on the services of Henry Owen, who was given responsibility for the preparation of summit meetings[6], and Zbigniev Brzezinski, who quite apart from his writings on international affairs, had been primarily responsible for introducing Mr Carter to the Trilateral Commission. Finally there was Mr Carter himself, who came to office pledged to revive the Atlantic Community on the basis of partnership rather than hegemony[7].

Why, it might be asked, were the early hopes not fulfilled? It would be tempting to explain the deterioration entirely in personal terms: Mr Carter and Mr Schmidt, as the popular press on both sides of the Atlantic soon discovered, simply did not hit it off. The explanation is particularly tempting in this case, because the breakdown in confidence between the two men was undoubtedly important and gave the crisis a sharpness that had not often been apparent in German–American relations. Mr Schmidt had taken exception to Mr Carter's style even before the latter became president and, unwisely perhaps, made no secret of the fact that he wanted Mr Ford to win the campaign. Whether because of this episode, or because of a more fundamental preference for the British, Mr Carter appeared to make very little use of the opportunities offered by the first few months of his presidency, when he was free of troubles at home and viewed with a mixture of ignorance and enthusiasm abroad, to breathe life into the relationship with the German chancellor. There were, it was said, a few transatlantic telephone conversations and Mr Carter sent his vice-president to brief his European allies[8] and in his turn received German ministerial visitors, such as Mr Genscher and Mr Leber[9]. But it was evident some time before the London summit of the Seven that he preferred the company of Mr Callaghan and Mr Jenkins, both of whom he welcomed with conspicuous warmth to Washington[10], to that of Mr Schmidt and M. Giscard d'Estaing. Although at the London summit itself he invited the German leader to a widely publicized breakfast, Mr Callaghan was still manifestly his favourite partner[11]. Subsequently, in July 1977, Mr Schmidt paid a visit to Washington, but again, despite energetic public relations work on both sides, the relationship seemed cold and fragile to those in a position to observe it at close quarters[12].

There was, therefore, a serious problem in personal relations and, given the increasing emphasis on summitry and the concentration of power in the hands of national leaders that this tendency reflected and encouraged, a development of this nature was bound to be of some consequence in relations between Bonn and Washington in general. There were, however, deeper reasons for the growing disillusionment of the German chancellor with the American leadership. Mr Carter may have personalized certain issues and made them worse, but the differences over priorities and interests that soured the bilateral relationship were not simply the product of the two leading personalities. Four issues merit special mention: the disquiet caused in Bonn by the administration's emphasis on human rights in its dealings with the Soviet Union; the dispute about the export of nuclear technology; alarm at the American authorities' dollar policy or lack of it; and resentment at the apparent ease with which the American administration and certain other governments could shrug off their own responsibilities for the seriousness of the international economic crisis by counterattacking on West Germany's failure to reflate. With the possible exception of this last point, the German government's position was mirrored or anticipated in Paris and the breakdown in Washington–Bonn relations was accompanied at each stage by consolidation of the Bonn–Paris axis.

President Carter's commitment to a compaign for human rights, promised before he became president and implemented in a series of rather dramatic gestures shortly after he came to power, was perhaps the clearest indication that the new administration's foreign policy differed in both substance and style from that of its Republican predecessor and of Henry Kissinger in particular[13]. The change was not unwelcome to many Western Europeans. The European Community governments had after all themselves attempted a similar link in their contribution to the Helsinki negotiations. Whatever enthusiasm the Carter policy may have aroused in London or even in France and Germany, however, it was not shared, it would seem, at any stage by Mr Schmidt or M. Giscard d'Estaing, who saw the new policies as a threat to their countries' increasingly important and profitable, but nonetheless delicate, relations with the Eastern bloc in general and the Soviet Union in particular. American–Soviet detente without adequate consultation between the United States and their European allies – Dr Kissinger's sin – had been bad enough; a policy that seemed likely to halt or even reverse the process was still worse. Their anxieties on this score were already evident in February 1977 at the first Franco-German summit after the new president came to power, when, it was widely noted, they devoted much more of their time to the discussion of global, as distinct from bilateral or Community, affairs than they had been accustomed to in the past, precisely because they felt uneasy about the implications of the new American foreign policy[14]. It was a trend that was to become ever stronger the longer president Carter remained in office.

For the first few months of the administration's life the anxieties that its policies aroused were mentioned relatively discreetly and tactfully in conversations with vice-president Mondale, with Mr Vance, the secretary of state, and finally, at the London summit in May 1977, with Mr Carter himself[15]. When it became obvious however that these private representations were not having any significant influence on the development of American policy, both the French president and the German chancellor would seem to have decided that the moment had come to register their disquiet more ostentatiously. M. Giscard d'Estaing's initiative took the form of a long interview in the American magazine *Newsweek* in July, in the course of which he openly criticized President Carter's foreign policy[16]. Though claiming that it was not his task to pass 'editorial judgement', and that he was 'most gratified by the excellent relations that he had established with President Carter', he could not help noting that the president had introduced 'a fresh ideological dimension' into his foreign policy.

> This undoubtedly met certain needs – such as non-proliferation, arms limitation and human rights – just as it met some of my own preoccupations, but it has compromised the process of detente. The question now arises whether or how new ideological themes can be applied without provoking negative reactions.

The French president had recently had conversations with Mr Brezhnev, and he professed some 'understanding' for the latter's views:

> Mr Brezhnev feels that some of President Carter's decisions have broken what I will call the code of conduct of detente ... [he] does not understand the objectives sought by breaking this code. The code for example calls for non-interference in the other's internal affairs, and you will never find in the Soviet press direct or personal attacks against the leaders of countries that subscribe to detente. ... When they saw a proposal that was completely out of phase with these rules of conduct, they understandably wondered why the code had been broken and what the ulterior motive was.

Mr Schmidt was more circumspect, but neither he nor his advisers made any secret of their views during the chancellor's visit to Washington in July, and he underlined his solidarity with the French president still more strongly after his return by arranging a 'private' dinner at an exclusive Strasburg restaurant, where, it was disclosed, the two men had exchanged views and information about the American administration's policies[17].

These skirmishes over human rights did not, however, compare in significance or in the depths of passion that they aroused with the dispute between Washington and Bonn over the nuclear issue. Karl Kaiser, in an admirable analysis of the origins and development of this controversy[18], has described it as the most serious clash in US–German relations since the war, and although subsequent developments between 1977 and 1980 may now call for a revision of this judgement, there can be little doubt that it was valid from the perspective of 1977 or early 1978. The dispute centred on an agreement negotiated between Germany and Brazil in 1975, under the terms of which the Germans promised to supply nuclear reactors and enrichment and reprocessing technology to Brazil, in exchange for supplies of uranium that, it was expected, the Brazilians would soon be able to mine. The issues involved were numerous, ranging on the American side from alarm that the deal might open a way to the development of nuclear weapons elsewhere in the American hemisphere, to outright hostility to the exploitation of nuclear energy as such, and on the German side from outrage at what was regarded as an unacceptable manipulation of the rules of the nuclear game for their own commercial advantage by the Americans in their capacity as senior partners in the Western alliance and principal suppliers of uranium, to fear for the long-term security of their very considerable investment in nuclear energy as an alternative to oil. Prior to the autumn of 1976, tension and misunderstandings at intergovernmental level had been kept under control. Despite considerable domestic pressure to block the sales, neither Mr Ford nor Dr Kissinger seems to have been sufficiently worried about it to intervene. The Germans for their part went out of their way to strengthen the safeguards against the abuse of the technology and, following a meeting between the German foreign minister and Dr Kissinger in June 1975, in the course of which the American secretary of state implied that the administration was satisfied with the guarantees that the Germans had built into the draft agreement, the latter concluded the deal.

In taking the course they did, Mr Ford and Dr Kissinger had, however, run the gauntlet of very sharp criticisms from both within and outside Congress, and it was not perhaps surprising therefore that, as the 1976 presidential elections approached, the Democratic candidate, Mr Carter, should have attempted to make the question a campaign issue. The attack was sufficiently successful to provoke Mr Ford into proposing, on 28 October 1976, a three-year moratorium on the domestic licensing and export of reprocessing, as well as new international agreements for stronger control of plutonium and for storage of spent nuclear fuel. The German government was not unnaturally alarmed by this development and, as both they and the French had been singled out for special criticism in the Carter campaign speeches, there was a real fear that the Democratic candidate, if elected, would block the Brazil agreement and exploit America's privileged position as the supplier of uranium to maim or even kill Germany's nuclear programme. As the sanctions proposed by critics of the Brazil deal in the United States included the threat of the withdrawal of American troops from German soil, the potential ramifications of the dispute were frightening and it was doubtless his anxieties on this score that prompted Mr Schmidt to make a celebrated, but singularly maladroit, intervention in the American campaign. Once the German chancellor's hopes that Mr Ford would be re-elected had been frustrated however, his government set about trying to ensure that the Carter administration did not come out against the agreement. A senior official was sent to Washington several days before the president's inauguration in January 1977. These talks were conspicuously unsuccessful, and were followed by equally fruitless exchanges involving, amongst others, vice-president Mondale, Cyrus Vance, Christopher Warren, Mr Genscher and Mr Schmidt himself.

Eventually the atmosphere began to change, and from March 1977 onwards progress was made towards a compromise of sorts. But there seems no doubt that this uncomfortable reminder of Germany's vulnerability to American power and the resentment caused by what seemed to the Germans at least to be an unacceptable mixture of appeals to higher morality and power politics, seriously scarred relations between Bonn and Washington and left a residue of mistrust, and personal animosity that could be and was drawn upon as further evidence of a growing divergence of interests between the United States and Western Europe emerged. The controversy also consolidated still further the Franco-German relationship since, although the Germans were the chief butt of American criticisms, the French, who had negotiated agreements with Pakistan and South Korea and whose nuclear programme was no less ambitious than Germany's, were also directly threatened by the new administration's policies[19].

The alarm caused by Mr Carter's policies on human rights and his initial handling of the nuclear issue helped, along with other episodes, such as the dispute over the Leopard tanks[20], to create the climate of opinion in which the German chancellor's decision to launch a new monetary initiative was taken, and it ensured that this decision was invested with more political passion and significance than a technical proposal designed to overcome short-term difficulties in the international monetary system could ever have been. The EMS emerged, in other words, against the background of the German chancellor's diminishing confidence in American leadership in general and not simply in the monetary sphere. That said, the initiative was in the final analysis triggered off by developments in the international economy.

3.2   The dollar and growth

The misfortunes of the American dollar from mid-1977 until March 1978 can be traced in detail in the tables in Appendix 2. Over the nine months from June 1977 until March 1978, the DM–dollar rate moved from DM 2.35 = \$1 to DM 2.06 = \$1; the Swiss franc from 2.49 = \$1 to 1.97 = \$1; the Japanese yen from 272 = \$1 to 236 = \$1[21]. The immediate origins of the crisis lay in a sharp deterioration in the United States' balance of payments, coupled with widespread doubts about the capacity or willingness of the Carter administration to adopt appropriate measures to meet the situation and, in some quarters at least, a fear that, if they did, the cure might be more dangerous to the world economy than the disease. The deterioration in the United States' balance on current account began under the Ford administration, but its extent was not widely appreciated until the summer of 1977. In 1976, the last year of the Republican presidency, the balance on visible trade had already moved from a surplus of \$9 billion in 1975 to a deficit of \$9.5

billion but, with a surplus on the invisible account of $18 billion, the current account as a whole remained comfortably in credit. In 1977, however, the trade deficit rose to $31 billion and, despite a rise in the returns on services and private transfers to $20 billion, there was a deficit on current account of over $11 billion. Furthermore, there seemed to be little prospect of any improvement in 1978[22].

As apologists for the administration both inside and outside the United States frequently pointed out, the American deficit could be seen as a benefit to the international community as a whole, since it made a significant contribution to the fight against recession. Better let well alone, the argument ran, than talk the dollar into decline and the world into recession. The underlying health of the American economy was strong and it could brush off this crisis without a run on the dollar if only critics and speculators would keep quiet[23]. There were, however, at least two fundamental weaknesses in this argument. The first was that the deficit on visible trade could only partially be explained away as a service to the international community. Much of it was the direct result of a massive increase in oil imports required to sustain energy consumption at levels that in the latter half of the 1970s were no longer either acceptable or responsible. Secondly, there was widespread doubt about the new administration's wish to sustain the exchange rate at its mid-1977 levels. For every speech by Mr Blumenthal, the Treasury secretary, that implied that a certain depreciation might be useful or welcome, there was it is true almost always another by secretary Blumenthal himself or one of his lieutenants, Mr Solomon or Mr Bergsten, or the chairman of the Federal Reserve, Arthur Burns, that stated the contrary. But the suspicion remained and was heightened by the increasingly acrimonious transatlantic and transpacific debate about refla-tion, of which more will be said shortly. Few Europeans would have rated the authorities' dollar policy better than benign neglect in the latter half of 1977, and many preferred M. Simonet's definition of it as 'aggressive neglect'[24].

In December and early January 1978, the administration made determined efforts to prove that it was genuinely concerned about the decline of the dollar. Arthur Burns, who was still the chairman of the Federal Reserve, returned from a Basle meeting of the central bank governors with fresh evidence of the disquiet that was felt throughout the Group of Ten about the situation and with a certain number of practical suggestions about what ought to be done in the short term. The result was a presidential 'sermon' on 21 December, part at least of which was drafted by Dr Burns, and the announcement on 4 January that, as a token of the seriousness of the president's declared intention not to let the dollar fall out of control, the Federal Reserve and the Treasury had decided to 'activate' both the Exchange Stabilization Fund of the Treasury and the $20 billion swap network that the Federal Reserves Board had negotiated with other central banks. Particular stress was laid on the new swap agreement that had been reached with the Bundesbank[25]. The measures of 4 January were, however, only partly and temporarily successful. The American authorities did intervene to buy dollars, though scarcely on a massive scale, and there was a succession of statements from Treasury and Federal Reserve sources that the dollar was already 'more than competitive'[26]. But the slide began again in February despite these efforts, and although order was momentarily restored at the end of the month, following the announcement by the Swiss authorities of a ban on foreign purchases of Swiss securities[27], it was not until the second week of March that the markets calmed down – after the conclusion of a 13-week coal strike and a dramatic transatlantic telephone conference during the weekend of 11 and 12 March between Anthony Solomon of the United States' Treasury and Dr Lahnstein in Bonn, and officials of the Federal Reserve Board and the Bundesbank[28]. Even then the peace was fragile and the threat of a new run on the American currency persisted. In the end it materialized at the end of the summer.

There had, of course, been dollar crises before, and the Germans in particular had come to accept the necessity and see the benefits of regular revaluations of their currency against the Americans'. However, there were at least two features of the 1977–78 crisis that made it particularly disquieting from the German point of view. In the first place, it was the first major test of the international monetary system since the inauguration of the new regime in 1973. There had of course been massive and, for those involved, distinctly unpleasant currency movements in the period since then, involving amongst others the French franc, sterling and the lira, but, as Dr Emminger noted in the essay that has already been quoted in chapter 1 and that, ironically enough, appeared within days of the beginning of the first serious bout of speculation against the dollar in mid-1977, 'no serious monetary crises involving the dollar, the DM and other strong currencies have occurred since 1973, despite tremendous upheavals in the world economy'[29]. The process that began in the middle of 1977 had therefore something of the quality of a journey into the unknown. Those with strong nerves or sunny temperaments argued that what was happening was a perfectly normal readjustment, prompted by the need of the international monetary system to come to terms with certain fundamental disequilibria in the world economy. 'This is what floating is all about', was a remark that was bandied about Washington press conferences fairly frequently, particularly before the president's statement on 21 December 1977. And so, in a sense, it was. But with the minimum of ground rules, and a massive overhang of dollars in the hands of OPEC countries, multinational companies and sundry other elements beyond the writ of the central banks, it was not altogether clear where or how the floating would stop. Whatever foreign exchange analysts might say, no politician in either Germany or the United States could be expected to remain silent or inactive when, as happened in the winter of 1977–78, popular newspapers carried stories about American GIs being provided with chocolates and other goodies that they could no longer afford by the benevolent citizens of West Germany, or gave the dollar–DM rate the coverage normally reserved for sports stories. A semi-serious quip in *Der Spiegel* suggesting that, before 1978 was over, two commodities would cost DM 1.50 – a cup of coffee and the US dollar – gives a good idea of what was at stake. So, too, does the increasing tendency, particularly in the United States but also elsewhere, to talk about another 1929[30]. Rather a lot of people were simply very scared in a situation that had no parallel in postwar experience, and, as a senior German official observed, who did not share the chancellor's enthusiasm for the EMS but who was sufficiently close to him to appreciate the pressures that he was under, it was not particularly surprising that Mr Schmidt, who seemed to appear on television almost every other night assuring his people that everything would work out in the end, decided after many weeks of this pressure and no end in sight that he simply had to do something. It is not an adequate explanation of the origins of the EMS, but it is at least a partial explanation.

A second feature of the 1977–78 crisis that was particularly disquieting to the Germans, and may have prompted the German chancellor to look for a European solution, was that although every currency was affected, they were not affected evenly. Dollar holders who wanted to sell made in the main for three currencies – the yen, the Swiss franc and the DM – though in the later stages the pound sterling also moved up sharply. There was, of course, nothing novel in itself about the weakness of the pound, the lira and the French franc. The trouble in 1977–78, however, was that their renewed depreciation came immediately after a phase in which they had already fallen sharply and, in the opinion of many if not all observers, were as a result already seriously undervalued against the DM. This renewed weakness of the currencies of Germany's principal Community partners, coupled with the problems of the Scandinavian countries, gave a new twist to the forces of disintegration and division within the European Community and the Snake, and directly threatened German interests. In the case of the French franc, there were special, indigenous forces at work pushing it down more or less with the dollar. Not for the first time in French history the hint of a left-wing victory in important elections prompted innumerable right-of-centre patriots to sell the currency that between elections at least was represented by the parties for whom they normally voted as a symbol of national pride and independence. The lira, too, tended to move more with the dollar than the DM. As far as the pound was concerned, there were special factors working against a parallel fall with the dollar. The dramatic devaluation that had occurred in 1976 had by common consent been overdone and, as the British economy began to recover, it was only to be expected that the pound should too. Even so, the authorities tried to keep the rate low, and it was largely due to the heavy spending of the British (and

Swiss) authorities on the US government securities market in September and October 1977 that the dollar's precipitate fall was postponed until November. In the end, however, the British had to be warned off by the American authorities themselves and the pound rose[31]. But the rise was nothing like as spectacular as the DM's, and at the end of March 1978 sterling was still approximately 7% lower against the German currency than it had been in June 1977. Within the Snake there was trouble too. The Scandinavian currencies had been under pressure for many months and there had already been realignments of their rates in October 1976 and April 1977. On 28 August 1977, however, further changes became necessary and the Swedish krone left the system altogether, while the Danish and Norwegian krone were each devalued by 5%[32]. As over 50% of West Germany's external trade was with her Western European neighbours, currency movements of this degree so close at hand could hardly leave the authorities indifferent, and although the Bundesbank continued to argue that any attempt to defy the market through a return to fixed exchange rates would have serious destabilizing consequences inside Germany, there is evidence of a widespread, if unarticulated, concern amongst German industrialists and public opinion at large that appreciation of the DM against other European currencies of the order that occurred between 1977 and 1978 could not be accepted without serious risks to German exports. There is nothing to suggest that Mr Schmidt was lobbied by any organized groups, but he must have been aware of these anxieties.

The fate of the dollar was not, however, the only item that figured prominently on the agendas of international economic conferences in 1977–78. Discussions of how to revive growth took up just as much time and, disagreeably enough from the German point of view, aroused just as much passion. The threat that seemed to many commentators to loom over the western world in the second half of 1977 was defined in the following terms in the OECD's *Economic Outlook* of December 1977[33]:

Last June OECD ministers agreed that, to implement their medium term strategy for a progressive return to full employment and price stability, expansion in the OECD area taken as a whole should be somewhat faster in 1978 than in 1977. At that time, output was expected to grow by around 4% in 1977. Accordingly, a 5% target for 1978 seemed appropriate. It was recognised that policies might need to be adjusted to achieve this in some cases, and that the aims of individual countries should vary according to their success in restoring internal and external balance.

In the months that followed, the immediate prospects for economic expansion worsened. Real GNP for the OECD area now seems likely to have increased by only about 3.5% in 1977, with growth slowing down between the two halves of the year. As a result, it is now probable that efforts to achieve 5% growth in 1978 could require an acceleration in the course of the year so sharp as to risk the resurgence of stronger inflationary pressures and thus run counter to the strategy. But it would still be possible, given appropriate policies, to achieve a growth path that, during 1978, accelerated sufficiently to start reducing unemployment without provoking new inflation. A 4.5% growth of the area as a whole between the years 1977 and 1978 – to which the preliminary objectives set by individual governments roughly add up – would imply this sort of acceleration without building up new inflationary forces, and thus be in line with the intentions of ministers.

The pressure for counter-recessionary action and the particular form that it took in 1977 and 1978 are of fundamental importance for an understanding of the origins of the European Monetary System. In 1975 and 1976 the debate about growth had taken place against the background of an international economic situation in which, despite the recession, both the external and internal health of the big three economies – the United States, Japan and West Germany – remained virtually intact. By the middle of 1977, this relatively simple picture had begun to change[34]. Germany and Japan were still in current account surplus. The United States was not. In addition, at least two of the weaker economies – the United Kingdom and Italy – were moving back into surplus, helped by very significant currency depreciations in 1976 and by the stabilization policies that these had given rise to. France remained in deficit and so too did Canada (the other member of the Seven), but in the former case at least there was solid ground for hope that the position would soon improve. As a result of these changes, the emphasis in the debate about how the threat of recession and unemployment should be met was shifted. At first sight, the new doctrines might appear to have been a significant concession to the German standpoint. The locomotive theory, which had placed the main responsibility for recovery on the economies of the big three, gave way to a convoy theory under which convalescent economies, such as the United Kingdom and Italy, might also be expected to give a boost to growth. Despite the apparent widening of the circle of governments that were now expected to contribute to international recovery however, the most important consequence of the deterioration of the American balance of payments position was that the Japanese and the Germans found themselves under even greater pressure than before to reflate. The convoy was a convenient slogan. The reality looked suspiciously like a train that, owing to accidents along the line, would now have to be pushed by two engines rather than three.

In what seemed to many Germans a grotesquely unfair reward for virtuous economic management, the Federal Republic found itself accused of irresponsibility. Having maintained price stability, when all around were losing theirs, and a rate of growth beyond the grasp of economies with levels of inflation incomparably higher than their own, the Germans found

themselves an object of envy rather than approval. The American administration in particular was never slow to point out that if they had a
responsibility to tackle the fundamental problems that had given rise to the
dollar crisis, the Germans had an equally serious obligation to help towards
rescuing the world from recession. The message was repeated publicly and
privately, in words and in actions, at the London summit of May 1977, at
innumerable international gatherings, in speeches by Mr Blumenthal and his
colleagues throughout the summer and winter of 1977 and, by no means
least, in the initial stages of the dollar crisis itself. It amounted, as *The
Economist* observed, following one particularly outspoken intervention by
Mr Blumenthal, to 'a monumentally untactful, if needed attempt to persuade
Japan and West Germany to concede either a higher value for their
currencies or more domestic reflation'[35]. The Americans were, however, not
alone in this attack on the management of the German economy. The IMF
Annual Report of 1978 spoke 'of the gradual evolution of a consensus among
international financial officials regarding an appropriate strategy to restore
satisfactory growth and price stability'[36]. It was not a consensus that the
German government found particularly congenial, and at international
meeting after international meeting, sponsored by the OECD, the IMF and,
by no means least, the EEC, the Germans found themselves in a minority.

There were, of course, brave declarations of international solidarity, such
as the communiqué following the London meeting of the Seven in May
1977, which managed for a few days at least to suggest to the world that
everybody was doing their best and that, furthermore, everybody agreed on
what the best was. The *Frankfurter Allgemeine Zeitung*, commenting on
this particular summit, noted with some relief that there had been little
evidence of the recriminations against the Bundesrepublik that had been
characteristic of other international meetings or exchanges on the development of the international economy[37]. It marked, the newspaper hoped, an
end to a situation 'in which a country with a relatively healthy currency and
balance of payments was regarded as an international pariah'. The price that
Mr Schmidt had had to pay for this particular act of reconciliation was,
however, high, including as it did a pledge to 5% growth. Once it became
apparent that he could not honour it, the recriminations and the pressure
became more fierce than ever. At the IMF meeting in September 1977, for
example, the Germans, according to the *Economist*, found themselves 'in the
dock' together with the Japanese[38]. They had few if any allies even within
the EEC, where because meetings were more frequent there was an even
more rapid cycle of pressure, producing promises that in the end provoked
recriminations[39].

There is no doubt that the German chancellor himself shared to the full
both the resentment about international criticism of the Federal Republic
and the determination not to be pushed on to a reflationary course that his
ministers, and more particularly Mr Apel and his successor, Mr Matthöfer,

displayed on almost every occasion they faced an international gathering. His position was stated with characteristic bluntness in the course of the annual statement of government policy to the Bundestag on 19 January 1978[40]. The government, he pointed out, found themselves under fire from two directions. The opposition believed that government spending was already too high and that the deficit should be drastically reduced. International opinion on the contrary felt that the deficit should be increased as part of a general programme to stimulate economic activity in the Federal Republic that would benefit the rest of the world.

> We have not however followed this advice. We are of course willing to contribute to the expansion of the world economy, but we do not wish to have any part in starting off a new inflationary spiral. ... We are thus trying you might say to steer a golden, middle course between the demands of the opposition here ... and the insistence of some abroad that we should increase our deficit. ... Foreign observers and foreign politicians who like to see the Federal Republic as a locomotive which ought to pull other states out of the world recession exaggerate the economic strength of our country. Together with others something might be done, but alone? This is to grossly overestimate our significance.

These public words were backed up more forcefully still in private exchanges with the leaders of other western governments. One of the more interesting, and for the purposes of this book more significant, private consultations that the Federal chancellor had in the early part of 1978 was a meeting with Mr Callaghan over dinner in Bonn on the evening of 12 March[41]. The occasion will be discussed at more length in the next section. Its most notable feature in the present context was the fact that the British prime minister presented his German colleague with a five-point programme for international economic recovery, at the heart of which lay measures to stimulate growth. The package was not a particularly original or ambitious one and it seems to have aroused little interest in Washington when Mr Callaghan visited the American president shortly afterwards[42]. It is some measure of the German chancellor's sensitivity about the issues it raised, therefore, that he and his advisers dismissed it gruffly and almost contemptuously as 'Mr Callaghan's plan for world inflation', a judgement that if nothing else rather overrated its significance.

By the time he met Mr Callaghan in what one well-placed observer later described as 'a dialogue of the deaf', Mr Schmidt's mind was in fact already moving in quite a different direction. The run on the dollar and the almost uninterrupted pressure from the international community to reflate had brought him to the point where he was virtually bound to take action of some kind to satisfy his domestic constituency and to regain the initiative for the Federal Republic outside. However, given the openness of the German economy, the options open to him were not numerous, and consisted essentially of the two that Mr Jenkins had defined in the course of his Bonn speech on 8 December 1977: to 'embrace the locomotive theory' or to work towards the construction of 'a hard-core integrated Community economy'[43]. The first would have exposed the Federal Republic to the risks of inflation, and increased rather than reduced its vulnerability to the policy mistakes of an American administration whose handling of the dollar crisis seemed to have confirmed the chancellor's worst fears of the previous year. The second, by contrast, though not without risks, offered Germany a degree of protection and security that it could not for structural reasons hope to achieve on its own, and a basis on which it might in due course be possible to move on towards a broader anti-recessionary strategy.

3.3   The European political presuppositions of the EMS initiative

As the opening chapter suggested, the politics of the European Community over the two decades since the Treaty of Rome have been very largely conditioned by the internal politics and interrelationships of three major Western European states – France, Germany and the United Kingdom. The history of the making of the EMS was no exception, and before moving on to a consideration of the Copenhagen summit and the first round of negotiations, it is necessary to analyse the changes that occurred in the domestic politics of the three countries in the months preceding the launching of Mr Schmidt's initiative and the consequences that these changes had for the development of his plan.

Of the three governments in question, the German administration was the least weak throughout the period from the end of 1976 until March 1977. That does not however signify very much, since, although the SPD/FDP coalition survived the electoral setbacks of October 1976, the damage to the internal morale of the government that these disappointing results caused was serious and surprisingly long-lasting. The existence of the government may only rarely have been in question, but its authority and more particularly the authority of its leader, the Federal chancellor, was signifi- cantly reduced for the greater part of 1977. Even a summary catalogue of the government's woes suggests how accident-prone and vulnerable it was[44]. The emergence of a CDU/FDP coalition in Lower Saxony, for example, in the winter of 1976–77 suggested to some that the Bonn coalition itself might be in danger. Even if this outcome was not particularly likely, the discovery of yet another spy scandal in the Bundeskanzleramt in the spring, the difficulties that Mr Schmidt had in honouring the pledge that he had made on pensions in the 1976 election, the resignation of the mayor of Berlin at the beginning of May 1977, the scandal linking the SPD prime minister Osswald with the problems of the Hessische-Landesbank, the decision by the constitutional court in Karlsruhe that, while minister of finance in 1973, Mr Schmidt had exceeded his powers and the consequent threat of a Bundestag vote to remove him in June, the difficulties that the government faced in restraining inflation while at the same time providing some alleviation to the growing unemployment problem and the incessant sniping at the chancellor from the Young Socialists and other groups on the left of his party, all added up to a picture of a government and a chancellor in serious political trouble. German political society speculated openly and frequently about his chances of remaining in office and even the quality press carried long articles about his low morale, his ill-health and his inclination to resign, if only a suitable substitute could be found within his party. An article in the *Frankfurter Allgemeine Zeitung* in March 1977, entitled 'Schmidt kommt nur noch selten zum regieren', was not untypical of a genre[45]. It followed a widely reported visit by the chancellor to his doctor and it started with the words: 'How well or ill is Helmut Schmidt?' The picture that emerged in the following paragraphs was scarcely flattering and must have been distinctly disquieting to the representatives of Germany's allies who read it, since it portrayed a man who had lost his appetite for work yet lacked the ability to stop or to distinguish between what was important and what was not. It might, of course, be said that the *Frankfurter Allgemeine Zeitung* is scarcely an impartial authority when it makes comments on an SPD government, but on this occasion it was by no means out of line. Indeed, in the light of what has been said already about the performance of President Carter, it is worth recalling that to many observers in the middle of 1977 he seemed a distinctly more self-confident and forceful leader than his German counterpart. In an article anticipating the London summit in May 1977, *The Economist* went as far as to urge the American president, who represented a country that he himself had helped to a new self-confidence, to be magnanimous towards Mr Schmidt, who like the country that he led was battered by self-doubt[46].

As this article suggests, the chancellor's low morale seemed to some observers at least to match the mood of the country. The European Community was never as unpopular in Germany as it was in Britain or Denmark but there was a perceptible decline in enthusiasm in the course of 1976–1977[47]. One explanation was the increasing publicity given to the fact that Germany was now the paymaster of Europe. One of the members of the European Commission, Christopher Tugendhat, in a remarkably out-spoken speech to a German audience in March 1978, referred to German discussion of Community affairs in the following terms:

Perhaps the two most striking features in the current discussion of Community matters in the media and elsewhere in the Federal Republic are first the constant emphasis upon the fact that Germany contributes more than any other member state to what is alleged to be a grossly distended Community Budget; and, second, the almost equally constant complaint about how little Germany receives in return for undertaking the burdens of the role of the Community's paymaster[48].

Mr Schmidt's negative response to the Commission's budget proposals at the London meeting of the European Council in June 1977 corresponded well, therefore, with the political mood at home. So, too, did the line that his government took in the protracted dispute with Britain over the interpretation of Article 131 of the Treaty of Accession, and there is more than one hint that at least some of the reserve expressed about Roy Jenkins' monetary proposals stemmed from the feeling that, in the final analysis, 'what was at stake was German money'[49].

In the autumn of 1977, however, the situation suddenly changed and Mr Schmidt, 'the fixer', who seemed destined to live permanently under the shadow of his predecessor, Mr Brandt, both in his party and abroad, became almost overnight Chancellor Schmidt, the statesman. It is difficult to understand quite how and why the metamorphosis occurred, but a crucial factor was undoubtedly the success of the operation against the hijackers of a Lufthansa jet at Mogadishu in October 1977[50]. As a comparable episode in the Iranian Embassy in London two years later confirmed, dramatic, televised paramilitary coups can have an effect on national and political morale of surprising proportions[51]. A measure of the change was the chancellor's reception at his party's annual congress a few weeks later where he received the type of acclaim normally reserved for his predecessor[52]. In European Community affairs, too, the sudden transformation of mood bore almost immediate fruit. Amongst the first to benefit from the new-found confident generosity was Mr Callaghan, the British prime minister, who visited Bonn shortly after the rescue operation, in which he had himself played a small but significant part by authorizing the despatch of two SAS men to assist the German troops involved. In total contrast to the pattern of Anglo-German relations that had obtained for at least two years, this meeting achieved positive and significant results at surprising speed[53]. Contrary to expectations, the German chancellor conceded a new offset agreement to help towards the foreign exchange costs of the British Rhine army, agreed in principle to the siting of the EEC's nuclear research project at Culham rather than near Munich and expressed far more sympathy than he had done before to the British position on the enlargement of the Community. The long-standing dispute over Article 131 was now settled, but the will to find a solution was now evident in a way it had not been before, and it did not therefore come as a particular surprise to officials at the December meeting of the European Council that the two governments were able to find an acceptable compromise. Mr Schmidt's other contributions to the European Council meeting in December, which were commented upon in the previous chapter, provided further evidence of the change in mood and outlook and other examples could be given[54].

The transformation of the German chancellor's political fortunes and of his mood and approach when dealing with his European partners is of considerable significance in the history of the emergence of the European monetary system. As previous sections of this chapter have suggested, the proposal was undoubtedly designed to serve German national interests as the chancellor at least perceived them. (Subsequent chapters will show that many of his fellow countrymen perceived them differently.) But the plan was also both in detail and in the manner in which it was delivered and developed a highly personal initiative, which reflected a remarkable and at times almost reckless self-confidence on the part of its author. In the early stages, as the next chapter will show, the German chancellor acted towards his expert advisers and indeed, as the Dutch later complained, towards the majority of his European Council colleagues with a freedom, not to say highhandedness, that would have been unthinkable at any time before October 1977. His ambition and drive remained the most important single force behind the negotiations even when, after the Bremen Council, they moved out into a more open phase. His reply to one of the senior Italian representatives at the Siena talks on 1 November, who asked whether it might not be rather difficult for the Irish to break with sterling if the British did not come in, was typical: 'leave it to me'.

Despite this spectacular political recovery, the chancellor continued to abide by an axiom that he had enunciated on several occasions previously and that he continued to affirm after October 1977, namely that it was in the interests of neither Europe nor the Federal Republic that Germany should act alone. For reasons that have already been discussed in chapter 1, there were essentially two possibilities: a link with France alone or a directorate of three. As far as the least important member of the potential triumvirate was concerned, namely Mr Callaghan, his political position was considerably stronger in March 1978 than it had been 12 months earlier. The explanation of this change is to be found very largely in the economic recovery that had begun during 1977, following the drastic fall of sterling in the latter half of 1976 and the measures that had been introduced in response to it, and had continued into 1978[55]. The balance of payments moved back into surplus, sterling rose against most currencies, and inflation began to move down below 10% compared to the 25% it had reached in 1975–76. Growth rate was still poor by international standards, but it was at least better than in 1975 or 1976 and looked certain to be better still in 1978. As the gathering debate about 'de-industrialization' showed[56], there were still profound reasons for anxiety, and the prime minister's contributions to the discussion at Copenhagen and elsewhere indicate that he was not unaffected by the gloom that the debate generated. But in public, with an election in the not-too-distant future, government ministers very naturally made the best of these more optimistic economic indicators. Their efforts were greatly helped, firstly by Mr Callaghan's personal popularity and secondly by the successful negotiation in the first half of 1977 of a pact between the Labour and Liberal parties that, for an extraordinarily low price in political terms, guaranteed the Labour government a solid parliamentary base. Opinion polls, which a year earlier had suggested certain Labour defeat in a general election, were by March 1978 giving a rather different picture[57].

Mr Callaghan's political recovery was therefore in many respects comparable to Mr Schmidt's and, as with the German chancellor, it was reflected in a greater freedom to act on the international stage. Ironically enough, however, his new-found authority at home and ability to act abroad increased rather than reduced the obstacles to fruitful cooperation with Mr Schmidt, since it only served to show that they assessed and reacted to the problems of the North Atlantic and European Communities in radically different ways. The most striking indication of their divergence was the 'dialogue of the deaf' on 12 March, which has already been alluded to in section 3.2. The timing of the meeting was itself significant. The Sunday in question followed a week in which the dollar crisis had worsened dramatically. It was also the day of the first round of the French parliamentary elections, in which, as the following pages will show, it was widely assumed that the left would win, a result that, despite their political affiliations, neither the German chancellor nor the British prime minister relished. Finally, reports from Rome confirmed that Mr Andreotti had concluded an agreement with the Communists that brought them into the 'majority' for the first time since the immediate postwar period.

The combination of an international monetary crisis and a new threat of political instability in France and Italy was, it appears, very much in the mind of the British prime minister when he suggested a private meeting in Bonn without advisers[58]. He hoped, it would seem, to build on the anxieties that he knew they both shared, in order to develop the Bonn–London axis and secure Mr Schmidt's support for a fresh attempt to work out a common North Atlantic strategy to overcome recession and, should this be necessary, to contain the dangers of political instability. His principal contribution to the process was a five-point plan for international economic recovery, which included new measures in the sphere of energy policy, the increase of capital flows to developing countries and currency stability, which the prime minister wished to work towards in the framework of the IMF, where American participation was guaranteed. The centrepiece of the programme, however, was yet another proposal for higher growth[59].

Mr Callaghan's journey proved a costly failure. The sarcasms that his 'inflationary' proposals provoked have already been referred to. What is in some respects even more significant, however, was the immediate political conclusion that the chancellor would appear to have drawn from the prime minister's plan, since, although there was an obvious opportunity to do so, Mr Schmidt chose not to discuss his own ideas about an EMS with his British colleague with anything like the frankness that he showed in his conversations with Mr Jenkins and, still more of course, with M. Giscard d'Estaing. At the Copenhagen summit, the German chancellor and the French president were to take steps to bring Mr Callaghan into a directorate of three, and there is nothing therefore to suggest that Mr Schmidt wanted to exclude the British prime minister on principle. Rather the reverse. But a precondition of their cooperation was agreement on the domestic and international priorities that underlay the initiative: economic stability at home and a redefinition of the Atlantic partnership through the creation of a 'hard-core integrated Community economy'. Mr Callaghan's political recovery, which could have provided the occasion for the consolidation of the Anglo-German relationship that the prime minister himself evidently wanted, only served to highlight the conceptual gulf that separated the two leaders.

In these circumstances, the French assumed particular importance. It was precisely here, however, that up until the eve of the Copenhagen summit the most serious doubts about the domestic political situation persisted. The first Barre government was, as has already been noted in the first chapter, almost certainly the most European-minded administration since the beginning of the Fifth Republic. However, few of its members can have entertained serious hopes that the task of giving political expression to their European aspirations, let alone the economic programme that in the mind of the new prime minister was an essential concomitant of French Europeanism, would be simple. The speed and the extent to which the government ran into political problems were even so surprising. The recovery of the left and more particularly of M. Mitterand's Socialist Party had already been announced in the municipal election of 1976, and had led, *inter alia*, to French withdrawal from the Snake. It continued in the months that followed the appointment of M. Barre, fuelled by the grievances that his first austerity programme aroused, as well as by the dissatisfaction with the regime that had already been evident in March 1976. In the local elections of March 1977, the left made even more impressive progress than it had done a year earlier. The electorate's response to the appeal of the prime minister to vote for the majority, Raymond Barrillon wrote in *Le Monde* on 22 March 1977, had been 'terribly negative'. The left now controlled 150 of the 221 towns with a population of more than 30 000 as compared with 103 before the election. 'The victory of the Left', the director of *Le Monde*, Jacques Fauvet, noted, 'was geographically and sociologically so broadly based that it could only be interpreted as a sign of a profound desire for change'[60]. As the parliamentary elections fixed for March 1978 approached, the outcome became more questionable, because the stakes were so much higher. However, despite the breakdown of Socialist–Communist unity in the autumn of 1977[61], marked by the failure to produce a common platform and the increasingly shrill threats of the Communists that if they did not secure at least 21% of the votes in the first round of the elections they would not

Figure 3.1 *French opinion polls in the winter before the parliamentary elections of March 1978. (Ecologists account for most of the balance to 100%)*

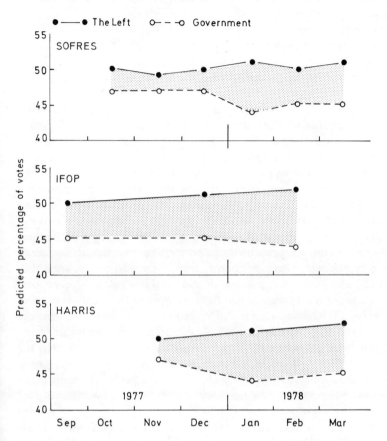

Source: *The Economist*, 11 March 1978

support the Socialists in the second round[62], opinion polls were unanimous until the very end that the left would emerge with an overall majority (see *Figure 3.1*). It was little wonder, therefore, that those who visited the French president in February or early March 1978 found him preoccupied and dispirited, unable or unwilling to consider any longer-term plans for Europe or for France until the election results were known.

The advance of the left was by no means his only preoccupation, however. There was a more immediate constraint on his freedom for manoeuvre in the emergence of M. Chirac as the undisputed leader of the Gaullists. M. Chirac's success in regaining and, still more important, rekindling the confidence of the Gaullists in November and December 1976[63], followed a few weeks later by an aggressive but conspicuously successful campaign to become mayor of Paris, followed in turn by an outright bid to determine the character and the strategy of the majority in the parliamentary elections, presented a formidable threat to Giscard d'Estaing's authority. When M. Mitterand proclaimed at the end of April 1977 that the French president was 'under house arrest'[64] he was perhaps carrying parliamentary rhetoric a little far, but M. Giscard d'Estaing's powers were nevertheless greatly diminished in the late spring and early summer of 1977.

In the event, M. Giscard d'Estaing and Raymond Barre stood their ground on a surprising number of occasions, not least in June 1977, when they sprang a counter-coup of their own and saved the French commitment to direct elections for the European Parliament[65]. But despite this and other acts of defiance, despite too the open avowal of the importance of the Bonn–Paris axis – demonstrated not only in the formal, bilateral summit meetings of that year, but also in the French president's attack on the wave of anti-German publicity in the autumn[66] – M. Giscard d'Estaing could not indulge in grand European gestures for fear of fragmenting his majority still further. As the elections approached, there were signs that the advantages of office were beginning to give M. Barre and the president new hope, but there was still little room for manoeuvre and even less for Europeanism.

In the end, the majority maintained their position in the most spectacular manner, winning 290 seats against 201[67]. However, the real victor in the elections was not the majority in general, so much as the president of the Republic and, to a lesser extent, his prime minister, M. Barre. Within the majority, the RPR, the Gaullist party, remained the biggest single group with 153 deputies, but this figure was 20 below the previous number and their success in hanging on to the majority of their seats was far outweighed in significance by the advance of the UDF, the loose alliance of groups identified more or less with the president, which secured 137 seats. These results, as many commentators at the time both inside and outside France observed, gave M. Giscard d'Estaing a political freedom that he had not possessed since he became president in 1974.

In its first leader following the election, *Le Monde* speculated that a 'relance diplomatique' would soon follow[68]. The author of the article assumed that the French president would act in the sphere of North–South relations or detente. In many respects, however, the decision to support the German chancellor's monetary proposals was even more logical, since it was at one and the same time a sign of the president's new-found independence of his Gaullist supporters and a reinforcement of the new Barre programme for the stabilization of the French economy on which the administration now embarked. To the German chancellor too, the internal consequences of the UDF's victories were hardly less important than the French president's hard-won external freedom because, with Raymond Barre confirmed as prime minister, there seemed solid hope that France would pursue not only a non-Gaullist, pro-European foreign policy, but also domestic policies that would enable the French, if no other non-Snake government, to remain within and prosper inside a zone of monetary stability. Mr Schmidt had frequently in the past given proof of his regard and affection for M. Giscard d'Estaing. What had not been so widely noticed was that he had also on a number of occasions gone out of his way to express his esteem for the French president's prime minister[69]. It would be an exaggeration to say that the political survival of Raymond Barre was an absolute precondition of the EMS initiative, but it was certainly a most important element in Mr Schmidt's calculations and, second only in significance to the personal relationship between chancellor and president, it was to ensure not only that the monetary initiative prospered, but also that the Franco-German partnership acquired a depth and durability that it had not had before.

1 For an interesting discussion of Mr Schmidt's motives, see Heinz Stadlmann in *Frankfurter Allgemeine Zeitung*, 14 October 1978

2 Karl Kaiser and Hans-Peter Schwarz (eds), *Amerika und Westeuropa*, Stuttgart and Zürich, 1977

3 ibid., p. 11

4 Richard Cooper, *The Economics of Interdependence: Economic Policy in the Atlantic Community*, New York, 1969

5 Robert O. Keohane and Joseph S. Nye, *Power and Interdependence: World Politics in Transistion*, Boston, 1977

6 See, *inter alia*, Henry Owen and Charles L. Schultze (eds), *Setting National Priorities: The Next Ten Years*, Washington, 1976

7 For Z. Brzezinski, see, *inter alia*, *Alternative to Partition: For a Broader Conception of America's Role in Europe*, New York, 1965

8 See Karl Kaiser, 'The Great Nuclear Debate', *Foreign Policy*, No. 30, Spring 1978, p. 98

9 *Frankfurter Allgemeine Zeitung*, 16 and 19 March 1977

10 See *The Economist*, 16 and 30 April 1977

11 *Frankfurter Allgemeine Zeitung*, 9 May 1977, an article entitled '"Helmut" bleibt beim "Mr President"'

12 *The Economist*, 23 July 1977

13 On the human rights policy see, *inter alia*, Arthur Schlesinger, Jr., 'Human Rights and the American Tradition' *Foreign Affairs: America and the World*, July 1978, Special Issue, pp. 503ff., and Sandra Vogelsang, 'What Price Principle? US Policy on Human Rights', ibid., pp. 818ff

14 For example, *Frankfurter Allgemeine Zeitung*, 5 February 1977

15 ibid., 6 July and 9 May 1977

16 *Newsweek*, 23 July 1977

17 *The Economist*, 23 July 1977

18 Kaiser, op. cit. (note 8), pp. 83–110

19 Pierre Lellouche, 'Frankreich im internationalen Disput über die Kernenergie', *Europa-Archiv*, **17**, 1978, pp. 541–52

20 *The Economist*, 2 April 1977

21 *International Herald Tribune*, 25 June 1977 and 11 March 1978

22 See OECD, *Economic Outlook*, December 1977, pp. 75ff

23 *The Economist* was a prominent representative of this school. See, for example, 18 June 1977

24 *The Economist*, 6 August 1977

25 See *Federal Reserve Bulletin*, March 1978, pp. 161ff

26 For example, US Treasury Press Releases, B. 683, Statement by Mr Solomon, 6 February 1978

27 *Wall Street Journal*, 1 March 1978

28 ibid., 13 and 14 March 1978

29 Otmar Emminger, *The D-Mark in the Conflict between Internal and External Equilibrium, 1948–75*, Princeton Essays in International Finance, No. 122, June 1977, p. 45

30 The *Wall Street Journal* followed the crisis with particular attention for obvious reasons, and the articles that Richard Levine and his colleagues contributed on the subject provide a well-informed and entertaining commentary on the subject, which should be read in conjunction with the more sober account in the *Federal Reserve Bulletin*, op. cit. (note 25)

31 See *The Economist*, 5 November 1977

32 *European Report*, 3 September 1979

33 OECD, *Economic Outlook*, December 1977, p. 3

34 Developments in 1977 can be most conveniently traced in the OECD *Economic Outlook*, July and December 1977

35 *The Economist*, 6 August 1977

36 IMF *Annual Report*, 1978, p. 2

37 *Frankfurter Allgemeine Zeitung*, 9 May 1977

38 *The Economist*, 1 October 1977

39 See, for example, *The Times*, 18 October 1977, *Financial Times*, 21 February 1978 or *Frankfurter Allgemeine Zeitung*, 23 March 1978

40 Deutscher Bundestag, *Stenographischer Bericht*, 65 Sitzung, 19 January 1978, p. 4970

41 See *The Guardian*, 13 March 1978

42 *Wall Street Journal*, 29 March 1978

43 Jenkins, 'The Integration of the Community in the Face of Enlargement', speech to the Deutsche Gesellschaft für Auswärtige Politik, Bonn, 8 December 1977; reprinted in *Europa-Archiv*, 1, 1978, pp. 1–10

44 *Der Spiegel, passim* 1977

45 *Frankfurter Allgemeine Zeitung*, 31 March 1977

46 *The Economist*, 30 April 1977

47 See *Eurobaromètre*, No. 9, July 1978, pp. 25–27

48 Christopher Tugendhat, speech to the Institut für Auslandskunde, Munich, 9 March 1978

49 *Frankfurter Allgemeine Zeitung*, 12 October 1977

50 See, for example, *The Economist*, 22 and 29 October 1977. There is however, alas, no substitute for the television coverage at the time

51 On the Iran embassy episode, see *The Economist*, 10 May 1980

52 *Der Spiegel*, 21 November 1977

53 *The Economist*, 22 October 1977

54 See p. 59 above

55 OECD, *Economic Outlook*, July 1978, pp. 77ff., covered the good news, but pointed also at some of the disquieting evidence of troubles to come

56 See, especially, F. Blackaby (ed.), *De-industrialisation*, London, 1979, which contains contributions from several of the economists most identified with the debate, and includes in addition an invaluable introduction to the problem by Sir Alec Cairncross

57 See e.g. *The Economist*, 28 January 1978, for a discussion of the changing political fortunes of the leaders of the two principal parties

58 *Frankfurter Allgemeine Zeitung*, 11 March 1978

59 For details, see Jocelyn Statler, 'The European Monetary System: From Conception to Birth', *International Affairs*, April 1979, pp. 206ff

60 *Le Monde*, 22 March 1977

61 *The Economist*, 10 and 24 September 1977

62 ibid., 4 March 1978

63 P. Crisol and J. J. Lhomeau, *La Machine R.P.R.*, Paris, 1977

64 See, *inter alia, Frankfurter Allgemeine Zeitung*, 30 April 1977, which is one of a series of articles in that period in the paper giving a German view of French political instability and 'the return of the Fourth Republic'.

65 *The Economist*, 18 June 1977

66 *Le Monde*, 15 September 1977

67 *Le Monde*, 30 March 1978

68 ibid.

69 For example, *Frankfurter Allgemeine Zeitung*, 5 February 1977

Three Summits: Copenhagen, Bremen and Bonn, April–July 1978

Between April and July 1978, the new European Monetary System ceased to be simply a public dream of Mr Jenkins or a private thought of Mr Schmidt and assumed more definite, if not yet definitive, form. The two most important moments in its emergence during these months were the meetings of the European Council at Copenhagen on 7 and 8 April and at Bremen on 6 and 7 July. Neither of these meetings, nor indeed much of the detailed discussion and negotiation that lay between them, can be properly understood, however, unless they are seen in relation to a third summit, which took place in Bonn on 16 and 17 July, when five European leaders – Mr Schmidt, M. Giscard d'Estaing, Mr Callaghan, Mr Andreotti and Mr Jenkins – met the American president and the Japanese and Canadian prime ministers.

4.1 The European Council meeting at Copenhagen, 7 and 8 April 1978

Mr Schmidt's conversion, the French president's political resurrection and the conclusion of Mr Jenkins' spell as a prophet crying in the wilderness, triggered off a few weeks of intensive pre-summit preparations. The German chancellor had made it clear to Mr Jenkins when they met in Bonn on 28 February that he proposed to outline his ideas at the Copenhagen meeting. Over the weeks that followed, he sought the views of a number of colleagues and experts both inside and outside Germany. The German Cabinet itself, it would seem, was not given any hint of what was in his mind, but Mr Schmidt did invite the new finance minister Mr Matthöfer to prepare a paper on the prospects for European monetary integration, and he also asked Dr Emminger, president of the Bundesbank, to explore the same problems with his French opposite number, M. Bernard Clappier. There is, however, little evidence to suggest that the results of either of these inquiries exercised any more than a negative influence on Mr Schmidt's own thinking. He had already worked out the most important features of his statement at Copenhagen by the time he saw the Commission president in February, and the subsequent exchanges with the Bundesbank and the finance ministry seem only to have reminded him of the scepticism that his initiative was almost bound to arouse amongst experts, and to strengthen his conviction that if anything at all was to be achieved it would have to be done against or without bureaucratic advice. It was to be an initiative, in other words, in the Monnet style with Mr Schmidt and M. Giscard d'Estaing operating outside the normal channels, through trusted agents, one at least of whom – M. Clappier – was a living link with the events that preceded the launching of the Schuman Plan in May 1950.

There were at least two other important preliminary meetings involving Mr Schmidt himself in the weeks before the Copenhagen summit. The first, the private dinner with Mr Callaghan on 12 March, which has already been referred to in the previous chapter, was notable more for what Mr Schmidt did not say than for what he did. Indeed, the British government was to hear more a week later, when Crispin Tickell, Mr Jenkins' chef de cabinet, spoke to Sir John Hunt, the secretary to the British Cabinet, and told him amongst other things of the conversations that the Commission president had had in Bonn at the end of February. Mr Callaghan himself heard from Mr Jenkins directly at the beginning of April. The consequences of this curious combination of non-communication in Bonn and disclosure via Brussels were not however particularly happy, since such was the scepticism with which information from the Jenkins Commission was viewed in Downing Street that Mr Callaghan went to Copenhagen singularly ill-prepared for anything save a Jenkins monetary gimmick, a fact that only increased his sense of resentment at having been excluded from the privileged circle of information when he discovered that he was wrong.

The second of Mr Schmidt's conversations, his meeting with the French president at Rambouillet on 2 April, was altogether more constructive and important. Like two dramatists preparing a performance in which they themselves were to be the principal actors, the two men sketched out the agenda for an informal meeting at which the Danish prime minister would preside and the Commission president would figure in a supporting role, but which they would dominate. The theatrical analogy is in fact not at all inappropriate, since there is ample evidence of careful stage management before the event and skilful timing during it. Formal responsibility for arranging the timetable for the European Council lay, of course, with the Danes, but the prime minister and his advisers found themselves subjected to a certain amount of polite but nevertheless firm pressure, particularly from the Germans, to plan the first day so that the plenary session, with foreign ministers present, could be cut down to a minimum, and the main business conducted in an informal, dinner-party setting. The Danes proved as obliging as possible, but even they baulked at the suggestion that the foreign ministers should be given no more than an hour between three and four in the afternoon of 7 April, with the result that in the end the formal session lasted until five. Thereafter, however, the evening proceeded almost exactly as the German chancellor and his French colleague wanted it to.

Eight government leaders, plus Mr Jenkins and Mr Andreotti's interpreter, were driven out to Marienborg Castle, some distance not only from the centre of Copenhagen, but also from the foreign ministers and officials. The eleventh member of the party, Mr van Agt, the Dutch prime minister, arrived an hour later, a fact that may not have been as insignificant as it seems, because it gave the Danish prime minister, Mr Jørgensen, an opportunity to summon his chef de cabinet, Mr Erik Holm, from a dinner table elsewhere in Copenhagen to act as notetaker. According to one of those present, Mr Jørgensen justified this procedural departure rather charmingly by claiming that as it would fall to him as president of the Council to tell the world's press what had been discussed at the meeting, it would be highly useful if he could consult the notes of somebody who unlike himself actually understood the matters at issue. If officials who participated in some of the other prime ministerial debriefing sessions later that evening are to be believed, he was not the only one present who emerged somewhat bemused by what had occurred.

The evening discussions[1] took place in two sessions, divided by dinner. Although some of the others intervened occasionally, the conversation was largely monopolized by Mr Schmidt, M. Giscard d'Estaing, Mr Callaghan and Mr Jenkins. The latter opened, taking as his point of departure a letter that he had written to all those present on 3 April, in which he had pressed for further progress on the monetary front, suggesting, amongst other things, much wider use of the European unit of account (EUA). Mr Jenkins was followed by the British prime minister, who immediately struck a note of gloom. The prospects for the world economy, he claimed, were considerably worse than they had been at the time of the London summit meeting of the Seven the previous May and hopes of arresting the spread of unemployment seemed to be receding fast. Mr Callaghan's assessment of the situation may not have been unaffected by the publication a few days earlier of the annual *Economic Policy Review* by the Cambridge Department of Applied Economics, which had been conspicuously pessimistic even by the standards of the university from which it came. As far as the United Kingdom was concerned, it predicted that in ten years' time unemployment would be rising towards five million unless mass emigration intervened. As for the world, there was 'no solution to the problems of structural trade imbalance through free trade unless it were really to be accepted that whole countries and whole regions of individual countries should be permitted to become impoverished and derelict'. Mr Callaghan did not advocate the protectionist solution favoured by the Cambridge economists, choosing instead to preach yet again the gospel of growth, but both the tone and the contents of his diagnosis bore a close resemblance to the Cambridge report[2].

The French president, too, confessed himself worried about the international economy, but developed an analysis of the crisis that ran counter to the one expressed by the British prime minister. Quite apart from problems posed by the uncertainty of oil supplies and of other essential raw materials, it had to be recognized, M. Giscard d'Estaing claimed, that the western industrialized nations were themselves divided by interest and geography into three distinct groups: the North American group, the Japanese group and the Western European group. It was essential therefore that Western European countries should work together in a highly vulnerable world, and one way in which they could lessen their exposure to external influences lay through monetary integration. If this path were to be trodden, however, something more than the Snake would be needed.

The German chancellor, who was the last of the four major figures to speak at any length in the pre-dinner session, agreed with those who had preceded him that the outlook for the international economy was deeply depressing. He was, however, particularly concerned to defend his own government's economic policies. The German economy too, he reminded Mr Callaghan, faced a serious structural crisis and, as for growth, his government was running the largest budget deficit in Germany since the days of Hitler. As far as he was concerned the most pressing problems lay elsewhere, in the shortcomings of the international monetary system and the inadequacies of the present American administration, which made these defects still worse. He recalled that when the French president and he had been finance ministers earlier in the 1970s, they had already tried to devise defences against the immense increase in international liquidity and in particular against the threat presented by the Eurodollar market. If the situation had been bad then, it was catastrophic now and it had been made much more dangerous by the policies of the United States' administration. The Germans, he declared, could not go on buying dollars. When Mr Callaghan intervened to ask what alternative he saw to propping up the American currency, Mr Schmidt replied that it would simply have to be allowed to fall.

It was after dinner that Mr Schmidt and M. Giscard d'Estaing disclosed their plan. They were urged to do so, ironically enough, by Mr Callaghan, whose suspicions would seem to have been aroused by the pre-dinner conversation. The French president began the double act by posing the two alternatives that his country faced: it could either rejoin the Snake, or it could work with its Community partners for something else and something more. Later in the evening, when it became evident that Mr Callaghan and perhaps also Mr Andreotti were worried by the proposals, M. Giscard d'Estaing made the same point even more sharply, saying in effect that if the United Kingdom or any other country could not join the new system, Western Europe, which was at a crossroads, would split and France would rejoin the Snake. What both he and Mr Schmidt wanted was something different and more ambitious.

The most important features of the plan were revealed by the German chancellor. Emphasizing that the proposals were personal and that they had not been cleared with either his Cabinet colleagues or the president of the Bundesbank, he outlined a scheme of which the most important characteristics were the following:

(1) the creation of a European Monetary Fund (EMF), which would take over the capital and functions of existing Community institutions and facilities, including the European Investment Bank (EIB), and the credit and swap arrangements connected with the Snake;

(2) the partial pooling of official reserves, with each member contributing between 15% and 20% of its reserves;

(3) increased use of European Community currencies rather than dollars in interventions on the exchange markets;

(4) the expanded use of the EUA, both as a means of settlement between central banks and in due course as a new form of reserve asset comparable to the SDRs.

The plan, the German chancellor insisted, was not as ambitious as the single currency zone for which Mr Jenkins had been pressing, and there would furthermore almost certainly have to be transitional arrangements, including possibly the use of wider margins of fluctuation in order to enable the weaker currencies to adjust to the new regime. In time, however, the new system would 'swallow up' the Snake and the EUA might eventually become a European currency of the kind that the Commission president had advocated.

M. Giscard d'Estaing added some observations of his own to the German chancellor's exposition, including the remark that the proposal amounted to a 'new Bretton Woods for Europe', but most of the rest of the evening was given over to a discussion of the merits and defects of the plan and of what steps if any should be taken to develop or publicize it. The most persistent questioner was Mr Callaghan. Most of the other participants would seem to have been so surprised by its scope that they either would not or could not react in any detail to it. Even those who like M. Tindemans or Mr Lynch had come expecting a discussion of monetary questions, did little more than express general approval. This reticence was particularly remarkable in the case of the Belgian prime minister, since he had come to the meeting armed with proposals drawn up by M. van Ypersele. Mr Callaghan, by contrast, though as surprised as anybody, did not feel any inhibitions about expressing his views. His chief preoccupation would seem to have been with the effect that the scheme might have on the dollar and to a lesser extent on the position of the IMF. On both questions, the German chancellor and the French president tried to reassure him, qualifying some of the sharper remarks made about the American currency earlier in the evening by insisting that the plan was not in any sense directed against the dollar. On the IMF, Mr Schmidt would appear to have been particularly explicit. The Fund, he claimed, would remain a powerful force in the international monetary system because it would continue to exercise surveillance over the non-communist world as a whole, including the other two major currency groups – the dollar and yen blocs – of which M. Giscard d'Estaing had spoken. It would also continue to be the lender of last resort. Mr Callaghan was not, it would seem, particularly reassured by these remarks, nor did he make any attempt to hide his annoyance at the way in which the scheme as a whole had been sprung upon the company without warning.

The British prime minister, however, was almost alone in his misgivings. Few of those present were competent to raise the technical questions that their advisers and subordinates would introduce into the discussion later in the year, but almost all of them would seem to have recognized the political importance of what was proposed. The atmosphere, one of them commented afterwards, was that of a Cabinet meeting when matters of real importance were being discussed. So positive indeed was the reaction of some of the other prime ministers, and notably M. Tindemans, that the only serious dispute that arose between them and Mr Schmidt was over the question of publicity. M. Tindemans, in particular, pressed for immediate disclosure of the main details of the plan. However, the German chancellor refused to countenance such a step, arguing that the ideas were his own, that he did not have the authority of his colleagues behind him, and that anyway there would be a serious threat to the plan if too many hands were allowed to get at it too early. In the end, Mr Schmidt's views prevailed and at the press conference the following day Mr Jørgensen confined himself to a few totally unrevealing remarks. Mr Jenkins, who as president of the Commission shared the platform with the Danish prime minister, was rather more explicit, but even he confined himself very largely to a restatement of his own position, thereby perhaps strengthening the feeling amongst some observers that little had in fact been achieved. He did not refer in any way to the roles played by Mr Schmidt or the French president and, as far as these latter themselves were concerned, their post-summit speeches could scarcely have given less away.

The question of what should be done next remained, however. At the evening meeting itself, no decisions were taken. The position was left so vague in fact that Mr Jørgensen, acting in his capacity as president of the Council, felt constrained to write to the chancellor some days later asking him what should be done. He did not receive a reply, however, a fact that prompted at least some of his advisers to conclude that Mr Callaghan's negative views, which it was assumed had been repeated at the bilateral Anglo-German summit at Chequers two weeks after the Copenhagen meeting, had finally put paid to the scheme. This surmise was, however, far from the mark, since a decision had been taken about how to proceed at Copenhagen itself, unbeknown to all but three members of the Council – Mr Schmidt, M. Giscard d'Estaing and Mr Callaghan. The three men had met at breakfast on the morning of 8 April and, despite Mr Callaghan's evident reservations and resentment, it was agreed that the next stage of the discussions should be restricted to a group of three specially chosen confidants and advisers. Mr Schmidt nominated Dr Schulmann, chief economic adviser in the Bundeskanzleramt (Chancellor's Office), and M. Giscard d'Estaing nominated Bernard Clappier, governor of the Banque de France. Mr Callaghan withheld his hand, however, and it was only later that he suggested that the British representative should be Mr Ken Couzens, second permanent secretary at the Treasury. He would not, however, appear to have objected to the procedure. A directorate of two was clearly unacceptable, but similar objections did not apply to a directorate of three.

The decision to keep these talks secret created considerable confusion in the weeks that followed. The embarrassment of the Danish prime minister has already been alluded to. Others who like Mr Jørgensen had a constitutional responsibility to consider monetary questions were no less perplexed. There was press speculation aplenty, some of it, as always, better informed than others, there were enthusiastic speeches as there had been for six months already from the president of the Commission, and there were other hints that something of considerable significance had been decided at Copenhagen, but when the finance ministers met in Luxembourg on 17 April they had no clear idea of what had happened, and even less idea of what should happen next. They took a rather half-hearted decision to invite the Monetary Committee and the Committee of Central Bank Governors to look again at prospects for European monetary integration, but several of them admitted afterwards that they did not know whether the decision was sensible or appropriate[3].

From then on, matters developed at a surprising speed, but they did so at different levels and in response to different pressures. It is difficult even now to establish a coherent account of discussions amongst the experts and negotiations between the three specially chosen advisers, but by examining each set of talks separately it is possible to see how the rather uncertain conclusions of the Copenhagen summit led to the much more public decisions of the Bremen meeting in July.

4.2   Discussions amongst the experts, April–June 1978

The post-Copenhagen discussions amongst the experts of the possibilities for progress towards monetary integration were initiated formally by the finance ministers at their meeting in Luxembourg on 17 April, ten days after the Copenhagen Council. Between then and 19 June, when the ECOFIN held their last meeting before the Bremen summit, there was a series of discussions in the Central Bank Governors' Committee, the Monetary Committee and the ECOFIN itself. A paper summing up the conclusions that had emerged in these various committees was drafted following the 19 June meeting and forwarded for consideration by the European Council.

In interpreting these discussions, it is essential to stress that almost all those involved proceeded in total ignorance of what was being said or achieved by Dr Schulmann, M. Clappier and Mr Couzens. Indeed, until *The Economist* revealed the existence of the small group on 26 May, it is almost certain that with the exception of one or two British members – Mr Healey and possibly Mr Jordan Moss – nobody knew that these parallel discussions were taking place at all. At the meeting of the central bank governors following the publication of *The Economist*'s story, one of his colleagues asked Dr Emminger, president of the Bundesbank, whether there was any substance in the report and received the rather abrupt reply: 'Ich kenne nichts davon' (I don't know anything about it). Dr Emminger had, it is true, been briefed by Dr Schulmann following the Copenhagen Council, but from then until shortly before the Bremen meeting he was systematically excluded from the circle of the initiated. So much so that when in the course of an evening in June given over to preparatory talks about the Bonn summit of the Seven he tried to broach the question with the chancellor, the latter is said to have replied: 'We can talk about that later.' On the eve of the Council, Dr Emminger was at last given an opportunity to 'talk about it' in a conversation with Dr Schulmann, but the Franco-German plan was already complete and all the president of the Bundesbank could do was insist that the chancellor should not enter into any binding commitments.

Dr Emminger's relations with the authorities in Bonn had not always, of course, been particularly close, and his constitutional position was further-more quite different from that of his counterparts in almost every other Community country, but there is nothing to suggest that even Dr Pöhl, the vice-president of the Bundesbank, who was widely believed to have closer contacts with the SPD/FDP coalition, was any better informed than his president. He certainly gave nothing away to his colleagues on the Monetary Committee if he was in on the secret, and the highly orthodox warning that he gave against any new monetary initiative in an article that was published towards the end of June confirms the impression that he was not[4]. Even Dr Lahnstein, who as Staatssekretär (permanent secretary) at the Ministry of Finance was to play a crucial role after Bremen, would not seem to have been a member of the inner group in the period between the Copenhagen and Bremen meetings. An article that he wrote for *Europa-Archiv* in May 1978 under the title 'Über die Währungsunion zur Wirtschaftsunion?' referred to the Copenhagen summit, but betrayed absolutely no sense of the political commitment to progress in the monetary sphere that the chancellor had conveyed to his colleagues[5].

A similar picture emerges on the French side. M. de la Genière, for example, who as deputy governor of the Banque de France was one of the French representatives on the Monetary Committee, confessed to one of his colleagues at a private dinner preceding the May meeting of the Committee that he had no knowledge of what had been said or decided at Copenhagen, or of what if anything had been done since. As for M. Monory, the French minister of finance, it is hard to believe that he could have been privy to the inner thoughts of the president or M. Clappier before he went to the last pre-Bremen meeting of the ECOFIN on 19 June, since, at almost exactly the same time as they were taking the decision to break with Mr Couzens in order to speed matters up, he warned his colleagues against 'excessive haste'. In fact, only the British representatives would seem to have been differently placed. Mr Healey, who with Harold Lever and the prime minister was one of the inner-Cabinet group of the three that determined British policy during this phase and indeed later, certainly knew about the existence and progress of the three-man talks. It is also possible, though by no means certain, that Mr Couzens' activities were known to certain British officials. Be that as it may, the relevance of this knowledge to the work of the expert committees as a whole was minimal, because, as we shall see in the following section, it was precisely the British who tried to play down the significance of the secret talks when these became publicly known and there was therefore little chance of the sense of political urgency, which was their principal distinguishing feature, being communicated to the experts by this channel.

Discussions amongst the experts developed, therefore, in something of a political vacuum. In these circumstances it is not particularly surprising that, even though they were formally commissioned to prepare papers on the question, many of those involved did not bother to conceal their scepticism or their feeling that other questions were more important. Perhaps the most striking example of official distaste for and boredom with a subject that many of them regarded as dead is to be found in the collective display of scepticism by the Committee of Central Bank Governors in the report that they delivered, through their chairman, M. de Strycker of the Belgian central bank, to the ECOFIN meeting of 19 June. It was an almost undiluted statement of the orthodox 'economist' position. There was, they claimed, no hope of all the member states rejoining the Snake at this particular juncture, even though this ought to be the ultimate aim. Before any monetary scheme could be contemplated, there would have to be a firm commitment to more effective coordination of economic policies. If and when there was evidence of real progress in this field, they would gladly examine the possibilities of linking Community currencies together.

A further and, in some respects, still more important consequence of the lack of any firm political guidance from the top was that many members of these committees maintained a sense of priorities in which the monetary question did not rate highly. With the advantages of hindsight, it is tempting to believe that from Copenhagen onwards monetary union dominated everybody's thinking. This was, however, far from being the case. Interest in the question may have been quickened by May and June 1978, but the major issue, particularly in the ECOFIN, was still economic growth.

However successful, therefore, Mr Schmidt may have been in regaining the political initiative at heads of government level, his subordinates found themselves in a minority and on the defensive at successive meetings of the ministerial Council. At Luxembourg in April and in subsequent meetings of the finance ministers in May and June, the pressure on the Germans to reflate intensified rather than slackened. The most pointed statement of the case was made in a document prepared by M. Ortoli and presented to the Council of Ministers at their meeting in May. The days of the locomotive theory might officially be over, but as the Ortoli paper showed there were some ships in the convoy that could be expected to pull more weight than others. The commissioner listed the Community states in order of reflation potential: Germany, Belgium, Holland, Luxembourg, France, Britain, Denmark, Ireland and Italy. As the Benelux states indicated that they accepted their obligations, the Federal Republic's position was not at all easy[6].

This preoccupation with other problems, the lack of any sense of urgency, not to mention the outright scepticism, that were so much in evidence amongst ministers and officials involved in the specialist committees between April and June 1978 might have been expected to prevent any useful contribution from the experts to the search for a new monetary system. In actual fact, however, a great deal of considerable importance was achieved. That this was so was due in large measure to the Monetary Committee in general and to its chairman, M. van Ypersele, in particular. The previous work of this committee has already been alluded to in chapter 1. The continuing obligation to think and think again about a relatively narrow, but extremely important range of technical problems, the freedom from the day-to-day problems of the management of the international monetary system that tended to dominate both formally and informally the agenda of the central bank governors, the relative youth of its membership compared with the Central Bank Governors' Committee, the development of what Conrad Oort, a former chairman, described as a 'club spirit' and, by no means least, the political commitment of several of its members, gave this committee a character and utility as a political instrument that the Central Bank Governors' Committee, for all its distinction, did not possess. It is no coincidence, for example, that a declaration put out by the Pamphilii Group in June 1978[7] calling on the Bremen Council to take steps to expand the role of the EUA, which was to be renamed 'Europa', included amongst its signatories two chairmen of the Monetary Committee, M. van Ypersele and Conrad Oort (his predecessor but one), and Giovanni Magnifico, who was one of the Italian representatives on the Committee. The activities of yet another chairman, Bernard Clappier, will be discussed later, but it is obvious that his association with the Monetary Committee in the past had been an important influence on the development of his thinking and that the connection remained a lively one. There is nothing to suggest that he broke the vow of secrecy even with his friend and colleague M. van Ypersele, but it is clear that he knew about and used material prepared by M. van Ypersele and his colleagues in the Monetary Committee during his own work for the committee of three. The dialogue developed in rather unusual circumstances, but there was a dialogue nonetheless, and the link between the two levels provided by M. Clappier more than offset in importance the link provided by Mr Couzens.

It would, of course, be a mistake to depict the Monetary Committee as a cohesive group of apostles, all equally devoted to the common end of European monetary union. Certain members made no secret at the time and have made even less since of their scepticism about the prospects as long as the economic priorities and performances of the member states were so disparate[8]. Left to their own devices the Alternates Committee, which had been asked to examine the implications of the Commission document on economic and monetary questions submitted to the European Council in December 1977, had come up with fairly timid and unexciting conclusions. The same might have happened in the Monetary Committee between April and June had it not been for the role of the Belgian chairman, Jacques van Ypersele. When one of his colleagues at the Copenhagen summit asked who was the father of the monetary plan that he and the German chancellor had just disclosed, M. Giscard d'Estaing is said to have replied with a quotation from Napoleon: 'En matière de paternité, Monsieur, il n'y a que des hypothèses'[9]. It would be stretching both history and biology a little far to put M. van Ypersele forward as an alternative candidate for the title of father of the EMS, but the child might not have been born and would almost certainly have been of a different size and shape without his help. Reference has already been made to his involvement in earlier episodes in the history of the search for European monetary integration. As monetary adviser to three Belgian ministers of finance, he had drafted a succession of ministerial statements and proposals at ECOFIN, including the Geens speech of July 1977. He was also the author of the section of the Tindemans report dealing with monetary union, though the original draft had been more radical than the version that was eventually published. In the winter of 1977–78, he had been consulted by Mr Jenkins and his Cabinet and had made various contributions of his own to the public discussion of the themes reopened by the president in his Florence and Bonn speeches. In December 1977, for example, he had given a lengthy interview to the Belgian journal *Trends*[10], in which amongst other things he took up once again the idea of monetary zones as a basis for a new international system, a theme that, as has already been noted above, was developed by the French president at the Copenhagen meeting in April 1978. In the months that intervened between the Brussels meeting of the European Council in December 1977 and the session at Copenhagen, M. van Ypersele contributed three papers of his own to the Monetary Committee, which were both parallel to and more important than the Alternates' report prepared during the same period. They are worth examining[11].

The first, completed in January 1978, set out four options that might assist the Community to recover the greater monetary cohesion for which the European Council had called. The argument was prefaced, it need hardly be said, by the orthodox caveat that new mechanisms for linking the exchange rates of the Community states could have only a limited effect in bringing about stability if they were not accompanied by more effective measures to coordinate economic and more particularly monetary policies. That said, there were four possible courses of action that might be followed. The first was the return of all the Community currencies to the Snake. The second, which was essentially the approach advocated some time earlier by M. Fourcade, involved linking the non-Snake currencies to the Snake but permitting the non-members to move within wider margins. The third was a revival of the Duisenberg plan, involving the creation of target zones. M. van Ypersele's own preferred option was, however, the fourth, which involved relating the non-Snake currencies to a currency basket composed of both European currencies and the dollar, in which the latter would account for 50% of the weight. The aim would be to reduce the dollar's weighting over the years, which would have the effect of gradually assimilating the three weaker currencies into the Snake. To make the option still more palatable in its initial stages, the obligations imposed on the three non-Snake currencies would be more akin to those advocated in the Duisenberg plan than to the much stricter and potentially more damaging commitments of the Snake. In time, however, the rules would approximate increasingly to those by which the Snake members were bound. The novelty in the proposal, as M. van Ypersele himself pointed out, lay partly in the use of a basket as a numeraire and partly, too, in the fact that it gave the Snake a less influential role in determining the exchange values of the three non-member states than either the Fourcade or Duisenberg plans had done, and that in doing so it met the objections of those, notably the British, who argued that so much of their external trade was done in dollars that they simply could not afford to link themselves to a non-dollar zone.

In a subsequent paper, written in March 1978, M. van Ypersele developed the plan still further, by examining arrangements of the coordination of economic and monetary policies, credit facilities and the means of interbank settlement. Under the first heading he called for the coordination of monetary targets, while under the second he advocated strengthening and extending both short-term and very short-term credit arrangements. As far as interbank settlements were concerned, existing arrangements under the Snake were, he observed, absurd, since they laid down that very short-term credits should be repaid in quotas reflecting the composition of the debtor country's reserves. As in every case dollars constituted the bulk of official reserves, the system involved, as Robert Triffin had earlier noted, the replacement of a credit given to a European partner by a credit from the former debtor to the United States. As an alternative, M. van Ypersele called for the progressive use of the EUA, which would be issued by the European Monetary Cooperation Fund (EMCF) and would be guaranteed in part at least by gold deposits from the member states. These deposits would remain the property of the member states and would be returned to them if and when the system was abandoned, unless of course the state concerned did not have the funds to repay outstanding debts. The plan, which as he noted was not unlike a set of proposals advanced independently by Giovanni Magnifico and Rainer Masera of the Banca d'Italia, amounted in effect to the creation of a new reserve currency, comparable to the SDR. In the final section of his paper, he turned to the political context, arguing that although there were undoubtedly difficulties in the way of any ambitious scheme, the present moment, in which there was a greater degree of convergence in economic performance than there had been for some time, was propitious for the adoption of a bold approach, which could, if embarked upon, reinforce the tendency towards convergence. There was also an external argument. Although some argued that a stable dollar was a precondition of European monetary integration, the opposite case could also be defended, namely that by working to create greater cohesion within the Community, the Community could make itself less vulnerable to shocks from outside.

When the German chancellor launched his monetary initiative at Copenhagen, therefore, M. van Ypersele was already trying to push his colleagues towards a serious reconsideration of the case for a new move towards monetary union. On 3 April, for example, he circulated members of the Monetary Committee with a paper entitled 'Intra-EEC exchange rate arrangements and related issues' in which he set out a questionnaire covering exchange rate arrangements, policy coordination, intervention, credit mechanisms and settlements of credits for discussion at their next meeting. At the Copenhagen summit itself, as has already been noted, the Belgian prime minister actually had a version of the van Ypersele plan in his pocket, but did not produce it because, to his surprise, the German chancellor developed ideas that were even more far-reaching. It was only to be expected, however, that when M. van Ypersele was told about what had happened at Copenhagen – and, unlike many and perhaps the majority of his colleagues, he was told – he did his best to ensure an effective contribution from the Monetary Committee. The agenda for the meeting of 11 and 12 May, circulated on 19 April, set aside a whole day for a discussion of prospects for a renewed attempt at economic and monetary union and in particular a convergence of exchange rate policy. As a basis for a discussion, the chairman suggested the questionnaire that he had circulated prior to the Copenhagen meeting.

Following a preliminary, oral presentation to the ECOFIN of 22 May, the Monetary Committee prepared a detailed report at the beginning of

June. It is an important document in the context of the emergence of the EMS because, four weeks before the Bremen Council, it sketched out the issues that, as we shall see in chapter 5, were to dominate the discussion of technical problems in the months that followed the Bremen meeting. Its point of departure was by now quite explicitly the decisions taken at the European Council in Copenhagen. It assumed, therefore, that member governments wished to see progress towards exchange rate stability even before they had entirely solved the problems of differences in inflation rates or balance of payments performance. Progress in this sphere, it averred, could contribute politically, psychologically and technically to improving the convergence of economic trends and policies in the member states. The committee presented three broad options, all of which, it was stressed, would permit the continuance of the Snake in its present form. As we shall see later in this chapter, this point was strongly defended, particularly by the Benelux countries, prior to and at the Bremen meeting. The first option involved essentially the extension of the current Snake to the rest of the Community. Participating countries would, in other words, be obliged to defend a nominal market rate vis-à-vis each partner currency. A possible variant to a straightforward enlargement of the Snake was, however, suggested, involving simplified procedures to modify central rates by small percentages, arrangements for temporary leave of absence and the development of common attitudes towards major countries outside the system to reduce tensions within. However, whichever variant was adopted would involve very strict discipline given the wide differences in the economic performance of member states. Deficit countries would have to pursue rigorous stabilization policies, while surplus countries should be expected to contribute towards equilibrium in the form of credits to their weaker partners and by the pursuit of the highest level of economic activity compatible with internal and external equilibrium. If these corollaries of the system were not accepted on both sides, exchange rates would have to be changed so frequently that the system's survival would be in doubt.

The second set of options involved the definition of intervention obligations in terms of a weighted index. Two possibilities were suggested: a trade-weighted basket including the dollar, or the existing EUA. Neither variant would rule out the survival of the Snake, but a basket system could form the basis of an entirely new Community system if this was desired. The first of the two variants was, of course, the proposal put forward by M. van Ypersele himself in January and March 1978. The second was a French proposal, and is the clearest possible indication of the interaction between the two levels of discussion in the months preceding the Bremen Council. Although M. Clappier's colleagues themselves would not appear to have known anything about his conversations with Dr Schulmann and Mr Couzens, the proposal that they outlined in the Monetary Committee was at the centre of M. Clappier's contributions to the secret talks, and news of how the idea was received fed back to the governor of the Banque de France even though there was not any reciprocal flow of information in the other direction.

The third option was essentially a revival of the Duisenberg plan. The three non-Snake currencies would be related to a common target zone, but the obligations that would arise if a currency drifted outside the zone would not include a commitment to intervene. Of the three alternatives it was therefore the least demanding and it was not discussed at any length.

The remainder of the report examined medium-term financing and the role of the EMCF. As far as the former was concerned, it was thought possible that a further increase in the amount available might be considered necessary as part of a general plan for greater exchange rate stability. Under the general heading of the EMCF, the possibility was mentioned of making greater use of the EUA as a means of settlement between the monetary authorities and as an additional monetary reserve. Any movement towards the pooling of reserves would, however, require detailed technical examination.

Behind this non-committal statement of the options, there were already serious differences of opinion and emphasis that foreshadowed the divisions of the summer. The Germans, the Danes and the Benelux representatives, for example, were insistent that, whatever new arrangements might be experimented with, the Snake itself should continue to exist. The principal advocates of an intervention system based on either the EUA or a trade-weighted basket of currencies including the dollar were the French and the Belgians, but whereas M. van Ypersele tended to see the new arrangement as an additional mechanism alongside the parity grid system used in the Snake, the French advanced it, and particularly the EUA variant, as the single basis of an entirely new Community system. Its principal attraction to those like the French who had a weak currency was that the point at which intervention became obligatory could be reached by one currency alone rather than by two, as was always the case in the parity grid system. As the deviant currency in question might be either strong or weak, this meant that the burden of taking corrective action could fall equally well on the strong as on the weak. The dispute that developed about the respective merits of a basket-based system as opposed to a parity grid will be discussed in more detail in chapter 5. What is most important in the present context is not so much the content of the debate as the fact that it took place at all. Independently of the secret talks, the Monetary Committee had managed to lift the discussion of prospects for a fresh monetary initiative to an entirely new level of seriousness several weeks before the European Council met at Bremen at the beginning of July.

The change that had occurred during the space of eight weeks was obvious in the meeting of the ECOFIN on 19 June. At the April meeting, most of the ministers had seemed mystified about what had happened and some were opposed outright to a fresh attempt to create a fixed exchange rate system. In June, by contrast, there was little or no disagreement on the general principle that a new effort to create a stable exchange rate system in the Community was desirable even before the problems of diverse inflation rates and balance of payments positions had been solved. M. Geens, the Belgian finance minister, was predictably the most outspoken of the ministers, pressing for firm conclusions that could be forwarded to the heads of government, including the retention of the Snake, the development of a wider system involving intervention obligations for all participants, modification of credit mechanisms, a more active role for the EMCF and greater use of the EUA. Even though his colleagues were more cautious, they too had begun to be affected by the momentum that had been generated in the Monetary Committee and, doubtless, by speculation about what the committee of three was engaged in. A striking example was provided by Mr Pandolfi, the Italian minister. In April, he had told his colleagues that Italy would find it impossible to return to a fixed exchange rate system, given the experiences of 1972–73. Now, in June, he appears to have argued that although there were many problems that would have to be examined, including not least the implications of the new arrangements for the dollar, he ruled out the third, looser Duisenberg option in favour of one or other of the fixed exchange rate options. He was also interested by the possibilities of developing the EUA mentioned in the Monetary Committee report. Similarly, Mr Matthöfer – the successor to Mr Apel as German minister of finance, and the inheritor therefore of the conventional scepticism towards proposals for monetary integration to which Mr Apel had been accustomed to give such blunt expression – was ready to admit that, although certain transitional arrangements might be necessary for the non-Snake members, it would be inherently undesirable to create a two-tier system and that the possibilities of extending the roles of both the EMCF and the EUA in the Community monetary system would be worth studying.

The task of summarizing the conclusions of the ECOFIN meeting and of preparing a paper for the European Council was entrusted to the Monetary Committee. The paper that emerged listed seven principles on which the new exchange rate arrangements should be based:

(1) The new system should embrace all Community currencies though there might be transitional arrangements for non-Snake members. Other European currencies might also be associated.
(2) It should achieve symmetry between the obligations of both strong and weak members.
(3) It should not be damaging to third currencies.
(4) The Snake should continue to exist for its members.
(5) Membership of the system should involve acceptance of an obligation to intervene where necessary and to undertake economic policy commitments where appropriate.

(6) Although the system should help to reduce divergences in economic performance, it should not be so rigid as to prevent changes in exchange rates when these divergences necessitated them.

(7) There should be modifications in the Community's short-term and very short-term finance support arrangements.

The Council also envisaged provision for the consolidation of short-term debts into medium-term obligations if the country that had incurred the short-term debts was not in a position to repay them. With this in mind, it proposed that the Community's medium-term financing facilities should be re-examined. It also 'expressed interest' in the possibility of a more active role for the EMCF. The fund might issue EUAs, which could serve as a means of settlement between central banks, and claims and liabilities resulting from operations in the fund could also be denominated in EUAs. The paper concluded by observing that the Community's own aspirations would be greatly facilitated if there was more stability in relation to the major third currencies.

It would perhaps be going too far to suggest that the finance and economic ministers as a body felt that they were sharing in the creation of a new monetary system, since several of them went out of their way after the meeting to declare that they expected no such thing to emerge from the European Council at Bremen[12]. But a momentum had nonetheless been created, and the terms in which the detailed technical discussions of the Schmidt–Giscard plan were to develop after the Bremen summit had been largely defined by the experts beforehand, even though the full implications of the most radical proposal – a basket-linked intervention system – were still not entirely clear even to its advocates.

4.3   The Gang of Three

At the same time as the finance ministers and the specialist committees were discussing the options open to the Community in the monetary sphere, secret talks were in progress between the three negotiators nominated by Mr Schmidt, M. Giscard d'Estaing and Mr Callaghan. The initiative for these private talks came from the German and French leaders, and more particularly from the former, and seems to have reflected at least two fundamental concerns of the German chancellor. The first was his conviction that if his plan were left solely or even partly in the hands of central banks or finance ministry officials it would be killed. The only hope of any real progress was therefore to entrust the task of working it out to special advisers, who had of course to be technically competent, but who needed above all else to be in the confidence of the three leaders themselves. As M. Clappier, the French president's nominee, told his colleagues in the Committee of Central Bank Governors at their first meeting after the Bremen Council, he had taken part in the preparations for the Bremen summit not in his capacity as governor of the Banque de France, but as the French member of a very restricted group formed by 'certain heads of state and government'. The second consideration in Mr Schmidt's mind seems to have been a genuine desire to bring the British in. Indeed, much of the significance of this episode lies precisely in the fact that it undermined a serious effort to create a directorate of three and confirmed a tendency, which was already strong, towards a directorate of two.

Details of how, when and where Dr Schulmann, M. Clappier and Mr Couzens met and worked together remain obscure. According to one usually well-informed source there were five meetings, at the fifth of which Mr Couzens was not present[13]. This is, however, almost certainly an oversimplification, since in a period in which there were frequent meetings between senior civil servants to prepare for both the Bremen and Bonn summits it was relatively simple for the three men to meet without attracting notice. There were also quite certainly informal exchanges on a bilateral basis.

The reasons that led to the breakdown between Mr Couzens and his two colleagues are rather easier to establish than the date, and will be discussed shortly. It seems likely that the breakdown occurred either on or a few days before 20 June, the day on which M. Hunt, the spokesman for the Elysée, announced that the French president would be paying a special visit to Hamburg on 23 June to meet the German chancellor[14]. As the main purpose of this working dinner (at which, in addition to the two leaders, Dr Schulmann, M. Clappier and M. François Poncet were also present) was to discuss the Schulmann–Clappier document, it is clear that the decision to hold it in the first place implied acceptance of the fact that there was no longer a serious prospect of agreement between the French and the German negotiators on the one side and Mr Couzens on the other. However, there is evidence to suggest that neither M. Giscard d'Estaing nor Mr Schmidt had entirely given up hope that the British might eventually be brought round. At a meeting with Mr Jenkins on 22 June, the French president spent some time discussing the British problem and expressed the hope that the Commission president would help in the effort to keep the connection open. There were also persistent rumours during the weeks between the Hamburg meeting and the Bremen Council that Mr Schmidt and M. Giscard d'Estaing planned to see Mr Callaghan either separately or together[15]. It is impossible to know whether these rumours had any foundation, but what is clear is that the two men asked Mr Callaghan to join them for special discussions about the monetary plan before the Bremen Council meeting. But Mr Callaghan refused the invitation, pleading urgent business in London, and the separate talks between the three leaders were therefore confined to a rather hurried session before dinner on 6 July. By then, however, it would have been too late anyway for the British to have any direct influence on the wording of the proposal. The document that was distributed to the heads of government after dinner on 6 July was thus to all intents and purposes a Franco-German plan. A few phrases from Mr Couzens' draft were incorporated and, unlike other officials with whom Dr Schulmann and M. Clappier spoke in the weeks following the Hamburg meeting, he was actually given a copy of the paper on 28 June, but this was definitely the product of M. Clappier and Dr Schulmann.

The text of their proposal, which was later published virtually intact as an Annex to the Bremen communiqué, is reproduced, together with the preamble that was drafted at Bremen, in Appendix 1A. The document repays careful analysis. On two points there would seem to have been total agreement. Firstly, the new system was not to be a soft option. Hence the opening sentence: 'In terms of exchange rate management the European Monetary System will be at least as strict as the "snake".' Upholders of the Snake system might later express doubts about how a system related to the European currency unit (ECU) could be as strict as the Snake, but it is evident that M. Clappier, no less than Dr Schulmann, endorsed the opening sentence in full. The second point on which they both agreed was that the system would be new, that it was not in other words simply the Snake by another name. It was, to quote M. Clappier himself, 'un nouveau pas vers une nouvelle organisation monétaire d'Europe'. Later, at the central bank governors' meeting at which he made this observation, he expressed his views even more strongly. Referring to the promise that, as we shall see, had been included in the preamble to the Bremen communiqué at the specific request of the smaller Snake countries, namely that the Snake would continue to exist alongside the new system, M. Clappier admitted that this might pose problems, since 'il s'agit de la coexistence de deux systèmes substantiellement différents l'un de l'autre'.

Both the French president and Mr Schmidt were equally insistent on the novelty of what was proposed. In the course of a visit to Spain at the end of June 1978, M. Giscard d'Estaing commented on recent reports that the Snake would be extended to include the franc and possibly even the pound. He admitted that plans to create a zone of monetary stability had been under review since the Copenhagen summit meeting earlier that year, but what was proposed was 'a new mechanism, and it would not be in the form of the French franc joining the Snake as it now worked'[16]. The German chancellor's comments, made in the course of a remarkably open interview with *Business Week* that was published only three days after the Hamburg meeting with M. Giscard d'Estaing, are even more interesting[17]:

> I'm not so much thinking in terms of enlarging the Snake, but of something which goes a little beyond the present Snake. I am thinking in terms of pooling some currency reserves. I'm thinking about a EUA that would also be the medium in which you settle accounts between the

European Central Banks. I could imagine additional instruments of monetary assistance, of broadening the existing instruments and extrapolating them into the long range field. ... of course there are ... some risks. ... It might mean for Germany ... that we have to sacrifice some of our reserves. It might also mean that we have to expand our money supply somewhat more rapidly than we have done until now.

This evidence of a determination to create something new is impressive and significant. However, it should not be allowed to conceal the fact that there were important differences between the two sides, which made the Bremen document more provisional in character than it seemed to be at the time. The most controversial phrase occurs towards the end of the first paragraph: 'The European Currency Unit (ECU) will be at the centre of the system.' The element of whimsy introduced into the proceedings by this happy blend of a serviceable Anglo-Saxon acronym with the name of a French coin, which as M. Giscard d'Estaing later reminded his television audience had been in circulation in the days of St Louis[18], should not be allowed to conceal the fact that the ECU was simply the European unit of account by another name, and that the same problems arose between the two special negotiators in connection with it as had already begun to emerge in the discussions of the Monetary Committee. There is, in fact, a striking parallelism between the two sets of discussions, even though the participants in the expert committees knew nothing of what was going on in the secret talks. For M. Clappier the ECU was intended to be at the centre of the system not just as its numeraire, nor simply as a means of settlement between central banks, but as the basis on which the intervention system itself was to be established. For Dr Schulmann the problem was more complex. Answerable only to Mr Schmidt, he was almost certainly more open to new ideas than official German representatives on the Monetary Committee and elsewhere. As the *Business Week* interview showed, the German chancellor was ready by the second half of June to say things in public that to a trained German ear must have sounded like intimations of a dangerous heresy, and it would seem only reasonable to conclude that both he and Dr Schulmann were even more relaxed in private discussions with the French president and M. Clappier. Even so, Dr Schulmann made it clear well before Bremen that his position differed from that of M. Clappier. The most explicit acknowledgement of this difference came in the course of a discussion that he had with some Dutch colleagues on 29 June. The French, he said, had a strong preference for an intervention system based on the EUA, but the Germans were in two minds. They could see the political attractions of 'showing the European flag', but they were not sure that it was technically feasible. He struck a similar note of caution the following day, when he spoke with the Belgians, who because of their linguistic divisions apparently enjoyed the unique privilege of visits from both M. Clappier and

Dr Schulmann and who were therefore particularly well placed to spot the differences in emphasis between the two men.

The Franco-German plan that was placed before the European Council at Bremen on 6 July was therefore by no means a definitive statement. There were still problems that had to be explored and discussed. Nor, however, was it simply a declaration of options or criteria of the kind drafted first by the Monetary Committee and approved subsequently by the ECOFIN. The essence of the Bremen Annex is to be found not in its detailed provisions, but in the political determination that lay behind it and that it faithfully reflected. By the same token, the roots of the breakdown between Mr Couzens and his two colleagues are to be found not in any specific divisions over technical questions, but in the fact that Mr Couzens and his masters at home did not share and failed to grasp the significance of the determination of the French and the Germans to get something done, come what may.

In analysing and explaining this initial breakdown between the British and their European partners over the EMS, it is important to draw a distinction between it and the subsequent episode when the British government decided not to enter the system. On the latter occasion, the reason was primarily, if not exclusively, party political. The decision to postpone the general election made Mr Callaghan the prisoner of his party for a further six months at least, and given the mood of the party conference in October there was little hope that he could carry his Parliamentary Labour Party let alone the National Executive Committee and the rank and file with him if he opted to enter the EMS before the election. Between April and July 1978, however, the situation was rather different. The general election seemed imminent of course – it was widely believed that it would be called in October – and it was therefore almost certainly impossible for Mr Callaghan to contemplate a final decision on the issue before he had cleared the electoral hurdle. In contrast to the later period however, Mr Callaghan was not being asked to take a final decision and this breakdown occurred when the main characteristics of the system were still to be determined and before the question had become a party political issue in any of the countries concerned. Although, therefore, electoral considerations may have been one of the factors influencing Mr Callaghan's behaviour, it seems difficult to believe that they are in themselves an adequate explanation of the initial rupture. The scepticism and political miscalculations that led to this crisis stemmed as much if not more from the prejudices of the senior civil servants involved as they did from the worries of party politicians. In a situation in which the German chancellor, having tried but failed to elicit any genuine enthusiasm from the Bundesbank or the ministry of finance, had decided to present the established bureaucracy with a *fait accompli*, Mr Callaghan appointed the representative of a department of state that, like comparable departments in Bonn and Paris, was known to be profoundly sceptical about the prospects for monetary integration, only more so. M. Clappier was also of course the holder of an independent position as governor of the Banque de France but, as he explained to his fellow central bank governors, he was careful to draw a distinction between the work that he did for the head of state on a personal basis and his normal official duties. Mr Couzens, by contrast, spoke and acted throughout as a senior Treasury official. The ultimate blame for this state of affairs lay doubtless with the prime minister himself who chose Mr Couzens in the first place and, having appointed him, failed to check or counteract his professional scepticism. The consequence of Mr Callaghan's uncertainty was however that the predominant voice in the initial British response to Mr Schmidt's initiative was the Treasury's.

There were doubtless some even inside the Treasury who felt or came to feel that it would be in the country's best interests to cooperate with the Germans and French in the construction of a new monetary system. There seems little doubt, however, that the early reactions of Mr Couzens anticipated what was to be the majority position inside the Treasury over the coming months. His and the Treasury's approach was characterized as much by the mental outlook that informed it as by the detailed arguments that were advanced to cast doubts on the wisdom of the scheme. As far as the former was concerned, there seems to have been a persistent compulsion to work out a system that was as intellectually satisfying and apparently water tight as possible coupled with an equally marked impatience with those, like the French or the Germans or the Italians, who cut corners or made exceptions for political reasons. The energy with which Mr Couzens and his colleagues threw themselves into the technical discussions in the second half of 1978 even when, in the later stages, they knew full well that there was no chance of the United Kingdom joining was frequently remarked upon. Devising a system was an intellectual challenge, which could be accepted and indeed relished without any sense of political commitment. By the same token, however, there was little patience with those like Dr Schulmann or M. Clappier who seemed inclined to leave certain key elements in the system unclear and ambiguous in the interests of political compromise and commitment. There was nothing particularly new about this Treasury order of priorities. In the history of postwar European integration, as earlier in the history of the wartime alliance, the real Cartesians, it sometimes seems, have been in London, while the French, who are normally reckoned to be the guardians of the tradition, have shown a remarkable grasp of the advantages of pragmatism and the possibilities of muddling through to goals determined by political considerations or passions.

The Treasury's arguments against a new European monetary initiative can be divided into two broad categories, the first international, the second domestic. Under the first heading, their reaction was undoubtedly conditioned by the fact that they had recently prepared a programme of their own for the stabilization of the international monetary system and the revival of economic activity, which, as we have seen already, Mr Callaghan took with him to Bonn and Washington in March. The essential element in this programme had, of course, been its implicit call for German reflation. What was almost more significant, however, was its global approach. To the Treasury officials who drafted it, the solution to the problems of the international monetary system lay not through the development of regional systems, but through multilateral diplomacy within the context of the existing international institutions and in particular the IMF, where American involvement could be guaranteed and where too, it might be pointed out, British influence was relatively stronger than it was within a Community framework, partly for historic reasons, but still more because Mr Healey was currently chairman of the Interim Committee. Distaste for a specifically European approach was strengthened still further by the fact that although British trade with the Community was growing both in volume and as a proportion of her total overseas trade, the United Kingdom's interests outside the Community were still relatively more important to the country's economy than the extra-Community business of any of her Community partners. A move that was even partly 'anti-dollar' in its motivation was therefore inherently suspect. (These 'structural' objections to British membership faded into the background in the negotiations themselves, following developments in the transatlantic dialogue that will be discussed in the next section, but they were referred to again informally by Mr Couzens in conversations with other officials 'standing by' at the Brussels meeting of the European Council in December. As the Council had just approved a British 'halfway house', partly at least because it was assumed that the only obstacle was the Labour Party in a pre-electoral period, Mr Couzens' admission of more fundamental grounds for reserve prompted one senior official from another Community country to observe: 'If this is now the line, when *will* they come in?')

The domestic considerations can also be summarized fairly briefly. They were not, it should be stressed, simply another example of the long-standing conflict between the British and the Germans over which should have priority, full employment or stability, even though at first sight this might seem to have been the case. Monetarist ideas and techniques had invaded Whitehall too and stability was now a fundamental object of British economic policy[19]. But in a nation of 'too few producers'[20], there were still limits to the commitment to monetary priorities. Full employment might no longer be a realistic aspiration, but 'de-industrialization' was a fate to be avoided at all costs. There is neither time nor space here to explore the way in which the preoccupation with de-industrialization came to dominate both official and public debate during 1978[21]. Suffice it to say that euphoria about the riches from the North Sea was rapidly giving way to gloom about the industrial wasteland that would be all there was left when the oil had gone. Proposals for a link between the pound and the mark were therefore almost inevitably seen in relation to this general problem, and although there were voices that argued that the only way out of the vicious spiral into which the British economy had drifted lay through the maintenance of a strong external exchange rate and the domestic policies necessary to sustain it, the predominant view inside the Treasury would seem to have been that any attempt to preserve a fixed exchange rate with the German mark would make the United Kingdom's bad position even worse. Some Treasury calculations of what the effect would be were apocalyptic, not to say hysterical, as an official paper, leaked much later in the year by Mr Brian Sedgemore, parliamentary private secretary to Mr Wedgwood Benn, conveniently illustrates[22]. The basic assumption underlying the calculations was that membership of the EMS, by depriving the British government of its freedom to allow the exchange rate to drift down, would keep sterling at an artificially and unacceptably high level. The consequences would be restrictive fiscal measures, a shortfall in gross domestic product (which by 1982 would, according to one scenario, be 9.5% lower than it would otherwise have been), rising unemployment and working-class unrest. Predictions such as these circulated Whitehall from April or May 1978 onwards, linked not infrequently with the suggestion that the whole EMS proposal was part of a Machiavellian German plot to boost their exports and ruin the United Kingdom's. The possibility that the market and North Sea oil might within less than a year lift sterling a long way above its 1978 parities with the major European currencies would seem to have occurred to nobody.

Views and reservations such as these did not provide a particularly promising basis for a major monetary initiative. As the weeks passed, partly it would seem because the Americans had made it clear that they were neither particularly interested in Mr Callaghan's scheme to salvage the dollar nor unduly worried about the development of the European zone of monetary stability, but partly too because rather belatedly the Treasury saw a possibility of negotiating a package deal with the Germans in which British membership of the monetary system was traded off against German measures to reflate, Mr Healey and presumably therefore Mr Couzens too began to adopt a more positive attitude towards talk of European monetary integration. Following the May meeting of the finance ministers, for example, *Le Monde* reported that the chancellor of the exchequer, who had been 'distinctly negative' at the previous Council meeting in April, seemed now to be much more understanding[23]. At the following meeting on 19 June, Mr Healey was if anything still more forthcoming on general principles. But there was still no sense of urgency. On the contrary, he and his officials made it clear to British journalists when they briefed them before the meeting that there was 'little likelihood of any agreement on a new currency regime within the Community before the Bonn summit'. While Treasury officials were not against currency stabilization in principle, *The Times* reported, they had 'many reservations'[24]. This was precisely the impression that Mr Couzens managed to convey to his partners, and against this background the Franco-German decision to drop him is not particularly difficult to understand. M. Clappier and Dr Schulmann had their differences of opinion on technical issues, and on a number of points, notably the role of the ECU, M. Clappier's ideas were a good deal closer or at least more congenial to the British than they can have been to either Dr Schulmann or Mr Schmidt. What distinguished Dr Schulmann and M. Clappier from their British colleague was not therefore their adherence to a precise idea of how the system should develop, but, much more, their awareness of and sympathy with the political commitment of their masters. The Bremen document that they drafted was above all else a declaration of intent, and nothing in the way that Mr Couzens himself or his political masters behaved between April and June suggested that they were willing to sponsor such a declaration. As a result, after almost six weeks of talks and with only three weeks to go before the Bremen Council meeting, he was left out.

In the final analysis, responsibility for the breakdown lies with Mr Callaghan, who failed to realize that, although for everything there is a season, the season between April and July 1978 was not for a Treasury official however capable he might be. There is evidence to suggest that the German chancellor himself hoped that his British colleague would nominate Harold Lever, who was a personal friend, a member of Mr Callaghan's Cabinet and also its chief link with the City. Later in the year Mr Schmidt actually sent Dr Schulmann to London on a special mission to Mr Lever, and much to the annoyance of both Mr Healey and his Treasury officials the German visitor did not call on the Treasury. It is difficult to believe that Mr Callaghan, however undecided he may have been about the merits or political feasibility of the monetary initiative, would have gone to Bremen so embarrassingly unprepared as he did had he accepted the chancellor's hint. Mr Couzens' political misjudgements remain nonetheless curious, and it is legitimate to ask whether even a Treasury official should have allowed himself to have been so dramatically and publicly wrong-footed and humiliated.

The initial mistakes during the secret talks were compounded still further by a series of blunders once it became clear that the conversations had broken down. Pique replaced indecision and prejudice as the determinant of policy, to the further detriment of British interests. Mr Couzens' feelings on being left out of the action were demonstrated most clearly in an extraordinary briefing that he gave to British correspondents on 10 July, shortly after the conclusion of the Bremen Council. *The Times* reported it thus[25]:

> While still accepting the goal of greater monetary stability, the Treasury remains sceptical to the point of contempt of most of the detailed content of the Franco-German scheme. ... There is considerable anger at the way in which the proposal was 'sprung' on the rest of the Community. ...
> More substantial criticisms revolve around the vague and often confused

terms in which the scheme is phrased, coupled with deep suspicion that the system is little more than a means of holding down the mark and imposing restrictive policies on Germany's partners. There is considerable resentment at what is seen as the success of the German government in presenting its national interest as being a move for the greater good of Europe.... The fact that the whole thing is dealt with in just a few hundred words is generally felt to show the danger of allowing enthusiastic amateurs to dream up schemes for monetary reform.

Mr Couzens himself later regretted the tone of the outburst and referred to it self-deprecatingly as the outpouring of 'a suspicious and elderly Treasury mind'[26]. Unfortunately, however, it was not an isolated explosion. British policy as a whole in the weeks immediately preceding the Bremen Council would seem to have been strongly influenced by sentiments such as these at both official and prime ministerial levels.

One of the more obvious manifestations of this tendency was a singularly clumsy approach to most if not all of Britain's other Community partners, aimed in effect at sabotaging the Schulmann–Clappier plan. British officials knew that in the last days of June and the beginning of July Dr Schulmann and M. Clappier toured the European capitals explaining their proposals. Taking these visits as its point of departure, the British note claimed that authorship of the plan was exclusively Franco-German, that in the British government's view insufficient attention had been given to the technical problems involved, that the European Council should not take a decision on the basis of the scheme and that the best way to proceed would be to authorize the ECOFIN and its associated committees to continue the technical studies that they had already begun. As will be noted shortly, the Dutch in particular were extremely unhappy about the way in which the follow-up to Mr Schmidt's Copenhagen initiative had been handled, but there is nothing to suggest that they were influenced in their attitudes by this ill-considered intervention by a government that had itself countenanced and connived at secret diplomacy until, largely through its own fault, it was dismissed from the privileged circle.

An even more striking demonstration of bad temper, comparable in many ways to Mr Couzens' press briefing, was to follow a few days later when, on the eve of the Bremen Council, Mr Callaghan himself gave an off-the-record interview to Peter Jenkins of *The Guardian*[27]. As evidence of the British prime minister's mood and aims on the day he left for Germany it could scarcely be improved upon. 'Britain', Mr Jenkins wrote, 'is on the verge of a new and serious quarrel with her European partners. Mr Callaghan [is] prepared to place virtually impossible preconditions upon British participation in a European currency stabilisation scheme favoured by Chancellor Schmidt and President Giscard.' These conditions Mr Jenkins described as 'virtually tantamount to a second renegotiation of the terms of British

Community membership', covering as they did the CAP, Britain's contribution to the Community budget and the transfer of resources from richer to poorer regions. Mr Callaghan even threatened to raise non-Community issues as well, notably the 'sore question of the British army on the Rhine'. The reasons for this sense of outrage are already familiar. The British prime minister was 'annoyed that he had not been consulted more fully by his two senior partners'. He regarded the plan as an act of German self-interest, 'thinly disguised by a veil of Community spirit', and Mr Schmidt's continuing refusal to take steps to reduce the German payments surplus as 'antisocial'. In sum, Mr Callaghan was 'simply not prepared to preside over the de-industrialization of Britain, which he believed would be the effect of currency stabilisation without a corresponding transfer of real resources'. As a sign of his ill-feeling, he had refused to take part in a pre-summit meeting with the German chancellor and the French president, pleading that he had an urgent British Cabinet meeting that he could not miss. Later in the article Peter Jenkins himself questioned whether Mr Callaghan would or should go as far as his mood inclined him to: 'He will probably swallow his resentments and play along at least until the general election is over.' He still hoped that it might be possible to slow down the momentum, but he recognized that the issues at stake were momentous. 'We are seeing a new two-tiered Europe struggling to emerge from the old Europe' and Mr Callaghan's task, however annoyed he might feel, was to 'seat himself firmly at the top table of three', since that was the only place from which he could hope 'to control events'.

Before describing the Bremen meeting itself, it is necessary to look briefly at the reactions of the other six Community partners to the Schulmann–Clappier paper and, in the next section, at the transatlantic discussion that developed in these months. Arrangements to tell the other member governments about what was proposed were coordinated between the French and Germans at or immediately after the Hamburg meeting. Dr Schulmann was instructed to brief the Danes, the Dutch and the Belgians, and M. Clappier, the Italians, the Luxembourgers and again the Belgians, who, because of their linguistic divisions and perhaps too because their role was recognized to be of critical importance, received both visitors. The task of telling the Irish was left open, in the hope, it is claimed that Mr Couzens would agree in the end to perform this task.

The Italians were for at least two reasons in a special category. Firstly, like the French and the British, they were not members of the Snake. Secondly, unlike the French and the British, though of comparable size, they had not been involved in the secret preparations of the monetary plan. This last point was commented on rather sourly in the Italian press shortly after the disclosure of the existence of the Schulmann–Clappier–Couzens group, and there is much to suggest that the Italian government itself shared the resentment at their exclusion from the inner circle expressed in the newspapers[28]. It is also clear that powerful elements within the Italian administration were hostile to any attempt to bring the lira back into a fixed exchange rate system; memories of 1972–73 were simply too fresh and too painful. Mr Pandolfi's comments at the April ECOFIN meeting have already been referred to above. They were echoed at other times and in other places by both Rinaldo Ossola, minister of commerce and a leading expert on monetary matters, and Dr Baffi, governor of the Banca d'Italia. As always in Italy however, political considerations soon began to make themselves felt. The importance attached to the continuing connection with Europe north of the Alps and in particular with Germany was underlined only days before M. Clappier's arrival in Rome, when, despite the major political and constitutional crisis precipitated by the resignation of President Leone on the previous day, Mr Andreotti, the prime minister, insisted on keeping his appointment with the German chancellor in Hamburg on 17 June[29]. The monetary plan was discussed at this meeting, even though it had not yet reached its final form, and it seems clear that despite the reservations felt by his advisers, which he outlined to Mr Schmidt, the Italian prime minister also emphasized that his government understood the potential political significance of the proposal and was therefore disposed to take it extremely seriously[30]. This new tone in official comments on proposals for monetary integration was confirmed two days later in the contribution by Mr Pandolfi at the ECOFIN meeting of 19 June and it became even clearer during and after the meetings with M. Clappier on 30 June. It can hardly be claimed that those involved relished the prospect of a new monetary system but the political argument won the upper hand. Following a discussion amongst ministers on 2 July, it was made clear that at Bremen and elsewhere the Italians would press for a more flexible system than the Snake, including wider bands for the weaker currencies and a transfer of resources, but that in principle Mr Andreotti and his closest colleagues were already disposed to join the new system, if it was in any way possible to do so[31].

The reactions of the Snake countries, Belgium, Denmark, Luxembourg and the Netherlands, were varied. The Danes, who were the first to be briefed (Dr Holm was told by Dr Schulmann when he was in Bonn on 27 June in connection with arrangements for the hand-over of the Community presidency), were also, it would seem, the least concerned. Their Benelux partners, by contrast, were much more active. The most outspoken, both behind the scenes and in public, were the Dutch, who made no secret of the fact that, whatever the merits of the scheme, they strongly disapproved of the procedure that had been followed. The day after Dr Schulmann's visit to The Hague, for example, the Dutch foreign minister, Mr van der Klaauw, commented: 'I want the Netherlands to be involved in Community decision making: if it appears that they are not being consulted, then I will rebel'[32]. Officials in the finance ministry and in the central bank shared these feelings and had in addition a number of serious reservations about the contents of the Franco-German proposal. To strengthen their position therefore, they called for a meeting with Belgian and Luxembourg officials in Brussels on 4 July. However, the meeting, at which the Dutch were represented by Mr Wellink, treasurer-general at the ministry of finance, and Dr Szasz, deputy governor of the central bank, the Luxembourgers by Mr Jaans, commissioner of banks, and the Belgians by M. Jansen of the Banque Nationale and M. van Ypersele, only served to illustrate once again the special position occupied by the Belgians in general and M. van Ypersele in particular. The difference between them and their partners was most marked in the exchanges on the procedural question, where the Belgians, though admitting that they did not particularly like the way the affair had been handled by the French and the Germans, insisted that what really mattered at Bremen was that there should be progress on the substantive issues rather than an acrimonious dispute about procedures. On the technical issues, the representatives of all three governments found it easier to agree. They all insisted, for example, that the Snake should continue to exist. Quite apart from any commitment in principle to the system, there was the purely practical argument that, unless a clear indication of this nature was given by the European Council, the foreign exchange markets might draw their own conclusions. On the ECU and in particular its possible use as the base for an entirely new intervention system, they were all extremely cautious, insisting that no final decision could be taken at Bremen, because the matter clearly required further study. Even here, however, it is possible to detect differing nuances. The Belgians, for example, did not exclude the adoption of an ECU-based system in principle, while the Dutch did or very nearly did. There were also differences over the proposal to pool reserves. The Dutch, supported by the Luxembourgers, felt that it was too early to take even a decision in principle; the Belgians, by contrast, felt that if progress was really to be registered at Bremen then it was important that the Council should decide in principle to work towards a new European currency, which implied the pooling of reserves. These differences amongst the experts were to be reflected at Bremen itself in the contributions of Mr van Agt, M. Gaston Thorn and M. Tindemans, though even the former allowed their fundamental political commitment to European unity to determine their attitudes in the final outcome.

It remains only to consider very briefly the Irish. For reasons that have already been referred to above, they were left out of the arrangements for a pre-Bremen briefing by the French and the Germans. As Mr Lynch stressed at the Bremen meeting, this oversight was resented. As he went on to explain however, the Irish had on their own initiative taken steps to repair the neglect, requesting and obtaining interviews between their ambassadors in Paris and Bonn and M. Clappier and Dr Schulmann. This small step was in many ways symptomatic of the Irish role in the EMS negotiations throughout. It was not only that they were interested in principle, they were also, as almost all those who negotiated with them afterwards acknowledge, remarkably well prepared. Part of the explanation is doubtless to be found in the personalities involved in the Cabinet and the bureaucracy. They operated, however, in a peculiarly favourable environment. Only days before Mr Lynch went to Bremen, for example, the Joint Committee of the Dail and the Seanad on the Secondary Legislation of the European Communities had concluded and published a report on the prospects for economic and monetary union, which had been begun in response to the Jenkins initiative at the end of the previous year[33]. In a single paragraph towards the end of the report the Committee anticipated what were to be the recurrent themes of official Irish policy throughout the EMS negotiations. European monetary union was to be welcomed for both political and economic reasons. Politically it would give the Irish a share in policy-making that they had never had in the monetary union with the British. Economically it would help to control inflation. However, in order to offset the burdens and dangers of association with countries that were both more advanced and geographically better placed, there would have to be a meaningful regional policy that would ensure a significant redistribution of resources from the richer to the poorer countries. Both the objectives of Irish policy and the criteria by which the government would be judged were therefore established in broad outline before the Bremen Council. Mr Lynch might regret the procedure that had been followed by the French and the Germans; he certainly resented the rather unnecessary slight given to national pride in the last weeks of June. But like his Belgian colleagues and in the final analysis all the other members of the Six, he was not prepared to allow irritation to prevent or delay the implementation of a scheme that he knew could count on the backing in principle of a broad consensus in Irish political society.

4.4   The transatlantic dimension

No account of the negotiations and controversies that preceded the European Council at Bremen on 6 and 7 July would be complete without at least some consideration of the transatlantic dimension. It was important for at least three reasons. Firstly because, as we have seen, the original proposal was provoked by concern about the quality of American leadership in general and the management of the dollar in particular. Secondly because, since its inception, the European Community had been so tightly meshed into a broader network of transatlantic ties and institutions that the Americans themselves and American-based international institutions, such as the IMF, had been to all intents and purposes important actors in the politics of the Community. Thirdly, and not least, because the pre-Bremen period was also the pre-Bonn period, and the calculations about the first of these mid-summer summits were not infrequently affected by estimates of what might be proposed or decided at the second where, in addition to the Europeans themselves, the Japanese, the Canadians and the Americans would be present. The preparations of the German chancellor for the second of the high-level meetings at which he was required to act as host will be discussed in the following section; for the moment, it is enough to concentrate on the formulation of American policy towards the EMS in this initial phase.

Discussion about the possible implications for the United States of a new move towards European monetary integration began within the administration well before the Copenhagen summit, and the most important points of principle had been rehearsed and largely settled by the first half of June 1978 – before, that is, most of the members of the European Council, let alone the great European public, had the slightest inkling of the contents or even the existence of a Franco-German plan. This rather curious timing can be explained to a large extent by two factors. The first is the tendency of a diplomatic timetable that revolves around regular summit meetings, if not to create problems, then certainly to demand answers before they may be required or relevant. Officials preparing for the Bonn summit knew that the question of European monetary integration might come up, and so rightly and properly they prepared appropriate papers to deal with the contingency. The second factor is the perennial capacity of senior American officials to engage in a debate with each other about the pros and cons of European integration that has a logic and a momentum almost entirely of its own. European integration is, it sometimes seems, a theological issue over which, with only the slightest provocation, those who believe in it (more often than not to be found in the State Department) and those who prefer to see it as a sinister, long-term threat to American power and influence (usually to be found in the Treasury, but also in some force in Congress) will engage in a glorious battle of words[34]. It is all highly entertaining, particularly to those involved, but it sometimes means that the discussion of serious technical issues is circumscribed in advance by the fact that the referee's decision has already been sought and given before the specific problems at issue have been identified let alone discussed. Something of the kind happened over the EMS. The administration gave its blessing to the scheme before they knew what was in it, for the *a priori* reason that the American government had always been in favour of European unity and that, as the monetary proposal was a step towards this goal, it ought to be approved and supported.

The somewhat philosophical character of the first round of the debate within the American administration can be deduced from the fact that the earliest exchanges occurred in response to the efforts of Mr Jenkins, which, as we have seen, few observers within Europe were disposed to take very seriously. However, Ambassador Hinton, the head of the United States' Mission to the European Community in Brussels, liked what the president said and wished him well, and, as an outstanding representative of a generation of American diplomats who had sometimes seemed prepared to work for and believe in the cause of European unity when many Europeans themselves had lost heart, he knew how to express his support in forthright terms. Many of those who heard his views remained sceptical about the possibility of anything substantial emerging from the Jenkins campaign, but there were apparently some, notably in the Treasury, who were ready to react even before Copenhagen in a negative sense, with the result that, when the earliest, vague and by definition inexact rumours on the Schmidt plan reached Washington, the battlelines were already drawn. Despite a certain amount of 'hard' information through London, the debate continued, as it had begun, at a high level of abstraction. It was not without significance, however, because senior Treasury officials would seem for a while to have persuaded Mr Blumenthal, the Treasury secretary, and perhaps even Mr Bergsten and Mr Solomon, that a European monetary system might constitute a threat to American interests. Their grounds for concern were summarized later in the year in an excellent paper on 'US attitudes and perceptions with regard to the European monetary initiatives', which was prepared in the EEC's Washington office. Those who felt perturbed, the paper suggested, wanted reassurance that a new EMS:

- —would not result in a closed currency block and restrictions on capital movements;
- —would not result in a systematic overvaluation of the dollar with regard to the European currencies;
- —would not provide a new lease of life for gold;
- —would not attempt to resume the Bretton Woods system or impose exchange rates so rigid as to prevent fundamental adjustments world-wide;
- —would have neither a low growth nor an inflationary bias;
- —would not be a threat to the IMF.

Some of these preoccupations were reflected in an important speech that Mr Anthony Solomon of the Treasury gave in New York on 15 May 1978[35]. The fact that he also by implication dismissed Mr Callaghan's offer of help for the dollar makes it doubly interesting:

Concerns about the possible effects on exchange rate instability have spawned suggestions which focus on efforts to achieve greater stability through financial means, including exchange rate zones supported by massive official intervention, greatly expanded credit arrangements, foreign currency borrowing by the US and 'substitution' arrangements to stabilise official currency reserves. Such proposals treat the symptoms rather than the causes of present economic problems. Experience of the past decade has demonstrated repeatedly that exchange rate stability cannot be imposed on the system but must be the result of sound domestic policies.

Later in the same speech Mr Solomon went on to acknowledge that 'expanded European monetary arrangements' of the kind that 'some European leaders seem to be considering' could be compatible with the new IMF framework symbolized in the amended Article 4, but scepticism, it seemed, retained the upper hand.

A few days later, Mr Blumenthal, secretary of the Treasury, gave a speech at Mexico City[36] in which, though he admitted that an expanded role for SDRs and European monetary integration were developments that might well occur anyway, he made it clear that he believed that 'such changes in the monetary system should be seen as possibilities for the future'. Present efforts 'must be conducted within the monetary system as it presently exists', which implied amongst other things that the dollar would continue to remain the pivot of the international monetary system. 'A change in the role of the dollar is not a cure for our problems.'

Over the following weeks a serious effort was made to work out a compromise between those, like Ambassador Hinton, who wanted the administration to give the new moves towards European monetary integration its full-blooded support and those, particularly within the Treasury, who damned them with faint praise – or inside the Treasury itself with worse even than that. Richard Cooper, who was in charge of US–EEC relations at the State Department, is generally acknowledged to have played the key role in this process, but he was helped not only by his officials, but also by Anthony Solomon inside the Treasury camp. Many questions of course remained to be asked. Indeed, as has already been suggested above, the more details became known about the scheme, the more questions they seemed to raise. But by the first week in June 1978, if not earlier, the administration would seem to have moved beyond what one might describe as the ideological phase. The new tone, though still laced with a strong hint of reserve and doubt, can be detected in an interview that Mr Solomon himself taped for the United States' International Communications Agency on 6 June, but that was not released until 18 June[37]. Asked by the interviewer how the United States viewed 'closer monetary ties amongst the European nations', Mr Solomon replied:

> Well, we have always supported, of course, the concept of fuller European economic integration, and I think it's a decision for the Europeans themselves. It's perfectly compatible with the broad international monetary system as we know it today, and if the Europeans make that decision, or if it evolves in a more gradual way, I would assume from everything I know about the way these things tend to operate, that it would be perfectly compatible and therefore we would have no problem with it.

When the interviewer went on to ask however how Mr Solomon would regard the emergence of a European reserve currency, rivalling the dollar in importance, his response was still rather cool:

If other currencies should develop more acceptance as reserve currencies, that is again, if it develops smoothly, that is a perfectly appropriate evolution from our point of view. You must understand, though, that for other currencies to become meaningful reserve currencies, they have to open their capital markets the way the United States has, and they have been reluctant to do that to the degree that we have. There is no way of having a really important reserve function for a currency unless it has large capital markets to which the rest of the world can have access, can borrow. The United States has played that role. We would not have had the post-war economic expansion in the entire world and the prosperity we have had unless the United States had been willing to do that. If other countries are willing to do that, or the European Community as a whole develops monetary union and a unit of account and is willing to do everything that is required ... for that currency to develop that reserve currency role, then assuming that it is a smooth evolution we would be perfectly happy with that. My own personal view is that there will be considerable reluctance to enter this role in any very rapid way, because I think the opening up of capital markets in Europe is something that most European governments would want to handle very, very cautiously.

The line that Mr Solomon developed in public was echoed in private by the president himself. As the German chancellor told journalists assembled at the press conference following the Bremen meeting, both he and President Giscard d'Estaing had spoken 'personally and separately' with the American president about the EMS several weeks before and he had given 'his political agreement in principle'[38].

This evidence of American benevolence had at least two consequences of immediate importance. The first was that it undermined still further the credibility of British opposition to the Schmidt proposals, since both at Copenhagen and thereafter British representatives had constantly reiterated their anxiety about the damage that the new system might inflict on the dollar and the priority of a global approach to the solution of the dollar crisis itself. At Mexico City, in the course of the IMF meeting, the Americans had already made it clear that they were not particularly interested in any plans that the British or anybody else might have for a grand stabilization programme along the lines of the Basle Agreements, which had been devised ten years earlier to deal with the problem of sterling balances[39]. With the administration's public endorsement of efforts to achieve European monetary union, the British arguments for caution and delay began to look distinctly ragged, and when Mr Jenkins and the French president discussed the British problem on 22 June, both of them had already come to the conclusion that, however sincere the preoccupations of Mr Callaghan and his officials might have been on this score at Copenhagen, the reasons for their continued reluctance to play a full part in the making of the system had now to be sought in London itself. The second consequence of the positive attitude taken by the Americans was in some respects still more important, since it paved the way for the Federal chancellor's concession on growth at the Bonn summit meeting. Had the advice of certain elements in the United States' Treasury prevailed, it is extremely doubtful that Mr Schmidt would have been prepared to make this additional commitment and it is quite certain that the Bonn meeting itself would have been thoroughly disagreeable. As it was, serious American questions still remained to be asked – Mr Carter himself indicated some at Bonn – but the ground rules of the debate had been decided and agreed, and, despite the 'Bergsten list', a document drawn up in the summer of 1978, which allegedly detailed all the problems that the EMS might pose for the United States, and the continuing concern of officials in the Treasury and in the IMF about the possible implications of the system, the next phase in the transatlantic discussion of European monetary plans was a good deal less emotional than the first, even though, as we shall see, it took place against the background of a dollar crisis that was in some respects even more dramatic than the crisis that had prompted Mr Schmidt to launch his initiative.

4.5   Bremen and Bonn

The agenda for the meeting of the European Council at Bremen on 6 and 7 July was a crowded one. At the press conference that followed its conclusion on 7 July, Mr Schmidt raced through ten points that, he claimed, had been covered in the course of the discussion[40]. They ranged from consultations about the negotiations with the three candidate countries, Greece, Portugal and Spain, to an extended discussion of North–South relations and the problems of Africa in particular, to a review of the 'economic and social situation', which included debate about youth unemployment, energy policy, Mediterranean agriculture and the possibilities of redressing regional disparities, to 'the removal of all remaining obstacles to the holding of direct elections for the European Parliament'. 'A system of monetary union within the European Community', Mr Schmidt's own description of the EMS, was therefore only one of many matters dealt with in the course of the two days. It was, however, by far the most important, and in recognition of its peculiar significance it was dealt with, as at Copenhagen, in the informal post-dinner session attended only by the heads of government themselves, two interpreters (one for Mr Andreotti and the other for Mr Jørgensen) and, on this occasion, Dr Schulmann, who was admitted on the basis of the precedent created by Mr Holm at the April meeting.

Before the main discussion began however, there were a number of informal conversations within smaller groups. The German chancellor for example sought out Mr van Agt before the opening session and attempted to soothe his feelings about not being kept informed about the Schulmann –Clappier–Couzens meetings. The most important of these informal meetings, however, was one between Mr Schmidt, M. Giscard d'Estaing and Mr Callaghan, which took place between the main afternoon session and dinner. It had originally been hoped that the British prime minister would arrive at Bremen much earlier in the day, and that these preliminary discussions could therefore take place before the formal Council meeting began. For reasons that have already been alluded to however, Mr Callaghan refused to oblige, and this belated attempt to repair the breach between the French and German leaders on the one side and the British on the other had to be fitted in between the conclusion of the afternoon session shortly after 6 pm and dinner at 7.30 pm. As might have been expected from Mr Callaghan's mood on leaving London, nothing came of the conversations and, when Mr Schmidt eventually arrived at the dinner table, he was quite open in saying that he and the French president had failed to secure the British prime minister's support for the proposals that they would later put to the Council.

The discussion that followed dinner was in some respects less structured and orderly than the comparable session at Copenhagen[41]. Then, Mr Schmidt, M. Giscard d'Estaing, Mr Callaghan and Mr Jenkins had virtually monopolized the evening; now, following an opening exposition of the Franco-German paper, everybody would seem to have had views to contribute, and they did so not in any order of precedence, often at length and occasionally repetitiously. Certain issues did however dominate the occasion and for the sake of convenience they can be divided into two main groups: procedural and substantive. Of the procedural issues three were of particular importance: complaints about the way in which the proposals had been prepared, reservations about the extent to which any firm commitments could be entered into at this point, and publicity. The first of these issues had, of course, already been raised before Bremen. On this occasion, it was the Irish prime minister, Mr Lynch, who would seem to have made most of the matter, complaining that his government had not even received the type of briefing that had been made available to the other smaller states before the Council. There was, however, no suggestion either in Mr Lynch's contribution or in the comments of any of the other leaders present of a 'revolt' by the small states. One reason was that, as we have seen above, the Belgians had made it clear before the Council that they would not be party to an acrimonious dispute about the past. Another reason almost certainly was that, earlier in the day, Mr Schmidt had had a private meeting with Mr van Agt at which he had explained why he and the French president had felt it necessary to go about things in the way that they had done and called on the Dutch prime minister as 'a European' to support the proposal.

Although protests about the past were not as vigorous or as sustained as might have been expected in the light of certain pre-Council observations, the feeling that they had not had sufficient time to consider the Franco-German plan did nonetheless figure prominently in the discussion of the second procedural issue referred to above. It was the British prime minister, predictably, who displayed the greatest reluctance about entering into any kind of commitment to the ideas set out in the Franco-German document. His Cabinet, he said, had authorized him to agree to further studies of the possibilities of monetary integration but not to put his name to a particular plan. Mr Callaghan was not, however, alone. There were others who, for a variety of reasons, felt that they could not endorse a document that some of them admitted they could not understand until they had had a chance to discuss the matter with expert advisers. The point was made with greater or lesser force by at least three prime ministers – Mr Jørgensen, Mr van Agt and Mr Andreotti. According to several reports, feelings ran high on the matter, sufficiently high indeed for the British prime minister or one of his associates to give a late-night briefing to North American correspondents that implied that the French president had been isolated on the question by colleagues who did not want to move as far or as fast as he did[42]. Mr Callaghan in fact seems to have believed, even after the meeting, that the issue had not yet been settled, because on the following morning he lobbied at least two of his colleagues before the formal session began and when the latter opened demanded further discussion of a question that, as he was eventually forced to accept, the rest of his colleagues regarded as closed.

The proposal that probably saved the Council from an inconclusive and possibly even an embittered outcome appears to have been made by the Luxembourg prime minister, M. Gaston Thorn, shortly after Mr Callaghan's most extended statement of his position during the evening session. M. Thorn proposed that the Franco-German document should be allowed to stand intact, but that it should be prefaced by a preamble approving the document as a starting point for detailed, technical discussions, and explaining in more detail the procedures that were to be followed and some of the reservations on points of substance that had emerged in the course of the evening. This suggestion met with general approval and prompted the French president to propose a sentence in the preamble defining the special position taken by the British government. Mr Callaghan dodged this poisoned chalice, however, claiming that he did not want to be publicly isolated. As a result, the preamble contained no specific allusion to the British or indeed any other government.

This left only one major practical problem outstanding, namely the question of whether or not the Franco-German document should be published. Mr Andreotti appears to have been almost as cautious on this issue as Mr Callaghan, since he felt unable to commit himself to the proposals on the spot and thought that he would not even be in a position to do so the following morning, when he had had a chance to discuss the matter with his advisers. He therefore suggested that circulation should be limited to the finance ministers and the other 'competent Community bodies' alluded to in paragraph 6 of the Schulmann–Clappier paper. Both the French president and the German chancellor fought vigorously against this argument, but in the end it was probably M. Tindemans who did most to ensure that both the preamble and the Franco-German document were published, arguing that this was too big and exciting an initiative to conceal any longer, since it offered a real chance of reviving interest in and progress towards European unification.

Two of the more substantive issues raised in the course of the evening's discussions were reflected in the preamble, which, together with the Franco-German document, is printed in full in Appendix 1A. One was the pledge that the Snake would continue to exist. This point, it will be recalled, had been stressed repeatedly by representatives of the Snake countries both in the ECOFIN meeting of 19 June and in subsequent pre-Bremen meetings between the Benelux states. The matter was given particular urgency on the evening of 6 July itself by the feeling that, unless some public statement was issued immediately to this effect, there was a real danger that currency speculation would build up on the exchange markets on the following morning. Indeed, so acute was the anxiety about what might happen on the markets that the German government took the unusual step of issuing an interim statement at midnight in order to prevent speculation on the Tokyo exchanges. The more profound issues raised by the proposal to allow the Snake and the new system to coexist were not, however, touched upon. On the role of the ECU, for example, the French president would appear to have restricted himself to saying that the ECU would have a monetary function and would act as numeraire of the system, which, as we shall see in subsequent chapters, could mean either a great deal or relatively little. The German chancellor, too, was not particularly forthcoming. He acknowledged the need for symmetry in the obligations of both strong and weak – though, as the subsequent debate was to show, symmetry meant different things to different people – and he admitted that transitional arrangements, involving for example wider bands of fluctuation, could be allowed to non-Snake currencies. He stressed, however, that these arrangements should be no more than transitional and that in his view little was to be gained by excessive indulgence. The ideal, to be achieved as quickly as possible, should be very narrow margins of fluctuation, of probably no more than 1%.

The other substantive issue specifically mentioned in the preamble was the approval given to 'concurrent studies' of action that might be needed to strengthen the economies of the less prosperous countries. The subject had already been anticipated during the more formal session in the afternoon, when Mr Andreotti had made a vigorous attack on the irrelevance of the CAP to the problems of Mediterranean agriculture. The discussion that followed, which went on for over an hour, was later described by Mr

Callaghan as 'the most thorough and frank discussion of the defects of the CAP' in which he had participated[43]. In the evening session, it was Mr Lynch who first raised the problems of the weaker economies, but he was strongly supported by Mr Callaghan and Mr Andreotti. The arguments that they advanced had already been aired in public before the Bremen meeting and, to judge by the speed with which the central point was conceded in principle, it seems likely that both Mr Schmidt and the French president arrived prepared to be cooperative. That said, however, there was already a foretaste of a difficulty that was to be of some significance in the negotiations between the Germans and the Irish later in the year, in an exchange between the German chancellor and Mr Lynch. One way, Mr Schmidt suggested, in which the less prosperous countries might be helped would be through an extension of the activities of the EIB. The Irish prime minister responded that, although the EIB might be good in itself, it could not, no matter what it did, meet the main point of his demand, which was for an outright transfer of resources and not simply loans.

The question of loans was clearly linked with another major issue, namely the scope and functions of the EMF. In the light of subsequent controversies, particularly inside Germany, it is significant that at Bremen, as earlier at Copenhagen, both the French president and the German chancellor obviously saw the Fund as a key element in the whole system. Mr Schmidt in particular stressed that it would be administered by a special institution, with a full-time staff and director of high calibre, helped possibly by the Committee of Central Bank Governors and supervised by the ECOFIN. The Fund, he is alleged to have said, should be such as to ensure that 'nobody could push us around'. As far as the dollar was concerned, however, his own feeling was that it would not suffer and that if any major currency were to be caused embarrassment by the new system it would be the yen. Both he and the French president, he stressed, had discussed their proposals with President Carter, who had made it clear that from a political point of view he would favour an initiative of this kind. Significantly enough perhaps, Mr Callaghan, who had laid such stress on the transatlantic dimension during the Copenhagen meeting, would not seem to have emphasized the matter on this occasion.

By the end of the evening, and still more by the end of the additional two hours of discussions the following morning prompted by Mr Callaghan's continuing doubts, Mr Schmidt and M. Giscard d'Estaing had in fact established total dominance over the Council. The reservations of their colleagues on points of procedure and substance had been allayed or neutralized and, although the preamble, drafted after the evening session by Dr Schulmann, Mr Jenkins and Mr Lynch, did not completely identify the Schulmann–Clappier paper with the Council's feeling that a zone of monetary stability 'was a highly desirable objective', the Franco-German document had to all intents and purposes been accepted as the point of departure for the detailed drafting that was now to begin in the competent Community bodies. Even the time-scale of the programme set out in the preamble reflected the wish of the French and German leaders to progress at the greatest possible speed. The sixth paragraph of the original document was omitted, but despite their very serious reservations about entering into commitments on the basis of inadequate information and without sufficient preparation, all the prime ministers, including Mr Callaghan, agreed in the preamble to a timetable that was identical with that proposed in the Franco-German document[44]. Expert discussions were to be finished by the end of October, so that a decision could be taken at the next European Council meeting in Brussels at the beginning of December. After the Council meeting, correspondents gained the impression that Mr Callaghan was still extremely unhappy about the Franco-German plan, that Mr van Agt was still annoyed about the procedures that had been followed before the meeting and that Mr Andreotti was still unable to make up his mind[45]. But the evidence suggests that, however much they or any of their colleagues may have resented the Franco-German initiative, they accepted the need to come to terms with it. There could have been no clearer indication of this than the semi-public rebuke given by Mr Callaghan to Mr Couzens following the latter's outburst to the British press on 10 July[46]. If one compares what Mr Couzens said on 10 July with what Mr Callaghan himself had told Peter Jenkins on 6 July, there are similarities in both tone and content. What could be said before Bremen, however, was quite different from what could be permitted afterwards, and by the time the luckless Mr Couzens unburdened himself of his resentments and doubts, his prime minister had come belatedly to recognize the political force that lay behind the Franco-German initiative.

The atmosphere in which the new phase of the negotiations opened therefore was determined very largely by the victors – the German chancellor, the French president and, to a lesser extent, the president of the European Commission, Mr Jenkins. Mr Jenkins' claim that the Bremen meeting had been 'much the most significant and worthwhile' of the five that he had attended as president of the Commission was widely quoted. So too was his praise for Mr Schmidt's chairmanship. In some respects indeed, the most significant result of the Council as a whole was the public proof that it gave of the German chancellor's emergence as the dominant leader in the European Community. Only a few days before the Council, *The Economist* had still seen M. Giscard d'Estaing in the role[47]. From Bremen onwards, the French president became increasingly the 'brilliant second'[48].

The meeting at Bonn, which took place ten days later, does not require extended treatment, but it is important in the history of the emergence of the European Monetary System because the fact that it was coming influenced the preparation of the German monetary initiative, and its outcome created a better political environment for the implementation of the plan in the months that followed. The link between the German chancellor's renewed interest in European monetary stability and his preoccupation with both the problems of the dollar and international pressure on the Federal Republic to reflate has already been discussed at length in chapter 3. The relationship between these concerns was not, however, a static one and the EMS that was born in anger and frustration became increasingly, as the months passed and the Bonn summit approached, part of a complex strategy aimed at what Mr Schmidt himself described after the Bremen Council as 'a set of complementary agreements' involving all the major industrialized countries of the western world and covering a wide range of problems, including the struggle against inflation, the expansion of trade, the avoidance of protectionism, the effort to achieve more balanced energy policies, the reduction of regional disparities and 'demand management in Europe'[49]. The language of conflict and anti-Americanism, of 'banning the dollar from Europe' or 'letting it fall', gave way to the language of package deals and compromise.

Several explanations could be given for this change, each of them probably containing an element of truth. At one level, the shift in emphasis and atmosphere is yet another proof of the increasing importance of the diplomatic timetable in an interdependent world. The fact that Mr Schmidt had to act as host to two major international conferences within the space of two weeks made it imperative that nothing should be done at the first that could be considered as hostile to the interests of those who would attend the second. The force of the timetable explanation is underlined still further when it is realized that the Bonn summit of 16 and 17 June was preceded by a state visit by the American president to the Federal Republic. Shrill, neo-Gaullism was out of place at a moment when President Carter was engaged in offering ritual, but essential reassurance to the citizens of West Berlin or visiting United States military bases in West Germany itself. The coincidences of a diplomatic agenda worked out many months before the EMS was conceived by the German chancellor were therefore almost certainly a powerful influence in the period between Copenhagen and Bremen. They are not, however, sufficient in themselves to explain the increasingly conciliatory tone of Mr Schmidt. Still more important, one suspects, were the realities of interdependence and dependence that the timetable itself reflected. In the informal atmosphere of a post-dinner discussion in a Danish castle, remarks were made that, taken out of context, might seem to suggest that Mr Schmidt was contemplating a European dash for freedom. At the Copenhagen meeting itself this was probably not the case, but, even if it was, the mood did not last long. Although the EMS is a highly significant episode in the redefinition of Euro-American relations that changes in the international system and accidents of personality provoked, it was not, even to the French president, still less to the German chancellor, a latter-day version of the dream of autarky that Germans of another generation had once indulged in and that some of the majority in

France liked to toy with. It was an act of self-defence in case, as in his worst moments Mr Schmidt must have feared, the American president possessed neither the skill nor the capacity to deal with the fundamental problems underlying the weakness of the dollar; but in the absence of adequate American policies, it would not suffice for long. In the final analysis a durable EMS required a healthy dollar: it could only in the short run be a substitute for a weak one. Hence the talk of packages and compromise, rather than conflict and confrontation.

Probably the clearest public indication of Mr Schmidt's thinking in the days immediately preceding the two summits is to be found in the interview that he gave to *Business Week* at the end of June[50]. It dealt amongst other things with his plans for the European Monetary System, but it placed the EMS firmly within the context of a global and, more particularly, a transatlantic deal, involving serious efforts by the American administration to tackle the problems of their economy, and in particular their wasteful energy consumption, in exchange for German action to stimulate demand. Asked whether he was contemplating some stimulus to the German economy, the chancellor replied:

> If other countries do something, I would of course strive for international compromise and package deals and would be willing to take some steps even if I'm not convinced that they would be helpful.

The British chancellor of the exchequer, Mr Healey, seems to have concluded on the basis of Mr Schmidt's hints on this score that the German chancellor might be ready to trade concessions on growth for acceptance of the EMS both in Europe and in America. In fact, the *Business Week* interview and Mr Schmidt's performance at the Bonn summit suggest that the stakes for which he was playing were higher still. He wanted not just the EMS, but a public commitment by the American administration in the most august setting possible that it really would deliver on the economic policies that it had promised, but failed to implement, for so long. That is why the concession on growth, despite general support for the Commission's paper on the subject at Bremen, was not made at the European Council meeting. Far from being an anti-climax in fact, the Bonn summit was an essential complement to the European meeting that preceded it.

The scene on the eve of the Bonn summit suggested that compromise was in the air. On the day before the meeting began, President Carter finished a state visit that both he and his German hosts seemed genuinely to have enjoyed. German newspapers claimed to have discovered facets of his personality that had not been appreciated before and there were loud indiscretions from the Bundeskanzleramt (Chancellor's Office) and the American Embassy that the president and the chancellor had broken through to a warmer and more positive personal relationship[51]. This impression of amity was reinforced still further by the normal run of 'spontaneous' gestures of solidarity, including on this occasion a widely publicized dance in the streets by Mrs Carter and a small town mayor. In fact, so successful was the visit that one nameless American spokesman observed, without any obvious irony, that it was a pity that the president did not travel abroad more frequently[52]. There were other more mundane pieces of stage management on the German side, the most important perhaps being the leak of a letter from the German minister of economics, Count Lambsdorff, to Mr Schmidt suggesting that the time had come on domestic grounds, quite apart from any international considerations, for a package of measures to stimulate the economy. The letter had been written on 3 July, but its contents were first revealed to the media on 16 July, the day on which the summit meeting began[53].

Despite these preparations however, the package deal was no easy accomplishment. As the final communiqué showed[54], discussions covered a large number of problems: growth, employment and inflation, energy, trade and international monetary policy. On international monetary policy, the document confirmed American goodwill as far as the European Monetary System was concerned but did not go into any details:

> The representatives of the European Community informed the meeting of the decisions of the European Council at Bremen on 6/7 July to consider a scheme for closer monetary cooperation. They welcomed the report and noted that the Community would keep the other participants informed.

Mr Blumenthal, the American secretary to the Treasury, saw Mr Matthöfer, the German finance minister, in separate meetings, but neither there nor in the meetings between heads of government would the EMS appear to have aroused the heat that it seemed likely to only weeks before. The German chancellor apparently reminded his American guest that whereas the Americans enjoyed the benefits of a massive integrated market that stretched from New York to Los Angeles and from San Francisco to Houston and that was relatively independent of international trade, the Europeans had no such privileges, and it was therefore perfectly rational for them to try to acquire these advantages as far as was possible[55]. The American president for his part is said to have asked a number of questions about the EMS but, somewhat to the relief of the advisers who prepared his brief, he did not go beyond the rather general problems dealt with in the first section of the paper in front of him and avoided the more detailed and potentially controversial questions listed in the second part.

On growth and energy by contrast, the seven leaders, plus Mr Jenkins, talked at great length and as it proved to some effect. The relevant parts of the communiqué are worth quoting. On growth, for example, the Germans made the following pledge:

As a contribution to avert the worldwide disturbance of economic equilibrium the German delegation has indicated that by the end of August it will propose to the legislative bodies additional and quantitatively substantial measures up to 1% of gross national product, designed to achieve a significant strengthening of demand and a higher rate of growth. The order of magnitude will take account of the absorptive capacity of the capital market and the need to avoid inflationary pressures.

On energy, the Americans for their part spoke in the following terms:

Recognising its particular responsibility in the energy field, the United States will reduce its dependence on imported oil. The United States will have in place by the end of the year a comprehensive policy framework within which this effort can be urgently carried forward. By year end, measures will be in effect that will result in oil import savings of approximately 2.5 million barrels per day by 1985. In order to achieve these goals, the United States will establish a strategic oil reserve of one million barrels. It will increase coal production by two thirds. It will maintain the ratio between growth in gross national product and growth in energy demand at or below 0.8 and its oil consumption will grow more slowly than energy consumption. The volume of oil imported in 1978 and 1979 should be less than that imported in 1977. In order to discourage excessive consumption of oil and to encourage the movement towards coal, the United States remains determined that the prices paid for oil in the United States shall be raised to the world level by the end of 1980.

Of the two sets of promises, the first was the hardest to obtain but proved in the event to be the more speedily honoured. The German chancellor was disposed to make concessions on growth before the meeting began. What he wanted to avoid, however, were precise figures. Experience since the London summit of the previous year, not to mention meetings of the European Community, had shown that large promises lightly entered into could become a political embarrassment within a very short time. Mr Schmidt therefore resisted the efforts of President Carter and Mr Callaghan to pin him down to figures far into the second day of the meeting. In the end, however, he gave way, and the German government emerged with a commitment that, though not as precise as the British prime minister would have liked, was a good deal more substantial and specific than Mr Schmidt wanted.

Given the disappointments that had followed earlier summits in the series, it was not surprising that many commentators viewed the pledges made at Bonn with more than a little scepticism. *The Economist* probably spoke for many when it described the outcome of the conference as 'a small deal at Bonn'[56]. In actual fact, however, it proved to be of more practical consequence than any of the meetings that had preceded it. Both the

Germans and the Japanese took real steps to stimulate their economies with results that in the short term at least were as beneficial for the rest of the western world as had been predicted[57]. The Federal government announced a fiscal programme before the end of July that was designed to strengthen demand and improve economic growth by DM 15.5 million from the beginning of 1979, a figure that actually represented more than the 1% of GNP promised in the Bonn communiqué. This programme was approved by parliament later in the autumn. As for the United States, the energy bill was also approved in October, after 18 months, and although it was less ambitious than had originally been hoped, and less even than had been promised at Bonn, it did represent real progress. By the time it was passed, however, the western world was experiencing yet another major dollar crisis and it was not until this had provoked a much more determined response from the American authorities in the form of the 1 November package, which will be discussed in chapter 6, that the Europeans could reckon on the sort of exchange rate stability that was essential if the EMS was not to run into immediate problems.

The importance of the Bonn summit did not only lie in the measures to which it gave rise on both sides of the Atlantic. In the story of the emergence of the EMS, it was significant chiefly because it rounded off the political strategy that Mr Schmidt had pursued since the Copenhagen summit and left him in a position of incomparably greater strength and authority. Before Copenhagen, as we have seen, the Germans were under pressure from almost every western government. At Copenhagen, Mr Schmidt had begun his outflanking operation, but for reasons of his own he concealed the extent of his proposals from all but a very small circle of leaders from whom he extracted a promise of secrecy. At Bremen, he was able to come out into the open, at least in European Community terms, with results that have already been referred to and assessed. Bonn represented the culmination of the strategy. Through his concessions on growth and still more through the speedy implementation of them, Mr Schmidt wrested for his country a moral advantage that it had not possessed at any other stage of the world recession. This political triumph was to become particularly important in the next phase of the EMS negotiations when, to quote the chancellor himself, 'the rats' began to nibble at the Franco-German plan.

1 On 4 December 1978, Granada television broadcast a reconstruction of the European Council meetings at Copenhagen and Bremen that was based on the investigations of ten of the best-informed European political commentators. Several of those in a position to know have vouched for its accuracy. I am grateful to Mr Brian Lapping, executive producer of the programme, for making a transcript available to me (hereafter cited as, Granada television). However, the information contained in the following pages and in the account of the Bremen Council on pp. 122–7 is also drawn from other, primary sources, including doubtless in certain instances materials used by the journalists themselves

2 *Economic Policy Review*, March 1978, *passim*
3 *The Economist*, 21 April 1978
4 *Frankfurter Allgemeine Zeitung*, 28 June 1978
5 *Europa-Archiv*, **9**, 1978, pp. 263–70
6 *The Times*, 20 June 1978
7 ibid., 28 June 1978
8 Amongst the most openly sceptical both at the time and since was (is) Dr A. Szasz, deputy governor of the Netherlands central bank. See his article, 'Het Europees Monetair Stelsel', *Internationale Spectator*, February 1979, pp. 79ff. and the lecture, 'EMS: Controlled exchange rates in a world of uncontrolled capital flows', that he delivered to the Euromarkets Conference, London, 22 January 1980
9 Granada television, op. cit. (note 1), p. 15
10 *Trends*, 22 December 1977
11 They were published in *Trends*, 8 February and 22 March 1978. See also *The Economist*, 8 April 1978
12 See especially *The Times*, 20 June 1978
13 Granada television, op. cit. (note 1), p. 21
14 *Le Monde*, 21 June 1978
15 For example, *Le Monde* and *Neue Zürcher Zeitung*, 29 June 1978
16 *Le Monde*, 2 July 1978
17 *Business Week*, 26 June 1978
18 See *Europa-Archiv*, **5**, 10 March 1979, pp. 129ff
19 *The Economist*, 2 July 1977, has a useful article on the spread of monetarism
20 See R. Bacon and W. A. Eltis, *Britain's Economic Problem: Too Few Producers*, London, 1976
21 See chapter 3, note 56
22 *The Times*, 4 November 1978
23 *Le Monde*, May 1978
24 *The Times*, 19 June 1978
25 *The Times*, 11 July 1978
26 *Financial Times*, 14 July 1978
27 *The Guardian*, 7 July 1978
28 As an example of Italian feelings on the subject, see *Corriere della Sera*, 7 June 1978
29 *Corriere della Sera*, 17 June 1978
30 ibid., 18 June 1978
31 ibid., 4 July 1978
32 *Frankfurter Allgemeine Zeitung*, 1 July 1978
33 *Fourteenth Report of the Joint Committee on the Secondary Legislation of the European Communities*, Stationery Office, Dublin, June 1978
34 For an earlier example of the 'worst case' approach to the Community by the departments of the Treasury, Commerce and Agriculture, see H. Kissinger, *White House Years*, Boston, 1979, pp. 425ff
35 US Treasury Press Releases, B. 905, 15 May 1978
36 ibid., B. 937, 24 May 1978
37 ibid., B. 983, released 18 June 1978
38 Transcript of the presidential press conference following the Bremen Council, 7 July 1978
39 US Treasury Press Releases, B. 899, 30 April 1978. See also B. 905, 15 May 1978
40 See note 40 above
41 See Granada television, op. cit. (note 1), pp. 21ff
42 For example, *Wall Street Journal*, 7 July 1978
43 *Hansard*, House of Commons, 10 July 1978, col. 1026
44 See the unpublished final paragraph of the Schulmann–Clappier document in Appendix 1A
45 See, *inter alia*, *Le Monde* and *Corriere della Sera*, 8 July 1978
46 *Financial Times*, 14 July 1978
47 *The Economist*, 1 July 1978
48 *Corriere della Sera*, October 1978
49 Transcript of presidential press conference, 7 July 1978
50 *Business Week*, 6 June 1978
51 The visit was fully covered in *Frankfurter Allgemeine Zeitung* and *New York Times* between 13 and 17 July 1978
52 *Frankfurter Allgemeine Zeitung*, 15 July 1978
53 ibid., 17 July 1978
54 Full text in *New York Times*, 18 July 1978
55 Mr Pandolfi, in *La Lira e lo Scudo*, Bologna, 1978, p. 133
56 *The Economist*, 22 July 1978
57 OECD, *Economic Outlook*, December 1978

Filling in the details: technical and political discussions, July–September 1978

With the conclusion of the European Council at Bremen, preparations for the EMS moved into a new phase and acquired a different character. Prior to the Bremen meeting, the initiative had lain primarily at heads of government level. There had, it is true, been important discussions amongst the experts, particularly in the Monetary Committee, but those involved were working to instructions that were at best vague and in some cases non-existent. After Bremen this was no longer the case. The Council had committed itself to a timetable that involved the preparation of a detailed draft agreement before the end of October 1978, with a view to a final decision on whether or not to inaugurate the new system at the following European Council meeting, which was due to take place in Brussels at the beginning of December. It was a major task, involving not only a considerable amount of study and discussion amongst the experts, but also a far greater degree of political consultation within each of the member states than had occurred before the July summit.

Most of the technical work was carried out within the orbit of three committees: the Monetary Committee and the Committee of Central Bank Governors, both of which worked on the details of the monetary system itself, and the Economic Policy Committee, which was instructed to carry out the 'concurrent studies' of what if any transfers of resources might be needed to enable the less prosperous countries to participate in the system. The work done by these committees between July and September will be considered in sections 5.2 and 5.3. The committees did not, however, operate in a political limbo, and the discussion of their activities must therefore be prefaced by an analysis of the domestic political consultations and bilateral international negotiations that determined the context in which their discussions developed.

5.1   Position-taking, 8–25 July 1978

As the previous chapter has shown, the contacts made by Dr Schulmann and M. Clappier with the other member governments, the deliberations of the Monetary Committee and, in the Irish case at least, the Jenkins initiative of the autumn of 1977 had already prompted ministers and officials and, in certain instances, other interested groups to take up preliminary positions on the fundamental issues before the meeting of the Bremen Council. These early discussions did not, however, compare in either intensity or scope with those that began immediately after the heads of government returned to their capital cities. The positions adopted in the course of the following fortnight were not by any means final, but by 25 July it was nonetheless possible to discern the basic objectives of each of the governments, the key figures who would represent them in the new phase, the pressures to which they were subject and the informal alliances that they hoped to preserve or foster.

The Snake countries

Despite the Franco-German origins of the new initiative, developments between July and September were to prove that the bonds of common interest that underpinned the Snake were still in many respects stronger than the links that had been forged between the Germans and the French on monetary matters. This first section will therefore examine the earliest expressions of views and intentions in the Snake countries, while the next section will consider in turn the preliminary negotiating positions of the French, the British, the Italians and the Irish. Of the Snake countries, by far the most important needless to say was West Germany and it was here that some of the most important changes in personnel and perspectives occurred during the first three weeks of July. In order to launch his plan, the chancellor had chosen to dispense with the advice of the ministers and officials responsible for monetary questions in Bonn and Frankfurt and to pursue a path of secret diplomacy. It was, however, obvious that if a new monetary system was to become a reality he would sooner or later have to consult those who were constitutionally responsible, not to mention a much larger number of party politicians and interest groups. It says much for the depth of Mr Schmidt's commitment to the plan that he devoted if anything even more energy to this more difficult and more frustrating task than he had to the development of the original scheme, spending it was later reckoned at least 200 hours coaxing and cajoling a predominantly sceptical and in many cases hostile domestic constituency into acceptance of his ideas.

Both the scepticism and hostility that awaited his proposal had already been apparent immediately before the Bremen meeting. Dr Emminger's rather terse advice to Dr Schulmann to be careful not to enter into any binding commitments at the Council has already been quoted. There were also more public expressions of concern. One of the clearest came significantly enough from Dr Poehl, Dr Emminger's deputy and eventual successor at the Bundesbank, who was normally reckoned to enjoy much better relations with the Bonn government than his president and who was to be used by the chancellor in at least one of the more critical meetings connected with the EMS in the following months. In an article that appeared in the *Sparkassenzeitung* in the last week of June[1] Dr Poehl expressed fundamental reservations about the proposals to extend the European currency group beyond the present Snake countries and to increase the funds available for intervention. Although there were welcome signs that the non-Snake countries were making strenuous efforts to reduce their inflation rates, he noted, the gap between them and the Snake group was still too large to sustain a common exchange rate system and no amount of funds or experimentation with new mechanisms could overcome this fact. A currency link was only conceivable if participants were ready to submit to the 'strict rules' of the present Snake. Dr Poehl's warnings were echoed in the days that followed by several other prominent spokesmen of political or interest groups. The chancellor himself was directly exposed to views of this sort at a four-hour meeting in Bonn on 5 July with a group of about 20 leaders of industry, finance and the trade unions[2]. In a statement issued after the meeting, the Bundesverband der deutschen Industrie, though admitting that an extended European currency grouping could be useful, stressed as a precondition of any such experiment the acceptance by prospective members of strict discipline in their monetary and economic policies. There were serious dangers in precipitate action, the association declared. Another participant in the meeting, Dr Manfred Schäfer (chairman of the Saarland Chamber of Industry and Commerce), went even further, claiming that despite the rather hectic movements on the exchanges in recent months, floating was a lesser evil than fixed rates. As if this was not enough, on the day that the summit meeting began there was also a broadside from Franz Joseph Strauss, calling on the Bundesbank and the economics minister to block the Schmidt–Giscard plan and warning dire action by the opposition if they did not[3].

This pre-Bremen crossfire was only a foretaste of what was to come. Indeed, in the days that followed the Council, it was sometimes difficult to find any major figure in either the economic or political establishments, outside the SPD, who did not seem to harbour doubts about the chancellor's plan. At a political level, Mr Strauss repeated his attack, announcing that the CDU/CSU would reject the proposal[4]. At the time it was difficult to know whether Mr Strauss spoke for the opposition as a whole, but it soon became apparent that a very large number of CDU/CSU deputies, including eventually Dr Köhl, the leader of the CDU, shared the Bavarian leader's feelings that the Schmidt–Giscard plan threatened to produce a 'European Community of Inflation'. As Heinz Stadlmann noted in an article in the *Frankfurter Allgemeine Zeitung*, the traditional bipartisan approach to major Community questions seemed at risk[5].

Significant though this potential development undoubtedly was, it did not at this stage compare in importance with the open hostility of the Frankfurt establishment. As an example of the feelings of the financial community in general, one could scarcely do better than to quote from the long interview that Dr Emminger's predecessor, Dr Klasen, gave to *Die Zeit* on 14 July. Entitled 'Es geht um unser Geld' (it is our money that is at stake), it dedramatized the chancellor's initiative with a remarkable mixture of loyal scepticism and faint praise.

> I followed the Bremen summit with considerable curiosity, particularly those aspects of it that touched on currency questions. I would welcome real progress towards currency union. Having said that, I must admit that the Council decision that pleased me most was the agreement not to take a final decision, but to work out the details in peace. I only hope that those concerned will approach their task with the utmost caution.

The German authorities, Klasen argued, would have to make absolutely certain that 'Europa Begeisterung' (Euro-fanaticism) did not lead them into a sacrifice of the control that they still had over their money. He was particularly wary about the French. If the EMF was once established, he claimed 'we would not be dealing with M. Giscard d'Estaing but with the French bureaucracy. And if there is one thing I admire it is the French bureaucracy: it has been trained to the highest level by centuries of experience and is vastly superior to us in the diplomatic pursuit of national interest.' Later in the interview he appeared to moderate his criticisms somewhat, going as far as to say that he welcomed the chancellor's initiative. But his reservations had the last word: 'I would however advise extreme care in the practical implementation of the idea.'

It fell to Dr Emminger, who, it would seem, shared these misgivings to the full, to state them officially and to work through constitutional channels for the safeguards and amendments that the financial community in general and the Bundesbank in particular regarded as essential. He had his first opportunity at a special Cabinet meeting in Bonn on 12 July[6]. It was, it should be stressed, a preliminary *prise de position*, delivered in response to an hour-long speech by the chancellor explaining his scheme, and Dr Emminger emphasized that before arriving at any final judgement he would have to consult the Central Bank Council (Zentralbanksrat). But on the assumption that the chancellor had not entered into any irrevocable commitments, he continued, he wished to make three preliminary observations. Firstly, there could in his view be no question of a return to a Bretton-Woods type fixed exchange rate system. The arrangements for adjustments of parities must therefore be simple. Secondly, great care would have to be taken to avoid an increase in international liquidity, either through the credit arrangements in general or through the proposed EMF in particular. Thirdly, there seemed a real danger that the Federal Republic might lose control over DM creation, because of the provision advocating intervention in Community currencies, which would more often than not lead to interventions in DM. Safeguards would therefore have to be built into the system to limit excessive intervention obligations. The chancellor's response was, it would seem, reassuring on all three points. From Dr Emminger's viewpoint, however, what was still more important in many ways than the provisional acknowledgement of his reservations was the assurance that he received that in this new phase of the negotiations he and his colleagues at the Bundesbank would be fully involved in the preparation and negotiation of the German position.

It was this shift in the composition of the inner group responsible for making policy in the Federal Republic, rather than any specific criticisms or reservations uttered by this or that authority, that constituted the biggest single change in the days immediately following the Council. Before Bremen, matters had been handled almost exclusively by Mr Schmidt and Dr Schulmann. After Bremen, the chancellor remained the most important figure, particularly in the period from 14 September to the Brussels meeting of the European Council, but the detailed preparatory and negotiating work was left to officials in the Bundesbank and finance ministry. Details of their objectives will become apparent in the following pages, but a few general observations on the personnel involved and in particular on the relationship between the chancellor and the experts are necessary at this point. The partnership that developed between Mr Schmidt and officials who, as he had commented on at least one occasion, would probably have done their best to prevent the Bremen proposals if they had been consulted at an earlier stage, was not exactly a simple one. What is, however, quite clear is that claims made by critics of the system, both at the time and since that in the post-Bremen period Mr Schmidt allowed himself to be overridden by Dr Emminger and his colleagues and allies are seriously misleading. Both in the general sense of insisting that the momentum should be kept up and over detailed points the chancellor, as we shall see, won his way as often as not. But he did undoubtedly have to make concessions, and the package that emerged in the course of the summer and autumn of 1978 was greatly influenced by the reservations felt by the German financial establishment and defended at both internal discussions and in international settings by Dr Emminger. In making these compromises with German orthodoxy more palatable and tolerable, both to the chancellor himself and to Germany's Community partners, a crucial role was played by Dr Manfred Lahnstein, Staatssekretär (permanent secretary) in the finance ministry, who after Mr Schmidt himself was the most important figure on the German side between the Bremen and Brussels Councils. It was he who, more often than not, stated and defended the German decision at both the ECOFIN and the Monetary Committee. He was also almost always at the chancellor's side when the chancellor had bilateral meetings with other Community leaders and it was he who, as we shall see, was drafted in to chair the important *ad hoc* meeting at Frankfurt airport shortly before the Brussels summit and who at the Council itself made energetic efforts to build bridges between the French on the one side and the Italians and the Irish on the other. As a former official in the European Commission and Dr Schulmann's predecessor in the Bundeskanzleramt (Chancellor's Office) he had an ideal background for the role to which he was assigned. It was inevitable that, with the expansion of the German negotiating team, and more particularly with the increased importance of Dr Lahnstein, Dr Schulmann's role was less prominent in the post-Bremen phase than it had been before, but he was still, as the chancellor's senior economic adviser, extremely well placed to exercise an influence, and he was to be found, more often than not assisted by Dr Thiele, at all the key meetings in which the chancellor was personally involved. He was also on occasions used for special missions, one being the visit to Harold Lever in London, of which mention has already been made.

The Germans' closest allies throughout the technical discussions between the Bremen and Brussels summits were the Dutch, though there was rarely if ever prior collusion between them. Their near identity of interest, which had its roots in a common approach to international monetary questions that had been evident at the IMF and elsewhere long before even the Snake came into existence, was illustrated in no uncertain terms by the contribution of Dr Zijlstra at the meeting of the central bank governors in Basle on 11 July, three days after the conclusion of the Bremen Council. It was indeed the Dutch governor, even more than Dr Emminger, who started to ask fundamental questions of their French colleague, M. Clappier, following the latter's exposition of the origins and intentions of the Franco-German paper. There were, Dr Zijlstra observed, three problems that would need to be clarified. The first was the nature and scope of the EMF, the second the composition and the character of the ECU and what would happen, for example, if one of the Community countries did not join the EMS, and the third the practical implications of an intervention system that was linked to a basket and in which interventions were apparently to be carried out in Community currencies. There was also the more general problem of how this new system could coexist with the Snake, because even if the latter would in due course be phased out, the Dutch governor commented, the transitional phase might last for a long time. M. Clappier duly replied to these questions but, despite his efforts to explain the meaning of the Bremen Annex, Dr Zijlstra remained obdurate to the end, suggesting that it might be useful to ask the heads of government what they actually meant and that it would certainly be necessary to carry out detailed studies to see whether the proposed system was technically feasible. As a former prime minister as well as a long-established central bank governor, Dr Zijlstra was a formidable figure in the negotiations that followed, but the Dutch position was hardly less ably and energetically defended on the Monetary Committee, where they were represented by Dr Wellink (Dr Oort's successor as treasurer-general in the ministry of finance) and Dr Szasz, deputy governor of the central bank. Indeed, in the absence of strong prime ministerial leadership – Mr van Agt admitted quite openly on several occasions that he was not qualified to judge the issues at stake – and despite foreign ministry pleas to moderate technical doubts with an occasional dose of European spirit, the Dutch seemed to some of their partners to be even more uncompromising defenders of the orthodox verities than the Germans.

Of the remaining European Community members of the Snake – the Danes, the Belgians and the Luxembourgers – less need be said at this point. The Danes usually sided with the Dutch and the Germans on matters of monetary discipline, an attitude that, with their history of current account deficits, public sector debt and above average inflation, seemed to one observer not unlike that of an inveterate drunkard who continues to sign the Pledge in the hope that one day he will end up a teetotaller or, at the very least, be saved from still greater lapses into insensibility. As far as the EMS negotiations were concerned however, their most distinctive objectives were twofold: to do all possible to enable and encourage the Norwegians to remain associated with Community currency arrangements and the Swedes to renew their link, and to prevent the reform of the Community budget and more particularly of the CAP for which the British and the Italians began to press with increasing determination. Their efforts in both directions will be noted in the course of this and the following chapters, but, as far as the link with Norway was concerned, the first signs immediately after Bremen were encouraging, since the finance minister, Per Kleppe, though reserving his position until more details became known, reaffirmed his personal preference for a stable exchange rate system as compared with a floating regime[7].

As for the Belgians (and the Luxembourgers with whom their currency was linked), enough has been said already and still more will be said in due course to indicate the very special position that they held both within the Snake and in the Community as a whole on monetary questions. The role of M. Tindemans at the Bremen Council and his public pronouncements in the days that followed made it clear that, while the Belgians had a strong interest in the maintenance of the Snake, they were more open than any of their partners to new ideas. As before, the key role in preparing and defending their initiatives was played by M. van Ypersele, who became chef de cabinet to the prime minister in the second half of 1978, but he worked closely throughout the new phase with officials at the central bank, whose governor was his counterpart as chairman of the Committee of Central Bank Governors. The Belgian compromise was advanced and explained simultaneously in both the Committee of Central Bank Governors and M. van Ypersele's Monetary Committee.

The non-Snake countries

Of the non-Snake group of governments, much has already been said in the previous chapter about the aims and reservations of the French and the

British, and much less about the Italians and the Irish. As far as the former are concerned, therefore, it is only necessary to note how, if at all, their personnel and policy objectives changed in the aftermath of Bremen. In the French case the answer is very little at all and the reasons are for once relatively simple. Firstly, despite the reservations of Dr Schulmann, both the president and M. Clappier evidently believed that in the Bremen Annex they had laid the foundations of a genuinely new monetary system, which was quite different from the Snake in both its scope and objectives. Their aims, and still more perhaps the spirit that lay behind them, were explained with almost disarming candour by M. Clappier himself at the first meeting of the Committee of Central Bank Governors after the Bremen summit. The plan, he declared, had been prepared with two primary considerations in mind. The first was the need for a zone of monetary stability in Western Europe, which would make a significant contribution to both the struggle against inflation and the recovery of economic growth. The second was more political: it amounted to a decision to seize the opportunity provided by the present international monetary crisis to attempt a fresh step towards a new monetary organization of Western Europe. M. Clappier then proceeded to a detailed discussion of the Bremen document, concluding with some words about the forthcoming work of the central bank governors that are worth quoting in full: '... il est souhaitable que les gouverneurs des banques centrales ne cèdent pas à la tentation facile de critiquer par principe les différentes propositions, mais contribuent plutôt de manière constructive à la réalisation de la nouvelle tentative. Les moyens existent, il suffit d'avoir la volonté de les utiliser.'

The French negotiators, of whom M. Clappier remained the most important, therefore started out on this new phase in the conviction that a new monetary system was not only desirable in principle but feasible in practice, because the political will existed. Its cornerstone, in technical terms, was to be the ECU, and throughout the summer, and indeed in M. Clappier's case well into the period after the Aachen summit, they negotiated and planned on the assumption that, whatever compromises with the Snake countries might be needed in the short term, the ECU was to be at the centre of the new system, both as an embryonic reserve currency and as the basis of the intervention system. In other words, the Bremen Council had not given the experts a chance to question the fundamentals of the new system, as the Germans and the Dutch seemed on occasions to imply; it had instead instructed them to work out the details of a ground plan that had already been laid down. The Bremen Annex, one senior negotiator from another country observed, seemed to the French like the laws of Moses, written in stone and unalterable.

The second factor explaining the continuity of French personalities and policies was political. The Bremen paper had been prepared at the behest of the president, who for once in his reign did not have to worry about domestic political constraints. It was not simply that he was free to ignore the scepticism and criticisms of officials and ministers: his constitutional position in relation to government personnel, as the use of M. Clappier as his personal representative had already shown, had always been radically different from that of Mr Schmidt, for whom it would have been constitutionally impossible to employ Dr Emminger in a similar role, even if the latter had been more sympathetic towards his views. It was still more that, four months after the parliamentary elections of March 1978, the president had a room for manoeuvre in his relations with both the majority and the opposition that he had not possessed since 1974.

Paradoxical as it may appear, M. Giscard d'Estaing's freedom was underlined and his authority confirmed by the fact that, on the eve of the Council, he decided of his own accord to consult leaders of the major political parties at the Elysée about the issues that were likely to come up at the Bremen meeting and in particular about the monetary system, with results that were both surprising and, from the president's point of view, highly gratifying[8]. The support of the UDF was only to be expected, but what was more surprising was the guarded approval of M. Mitterand, who stated as he left the palace that 'any well thought out monetary system capable both of ensuring national independence, observing the interests of the Third World and of not confining to a few the absolute mastery of monetary channels, any effort towards a certain monetary order or stabilisation or union seems to us desirable'. M. Chirac did not say anything after the meeting, but following the Bremen Council the Gaullist paper *La Lettre de la Nation*, in a comment entitled 'A little ray of hope', admitted that for the first time for years there was evidence of a new European solidarity of the kind desired by the RPR in its proposals to the nation: '... it is essential both for France and for Europe that the president's initiatives should succeed. ... The task is already very difficult. In a Europe of twelve, it will be impossible'[9].

In due course both the president's domestic freedom and the belief that the European Community was on the verge of an almost painless rebirth were to be severely dented: the former by the revival of political debate and division in anticipation of the direct elections to the European Parliament, the latter by the mauling that the ECU received from the Germans and the Dutch and by the unforeseen opening of Pandora's box by the British in the concurrent studies. But in July at any rate, there seemed ground for hope that the process begun before Bremen could be carried through to what, in French eyes at least, was the logical conclusion of the Franco-German initiative.

By contrast with the French, the British were obliged to carry out a fundamental review of their approach to the monetary negotiations in the days that followed the Bremen Council. Indeed, the process had begun at the meeting itself, where, as we have seen, Mr Callaghan had been confronted by a display of political determination on the part of Mr Schmidt and M. Giscard d'Estaing and a willingness to go along with it amongst his other colleagues for which he had not been prepared. Instead of leading a rebellion, he had found himself in danger of being isolated, an outcome that it would seem he decided was still worse than the monetary scheme itself. The Bremen communiqué, including the Annex, had therefore been released with his approval as well as that of his fellow heads of government. Despite Mr Couzens' public demonstration of the fact that the Treasury was still behind the times, the new direction begun rather grudgingly at Bremen was confirmed and developed in the days that followed.

The clearest exposition of his government's position was given by the prime minister himself in a statement to the House of Commons on 10 July[10]. Not unnaturally, in the light of the publicity that Mr Callaghan had chosen to give to his hostility to the scheme before the summit, there were still some indications of residual reserve and a certain tendency to play the monetary plan down. 'A number of heads of government, including myself, wished to see the details fully worked out before entering into any commitment by our respective governments.' But, as the prime minister went on to say, 'the outlines of the Franco-German proposal contain some new features and the government will play their full part in the forthcoming studies', including of course the parallel studies, the credit for which Mr Callaghan claimed for himself. The formal part of his statement closed with the following words:

> This was a constructive meeting in which there was some hard talking because we were getting to grips with important problems. If, as a result, some new solutions can be agreed on the convergence of our economies, on a zone of monetary stability and on the transfer of resources inside the Community, including a better use of resources in the CAP, it could turn out to have been a historic occasion.

The questions and answers that followed were in some respects more revealing than the statement, because they brought out the extent to which not only the prime minister, but also the opposition were at this stage aware of the 'high political' issues raised by the Bremen meeting and, in Mr Callaghan's case, the openness with which, in the light of these larger issues, he was ready to rebuke critics within his own party, election year or no election year. The Conservative Party's initial reactions to the Bremen statement had been muddled and unsure. Though welcoming a move back towards greater currency stability in principle, the party's shadow chancellor, Sir Geoffrey Howe, had been singularly unenthusiastic about this particular set of proposals in a radio interview on the day after the Bremen summit[11]. As so far disclosed, he observed, he would not favour the present plan as a way of helping towards the convergence of Community economies. Mrs Thatcher was more forthcoming in her comments to the House of

Commons on the following day, influenced no doubt by a great deal of press comment, which like the *Daily Telegraph*[12], a paper of her own persuasion, saw Britain 'on the point of relegation to the Third Division'. 'We are more likely', she claimed, 'to get out of the problem of world recession by cooperation with our partners than we are by standing aside from the scheme which they have put up.' However, the problems of linking an economy that, owing to the mismanagement of the present government, was now 'in the second division' amongst European countries (the *Daily Telegraph* had spoken in terms of a global football league) with others that were better run remained a fact that, 'since Britain was the victor in Europe', came 'very hard' to the British people. Despite these formidable problems, she clearly implied that the government's duty was to ensure that the British participated in the scheme[13].

Mr Callaghan's handling of his critics provided an even better guide than his formal statement to the shift in perspectives that the near isolation at Bremen had induced. It is true that when answering Mrs Castle, who thought that the proposals might be 'the beginning of a process that would lead inevitably to a Federal Europe', he reassured her that in his view it would be a 'long way' from a zone of monetary stability to even a common currency[14]. Even in this answer, however, he went on to say that if the necessary convergence of European economies 'happened and raised the standard of life of the British people', he would be 'the first to cheer'. Later on, in reply to other questions, he was more explicit still, first in begging 'some honourable members not to enter this matter with all their antennae quivering because of preconceived ideas', but still more in a fairly sharp rejoinder to a Labour member who remarked that, even if the scheme promoted stability, it would do so at the expense of the government's powers to regulate the country's own finances as they wished. Mr Callaghan's reply is worth quoting in full in the light of the widely held belief that because of the forthcoming elections he was more a prisoner than a leader of his party:

> He [the labour member] asked whether he would remove some powers from us. The answer is 'yes': all these matters remove powers from us. When we joined NATO we removed some powers from ourselves but it was the general view of the House, continued for a quarter of a century, that in removing these powers we increased our security. That is surely the test that one needs to apply to this sort of proposal. If it means less powers in order to increase prosperity, the House would have to take a decision whether it wished to remain poor and independent or whether it was willing to sacrifice some powers and be more prosperous[15].

Mr Callaghan's determination that British ministers and officials should play a constructive part in the negotiations that followed was reflected in the contributions made by British personnel to the expert committees between

July and September. Several members of the Monetary and Central Bank Governors' committees and subcommittees went out of their way both at the time and subsequently to praise the efforts of Mr McMahon and Mr Balfour of the Bank of England, and of Mr Couzens and Mr Jordan Moss of the Treasury[16]. And yet, as will be seen in the final section of this chapter, the British found themselves as isolated at the end of this second phase as they had been at the end of the previous one. The reasons should become clearer as the chapter develops, but at least some of the problems that will be discussed more systematically in the final section were already apparent during the fortnight following the Bremen Council, notably in the meetings with Italian representatives in London on 25 July and in the preliminary statements about and preparations for the so-called concurrent studies. The Anglo-Italian conversations will be better discussed following a review of the Italians' preparations for the negotiations, but the preliminary statements on issues likely to come up during the concurrent studies can be conveniently discussed at this point.

The arguments in favour of a transfer of resources in connection with the creation of a new European monetary system had a validity and force quite independent of the existing budgetary arrangements of the EEC. As the Irish in particular stressed continuously, a new step of such major potential consequence required fresh financial measures to underpin it. Before the formal negotiations within the Economic Policy Committee began, however, it was already clear that the discussions of the committee were going to be complicated by the wholly fortuitous coincidence between the Franco-German proposals for an EMS and the beginnings of the British budgetary crisis. Storm signals on this latter question had been hoisted in public in March 1978, before the Copenhagen summit, when the *Cambridge Economic Policy Review* published an article by Richard Bacon, Wynne Godley and Alister McFarquhar on 'The direct costs to Britain of belonging to the EEC'[17]. As this article showed, the imminent end of the transitional phase of membership meant that Britain would have to make an increasingly heavy net contribution to the Community's budget. Although, as the article admitted, these costs had been predicted with remarkable accuracy in a White Paper published as long ago as July 1971[18], it was only to be expected that the British, no less than the Germans, would complain about and attempt to make political capital out of their role as the paymasters of Europe. In these circumstances, it was also predictable that, offered an opportunity to discuss the financial instruments of the Community in the concurrent studies, the British should have decided to raise the budget problem. Properly exploited, indeed, this coincidence might have been an ideal opportunity to achieve a long-term, though doubtless phased, solution to the budget problem. However, it was already clear by 25 July, before the Economic Policy Committee began its work, that ministers and officials were likely to handle the budgetary problem in the context of the concurrent studies in such a way as to ensure maximum unpleasantness for months to come and self-exclusion from the EMS. Reform of the CAP, Mr Healey implied in a speech to the Foreign Press Association on 11 July, a day after Mr Callaghan's eirenic statement to the House of Commons, was to be in effect a price 'of Britain's entry into the system'[19]. A few days later, acting it would seem on the basis of calculated indiscretions in Whitehall, the *Sunday Times* spoke of a British 'counterattack' on the EMS proposal[20]. Mr Joel Barnet, chief secretary to the Treasury, was, the paper later reported, sent to a Brussels meeting on 18 July to 'kick off a new campaign ... to improve Britain's financial arrangements'[21]. References to the perversity and inequity of the CAP multiplied and were doubtless noted in Paris. The budget question and the opportunity that the concurrent studies offered for an airing of it were in fact beginning to assume an importance in their own right quite unrelated to the discussion of the EMS. As Mr Heath noted in a speech that he gave in London in the middle of July, the evident desire of British ministers to have a go at the CAP and other inequities in the Community's budget in the context of the discussions to which the EMS had given rise threatened to nullify the very real opportunities that the latter opened up: 'If the British government is seeking to destroy the common agricultural policy it will fail and in failing it will ruin Britain's chances of securing other changes it wants to bring about in the proposed EMS...'[22].

Despite therefore the newfound seriousness with which Mr Callaghan himself approached the EMS negotiations, there were clear signs that a misconceived approach to the concurrent studies, which will be analysed in greater detail in section 5.3, was likely to undermine the new strategy. Taken together with the 'constructive caution' and the marked lack of interest in an Italian connection that, as will be noted, were characteristic of the British contribution to the Anglo-Italian talks of 25 July, it is not difficult to understand why, in spite of the prime minister's personal convictions, the United Kingdom's isolation was to be as apparent in September as it had been in June.

Like their British counterparts, Italian ministers and officials had to define their approach to the detailed discussions of the Franco-German plan against the background of economic weakness. Italian experience of the Snake in 1972–73 had been somewhat less short than the United Kingdom's, but rather more nasty and brutish, while the country's economic fortunes in the intervening period had been on a par with Britain's. Italy's balance of payments problems, its high inflation and its massive public sector borrowing requirement had all contributed to and been reflected in the behaviour of the lira on the foreign exchange markets, where its trade-weighted value had declined by over 42% between February 1973 and July 1978[23]. In the 12 months immediately prior to July 1978[23], there had, it is true, been at least some signs of recovery. The balance of payments had moved back into surplus, a major attack on the country's huge foreign debt had begun to have significant results and Italy's official reserves were for the first time for several years about the equivalent of her total external liabilities. Inflation was beginning to drop (though slowly) and the index of industrial production was moving upwards again, though not yet at the rather dramatic rate achieved in 1979. Despite these more encouraging signs however, Italy was still quite definitely both 'less prosperous' and fragile, and even the most sanguine and pro-European Italians had to admit that, in strictly economic terms, life with the DM would probably be difficult and uncomfortable.

In the first two months following the Bremen Council, economic considerations would seem to have been paramount in the minds of those responsible for planning Italian negotiating tactics. The prime minister does not appear to have consulted the parties that made up the majority after his return from Germany, and public discussion in the press and in the media was for the time being at least relatively slight. Both the objectives and the tone of Italy's approach to the negotiations were set by a small group of technocrats to whom Mr Andreotti entrusted almost entire responsibility. The most important members of the group were Mr Pandolfi, minister of the Treasury, Dr Baffi, governor of the Banca d'Italia, Dr Ciampi, director-general (the equivalent of deputy governor), Dr Rainer Masera, a young Oxford-trained member of the study department of the bank, and Renato Ruggiero, who had been given ministerial rank at the ministry of foreign affairs following his return from the Commission.

Despite the considerable latitude that they were allowed, none of those involved even in the most technical phase of the discussions between July and September could ignore two fundamental, political constraints. The first was the constant possibility of domestic political upheaval and, as a result, the no less constant possibility that their own endeavours and they themselves might be used in the interests of precipitating, averting or settling the crisis. The second was the near universal consensus in Italian politics about the central importance of the European connection from the point of view of Italy's security, political stability and prosperity. In the second half of 1978, when Mr Andreotti's Christian Democrat government survived by courtesy of a pact concluded in March 1978 with four other parties – the Republicans, the Social Democrats, the Socialists and the Communists – who together with the Christian Democrats constituted 'the majority', fissionable material was even more liberally strewn about than usual, and as the next chapter will show, pre-crisis manoeuvrings intruded increasingly into the discussions of the EMS as the climax of the negotiations approached. Important though the domestic political dimension undoubtedly was, however, the second constraint was ultimately still more significant. It is easy to deride the repeated insistence of Italian politicians on their European commitment. In the wake of the Bremen Council, cliché-ridden speeches and articles demanding that Italy should not 'miss the European train' provoked Luigi Spaventa to write sarcastically of what he called the

'Tonio Kröger complex': 'we' small and brown cannot afford to drop out of the company of 'them', tall, blonde, calm and clear-eyed[24]. Reading through much of the rhetorical verbiage that passed for political analysis, his reaction becomes entirely intelligible. But the cloudy federalist nonsense that he justly denounced was only one of the ways in which the consensus on the European connection showed itself. Of much more significance was the way in which it shaped the judgements and reactions of those who were responsible for defining Italian strategy in the post-Bremen period. In total contrast to their British counterparts, for whom the alternatives were still essentially those of renegotiation – that is, membership or non-membership – Italian negotiators from Mr Andreotti downwards began with the presumption that participation in any new Community initiative was the proper objective, which could only be abandoned if the material obstacles were such that even special transitional arrangements could not overcome them. Given the experience of the Snake, the possibility that membership might in the end prove intolerable was never excluded, but, for Dr Baffi as much as for his more politically committed colleagues, the obligation to find a solution that was justifiable in European terms as well as technically was always present.

This general characteristic of Italian policy had already been evident before Bremen and Mr Andreotti's contributions to the Council meeting itself, but, as he had insisted, the detailed implications of the plan and the safeguards and assistance that would be needed to enable Italy to participate would require a more considered judgement than he could give on the spot. Work began immediately, and by 25 July Mr Pandolfi, Dr Baffi and their colleagues had already worked out the main features of their strategy. It consisted of four principal elements:

(1) the systematization and reinforcement of the domestic stabilization programme that had already been under discussion within the majority for several months in the light of the obligations that membership of the EMS would entail;
(2) the achievement of a monetary agreement that at one and the same time placed obligations on the strong comparable to those that rested on the weak in the Snake, and provided wider bands of oscillation for the latter;
(3) a significant revision of the Community budget and more particularly of the CAP, so that the latter gave greater assistance to Mediterranean producers;
(4) the coordination of strategy and tactics with the British, with whom, understandably in the light of the second and third points, it was believed there was a strong community of interests.

The intention to introduce a far-reaching stabilization programme as part of a general strategy designed to equip Italy to play a constructive role in the

EMS and the wider international grouping of Seven was indicated at the Bonn summit on 16 July and in more detail at the ECOFIN meeting in Brussels a week later[25]. Preparation of the document, which subsequently became known as the Pandolfi plan, proceeded *pari passu* with the technical negotiations in the Community committees and it was eventually published on 31 August[26]. Most of the detailed proposals in the plan, including in particular those designed to tackle what the authors claimed were the two principal sources of instability – the public sector borrowing requirement and labour costs – had already been subject to long and hitherto inconclusive negotiations within the majority and with the trade unions. The 'appointment with Europe' did not therefore provoke any fundamental revision of the government's economic strategy. It was used instead as an occasion to place the strategy within a broader perspective and by doing so to reinforce its authority. The point was made in the clearest possible manner in paragraphs 58 and 59 of the document itself:

58. A new direction for our economy and therefore for our society can also be seen as a vote for Europe.

59. The decisions taken by the European Council last July have accelerated the movement towards the integration of the member states of the European Community. The Community is beginning to work towards stricter monetary discipline. The integration process will be advanced still further next year with the direct elections for the European parliament. The road forward is a difficult one, but we are now beyond the point of no return. Italy cannot opt out of this endeavour. Everything, our cultural tradition, popular sentiment, the basic orientation of our politics, point us towards Europe. But much in our economic life, by contrast, tends to push us towards the margins. It is a contradiction that it is up to us to resolve. The road that leads us towards Europe is the same one that leads us towards the objectives of growth on the basis of stability: it is the same in other words as the one proposed in the strategy outlined in this document.

There were obvious political risks in identifying a vote for Europe, which included by definition entry into the EMS, with a domestic strategy that was bound to be unpopular, and, as the next chapter will show, the close association between the two proposals undoubtedly helped to bring the European issue further into the centre of political manoeuvrings than it might otherwise have been. But the calculation that lay behind the move was both sound and shrewd: sound because, if Italy was to live with the EMS, policies of the kind proposed in the Pandolfi plan would in fact be necessary; shrewd because, as the outcome of the tactical game played by Mr Andreotti in the week following the Brussels European Council of December showed, even the Communists accepted that the onus of proof in Italian politics lay on those who proposed an anti-European course rather than on those who preached their European credentials.

The second and third elements in the Italian strategy will become clearer in the following sections of this chapter. It is enough for the moment to show how the Italian negotiators attempted to give immediate effect to their hope of forming an alliance with the British, through a visit to London by Mr Pandolfi, Dr Baffi and several advisers on 24 and 25 July, immediately after the ECOFIN meeting in Brussels. The ministers and officials whom they met on the British side were Mr Healey and his most senior Treasury officials, Sir Douglas Wass and Mr Couzens, the governor of the Bank of England, Gordon Richardson, and Mr McMahon, and, on a separate occasion, Harold Lever. There were also exchanges of views and papers at lower levels in both the Bank of England and the Treasury. The discussions ranged far beyond the technical issues that, as the next sections will show, dominated the agenda of the experts' committees, covering, in addition to the Bremen document itself, the fight against inflation and in particular the possibilities and problems of incomes policies and the control of public spending. The Italians made it clear that they had in a certain sense come to learn; the British, particularly in the Treasury, made it rather too obvious that they felt that they had something to teach, a tendency to which, as students of the interwar period not to mention the wartime alliance can verify, officials in Great George Street have long been prone, but that was reinforced on this occasion by the success, however temporary, of three years of incomes policies and an IMF-induced attack on public expenditure.

The main purpose of the discussions was obviously to explore the prospects for a coordinated approach towards the monetary negotiations. The Italians repeatedly stressed the common interests that in their view bound the two countries. The point was made deftly and elegantly in a speech by Mr Pandolfi, to a mixed gathering of Whitehall and City personnel at dinner in the Italian embassy on 25 July: 'The most famous ECU in history was in fact ECU de marc, used in the fairs of the middle ages and not many would wish, I presume, this newly suggested ECU to become too closely identified with the *mark*'. On this point at least there was complete agreement. Both sides wanted to avoid a parity grid system of the type used in the Snake and to replace it by some new system that would achieve a greater symmetry of obligations on the strong and the weak and, by no means least, on the small as well as the large. Strong interest was expressed in the French proposals, but, in the light of developments that will be discussed in the next section, it is interesting to note that representatives of both governments emphasized strongly the need for further study lest some of the side-effects of the solutions that the French proposed to the problems of asymmetry might be worse than the problems themselves. There was also agreement on the need to develop an adequate and responsible policy towards the dollar and on the importance of ensuring that dollars in official reserves that were not transferred to the EMF should not be frozen. Finally, both sides declared their intention of working towards a more equitable distribution of wealth between the different parts of the Community.

There were also differences of opinion however, not only over specific issues, but also at more profound and less obvious levels. At the technical level, there were signs that the role of gold in the new system might in due course give rise to trouble – the Banca d'Italia had traditionally kept a high proportion of its official reserves in gold, whereas the Bank of England had not – but the principal disagreement arose over the question of margins of fluctuation. From the very beginning in fact, the Italian negotiators aimed at a looser system for at least a transitional period. The reasons were partly economic and partly political. In the present state of the Italian economy, the Italian representatives argued, the lira was likely to come under serious pressure if it was linked to a rigid exchange rate regime. It was to be hoped that the three-year plan that the government was working on would in due course create the conditions in which the lira could live with the mark; but if the link was attempted too soon, the consequences could be serious. On the other hand, not joining could also have significant destabilizing effects both inside Italy and in the European Community as a whole. It was necessary, therefore, to construct a system that not only distributed burdens more effectively than the Snake had done, but also gave weaker and more volatile currencies such as the lira, and by implication the pound sterling, a greater chance of avoiding speculative attacks.

The British were not interested, however. There seem to have been several reasons for this attitude, two at least of which throw considerable light on their underlying approach to the negotiations, Mr Callaghan's House of Commons speech notwithstanding. The first was the general, almost philosophical, preference for a system that was precisely drafted and in which the obligations and responsibilities of those who joined were clearly spelled out, which was discussed earlier in connection with Mr Couzens' contributions to the secret conversations in May and June: 'If you are going to have a system at all, you might as well have a proper system.' Special cases, wider margins and other concessions to political reality were an untidy and unacceptable nuisance. The second reason was that the resort to wider bands would reduce one of the principal benefits that might be expected to flow from membership, namely the reinforcement that the external discipline would give to domestic anti-inflationary policies. This point was stressed with particular force by the ministers concerned and by the Bank of England, who pointed out that this additional element of discipline might be particularly welcome because, as the White Paper describing Phase Four of the incomes policy indicated, control over wages would be much looser during the next 12 months than it had been over the previous three years[27].

The difference of opinion over fluctuation margins in the new system pointed at other, fundamental differences that pervaded the talks as a whole and that were to be illustrated repeatedly in the months that followed. The principal virtue of wider margins to the Italians was that it would enable them to become members of the system, which was politically desirable, without incurring intolerable economic costs. To the British, the most important safeguard would seem to have been a clause allowing members to opt out. Given the experiences that the two governments had had in the Snake, both reactions were understandable. The first, however, was the solution of a government predisposed to join, while the second was the proposal of an administration that was still agnostic. The predominant impression left by the talks indeed was precisely that, despite Mr Callaghan's change of course and despite detailed preparations in Whitehall for the technical negotiations, the British authorities were still unclear about what they wanted. As Samuel Brittan observed in the *Financial Times* shortly after the Pandolfi–Baffi visit[28]:

> One difficulty about forming any Anglo-Italian front on monetary union is that there is no really agreed British position as yet ... the Anglo-Italian meetings were notable for the invention by a very senior British representative of the phrase 'constructive caution', which covered the whole spectrum of UK official responses to monetary union.

As Mr Brittan's article also suggested however, there was another feature of the talks that helps to explain why the Anglo-Italian partnership on which the Italians set such store never developed its full potential, namely the evidence that they provided of an 'unspoken assumption' of superiority by British ministers and officials when dealing with their Italian counterparts. There was, of course, nothing particularly new about this attitude: it has discoloured Anglo-Italian relations on many occasions in the past, sometimes to the considerable disadvantage of the British themselves. Whatever its origins, it was not a particularly firm base on which to form an alliance.

The fourth of the non-Snake countries, Ireland, though linked in some respects with the others and in particular with the two less prosperous countries, Italy and the United Kingdom, faced special problems as a result of the EMS proposal and, as this and the following chapter will show, pursued a distinctive path in the effort to overcome them. The all-party report on the opportunities and the implications of EMU for the Irish economy had concluded that although Ireland would need direct financial aid to meet some of the difficulties involved in association with the stronger European currencies, there were strong arguments in favour of the link. At Bremen, confronted by the EMS initiative, Mr Lynch spoke in essentially the same sense, welcoming the initiative in principle, but stressing that Ireland would need a substantial transfer of resources. The Bremen meeting itself had, however, introduced a new complication from the Irish point of view, since Mr Callaghan's caution – bordering on hostility – suggested that they would have to reckon with the possibility that sterling would not be part of the new system. But, far from being dismayed by the prospect, Mr Lynch would seem almost to have relished it in his post-Bremen comments. While stressing that it was still possible that the British government would decide to join the system, and expressing hope that it would in fact do so, the prime minister claimed that the Bremen proposals gave the Irish the first practicable chance since the foundation of the Republic to end the monetary union with the UK[29].

One of the more curious features of the Irish debate about the EMS during the months that followed is that of the two problems that entry raised (namely the strains that might arise from closer association with the continental economies and the difficulties that would be bound to flow from a break with sterling), the latter gave rise to much less debate and controversy in the Dail and elsewhere in Irish political society. This is not to say that the risks and discomforts that the break might entail were ignored. As the next chapter will show (see section 6.3), there was a good deal of lobbying by industrial and commercial interests with a special stake in the British market, while the central bank had to cope with currency movements between the two countries in the weeks immediately before the Brussels European Council of an unparalleled scale and prepare detailed legislation and regulations to deal with a range of practical problems that had no precedent. But important, even frightening, though these questions were, they were treated by almost all concerned as essentially logistic problems. The strategic decision, already implicit in Mr Lynch's public comments immediately after Bremen, was rarely called into question by leading politicians in either of the main parties or by senior officials in the bank or the ministry of finance.

The reasons for this apparent equanimity were both political and economic. As Mr Lynch implied, a break with sterling had long been on the agenda of Irish politics. It was anomalous, to say the least, that a country that had broken with the British Empire earlier than any other colony or dependency should have remained tied to the imperial currency long after almost all the other former colonies had severed the connection. By 1978, in fact, only four currencies other than the Irish punt remained linked with sterling: the Bangladeshi taka, the Gambian delasi, the Seychelles rupee and the leone of Sierra Leone. In these circumstances, it was understandable that calls for a break were part of the standard baggage of politicians, particularly at election times. What was much more significant, however, was that a step that would long have been popular in political terms had in the course of the 1970s become increasingly attractive and feasible in economic terms. The principal factors explaining this change were two: the dramatic reduction in the Republic's commercial dependence on the UK, which had begun before entry into the EEC but which the latter had accelerated, and the complications and unpredictability that sterling's erratic behaviour on the exchange markets had introduced into the management of the Irish economy.

The diversification of Irish trade in the 1960s and more particularly the 1970s had been quite dramatic[30]. In 1958, when the original Community was formed, 78% of the Republic's exports had gone to the UK and only 5% to the seven countries that Ireland was later to join in the Community. The import figures were less striking, but even in this case 56% of all Irish imports came from Britain in 1958 and only 12% from the Seven. By 1978 the position was radically different. Britain's share of Irish exports was now only just above 47%, while the rest of the Community took over 30%. Imports from Britain had changed much less, and still ran at or slightly above 50%, but the rest of the Community's share had risen to 20%. As these figures suggest, the commercial ties with the United Kingdom were still extremely important, but the Republic's dependence had been sharply reduced and the trend suggested that, particularly on the export side, it would diminish still further. Whereas in 1958 a break with sterling would have been utterly inconceivable, by the mid-1970s it had become an option that could at least be contemplated.

Figure 5.1 *Response to question 'Is Common Market "a good thing"?'* *1973–78*

*Great Britain 1973–74
Source: Eurobaromêtre, No. 9, July 1978, p. 27

The inclination to work out possible alternatives had been considerably strengthened by the behaviour of sterling throughout the 1970s on the foreign exchange markets. It was never suggested, of course, that the familiar symptoms of Britain's economic illness – slow growth and high inflation – from which the Irish themselves had suffered, were communicated exclusively through the currency connection. But there was a growing feeling in the central bank and the ministry of finance that the Republic might stand a better chance of coping with these problems if it did not have to deal with the added complications that flowed from such a close link with an ailing neighbour. This feeling found practical expression in a number of studies of possible alternative arrangements that were carried out in the bank in the mid-1970s, and that were discussed very seriously indeed during the sterling crisis of 1976. The alternatives were all essentially variants on the basket theme. In other words, instead of a 1:1 link with sterling, the Irish punt would be allowed to float, but the authorities would attempt to keep its movements as closely as possible in line with a basket of currencies, weighted according to their importance in Ireland's external trade. This meant, of course, that the value of sterling would continue to be the most important external influence on the value of the punt, but its importance would have been much reduced and would almost certainly be reduced still further as the years passed and Ireland's commercial links with the Community and other parts of the world acquired increased significance. The recovery of the British pound from its low point in 1976 and the general improvement in the United Kingdom economy that it reflected postponed the need to take a decision, but contingency plans were available, and in understanding official Irish reactions to the Bremen proposals and the prospect of ending the link with sterling that they opened up the existence of these alternative ideas is clearly a factor of some importance[31].

The political and economic arguments in favour of releasing the punt from the pound were complemented and enhanced by the positive attractions of a stronger link with the EEC. In marked contrast to the Danes and the British, who seemed to like the Community less the more they had to do with it, Irish public opinion remained favourable, as can be seen from *Figure 5.1*. A comparison of elite opinion is even more striking. According to a poll taken in the spring of 1978[32], 63% of Irish 'leaders' thought that Community membership was in the country's interest, compared with only 34% of the same groups in Denmark and 36% in the United Kingdom.

This comparatively favourable attitude towards the Community can be explained in many ways and at several levels. As Dr Keogh has recently argued, the Catholic dimension of Irish society meant that there were important webs of interest and sentiment linking parts of the Irish elite with Community countries long before the formal association with the Community began[33]. In a more general sense, membership of the Community had enhanced the Republic's sense of independence and put even the problem of Northern Ireland in a new perspective. The link with the Community had had other, more tangible consequences too. The diversification of Irish external trade has already been referred to. Community membership had also, however, been an important stimulus to growth, particularly in the industrial sector[34] but also in agriculture. The discussion in section 5.3 will show how difficult it is to evaluate the significance of direct costs or benefits when assessing the overall advantages or disadvantages of Community membership, but *Tables 5.1* and *5.2*, published by the

Table 5.1 *Ireland's receipts from, and payments to, the European Communities, 1973–78*

	1 January 1973– 31 December 1977 £m.	1978 (estimate) £m.
(a) Receipts by way of Grants and Subsidies:		
FEOGA–Guarantee Section	549.7[a]	350.0[a]
–Guidance Section	10.6	12.0
European Social Fund	20.4	20.0
European Regional Development Fund	18.8	17.0
Regional Studies jointly financed by Ireland and the Communities		
Pilot projects and studies to combat poverty		
Research and Investment projects	1.9	1.0
Projects in the hydrocarbons section		
Moneys for miscellaneous surveys and studies carried out by Irish agencies for the Commission		
Total[b]	601.4	400.0
(b) Payments to the European Communities and other contributions arising as a result of membership:		
Contribution to the budget of the European Communities	57.3	42.0
Contribution to the EIB	2.4	0.6
Contribution to the ECSC		
Contribution to EURATOM research programmes	3.7	1.4
Miscellaneous contribution		
Total	63.4	44.0

[a] Receipts under the Guarantee Section include amounts of £152 million for the period to 31 December 1977 and an estimated amount of £140 million for 1978 in respect of UK and Italian MCA import subsidies which have been administered by Ireland in the case of Irish exports to the UK and Italy since 17 May 1976

[b] In addition to the above amounts, receipts also arise as a result of Community regulations on social security for migrant workers; Ireland's receipts under this heading amounted to £10.3 million in the period 1 January 1973–31 December 1977 and are estimated at £3.3 million for 1978

Source: Dail Eireann. *Parliamentary Debates, Official Report, Vol. 308, columns 271–272*

Table 5.2 *Loans approved for Ireland, 1973–78*

	1 January 1973– *31 December 1977*	*1978 (estimate)*
EIB	145.4	75–80
ECSC	1.4	–
Community loan	156.0	–
Total	302.8	75–80

Source: Dail Eireann. *Parliamentary Debates, Official Report, Vol. 308, columns 271–272*

ministry of finance in response to a question in the Dail in October 1978, give some idea of the variety of economic benefits that the Republic derived from Community membership.

Despite the budgetary benefits that the Republic already received, the principal aim of Irish policy in the months that followed the Bremen Council was to ensure that entry into the EMS was linked with a fresh transfer of resources from the richer member states, and it was this question, rather than the sterling problem, that was to dominate public debate and in the end to postpone for a few days Ireland's entry into the system. The strategy that the Irish pursued had already been anticipated in the pre-Bremen period, but serious work in both the ministry of finance and the ministry for economic planning and development on detailed proposals began only after the Bremen Council. The general case that the Irish made for a transfer of resources was, as section 5.3 will show, broadly similar to the argument advanced by both the British and the Italians. This was scarcely surprising. With one of the authors of the MacDougall report, Professor Martin O'Donoghue, in the Cabinet, the Irish government was as well placed as any to quote effectively from the report and the body of ideas that underlay it.

There were, however, certain elements in the Irish situation that separated them from their potential allies and that led to a significant difference in tactics. The first was that the Irish stood to lose under virtually any conceivable reform of the CAP. The second was that, largely because of the access that Community membership had given to new sources of investment and new markets, successive Irish governments, but more particularly the Fianna Fail government led by Mr Lynch, had committed the country to high growth policies that had put it in a highly vulnerable and, by Western European standards in 1978, quite peculiar position. In pursuit of its growth targets, which were defined in a succession of official papers, the most important of which were entitled *National Development 1977–1980* and *Development for Full Employment*, the Lynch government had consciously reckoned with an increase in the public sector borrowing requirement, greater foreign borrowing in general and a further deterioration in the balance of payments. Even the most optimistic government ministers were aware that the health of the economy could be seriously impaired if borrowing was increased still more and if there was any further import growth. As an indication of their concern on this latter score, they had themselves sponsored a Buy Irish campaign, and later in the autumn of 1978 they were to revise credit guidelines with a view to limiting the imports of consumer goods. Thus, although they welcomed the EMS proposal, not least because, it was argued, it would reinforce efforts to reduce inflation and as a result create a more stable base for further growth, ministers and officials were acutely aware of the risks of Ireland joining at this particular juncture. The government's determination to take the Republic into the new system hardly faltered, but with an economy as near the margins as the Irish one was in 1978, Irish negotiators, and particularly those involved in the concurrent studies, had particular problems and objectives in view[35].

5.2   The technical discussions of monetary problems, 25 July–13 September

The task of working out the details of the monetary system based on the ideas outlined in the Bremen Annex was entrusted by the ECOFIN at its meeting in Brussels on 24 July to the Monetary Committee and the Committee of Central Bank Governors. Most of the detailed preparatory work was done in reality however by two subcommittees: the Alternates Committee of the Monetary Committee and the Heyvaert group, a subcommittee of the Central Bank Governors' Committee, named after its chairman, which had often in the past prepared technical papers for the governors and their deputies. The Monetary Committee also set up a special Legal Committee to examine the juridical problems that were bound to arise, particularly if it was intended to establish an EMF. No attempt was made to differentiate between the functions of the two main committees and both produced lengthy reports covering essentially the same ground for the ECOFIN meeting of 18 September. The identity of the subject matter tackled by the two committees was matched at the most senior level by a considerable overlap of personnel, since the deputy governors of the central banks or their equivalents attended both major committees. As, in addition, in almost every case both elements in the national teams – bank and finance ministry officials – worked very closely together before and during the meetings of the Monetary Committee, the duplication of labour might at first sight seem hard to justify. The problems raised by the Bremen Annex were, however, too important for the central bank governors to be left out of the process and, as the Belgian governor said at the July meeting, there was no way in which they could reasonably divide the subjects up between them. A request by the IMF to be allowed a place on the Monetary Committee was refused, but the central bank governors continued to use the services of the staff of the Bank for International Settlements (BIS) in Basle, so that by this means if by no other non-Community views and perspectives were admitted to the discussion.

Much of the documentation produced for or by the various committees was of a highly technical, not to say academic, character, and contributions such as a BIS paper of 24 August discussing the 'technical implications of pegging an exchange rate against a currency basket', or a UK Treasury paper submitted two weeks earlier entitled 'Recognising when exchange rates may need changing', will have to be discussed by another scholar in a book of different size and scope from this one. The discussions that went on in the expert committees are nonetheless of fundamental importance for understanding not only the detailed provisions of the Resolution that was eventually approved at the European Council in December 1978, but much of the politics and diplomacy at the highest levels that preceded it. The outcome of the discussions between July and September was inconclusive but, as the following paragraphs should show, the expert committees had already by the second week in September closed some important doors and opened others. Even their semi-formed judgements set limits on the freedom for manoeuvre of their political masters.

On at least two points, all the members of both main committees would seem to have been in total agreement. The first was that, however strict the system might eventually become, flexibility, and more particularly provisions for changes in exchange rates, would have to be written into the arrangements from the beginning; the second, that unless substantial progress was made towards the coordination of economic policies, parity changes would be so frequent as to render the system worthless. That said, the difficulties began and they were numerous. There is neither space nor need to discuss all of them here, but the more significant can be grouped under two headings: firstly, the problems associated with the use of the ECU as the basis of the intervention system and, secondly, the scope and resources of the proposed EMF, both in its final form, which the Bremen Annex had reckoned would be achieved within two years, and in the transitional stage, in the form of the credit arrangements that would be needed to underpin the system.

The Bremen Annex had decreed that the ECU should be 'at the centre of the system'. However, as both the Schulmann–Clappier talks and the preliminary studies of the Monetary Committee had already suggested before the Bremen meeting, there were a number of issues that had to be resolved before anybody could be quite sure what the implications of a basket-centred currency system were. Some of these issues have been referred to above, but for the sake of clarity they need to be reiterated and expanded upon here. The fundamental question was whether or not the ECU should be used as the instrument for determining when currencies had reached their intervention limits. At the outset of the discussions there were essentially two approaches – one minimalist, the other maximalist. The *maximalist* position, supported principally by the French and identified in particular with M. Clappier, envisaged the ECU as the sole means of defining a currency's fluctuation margins. At the inauguration of the system, both the central rate and the margin within which each currency might fluctuate would be calculated exclusively in terms of the ECU. There would be no fixed, bilateral crossrates and one currency could therefore reach its upper (or lower) limits without any other currency necessarily reaching its limits at the same time. When it did so, the central bank in question would be obliged to intervene on the markets to check its rise or fall. The *minimalist* interpretation, advanced by the Germans and the Dutch, assigned the ECU a much more modest role. Central rates would be determined in relation to it (and in this sense it could therefore presumably still be said to be at the centre of the system), but a parity grid system, comparable to the one already in use in the Snake, would be superimposed, assigning currency limits not in relation to the ECU, but in relation to each other. In other words, the ECU reference would be no more than a point of departure and a central bank would only be required to intervene when its currency reached margins calculated in relation to the bilateral central rates. By definition, therefore, there would always be at least two deviants, since if one currency went to its upper limits there would always be another at the bottom. The characteristics of the system can be seen in *Table 5.3*, which indicates the central rates and margins of the Dutch guilder.

Table 5.3 *Central rates and margins of the Dutch guilder*

	Amsterdam HFl	Brussels BFr	Frankfurt DM	Copenhagen DKr
+ 2.25%		1483.25	94.375	266.365
bilateral central rates	100	1450.26	92.2767	260.439
− 2.25%		1413.00	90.225	254.645

Source: European Economy, July 1979, p. 74

The issues raised by the two approaches to the problem were profoundly important. Under the minimalist interpretation, the exchange mechanism would always identify at least two currencies as being out of line and both central banks concerned would be obliged to intervene. However, as governor Baffi pointed out in his evidence to the Italian Senate Committee on Financial and Treasury Affairs, though formally symmetrical, the obligations under this system were in fact asymmetrical, since the obligation on the strong was to buy foreign currencies, thereby augmenting their official reserves, while the obligation of the weak was to sell, thereby diminishing their reserves and domestic liquidity. Despite the fears of the Germans and others about the expansion of domestic liquidity that followed an inflow of foreign currencies, history showed, Dr Baffi argued, that it was much easier for a strong currency country to absorb an inflow than for a weak currency country to resist an outflow. The Snake had only lost the weak, it had not expelled the strong[36].

What the maximalist or French interpretation attempted to do was to identify one deviant rather than two. The deviant might, of course, be a weak currency, but it could equally well, the history of the Snake suggested, be a strong one. The way would therefore be open under this system to place obligations on the strong independently of any that might fall on the weak. To both M. Clappier and his colleagues this interpretation of the Bremen Annex statement assigning the ECU the central role in the system was of fundamental importance if the EMS was to be more than the Snake in any real sense. M. Clappier's antipathy towards the Snake was frequently in evidence during the summer negotiations and discussions and was illustrated with particular clarity in the course of a bilateral meeting with the Italians at Bergamo on 8 September. The French, he declared, wanted a mechanism that was different from that of the Snake. They had left the Snake twice and they did not want to be forced out of it a third time. It had its virtues of course, but it was only workable in what was in effect a DM zone, and it could not therefore be used to advance progress towards European unity. In the Snake, M. Clappier continued, three times out of four problems had arisen because the strongest currency, in almost every case the DM, had reached its upper limits. It was for this reason that the Germans wanted to retain a parity grid system, since although they had more often than not been the deviants, the system was so biased against the weak that the latter had always had to pay the consequences. For precisely the opposite reason he wanted the basket mechanism. The latter had, in addition, a major political advantage. Given the differences that existed in inflation rates within the Community, there would clearly have to be parity changes in the future, but it would be in the interests of both the French and the Italians if a mechanism could be found that took some of the drama out of these changes. By using the ECU, he averred, progress could be made in this direction too.

The political calculations and objectives that lay behind the French insistence on the ECU as the basis of the intervention system were for obvious reasons congenial to the British and the Italians. A Bank of England paper written in July observed that the idea had no precedent and that the possibility that it provided for imposing real obligations on the strong deviant should be explored and expanded. The paper itself suggested that the EMCF or the EMF might open two types of account, an A account for borrowers and a B account for creditors. If the B accounts became excessively large for more than a period of say six months, there would be an automatic obligation upon the holders to carry out a fundamental review of their economic policies in conjunction with EMF officials, in much the same way as countries that ran persistent deficits at present had to undergo surveillance by the IMF. It is a moot point whether the Bank of England would have felt the same way two years later, but it is easy to see why, with ideas such as this floating abroad, the Central Bank Council of the Bundesbank, at a meeting devoted to the EMS on 7 September, argued in no uncertain terms against the French proposal. If implemented, it was claimed, it would almost certainly necessitate German interventions on a much larger scale than hitherto and the general effect of the system would be to push the Federal Republic towards accepting inflation rates at or near the Community average. This would be totally incompatible with Germany's fundamental commitment to stability.

There was thus a clear-cut conflict of interest between the Snake and the non-Snake countries. What was not widely appreciated at the time, however, was that, even though the non-Snake countries remained united in their fundamental aim of devising a system that placed constraints on the strong as well as on the weak, hopes of achieving the objective through the *French* proposal were already diminishing and, in the case of at least some key figures, had totally vanished before the expert committees drew up their preliminary reports in September and, more important still, before the Aachen meeting between the French president and the German chancellor on 14 September. The Belgian compromise, which will be explained in more detail shortly, was usually represented as an attempt to bridge the gap between two incompatible positions. It can equally well be seen, however, as an attempt to salvage what could be salvaged of a proposal that had run into serious and possibly insuperable technical problems. Many observers, particularly the British, saw French behaviour at Aachen and French, Irish and Italian behaviour at the ECOFIN meeting of 18 September as a capitulation to the Germans. The reality, as the final section of this chapter will suggest, was complex. As the French finance minister admitted at the meeting of 18 September, the basket proposal in the form that it had been defined in earlier stages of the post-Bremen discussions was simply not feasible in technical terms.

The objections to the ECU proposal that began to persuade officials of even the non-Snake countries that it could not be used as the basis of the new system in the sense originally envisaged by the French were essentially two: firstly it was too complex and secondly, though it might bruise the strong, it could in certain circumstances cause considerable difficulties to the weak. It is impossible to give an exhaustive list of the operational problems that quickly arose and that made it certain that even if it was politically acceptable the ECU proposal would be extremely difficult to manage. Most of these objections arose from the nature of the basket itself, which was not a constant, but a variable. In an ECU-based system, currencies would have different weights that would vary over time, according to whether or not they were appreciating or depreciating. It followed, therefore, that if one of the currencies changed its central rate this would necessitate the revision of all central rates vis-à-vis the ECU, the redistribution of the weights of all the currencies in the basket and a change in the market value of the ECU itself vis-à-vis third countries. In fact, far from being an undramatic event, a revaluation or devaluation would have exceedingly complex consequences. So, too, would a decision by one of the member states not to participate in the system, since short of the country concerned leaving the Community, its currency would remain part of the basket and its movements, which might well be more volatile outside the system, would affect the currency relationships of those who stayed inside. Another by-product of the system, which followed from the demand in the Bremen Annex that intervention should 'in principle' be in currencies of the participating countries, was that the authorities whose currencies deviated would have to intervene in the currency of another member. The latter would thereby incur 'involuntary' debts or credits, which might in due course be transformed into real losses if, as was quite possible, values shifted between the moment of intervention and the moment of settlement.

Probably the single most important problem, however, which was bound to make the system complicated to manage but which was also a considerable threat to the interests of the weak and the small, was the inherent bias of the basket towards its heavy components. The greater the weight of the currency, the larger the margins of fluctuation available to it in bilateral terms. This bias against the small, as well as the untidiness and complexity of the system, can be illustrated by a comparison of the bilateral margins for the DM and Danish krone if both belonged to a system that allowed a 3% margin vis-à-vis the ECU. Because of its weight, the DM could appreciate or depreciate against all the other currencies by 4.4% before reaching its intervention limits, while the Danish krone's fluctuation would be limited to 3.1%. Both central banks and market operators were likely to be reduced rather quickly to despair by such a system. What was still more important, however, was the political aspect, since, far from favouring the weak, the system could very well operate against them. The extreme case would arise when one currency achieved a weighting higher than 50%. In this position it could never reach its upper or lower limits, because before it did it would by its own weight have pushed some other currency to its limits in the other direction. This contingency was not as remote or as irrelevant as it might at first seem, since the DM itself, which had had a weight of 27.3% when the

EUA was first defined in 1975, had already by September 1978 appreciated by over 5% within the basket to a weighting of 32.35%. Still more to the point, the DM zone (alias the Snake), which in 1975 had had a combined weighting of 47.5%, had by September 1978 reached 55.13%. The Snake currencies would therefore start off with a preponderance in the system, which, given the tendency of even the weakest amongst them to appreciate against the non-Snake countries, would probably delay and quite possibly thwart the 'exposure' of the DM that the French and their allies desired. More generally, the bias towards the strong made it not at all unlikely, as governor Baffi observed in the Franco-Italian meeting at Bergamo on 8 September, that a conspicuously weak currency like the lira might be singled out by the ECU just as frequently if not more so than the DM, with consequences that could be still more disagreeable than those that resulted from reaching the lower limits in a parity grid system.

Various suggestions were made in the course of the summer discussions to overcome this problem. The most radical came from the Bank of England and was identified in particular with Mr Balfour, who argued that currency weightings should remain constant and that all that would change when the currency appreciated or depreciated would be the amount of that currency in the basket. German reactions to this proposal, which seemed to them to be a sure recipe for a 'Community of inflation', were predictably hostile; they were even worried about more moderate variants on the theme, involving for example infrequent reviews every three or five years. Even if agreement had been possible on some way of overcoming this problem however, there were still other unexpected difficulties. In the Italian case, for example, their preference for wider margins of fluctuation would have given rise to considerable difficulties. All in all, therefore, it is not entirely surprising that, well before Aachen, experts from two of the non-Snake countries, Italy and Ireland, should have expressed their indifference or even in one case hostility to the basket proposal in its original form. Amongst the Italians, the growing list of problems that the summer studies had revealed prompted Dr Baffi to tell the French on 8 September that on balance he actually preferred the Snake system, and Dr Masera to suggest at the same meeting that it might be better after all to work towards an ECU-based system in the long term, but in the meantime to operate within the less complex and problematical parity grid arrangement. The Italians had not, it need hardly be said, lost their enthusiasm for the original purpose of the proposal. It was simply that without much more protracted study and negotiation than could possibly be contemplated in 1978, there was no real chance of that purpose being achieved. They were therefore predisposed towards a compromise. So too, more reluctantly, were the French. At Bergamo, on 8 September, a week before the Aachen meeting at which, in British eyes at least, the French president 'sold out' to the German chancellor by agreeing to explore the possibilities opened up by the Belgian compromise, French and Italian experts, led in each case by the minister of finance and the governor of the central bank, agreed to do exactly the same.

It is against this background that one can best understand the motives that underlay the Belgian compromise. It was essentially a holding operation rather than a pre-packed formula to which both sides could give a final answer for or against. In the form in which it appeared in the interim report of the Monetary Committee of 7 September, it consisted of two propositions:

La grille de parités, établie sur la base des contrevaleurs en ECU des différentes monnaies, serait employée pour fixer les cours limites d'intervention en termes nominaux:

La formule panier ECU serait utilisée pour déterminer le degré de divergence des monnaies participantes de façon à en tirer certaines conséquences pour les règles d'intervention et/ou d'autres politiques.

Of the two propositions, the first was so much the clearer and more specific that the compromise might appear to have been biased in favour of the parity grid system as opposed to the basket. However, such an interpretation ignores the specific context in which the formula was drafted. Far from prejudging the issue, it bought time for the supporters of the ECU proposal to work out ways of dealing with the more important technical problems that the proposal had run into and created an environment in which these solutions stood a chance of gaining acceptance. By the time at which the compromise was tabled, it was becoming increasingly clear that, however meritorious its intentions, the ECU plan would never result in a system as intelligible and manageable in an operational sense as the parity grid. It was also apparent that, to achieve its purpose, measures would have to be agreed (such as the 'individualization' of fluctuation margins) that would not only make the system even more complex, but that would also require a degree of political tolerance from supporters of the parity grid system, against whom (as they and everybody else knew) the proposals were to some extent directed, that was inconceivable unless they received a substantial *quid pro quo* in return. This the Belgian compromise gave them in the form of the retention of the parity grid. But it still left ECU supporters with the chance of achieving their objectives too.

Although the role of the ECU in defining intervention limits in the new system was undoubtedly the most controversial problem that arose in the course of the technical discussions in July and August, there were also significant exchanges of view about the scope and role of the EMF in the long term, and about the transitional arrangements governing credit and interbank settlements in the phase preceding the establishment of the Fund. The importance of these issues should be obvious. At Copenhagen and again at Bremen both Mr Schmidt and M. Giscard d'Estaing had placed great stress on the Fund as the cornerstone of the new system, and it is evident that, however much their officials may have regretted their enthusiasm, they themselves intended the Fund to be much more than the EMCF in new guise. It is true that in the Bremen Annex it was recognized that the EMF could not come into existence immediately, but M. Clappier, who had after all drafted the document, was doubtless correct in suggesting that in terms of the spirit if not of the letter of the Annex those responsible for working out its detailed implications were expected to lay the foundations of the permanent system immediately. The transitional period, he argued, was a time for 'running in' a system, the essential components of which had already been put into place, rather than for leisurely studies related to an indefinite future. It was for this reason, he and others implied, that the Bremen document placed such emphasis on the immediate creation of a large supply of ECUs as a means of settlement between banks and as a source of credit.

In the discussion of these problems that developed in the Monetary and Central Bank Governors' committees, it was once again the Germans, and in particular the Bundesbank, who urged a minimalist interpretation of the Bremen proposals. Dr Emminger had already given notice of his reservations on these points at the Cabinet meeting of 12 July and, in the weeks that followed, he and his colleagues became if anything even harder on both the long- and short-term issues at stake. It is some indication of the strength of their feelings on the matter that over half of the paper summarizing the attitude of the Central Bank Council toward the EMS, following its meeting on 7 September, was devoted to this complex of problems. On the Fund, the Council was adamant. No German reserves could be transferred to it without special legislation and even if they were, the Council insisted, the creation of such a Fund should in no circumstances limit the autonomy of the Bundesbank in the sphere of monetary policy. Their determination to contemplate no loss of sovereignty in the future was matched by their insistence on the greatest possible caution in devising transitional arrangements. They acknowledged that credit facilities would be needed to sustain the new system, but they were openly critical of the provisions that seemed to be implied in the Bremen Annex. Credits of this magnitude, they argued, threatened to undermine the discipline that the system was meant to inculcate and might well encourage central banks to defend unrealistic exchange rates longer than was justifiable and wise, and put pressure on potential surplus countries to intervene on an excessive scale. In determining the scope and character of the financial backing for the new system, they suggested that the following criteria should be observed:

(1) the proposed creation of ECUs should not increase international liquidity;
(2) ECUs issued against deposits of national currencies should only be used to finance short- and medium-term support operations and should not therefore be automatically available;

(3) rules governing short-term credits should be no weaker than those that currently obtained in the Snake.

As far as the volume of credits was concerned, the Council believed that current Community provisions for short- and medium-term support operations were already sufficient. Proposals for an increase in the figures should therefore be handled with extreme caution and some at least of the suggestions made by other members since Bremen were quite clearly out of the question. They were also worried about the possible implications of the demand made in the Bremen Annex that interventions should, in principle, be made in Community currencies. What they feared would develop was a 'DM intervention system', which, particularly if credit facilities were significantly increased, would constitute a serious threat to the continuing capacity of the Bundesbank to control the availability of DM. The same danger threatened if member states were allowed to exchange their ECUs for DM when settling accounts. There would therefore have to be a ceiling placed on the amount of ECUs that the central bank was obliged to accept and, more generally, it was imperative that the Bundesbank should be authorized to call a halt to its interventions if these seemed in their view to put their control over DM liquidity at risk.

The fundamental character of the Bundesbank's reservations on the proposals for an EMF and other related issues placed a severe constraint on the discussion of these problems. On the crucial question of the Fund, however, the Germans found support not only amongst their allies, like the Dutch, but also amongst the credit-hungry, who feared its political implications. The preliminary reports of the specialist committees justified their lack of any detailed treatment of this problem by referring to the sentence in the Bremen Annex that implied that the Fund would not come into existence immediately and by pointing out the legal problems that would have to be overcome at both national and Community levels before any final decisions could be taken. These legal problems are worth considering in some detail, since they remain relevant to the discussions about the next stage that have been in progress sporadically since the inauguration of the system. The legal issues involved were discussed at length in a special subcommittee set up under the auspices of the Monetary Committee in July. Their studies covered a wide range of topics, but the central problem concerned the legal basis of the EMS in the Treaty of Rome. There were essentially two articles to which the system could be related. The first, Article 235, empowered the Council, acting unanimously on the basis of a proposal from the Commission and after consultation with the Assembly, to take appropriate measures to achieve an objective of the European Community that was implicit in the Treaty but for which the Treaty itself did not provide the necessary powers. Article 236, by contrast, dealt with amendments, and for these the procedures involved were more complicated, including not only a special conference of representatives of the governments of the member states, but also ratification of the agreed amendment 'by all the member states in accordance with their respective constitutional arrangements'. When the EMCF had been established in April 1973, the Council of Ministers had based its legality on Article 235, and the argument advanced by the majority of legal experts in the summer and autumn of 1978 was essentially that, unless the financial provisions of the EMS in its initial, transitional phase conformed with the provisions set out in the Regulations and Statutes governing the EMCF, recourse would have to be had to Article 236, which would almost certainly jeopardize the timetable implied in the conclusions of the Bremen Council.

It is possible, indeed probable, that in the case of several if not all of the governments that used this argument the appeal to legal propriety was a convenient cover for their lack of enthusiasm for the EMS in general and the EMF in particular. One of the officials concerned in the discussions of July and August noted in a report to his government towards the end of August that the majority of delegations wanted no more than 'a showcase for Community currencies', an institution that juggled with figures but had no control over money. Whatever their motives, however, the legal opinion of the majority, reinforced in certain cases by the claim that special national legislation would be required even if the provisions were permitted under Article 235, determined the framework of the debate about both the Fund and the credit mechanisms in the new system. The Fund, it was claimed and eventually accepted even by those like M. Clappier or the Italians who wanted a thorough discussion immediately, was essentially a matter for the future. For the time being, work should be concentrated on transitional arrangements and even here, it was implied, caution was essential if the law was to be upheld.

The 'transitional' issues covered were numerous, including as they did subjects as diverse as the basis to be used when calculating the exact quantity of central bank ECU deposits, ways of protecting participants against the consequences of fluctuations between the national currency and the ECU, the determination of interest rates on ECUs and the role of gold. There is neither space nor need to summarize the discussion of all the points that were touched upon, but two do merit particular attention: the legal basis of the ECU and the form and amount of credits that would be made available to participants.

As far as the first of these problems was concerned, the Bremen document had been a good deal more cautious than journalists, and indeed some participants, implied afterwards. The ECUs were to be 'created against deposits' of foreign and exchange reserves and member currencies. Like the phrase that decreed that the ECU would be at the centre of the system, this could mean either a lot or a little. The Monetary Committee distinguished between at least five possible interpretations of the word 'deposit':

(1)   deposits in the banking sense
(2)   swaps
(3)   collateral
(4)   trust contracts
(5)   definitive transfers.

Some of the more euphoric comments following the Bremen Council suggested that what had been intended was the equivalent of a definitive transfer. Even if this had been the intention of those who drafted the Annex, however, it was quickly apparent that neither the Bundesbank nor several other central banks were prepared to contemplate more than either the first or the second interpretations, and by the beginning of September if not earlier even M. Clappier was ready to concede that for the time being at least it would probably be necessary to equate the ECUs with 'swaps'. In his discussions with the Italians at Bergamo he emphasized that these arrangements were still to be regarded as the beginning of a process that would lead eventually to the creation of a European central bank. But despite its fine sounding name, the ECU was to emerge from the expert discussions with a legal basis similar to and as precarious as the funds earmarked for swap purposes under numerous existing central bank agreements. Like them, it would have to be renewed every three months and unless there was a unanimous vote to the contrary, it would simply cease to exist after two years. Despite the French governor's optimism, therefore, the reserve currency role remained, to put it mildly, a remote prospect.

The extremely cautious definition of the ECU that was more or less agreed to by the beginning of September and that, given the legal position, was probably inevitable, made it all the more important to those who wanted the scheme to be more than the Snake that the credit arrangements should mark a clear advance on the Community provisions already in existence. The discussions between July and September did little more than indicate the agenda of the debate and define its limits. As far as limits were concerned, the arguments about Articles 235 and 236 were once again of fundamental importance, forcing the participants to concentrate their efforts on modifying the existing credit mechanisms set up under the EMCF, rather than devising new ones. The debate therefore turned on the amount of credits that would be made available under the various headings. Even so, the issues were contentious enough, with the Bundesbank pressing for the smallest possible increase on existing facilities and others arguing for the opposite. The details of these discussions will be described in the next chapter, but by the end of September the battle lines were already clearly drawn.

5.3   The concurrent studies, July–September

To three of the non-Snake governments, the British, the Italians and the Irish, if not the French, the outcome of the concurrent studies was as important and, to the Irish at least, perhaps more important than the fate of the ECU or the amount of central bank credits that would be available under the new system. The committee that considered these views under the chairmanship of Dr Tietmeyer of the German ministry of economics, though formally labelled the EPC, was in fact an *ad hoc* group assembled for the occasion and liable to changes and additions to its membership as and when it suited the purposes of national governments. The air of improvisation that surrounded its proceedings throughout and that reached its acme in 'the secret meeting' at Frankfurt airport a few days before the European Council should not, however, be taken as a sign of its relative insignificance compared with the more orderly and established committees that dealt with the monetary issues. On the contrary, it was from the beginning a heavyweight group, and the changes in membership, not to mention the hastily convened meeting at Frankfurt, reflected the constant intrusion of high politics into its proceedings.

The countries with special cases to plead were for obvious reasons the first to show by their choice of personnel how seriously they rated the committee's work. The Italians nominated Dr Ciampi, deputy governor of the Banca d'Italia, and Renato Ruggiero, whose formal position at the ministry of foreign affairs after his return to Rome from Brussels never did justice to the multiplicity of his roles or, still more important, his closeness to successive prime ministers. The principal British representative was Michael Butler, a veteran of the 1974/75 renegotiations, who was shortly to become the UK's permanent representative in Brussels, but who was at the time the most senior Foreign Office official concerned with Community affairs on a full-time basis. The Irish entrusted their case to Mr Dermot Nalley, a senior permanent official in the prime minister's office. The decision by the French government to send Jean-Claude Payet, who was responsible for coordinating French policy on Community affairs and was generally believed to be close to the president, was a sign of the significance that they came to attach to the committee, while the Germans eventually mobilized Dr Lahnstein, who was drafted in as chairman of the *ad hoc* gathering at Frankfurt. The Belgians sent M. van Ypersele to the same meeting.

By the time that the committee had presented its first, oral report to the ECOFIN of 18 September, it was already apparent that the disagreements amongst its members were even more fundamental in many ways than those that divided the Monetary and Central Bank Governors' committees and that, without political intervention at a very high level, there was little prospect that they would be overcome. Various explanations could be given for this deadlock, but three are probably sufficient: the comparative vagueness of the brief to which the committee worked, which allowed for both sincere and tactical questions about the overall purpose of the operation; the negotiating position taken up by the British and to some extent the Italians; and the evident determination of the representatives of at least three other countries that, if what the British and Italians wanted was what the proceedings were really about, no progress would be the best possible outcome. All three points, are, needless to say, closely related.

Whereas the Monetary Committee had both a text and a tradition behind their work, the EPC had nothing but a short sentence tacked on to the Bremen preamble. It read:

> There will be concurrent studies of the action needed to be taken to strengthen the economies of the less prosperous member countries in the context of such a scheme; such measures will be essential if the zone of monetary stability is to succeed.

The statement begged more questions than it answered and two at least were of fundamental importance. The first concerned the definition and identification of the less prosperous countries, the second the problem of deciding what measures were appropriate to a scheme that would certainly fall short of full monetary union but whose final form was still a subject of negotiation and speculation. The problem of definition was clearly basic, but also extremely difficult. Like their prime ministers at Bremen, the Italian, Irish and British members of the committee were convinced that they represented less prosperous countries, but the British in particular had considerable difficulty in proving it. Various criteria were suggested and the following were eventually accepted as being of some use: a persistent need to import capital on a long-term basis, above average unemployment, below average growth rates, problems arising from demographic factors (emigration, etc.) and serious regional imbalances. But the greatest weight, it was decided, should be given to calculations based on GDP *per capita*. This in itself raised problems, however, since there were different ways of estimating it. The choice lay essentially between two sorts of figures, the first based on current exchange rates, the second on a version of this adjusted to reflect real purchasing power. As *Table 5.4* taken from the committee's final report suggests, the two methods produced significantly different results.

The British, as the most affected, were naturally enough the chief advocates of an approach based on current exchange rates, arguing that its statistical base was surer than the alternative proposal, since despite some excellent work by the Community's Statistical Office there was no internationally agreed method for comparing purchasing power, and that the exchange rate was the appropriate guide to an economy's capacity to effect international transactions. They were supported by the Italians and the Irish. But the majority took the other view and, although it was in the end

Table 5.4 *Per capita GDP in the Community, using different methods of calculation (The Nine = 100)*

	At current prices and exchange rates		PPP OSCE*: at current prices and levels of purchasing power parity	
	1960	1976	1960	1976
Germany	112.5	134.7	116.5	117.6
France	113.8	122.7	99.6	113.3
Italy	59.6	57.2	68.9	73.3
Netherlands	83.0	120.9	105.2	107.8
Belgium	105.7	125.1	97.7	108.1
Luxembourg	140.5	128.0	135.5	107.1
United Kingdom	117.5	72.8	112.1	92.8
Ireland	54.4	46.7	58.7	60.7
Denmark	111.5	141.1	112.6	113.4
The Nine	100.0	100.0	100.0	100.0
Greece	36.4	44.9	–	–
Spain	33.4	53.9	–	–
Portugal	24.3	30.4	–	–
The Twelve	88.9	90.9	–	–

* Purchasing power parities of the Office Statistique des Communautés Européenes

Source: Economic Policy Committee, *Final Report*, 13 November 1978 (11/579/78).

agreed that whatever criteria were adopted the Italian and Irish economies could certainly be regarded as less prosperous, references to the United Kingdom's position were notably reserved. Britain, it was indicated, was less prosperous than the Community average, but the Irish and the Italians were in a different category altogether.

The second of the major questions concerned the problem of defining measures appropriate to a monetary system that would certainly fall short of EMU but whose final form was not yet known. The difficulties that emerged were both conceptual and practical. One relatively neutral observer commented afterwards that as the discussions progressed it became increasingly obvious that the French, the Dutch and the Danes had no feel whatsoever for arguments that, however improbable it might seem in the British case, were derived in the last resort from a body of theoretical work that was federalist in character. There was little point in quoting the MacDougall report – as representatives of all three less prosperous countries did rather frequently – to those who had not only not read it, but who lacked the essential conceptual equipment to appreciate its force. It is perhaps a harsh judgement and, as the analysis of the negotiating tactics of the British and the Italians will suggest, it is certainly not a complete explanation of the deadlock that ensued. But it is a relevant point nonetheless, and it goes a long way towards explaining why the committee was never able to reach agreement that transfers of resources were an appropriate method of meeting the problems of the less prosperous countries. There were other difficulties too, however. The MacDougall report was all very well, but its immediate relevance to the problems under discussion in this committee were not self-evident. As Professor O'Donoghue, one of the authors of the report, pointed out in a debate in the Irish Dail in October (in reply to a call by the leader of the opposition that the government ought to make more effective use of it), the proposed EMS was not a monetary union of the kind that the authors of the report had intended when discussing the financial implications of their low-cost federal model[37]. It was not even obvious that the pre-federal model they discussed at length was relevant in the present case[38]. There was therefore an air of arbitrariness about most of the attempts to draw practical conclusions from the report when so much about what the EMS was or might become was still unknown.

Eventually, however, the committee did agree that, in addition to domestic policies by both the less prosperous countries and their richer partners that were conducive to greater convergence, additional help might conceivably be necessary to cope with the following problems associated with membership of the system:

(1) greater pressure on the balance of payments, which would put growth and job-creation policies at risk;

(2) the fact that by joining the EMS the governments concerned would by definition make less use of changes in the exchange rate as an instrument of economic policy, and would therefore lose a powerful method of adjustment if their economies became uncompetitive;

(3) the possibility that the EMS might accelerate a convergence of costs across the Community out of line with changes in the basic patterns of productivity, a tendency that could conceivably encourage a drift of capital and labour away from the less prosperous countries to the more prosperous ones;

(4) the probability that there would be a time lag in the reduction of inflation rates in the more inflation-prone countries to standards essential for participation in the EMS.

The difficulties that the committee experienced in defining its terms of reference were compounded by the negotiating tactics adopted by the British and to a lesser extent the Italians. This problem, which has already been alluded to in section 5.1, can be appreciated most easily by a comparison of the earliest statements and written submissions of the three delegations. The Irish approach was blunt and specific[39]. The need for Community action to strengthen the Irish economy in the context of the EMS, it was stated, arose from the country's level of development, which was low by Community standards, and the employment challenge facing it. The Irish government was itself engaged in encouraging a fundamental restructuring of the Irish economy in order to bring it up to Community standards, but the strategy might be made more difficult if Ireland were to become a participant in the EMS for the following reasons:

(1) In fulfilling its obligations as a member of the system, the Irish government would in normal circumstances have to reduce the balance of payments deficit on current account more quickly than was presently envisaged, which would have serious and damaging deflationary consequences for an economy characterized by above average unemployment and underdevelopment.

(2) In order to meet with the challenges of Community and EMS membership the best long-term solution would be to increase investment, a process that could be greatly assisted by the provision of Community funds to facilitate the financing of the public capital programme and to offset the adverse effects on the balance of payments that would result from increased imports induced by the necessary acceleration of investment.

(3) In the initial phase at any rate, the Irish punt would almost certainly have to be maintained at a level higher than it would otherwise have been, and Community funds would therefore be necessary to reduce the damaging consequences of the loss of competitiveness.

What distinguished the Irish case most clearly from those advanced by representatives of the other two less prosperous countries – Britain and Italy – was that the Irish attempted to put a precise figure on their needs and provided a detailed list of infrastructure-improving projects for which they wanted assistance. The figure, £650 million over five years, or 200 million EUAs per year over the same period, represented 10% of GNP or 2% per annum if the sum was spread over five years. It was also highly desirable, the Irish paper indicated, that this money should be made available in the form of grants rather than loans, since the government was committed to reducing the borrowing requirement as a percentage of GNP, an aim supported by the EEC Commission and in accordance with the Community guidelines for Ireland. Finally, it was emphasized rather pointedly, the Irish did not intend to raise any fundamental questions about the structure of the Community budget.

The Italian government's ideas were expounded in a document that, like its Irish counterpart, was circulated to the committee at the end of August[40]. It began with some general observations on the consequences that were likely to follow on the decision to join the EMS and the measures that might be adopted to alleviate them. The latter, it suggested, fell into two broad categories: policies designed to stimulate demand in the stronger currencies, and transfers of resources to the weak. As far as transfers were concerned, the paper argued, experience had shown that the initiative could not be left to the private sector alone. Official transfers on a substantial scale were therefore indispensable. Unlike the Irish, however, the Italians did not submit a precise list of desiderata, preferring instead to indicate the types of project that might be supported by Community funds if such funds were made available. These included environmental projects aimed at combating pollution and other consequences of industrialization, aid to research into alternative sources of energy and energy saving, public building programmes, investment in projects designed to overcome the social consequences of recession and unemployment, such as retraining schemes, and grants towards the improvement of the economic infrastructure in the underdeveloped parts of the country. Although no precise figures were mentioned, the paper did refer to the MacDougall report and in particular to the 2% of GDP that it had reckoned would be essential to ensure the necessary public finance backing for its pre-federal model. Expenditure on this scale, the Italian government pointed out, would require a rise in the Community budget from its present level of approximately 10.6 billion EUAs to approximately 24.6 billion. This objective could be achieved by a mixture of economies in the present budget and increased funds and loans. As far as the budget was concerned, the Italians urged more thorough control of the Guarantee Section of the Agricultural Fund and the division and expansion of funds available under the Guidance Section to ensure that more sectors were favoured, particularly those that were important in the Mediterranean agricultural economy. There should also, it suggested, be substantial increases in expenditure on both the Social and Regional Funds. A start could be made by making immediate use of the full 1% of VAT that was theoretically available to the Community instead of the 0.75% that was budgeted for in the current year. This alone would release an additional 2.3 billion EUAs. For the rest, much if not all could be raised through loans.

The differences between the Irish and Italian approaches, which as the next chapter will show were to become more rather than less marked as the months passed, were already evident in these two papers. The Irish stated what they believed they needed and why and asked no questions of the existing provisions of the Community budget. The Italians, though alluding to the types of projects that might be considered, were at one and the same time vaguer and more radical. The figures that they mentioned, though justified by reference to the MacDougall report, were massive by current Community standards and the measures that they suggested might help to overcome the gap would have involved a complete review and reform of the Community's financial instruments. Viewed in abstract, there was much to be said in favour of the bold approach. The Community budget was pitifully small and unbalanced and the negotiation of a new Community monetary system was a peculiarly appropriate moment for a fundamental reconsideration of the problem. The trouble, however, was that their demands were not made, and could not be considered, in a vacuum. Thanks to the MacDougall report and the popularization of some of the issues that it raised by Mr Jenkins and his associates, there was probably more awareness in 1978 of the financial implications of further integration than there had been before 1977 but, as we have seen, several of Italy's Community partners either could not or would not understand the issues at stake. As the final report noted, paraphrasing arguments advanced repeatedly and at great length by the French, the Dutch and the Danes, the Community budget appeared to these governments as essentially a means of advancing particular policies. Its redistributive effects were incidental to this principal purpose:

> Les mérites des politiques actuelles ne doivent pas s'apprécier essentiellement d'après les effets redistributifs du budget, mais leur efficacité doit plutôt être évaluée en fonction des résultats obtenus par rapport aux objectifs fixés. Dans ces conditions il se peut que des pays moins prospères soient contributeurs nets au budget communautaire et que des pays prospères en soient bénéficiaires nets.

It was a response of sufficient crudity and bluntness to ensure the frustration of the Italians' hopes virtually of itself. What made their position still worse, however, were the tactics adopted by their British 'allies'. The British handling of the EPC negotiations in the summer and autumn of 1977 was a copybook example of the scope and limitations of what is perhaps best described as the trench warfare conception of Community politics, which the French had pioneered but which the British had adapted to their own purposes from 1974 onwards. They began with a spectacular coup. On a hot August day when the Berlaymont and Council buildings were virtually deserted, they suggested to their committee colleagues that it would be extremely useful if the Commission could provide the committee with figures showing the net contributions of member states to the Community budget. Surprisingly enough their colleagues accepted the proposal, and still more surprisingly the Commission agreed to cooperate too, even though until then it had always refused to divulge this kind of information, because, as it subsequently stated in a reply to a written parliamentary question in the European Parliament, 'the figures give a false impression of what the member states do for the Community and of the economic benefits they derive from it [and] ... calculations of a fair return do nothing to create a spirit of European cooperation'[41]. Only shortly before indeed, the commissioner responsible for the budget, Christopher Tugendhat, had taken the Germans to task for making calculations of their own and discussing them at excessive length: this preoccupation with figures, he implied, was misleading and dangerous[42].

Speculation about why the information was provided – the commonest explanation seems to be that Brussels was simply rather hot and deserted – is of less importance than an examination of the uses that the British made of figures that, as *Table 5.5* shows, provided an impartial vindication of their claim that the contributions of member states were extremely uneven and that, once the protection offered by Article 131 of the Treaty of Accession was removed, their position, which was already bad, would become even worse[43].

As was only to be expected, the utility and accuracy of the figures were hotly disputed by several member states, notably Denmark and France, both arguing that monetary compensatory accounts (MCAs) should be credited to the importing country, a change that, as columns 2 and 4 in the table suggest, made a significant difference. But even if their less generous interpretation of the evidence was accepted, it was obvious that without Article 131 the British would already be net contributors to the budget, while their more prosperous partners, notably the Danes, the Belgians and the Dutch, were not, and that the situation was likely to be still worse in 1978 and 1979.

The British undoubtedly had a strong case therefore, as several German commentators were quick to concede when the figures became public knowledge. They also had an ideal opportunity to air their grievances in the context of a committee that had been specifically instructed to examine ways of assisting the less prosperous member states and where they could count on the support of the Italians, who had similar grievances and who, like them, were ready to press for radical redress. And yet they made no progress whatsoever. On the contrary, the prospects of achieving the kind of review that they wanted were if anything even bleaker at the end of their efforts than they had been when they began. Of course, not all the blame attaches to them. None of their negotiating partners was under instructions to be charitable, and some lacked even the modicum of political intelligence necessary to see that their determination to defend the *status quo* might be contrary to their own long-term interests. But it is difficult not to conclude that the British made matters worse for themselves, not because the negotiations were badly conducted in a technical sense – rather the reverse – but because of the air of opportunism, conditionality and reserve that characterized the underlying approach of those involved.

The fundamental ambivalence of the British position was to be illustrated even more clearly in the months that followed, and in particular in their undignified and confused reaction to the European Parliament's campaign for an increase in the Regional Fund, but it was already apparent in July and August. For all their quotations from the MacDougall report, the British simply could not persuade their Community partners at official or political level that they seriously wanted to lay the foundations of a monetary union. If the EMS was to provide an opportunity for a radical review of the

Table 5.5 *Net balances and monetary compensatory accounts, 1976 and 1977 (million EUA)*

| | Actual situation | | | | Unrestricted contributions | | | |
| | Incl. MCA 1 | | Incl. MCA 2 | | Incl. MCA 1 | | Incl. MCA 2 | |
	1976	1977	1976	1977	1976	1977	1976	1977
Germany	−1014.91	−1291.67	−1053.64	−1466.68	−647.93	−854.66	−686.66	−1029.67
France	+102.11	−46.49	+58.15	−309.88	+345.59	+171.05	+301.63	−92.34
Italy	+209.78	−66.43	+247.74	+293.60	+266.87	−171.74	+304.83	+188.29
Netherlands	+295.12	+286.05	+221.76	+87.48	+372.69	+284.64	+298.33	+86.07
Belgium/Luxembourg[a]	+357.59	+378.35	+346.24	+328.74	+430.65	+467.53	+419.30	+417.92
United Kingdom	−238.12	−624.06	−89.84	+125.86	−1000.82[b]	−1208.96[c]	−852.54[b]	−459.04[c]
Ireland	+194.22	+408.40	+154.93	+211.68	+166.73	+381.70	+127.45	+184.98
Denmark	+378.78	+519.62	+293.93	+293.14	+350.79	+494.22	+265.94	+267.74
The Nine	−284.57	+436.23	−179.27	+436.23	−284.57	+436.23	−179.27	+436.23

[a] Includes 400 million EUA in respect of administrative expenditure
[b] Excludes potential benefit of 200 million EUA under the Financial Mechanism
[c] Excludes potential benefit of 75 million EUA under the Financial Mechanism
Note: MCA in respect of imports: MCA 1 are paid in exporting country, MCA 2 in importing country
Source: Economic Policy Committee, *Final Report*, 13 November 1978 (11/579/78)

Community's financial instruments of the kind that the Italians wanted, those who pressed for it had to be prepared to advocate or at the very least accept the political limitations that would flow from it. The British were manifestly not; indeed, they were not even clear whether they wanted to join the EMS itself as a first stage on the journey. As a result, their approach to the concurrent studies seemed, and indeed in the final analysis was, no more than opportunistic. A British official, not one of those directly involved in the negotiations, summed up their attitude aptly as follows: 'We knew that there was not enough money in the EMS to meet our problems with the budget. We used these talks therefore principally as a means of drawing attention to our problem.' The negotiations, in other words, gave them a chance to take another swipe at the CAP and to prepare the ground for a campaign on the budget that, given the near certainty of a financial crisis in the Community as a whole within the following two or three years, would probably only be won when their partners were under material rather than moral pressure.

The documentation that they submitted to the committee and the arguments that they advanced orally were, even by comparison with the Italians' efforts, notable for their lack of any specific reference to projects that might be assisted or indeed to the connection between the problem that they described, namely the perversity of the Community budget, and the EMS. Like first world war generals, they were neither surprised nor particularly dismayed when the French and the rest, having been caught off balance, dug new trenches as near as possible to those that they had been forced to abandon during the August raid on the budget figures. The CAP, the French let it be known to all and sundry and the Italians in particular, was non-negotiable, and the demands that the British were making had little or nothing to do with the EMS. And in this latter respect at least they were almost certainly right. The connection between the concurrent studies and the EMS became increasingly tenuous, and the timetable to which the British worked had less and less to do with the deadlines imposed at Bremen. British officials would have concurred readily enough with M. Ortoli, who is alleged to have remarked to one of the Community finance ministers during the IMF meeting in Washington at the end of September that an overhaul of the budget of the kind that the British wanted would not be seriously considered until the Community itself began to run out of money in two or three years' time. That date, rather than the Brussels summit of December 1978, was crucial in their plans, and in the meantime it remained only to win the skirmishes and send bloodcurdling propaganda back from the front of the kind that began to appear with increasing frequency in the British press from August onwards[44].

Given the domestic political constraints under which they operated, the tactics adopted by British officials are in many respects intelligible and, in the light of what was subsequently achieved in 1980 as a result of these self-same tactics when the French were forced to give ground not by superior arguments but by material necessity, it is difficult not to admire the sheer professionalism and persistence of what one Italian newspaper described after the budget compromise as 'an ancient and arrogant diplomacy'[45]. But the costs of the 'victory' (which cannot by definition be calculated in terms of precise figures, but which are evident to anybody who has discussed Community politics for any length of time in Bonn, not to mention other Community capitals) were enormous, and it is legitimate to ask whether different tactics, which took account of the totally new situation created by an initiative sponsored personally and against the better judgement of their officials by the two most powerful leaders in Europe, might not have achieved comparable or still better results at much lower price to both Britain and the Community. It is a legitimate question because, although British participation in the EMS was finally made impossible by developments in domestic politics, the Labour Party conference, which as the next chapter will show was decisive in persuading Mr Callaghan that he could not take the British in, was not held until early in October, and during the weeks in which the EPC became hopelessly deadlocked the prime minister himself would seem to have wanted the negotiations to succeed. Like their counterparts in 1914–18, British officials had, one suspects, become so trapped in the habits and responses appropriate to campaigns characterized chiefly by immobility that they could not seize on an unexpected opportunity to break out of their entrenched positions and develop a new strategy.

Be that as it may, the polarization of opinion inside the EPC was virtually complete and irreversible by the end of September. According to the EPC report, there were certain members of the majority who believed that a review of the facilities currently available through the European Investment Bank, the Regional Fund and the Social Fund would be justified 'dès lors que seraient satisfaites les exigences fondamentales d'une coordination efficace des politiques pour un SME stable et durable'. But this qualification brought only limited comfort to the Irish and the Italians, not only because of the conditional character of the concession, but also because the whole tenor of the discussion about measures that might be taken if the governments did eventually decide that they were justified or necessary had revealed a strong preference on the part of the majority as a whole for loans rather than grants. The Irish in particular, with an economy that was dangerously overheated and a loan requirement that was already excessive, could not have relished the promise of more loans at an unspecified date in the future.

5.4   Aachen, Brussels and Washington, 14–30 September

By 14 September, the expert committees had completed the first phase of their work on the implementation of the decisions taken at Bremen, in time for the ECOFIN meeting scheduled to take place at Brussels on 18 September. Before this meeting was held, however, there was a meeting between the French president and the German chancellor at Aachen on 14 and 15 September that was the subject of widespread speculation and suspicion at the time and that must therefore be considered at this point.

The Aachen summit was in one sense no more than a routine meeting in the long-established six-monthly series between the French president and the German chancellor. Various factors conspired however, to make it appear different and special. One was simply that it was the first occasion for the two men to meet since Bremen and, given the significance of their individual contributions to that meeting, it was widely assumed, as the *Frankfurter Allgemeine Zeitung* reported on 14 September, that they would use the opportunity to 'settle' problems that had arisen between the representatives of their two countries during the technical discussions. This assumption, which seemed to be vindicated by the announcement that the two men would be accompanied by some of their top economic aides, including M. Clappier and his deputy on the French side and Dr Lahnstein, Dr Pöhl and Dr Schulmann on the German side, provoked in turn a bout of semi-public and public position-taking by interested parties, particularly in the Federal Republic, that enhanced the significance of the occasion still further.

The most important of these advance warnings to the chancellor – for that, in Germany, was what they always were – were delivered by Dr Emminger and his colleagues at a meeting with Mr Schmidt in Bonn on 13 September and by the official opposition a day later. Dr Emminger used the occasion to summarize the reservations that had been expressed at the meeting of the Central Bank Council in the previous week. He made five points:

1. With a view to reducing the risks to stability inherent in a scheme of the kind proposed, it would be advisable to begin cautiously, and in stages. In particular, he and his Bundesbank colleagues urged that no attempt should be made to admit all three non-Snake countries at once. Of the three, France seemed to them to be the most determined in the pursuit of stability and was therefore the most suitable candidate. As far as the others were concerned it might be possible to negotiate transitional arrangements, but nothing more conclusive should be contemplated.
2. Parity changes would clearly have to be reckoned with in the not too distant future and the system should therefore be sufficiently flexible to allow for them. In this respect, the Snake, in which Denmark had altered its exchange rate four times within the previous 24 months, provided a good precedent.
3. Credit facilities available under the system should be limited.

4. So too should the Bundesbank's obligations to intervene and the possibility of partner countries' intervening in DM.
5. The intervention system should be based on the parity grid rather than the basket.

A sixth point, which Dr Emminger assumed would not be immediately relevant, was also mentioned, namely the necessity to ensure that, if and when it was decided to create an EMF, the Bundesbank's autonomy to determine its own monetary policies should not be affected either directly or indirectly.

The intervention of the official opposition was equally forthright and sharp[46]. On the day that the chancellor travelled to Aachen, the CDU/CSU parliamentary group, in a motion signed by both Dr Köhl and Mr Strauss, demanded that the government should not present the Bundestag with a *fait accompli*, but that before any final decision was taken deputies should be given the chance to make their views known. The CDU/CSU, the statement declared, were, as they always had been, committed to the economic and political unity of Free Europe. However, they felt bound to express their anxiety about the new proposal on the basis of the information that was available to them. In their view, a spokesman explained, the conditions simply did not exist for the creation of a viable system. Furthermore, the plan for a massive Fund threatened to provide fresh fuel to inflation and to undermine the autonomy of the Bundesbank.

Interventions of this character from the president of the Bundesbank and the official opposition only served to reinforce expectations that decisions of major consequence would be taken at Aachen. Speculation was encouraged still further by official advance publicity[47]. The symbolic significance of Aachen was stressed, and it was made known that the two leaders would visit the throne of Charlemagne and attend a special concert in the Cathedral. Parallels were drawn with the meeting between Adenauer and de Gaulle at Reims 16 years earlier. That had announced the birth of a special relationship; the present meeting signified its renewed vitality and increasing importance. Far from putting an end to these questions, however, the meeting itself increased them. The impressiveness of the ceremonial and the evident satisfaction of the two principals with what had been achieved, coupled with rather less than informative press briefings by M. Hunt and Dr Grünwald, conveyed an impression of success without any clear indication of what precisely it consisted of[48]. A comment by the French president matched the mood of the occasion: 'Perhaps when we discussed monetary problems, the spirit of Charlemagne brooded over us'[49]. It implied that agreement had been reached, but it said nothing about the nature of the agreement. Perhaps it was little wonder therefore that while German and French newspapers celebrated a 'historical meeting'[50], others, particularly in Britain, speculated about what had happened and, with few exceptions, concluded the worst. A *Times* headline summarized a common assumption that, as Mr Healey's performance at the Brussels meeting of the ECOFIN on 18 September showed, was shared inside government as well as outside: 'France shifts towards German viewpoint'[51].

What was myth and what was reality? The answer, one suspects, is that the myth was by and large the reality. The agreement itself, set out in a document drafted by M. Clappier, Dr Lahnstein, Dr Schulmann and their colleagues on the evening of 14 September and put into final shape by the two leaders on the following morning, was by no means as specific or conclusive as the British chancellor of the exchequer feared. It made four main points:

1. a precondition of the durability of the new system was the convergence of member states' economies, which the system itself would naturally encourage, but which would be ensured above all by the commitment of all concerned to anti-inflationary policies.

2. the ECU would be used as the numeraire of the system, but interventions were to be based on a parity grid. The ECU might however 'serve a useful purpose as an indicator of divergence'. Both parties agreed that they wished to avoid a system which placed pressure on only one currency.

3. the concurrent studies were to continue, but the speed at which they advanced was not to delay progress towards a monetary agreement which, it was hoped, would be concluded at the next meeting of the European Council.

4. the commitment to create an EMF 'modelled on the IMF' remained intact, and work would be carried out to this end. In the meantime, however, financial arrangements in connection with the monetary system would be administered by the BIS through the EMCF.

The element in the agreement that was subject to most intense speculation and, on the British side, suspicion, was the section concerning the intervention system. If, however, one compares the text of the agreement with what the French representatives had said a week earlier at the Bergamo meeting with the Italians and, more generally, with what had become evident to most of the advocates of a system based exclusively on the ECU during the course of the expert discussions, the novelty of the Aachen agreement is considerably diminished. As the French minister of finance, M. Monory, noted when explaining his government's position at the ECOFIN of 18 September, 'il y a des difficultés techniques pour le panier pur'. There is, it is true, some evidence to suggest that French officials at Aachen, notably M. Clappier, would have liked certain parts of the text and in particular the phrases referring to the possible use of the ECU as an indicator of divergence to have been more definite. The final draft submitted by officials to the French president and his German colleague included, it is alleged, several bracketed phrases, and it was, according to this version, M. Giscard d'Estaing himself who approved the weaker references to the Belgian compromise that appeared in the final text. Be that as it may, the formula that was eventually adopted did not prevent M. Clappier from fighting energetically at the Committee of Central Bank Governors in October for a rigorous interpretation of the obligations that would arise if the divergence indicator showed that a currency was out of line. In other words, the Aachen agreement on the intervention system did no more than settle what the French had already been forced to admit outside a bilateral and exclusively Franco-German context, namely that there was no more mileage to be made out of 'le panier pur' and that it was in their own interests to concentrate henceforth on the possibilities offered by the Belgian compromise. What these possibilities were remained to be seen.

The principal significance of the Aachen agreement, and indeed of the meeting as a whole, lies elsewhere. It was firstly a reaffirmation in a symbolic setting of the fundamental importance to each of the governments concerned of the Franco-German partnership, which was sanctioned by history, underpinned by the necessity to overcome the self-destructive conflicts of the past (a point made by Mr Schmidt in his after-dinner speech), cemented by a common commitment to the pursuit of economic prosperity and growth based on stability and freedom, and led by two men who, as the French president claimed in one of two conspicuously warm after-dinner speeches, enjoyed a personal relationship that was unique amongst world leaders. Secondly, it provided an indication of the determination of both leaders that, whatever the technical problems, the timetable agreed by the European Council at Bremen should, at least as far as the monetary agreement was concerned, be adhered to and therefore, by implication, if others did not agree, they would proceed without them. It was, finally, a declaration of intent that, although transitional arrangements might be necessary, the system should in principle be more than the Snake, both in terms of its membership, which, contrary to the wishes of the Bundesbank, both the chancellor and the president and more particularly perhaps the former regarded as open to all Community states, and in terms of its institutions, mechanisms, facilities and objectives.

The sum of their agreement, it might be said, was more important than its parts. The latter, as the events of the following weeks were to demonstrate, could still be argued about and fought over within their own countries as much as between them or amongst their partners. The Aachen summit could not create a consensus on detail when many of the details themselves remained to be clarified before sides could be taken. What it could and did do was silence those who were beginning to argue that the timetable could not be adhered to at all. It reminded the technical experts, and more particularly the French and the Germans involved, of the political context in which they had to operate; it could not and did not determine the detailed outcome of their discussions.

The British, mistakenly, assumed that that was what had been done, or at least attempted. The most outspoken expression of their suspicions was made by Mr Healey at the ECOFIN meeting in Brussels on 18 September[52]. The meeting opened with statements by the chairmen of the Monetary and Central Bank Governors' committees, summarizing the findings of their respective committees. They were followed by Dr Lahnstein and M. Monory. Both, without actually stating that this was what they were doing, expounded their government's positions in terms anticipated at Aachen. On the intervention system, for example, Dr Lahnstein admitted that the Germans favoured the parity grid but that they were open to a discussion of the Belgian compromise proposal. What perhaps emerged most clearly, however, from both statements was the determination of the governments concerned to keep to the timetable laid down at Bremen, even if, as M. Monory noted, the concurrent studies, which were concerned with longer term problems, had not arrived at any firm conclusions. The French finance minister was followed by Mr Healey, who proceeded to engage in an aggressive cross-examination of M. Monory and Mr Matthöfer, aimed at uncovering 'what had happened at Aachen', which, as the contemporary notes and subsequent recollections of several of those present suggest, seemed – to at least some if not the majority of his colleagues – as tasteless as it was inappropriate. It was also unsuccessful. Following the contributions from the representatives of other member states, the Council agreed, despite the disapproval of the British chancellor, to instruct the expert committees to carry out further study of the Belgian formula.

The manner in which Mr Healey spoke at both the morning session, which was devoted to monetary matters, and the afternoon session, which dealt with the concurrent studies, and the fact that he followed up this performance with a series of public and semi-public attacks on the Franco-German plan in North America immediately afterwards, suggest that the chancellor of the exchequer had already decided that it was not in British interests to join the EMS. The general impression conveyed by Mr Healey and his officials at both the Commonwealth finance ministers' conference in Montreal on 21 and 22 September and the IMF meeting in Washington a few days later was certainly that Britain was unlikely to join[53]. The objections that they had to the scheme were in the main familiar, but the tone in which they were stated, particularly when equating the new system with a DM zone, recalled the early July press briefings of Mr Callaghan and Mr Couzens rather than the more conciliatory line laid down by the prime minister after Bremen. There were also some additional, bombastic touches. The French, it was implied, needed to join the new system for short-term reasons, because they would require access to German funds to prop up the franc in the New Year. The British, by contrast, did not, because their economy, unlike France's, was strong enough to stand on its own. It was a line of argument that prompted a number of reflections in the British press of which one at least, a leader in the *Financial Times*, is worth quoting[54]:

Mr Dennis Healey, it seems, has yet to learn the elementary lessons of negotiating. ... For a chancellor of the exchequer publicly to proclaim an indifference bordering on hostility to a major European initiative, and to base his case on an illusory notion of British economic strength can hardly make the British position any easier. ... A great deal of the workings of the Community as we know it are effectively up for renegotiation, not perhaps in one fell swoop, but gradually as EMS gets underway. ... There may, of course, be legitimate fears about how EMS will develop [but] the worst ground of all for lack of commitment would be the belief that the British economy somehow no longer needs the Community. There is no way in which such an approach can improve the British bargaining position either now or later when the belief is found to be false.

The chancellor's reservations, if not his way of expressing them, were almost certainly noted with approval by his senior Treasury advisers. It was widely believed however that they were not, at this stage at least, shared by the prime minister. Frances Cairncross in *The Guardian*[55] summed up the position as seen by Treasury officials with whom she had spoken in the following terms: 'here is a nutty and possibly damaging idea which the prime minister is embarrassingly keen on. Why doesn't somebody generate a public outcry against it before it is too late?' A few days later, despite Mr Healey's statements in North America, and writing, it would seem, on the basis of information from those who were in the position to know, Samuel Brittan added fresh support to the belief that, official scepticism notwith-standing, Mr Callaghan was more determined to join than had so far been realized[56]: 'Indeed I would give odds of between 2 and 3 to 1 in favour of the UK joining. It would take a major calamity on the industrial front at home – rather than any foreseeable negotiating difficulties here or in Brussels – to force the change of plan.' The low profile approach, Brittan argued, had been deliberately taken to avoid troubles with the Labour Party.

Whatever the truth of Mr Brittan's and others' assertions about the prime minister's personal preferences however, one is left with the impression at the end of the first post-Bremen negotiating phase that, firstly, the prime minister had not communicated his positive convictions with sufficient strength or consistency to his officials and colleagues between July and September, and, secondly, as a result Mr Healey and at least some of his officials had conducted the negotiations in such a way as to ensure the United Kingdom's isolation and to make entry exceedingly difficult if not impossible. As far as the first point is concerned, the observations of a very senior official concerned are of some interest. In contrast to other occasions when Mr Callaghan, as chancellor, foreign secretary or prime minister, had been responsible for international economic negotiations, he never once convened a conference to discuss tactics with those principally involved. To the official concerned, this suggested that the prime minister could not resolve his own doubts. Whether or not this is the explanation, the evidence discussed in this chapter suggests that, in the absence of strong political leadership, the British had manoeuvred themselves into positions, particularly in the EPC, but also in the ECOFIN and other bilateral and multilateral settings, from which it was difficult to imagine them moving out to join the system. Not everybody, of course, was as sceptical or as hostile as the Treasury officials with whom Frances Cairncross spoke. It was widely believed both abroad and in London, for example, that the governor of the Bank of England, Mr Richardson, and Mr McMahon were more positively disposed than their colleagues in the Treasury. But 'constructive caution', scepticism and, in the last weeks of September, outright aggression prevailed. The Labour Party conference in October may have settled the issue finally, but critics and sceptics were already in the ascendant before then.

The Italian case was, as ever, quite different. The contrast was evident not only in the ECOFIN meeting, where both the tone and the substance of Mr Pandolfi's observations differed significantly from Mr Healey's, but still more perhaps in the practical steps that officials in the Banca d'Italia, who were in many ways just as sceptical on professional grounds as their British colleagues, took to develop a new negotiating position on the basis of the Belgian compromise. As far as the ECOFIN meeting is concerned, it is sufficient to refer to Mr Pandolfi's contribution to the discussion of the concurrent studies. Unlike Mr Healey, who had launched into a tirade against the 'absurdities' of the current budgetary system in the Community, the Italian minister argued that, although current arrangements were in many respects extremely unsatisfactory, particularly as far as the CAP was concerned, the fundamental principles were often sound and the Italian government's aim in these negotiations was not therefore to transform the CAP or the budget as whole, but to bring about significant reforms in the way the policies were implemented.

The Banca d'Italia's response to the breakdown of the hopes that had been placed in the ECU is still more revealing and important, since it formed a basic point of reference for Italian negotiators during much of the final phase of talks between October and November. The paper outlining the strategy, 'A Blueprint for the EMS after the ECOFIN meeting of September 18', was written by Rainer Masera[57] at the request of the governor, Dr Baffi, and on the basis of discussions with the governor himself and other officials concerned in the negotiations. An attempt was also made, significantly enough, to interest the British, when immediately after the ECOFIN meeting Dr Masera went to London at governor Baffi's suggestion. British officials remained wedded to the ECU, however, and in particular to the proposal for a redefinition of the basket that assigned currencies fixed weights, which would remain unchanged even if the currency appreciated or depreciated. The Italians, who considered this approach a lost cause in political terms, believed by contrast that the Belgian compromise offered a real opportunity to break out of the philosophy that underlay the Snake without running into the technical problems that not only they, but also the British, admitted would arise in an ECU system pure and simple.

It is clearly beyond the scope of this book to discuss the Italian 'Blueprint' at length but, at the risk of oversimplifying an argument that was advanced with considerable subtlety and elegance, a brief summary of two of its main proposals seems appropriate and opportune. They concerned methods of calculating and revising the weights assigned to each currency within the basket, and measures to combine both the parity grid and the ECU proposal that allowed real scope to both systems. There was, in addition, an extended and extremely interesting discussion of the Fund, but as this was not to be a major topic of concern over the following weeks, this section can be ignored for the time being.

The proposals concerning the definition of the ECU were prompted by considerations that have already been explained in section 5.2, namely the inherent bias towards the strong that would result from a straightforward identification of the ECU with the existing EUA, and the problems that currency realignments would be bound to pose if, as in strict logic they ought to, they led automatically to a revision of all the currency rates inside the ECU. Starting on the assumption that the concession towards the parity grid system represented in the Belgian compromise would be sufficient to unfreeze negotiating positions on both sides, the Italian paper argued that the problems of heavyweight bias could be overcome if the Community adopted a broader approach when calculating the initial weights to be assigned to participating countries, taking account of three criteria: the GDP of the country concerned (its financial wealth), the openness of its economy, and the size of its population. Applying these criteria, Dr Masera reckoned that the result would be weightings of the order set out in column 1 in *Table 5.6*. A comparison with column 2, which gives the weightings that would have resulted if the ECU had been equated with the EUA without any revision in September 1978, illustrates the greater protection that the Italian system would have given to the weak. The Snake element in column 1 accounts for 46.17% of the total weight, whereas under existing arrangements it amounted to 55.13%.

As far as the revision of weights was concerned, the Italians were prepared to make significant concessions to the stronger currencies, though arrangements for a general revision every three to five years (the solution eventually adopted) were not excluded if these could be negotiated. The Bank of England position was, however, regarded as unrealistic. The solution that the Italians proposed envisaged that when parities were realigned the amounts of each currency should vary in such a way that the weighting of the basket (and its third currency value) remained unchanged with respect to the market-determined values of the day before the realignment, values that would of course reflect earlier movements within the established margins.

Table 5.6 *Methods of calculating the weights assigned to Community currencies within the basket*

	Italian 'Blueprint' weighting (1)	Unrevised weighting (2)
Belgium/Luxembourg	7.09	9.42
Denmark	2.56	3.08
Germany	28.09	32.35
France	20.41	20.23
Ireland	1.13	1.15
Italy	15.23	10.11
Netherlands	8.43	10.28
United Kingdom	17.06	13.38
	100.00	100.00
Snake	(46.17)	(55.13)

Source: 'A Blueprint for the EMS after the ECOFIN meeting of September 18'

This would allow for change, but would prevent discontinuity with regard to third currencies.

If the system was equipped with an ECU that was shorn of the disadvantages and complexities that attended the EUA, it should be possible, the paper argued, to devise arrangements along lines already indicated in the Belgian compromise, which gave real force to *both* intervention systems. To achieve this, however, it was essential that the ECU divergence indicator should operate early enough to give rise to significant remedial action on its own account. If the ECU margins were too close to the parity grid limits, the importance of the margins would inevitably be greatly reduced. The Italians therefore suggested that margins in the parity grid system should be wide, at least for the non-Snake currencies, but that ECU margins should by contrast be narrow (below 2%) and that when these margins were reached, real obligations would be entailed. This mixture of looseness and discipline was most suited, it was argued, to the current state of the European economy, where divergences between the weak and the strong were still too great for both to be fitted into a narrow system like the Snake. In due course, the wider non-Snake margins might be reduced as economic performance converged. Discipline would be ensured for the Snake by their narrower margins and for all by a divergence indicator with real teeth.

In the light of the subsequent debate, this last point is worth developing. In understanding the argument, it is important to recall that the Italians themselves had strong reservations about the ECU indicator's ability to pick out a single deviant, on the grounds that they feared that the deviant could just as well be the lira as the DM. The divergence indicator did not therefore entail the same automatic consequences as the parity grid. Instead, the first result of the alarm going off would be to initiate a consultation procedure to analyse and study the reasons for the divergence and to prepare a set of economic policy measures to ward off the dangers to the system represented by the currency's deviation. It would, however, also be taken for granted that, unless specifically excluded in the consultations, intervention would be the normal response to the indication of divergence. Consideration should also be given, it was argued, to the possibility of devising penalties against a strong currency country whose currency remained above its permitted ECU limit for more than a certain time. As the following chapter will show, this subtle combination of flexibility and discipline was to be the main characteristic of the Italians' negotiating position in both multilateral and bilateral settings in the weeks before the main agreement was reached. It was, needless to say, tailored to afford maximum protection to the Italian lira, but both the tone and the content of the strategy were characteristic of a government that was predisposed for high political reasons to work within rather than outside the Community system.

The remaining development in the second half of September that requires a brief discussion in this chapter was the spate of international economic conferences that gave European Community spokesmen an opportunity to explain the results that had emerged so far from the negotiations and gave non-Europeans a chance to react[58]. The two most important occasions were a meeting of the OECD's Working Party 3 on 21 September, and the annual IMF meeting in Washington a few days later. At the former, the principal Community spokesman was M. van Ypersele, who gave a report in his capacity as chairman of the Monetary Committee, while at the latter, all Community finance ministers and central bank governors were present but, as the Germans held the presidency, Mr Matthöfer had formal responsibility for explaining the current position. It was only to be expected that both official representatives were bland and reassuring, particularly as far as the potential conflict between the purposes of the system and the recently revised Article 4 of the IMF Articles of Agreement and EMF/IMF relations were concerned. The more important exchanges occurred outside the formal meetings, and on these occasions it was possible to detect continuing anxieties about the potential implications of the system amongst both the Americans and IMF representatives. In the case of the Americans, the approval in principle worked out before Bremen, which was discussed in the previous chapter, was reiterated by President Carter in his address to the Fund on 25 September[59], but behind the scenes, administration and more particularly Treasury officials subjected some of their European colleagues to cross-examinations only a little less aggressive and suspicious than the one Mr Healey had inflicted on his German and French colleagues a week earlier in Brussels. The principal sources of concern had already been evident in the pre-Bremen period, but the preoccupations were now more specifically and insistently formulated and they can therefore be analysed in greater detail at this point.

The first, and from the American point of view naturally the major, concern was about the possible implications that the EMS might have for the dollar. These anxieties were given extra point in September by the renewed pressure on the American currency that had built up since the end of July. The preparation of what was eventually to become the November package had already begun, and the curious mixture of anxiety that the dollar should remain at the centre of the international monetary system and fear about the risks involved in keeping it there was more in evidence than ever. In a global sense, therefore, the EMS could and did appear as either a rival moving in to put an end to the dollar system or a possible source of support in a role that was by now beyond the means of only one country or currency to sustain. There were, however, even to those disinclined to view the proposal in these universal and rather apocalyptic terms, at least four more specific sources of concern. Firstly, administration officials were worried that the European pool of reserves could be used to maintain an artificial dollar rate out of line with long-term market trends, by, for example, preventing or delaying the appreciation of the DM. Secondly, there was concern that to the extent that interventions in the EMS were to be made in dollars – and it was evident by September that this would be at least partly the case – pressures might build up on the dollar even greater than those that had been exerted in the past by sales of dollars in support of Snake members. Thirdly, despite the assurances of Mr Schmidt at the Bonn summit, officials still feared that the EMS might have an overall deflationary effect on the European economies, which would in turn have adverse repercussions on the American currency. Fourthly, whatever the declared intentions of the EMS, central banks might be encouraged by its emergence to unwind their dollar holdings still further.

The second major topic of concern involved gold. The administration was committed to a progressive reduction of the role of gold in the international monetary system, and its intentions on this score had been reaffirmed in both word and deed on several occasions over the previous months. The important place that certain Community central banks had always assigned to gold in their official reserves had long been a source of concern, and it was therefore only to be expected that the reference to deposits of gold in the new Fund in the Bremen Annex should have given rise to anxiety that the EMS might encourage a revival of the role of the metal in the international monetary system. Another, related point, which had already come up in the specialist committees on the other side of the Atlantic, concerned the valuation of the gold exchanged for ECUs, since if market rates were adopted this would mean an increase in official reserves and a possible boost to inflation.

The third potential source of problems concerned IMF personnel as much as the American administration. Despite widespread acknowledgement that the present international system was far from perfect, the majority of US and IMF officials remained convinced that the combination of floating, conscientious observation of the spirit as well as the letter of the amended Article 4, IMF surveillance and western summitry was almost certainly the best that could be hoped for in the immediate or even the medium-term future. Under the revised Article 4 and the interpretative guidelines that were endorsed by the Interim Committee at its meeting in April 1977[60], members were given a considerable latitude in their choice of exchange rate practices: they could float freely or manage their floating; they could peg their rates to one currency or a basket of currencies; they could even be part of a fixed exchange rate system of the Snake variety. But they were expected in return to avoid the manipulation of exchange rates in order to prevent effective balance of payments adjustments or to gain unfair competitive advantage over other members, to counter disorderly short-term conditions on the markets and to take account of the interests of others. They were also expected to accept the surveillance of the IMF, which might, if their own affairs were seriously out of order, mean submitting to investigation and adopting disagreeable policy recommendations. Against this background, the EMS was viewed with some suspicion as a covert threat to both the floating regime and the role of the IMF itself in its dual capacity as the supreme supervisor of the international monetary system and the most important source or guarantor of funds for countries in payments difficulties. As a 'mini-Bretton Woods', the EMS would, it was believed, inevitably fail for the reasons that Bretton Woods had failed, and its failure would increase the western world's woes. As a mini-IMF, it would undermine the authority of the IMF itself in the international monetary system, tending inevitably to make the IMF a Third World or minor powers' bank, and it might, if the rules governing the conditionality of credit were weaker than those applied under the IMF, contribute towards an increase in international liquidity. (Given the role of the Dutch and the Germans in IMF affairs over the previous decades, this particular fear seems, to say the least, a trifle far-fetched.) There was an additional anxiety that, in their efforts to make it successful, the European governments might introduce capital controls.

These and other questions about the EMS were widely aired in the course of the September meetings in Washington. It would be a mistake, however, to imply that everybody felt equally concerned and that anybody indeed felt excessively alarmed. It was still too early to judge, and the combination of those Europeans, by no means all British, who suggested that nothing would come of the plan anyway and those who believed in it, but stressed its benign intentions and implications, was distinctly reassuring. There were even some officials who welcomed the initiative, and even those who did not were under strict instructions to bridle their anxieties in public. It was alleged, for example, that Mr Blumenthal's speech to the IMF meeting was censored by the White House itself and, although a less direct control was exercised within the IMF, it was evident from early on in his reign that the new managing director, M. de Larosière, did not share the strong feelings on the subject held by some of the senior officials at the Fund. The net effect of the Washington meetings in terms of the development of the EMS negotiations was, in other words, neutral.

1 *Frankfurter Allgemeine Zeitung*, 26 June 1978
2 ibid., 6 July 1978
3 ibid.
4 ibid., 8 July 1978
5 ibid., 13 July 1978
6 ibid.
7 *Le Monde*, 11 July 1978
8 *The Times*, 7 July 1978
9 *La Lettre de la Nation*, 10 July 1978
10 *Hansard*, House of Commons, 10 July 1978, cols 1025ff.
11 *The Times*, 10 July 1978
12 *The Daily Telegraph*, 10 July 1978
13 *Hansard*, House of Commons, 10 July 1978, cols 1027ff.
14 ibid., col. 1032
15 ibid., col. 1034
16 See *The Financial Times*, 1 December 1978, for a useful description of the British negotiating team
17 *Economic Policy Review*, March 1978, pp. 44ff.
18 *The United Kingdom and the European Communities*, Cmnd. 4715, July 1971, HMSO, London
19 See *The Guardian*, 12 July 1978
20 *Sunday Times*, 16 July 1978
21 ibid., 23 July 1978
22 *The Times*, 13 July 1978
23 Banca d'Italia, *Abridged Version of the Report for 1979*, p. 72
24 *La Repubblica*, 2 August 1978
25 See *Corriere della Sera*, 25 July 1978
26 ibid., 1 September 1978
27 *The European Monetary System*. Prime Minister Cmmd. 7419, HMSO, London, 1978
28 *Financial Times*, 9 August 1978
29 *Irish Times*, 8 July 1973
30 See *European Economy*, 1979, no. 4, Statistical Annex
31 See Dail Eireann, *Parliamentary Debates*, *Official Report*, vol. 308, col. 426, Statement by Mr Colley, 17 October 1978
32 *Eurobaromètre*, no. 9, July 1978, p. 28
33 D. Keogh, 'Ireland, The Vatican and Catholic Europe 1916–39', unpublished doctoral thesis, European University Institute, Florence, 1980
34 *European Economy*, 1970, no. 4, Statistical Annex
35 For an official view of the dangers in the current situation, see the White Paper, *National Development 1978–81*, Stationery Office, Dublin, December 1978
36 Italian Senate, *Rassegna della Stampa, Il sistema monetario europeo*, vol. I, *documento presentato dal Governatore della Banca d'Italia alla Commissione Finanze e Tesoro del Senato*, 26 October 1978
37 Dail Eireann, *Parliamentary Debates*, Official Report, vol. 308, cols 1041ff
38 See above ch. 2, p. 51f.
39 The essence of the Irish case is contained in the White Paper on the EMS, *The European Monetary System. Paper laid before both Houses of the Oreaditas*, the Stationery Office, Dublin, December 1978. See especially pp. 9–11. The paper prepared for the EPC in August 1978 was leaked to the *Irish Times* in October; see *Irish Times*, 19 October 1978
40 This too was leaked; see *La Repubblica*, 14 September 1978
41 *Official Journal of the European Communities*, 31 January 1979, European Parliament, Answer to Written Question by Lord Bessborough, no. 607/78 (22.12.78)
42 Speech to the Institut für Auslandskunde, Munich, 9 March 1978
43 Most of the information contained in table 5.5 was conveyed in the Answer to Lord Bessborough; see note 41 above. It was also leaked to many newspapers in November 1978
44 See, for example, *The Times*, 11 August 1978

45 *Corriere della Sera*, 31 May 1980
46 *Frankfurter Allgemeine Zeitung*, 15 September 1978
47 For example, *Frankfurter Allgemeine Zeitung*, and *Le Monde*, 14 September 1978
48 *Frankfurter Allgemeine Zeitung* and *Le Monde*, 16 September 1978
49 Quoted in *Corriere della Sera*, 16 September 1978
50 For example, *Frankfurter Allgemeine Zeitung*, 16 September 1978
51 *The Times*, 16 September 1978
52 See *The Guardian*, 19 September 1978
53 See *The Times*, 22 and 28 September 1978

54 *Financial Times*, 25 September 1978
55 *The Guardian*, 23 September 1978
56 *Financial Times*, 5 October 1978
57 Dr Masera's numerous writings on the EMS include:
L'unificazione monetaria e lo SME, Bologna, 1980; 'The operation of the EMS; a European view', *Economia Internazionale*, **XXXII**, (45), 1979, pp. 371–96; see also references in Conclusions, note 1, below.
58 See *Europa-Archiv*, 22/1978, D 609ff
59 ibid., D 625ff
60 See IMF, *Annual Report*, 1977, pp. 45ff. and 1978, p. 55

The launching of the EMS:
October 1978–March 1979

Work in the technical committees and the ECOFIN continued in October and November 1978 and, by the beginning of December, draft agreements covering both the monetary system itself and the 'measures designed to strengthen the economies of the less prosperous member states of the EMS' were ready for consideration by the European Council at its meeting in Brussels on 4 and 5 December. The final phase of the negotiations was, however, still more heavily politicized than the previous one and an account of the events that preceded the Resolution of the Council on 5 December must therefore include an analysis of the domestic political debate in the five countries for whom the EMS proposal raised special problems and offered special opportunities (France, Germany, Ireland, Italy and the United Kingdom), the bewildering sequence of bilateral discussions that accompanied and influenced the more formal multilateral meetings of ministers and officials and, by no means least, the European Parliament's unexpected intrusion into the subjects raised by the concurrent studies.

The complex interaction of domestic and international developments during these months makes it extremely difficult to organize the material concerned into meaningful and intelligible shape without either oversimplification or duplication. The following pages doubtless contain examples of both, but the arrangement adopted attempts to do justice to both the primacy of national governments and the relative autonomy of the technical negotiations, which, though now conducted in more numerous settings than they had been previously, still possessed a coherence and momentum of their own. The first section therefore contains an analysis of developments at national level in the five states mentioned, while the second and third examine the discussions of monetary issues and the question of resource transfers, both in the multilateral settings provided by the ECOFIN and its related committees, and in some of the numerous bilateral meetings of ministers and officials that were such a conspicuous feature of these months. Against this background, it should be possible to understand both the nature of the agreement reached at Brussels in December and the curious obstacles that still had to be overcome in the European Council itself and then in a fresh round of multilateral, bilateral and domestic bargaining between December and March 1979 before, more than two months overdue, the EMS was eventually launched.

6.1 Aspects of the domestic political debate about the EMS and related issues in Germany, France, Italy, the United Kingdom and the Republic of Ireland, October–December 1978

Germany

The driving force behind the EMS negotiations in the period since the German chancellor decided to launch a monetary initiative had been the personal commitment of Mr Schmidt himself and the French president. For much of the period remaining before the Brussels meeting of the European Council this continued to be the case. Whether abroad or at home, apart or together, they dominated the scene. Not all roads led to Paris or Bonn – the French president went to Rome and the German chancellor to Siena – but few doubted that it was in the French and German capitals that the crucial decisions were and would be taken. The will to overcome the issues on which their own officials differed, which was demonstrated most clearly in the Rambouillet meeting at the beginning of November and in the contributions that both governments made to the ECOFIN meeting on 20 November, left them, it seemed, with a margin of largess sufficient to accommodate the special pleading of the Irish and the Italians. Then, rather suddenly, and to the great surprise it would seem not only of their seven Community partners but also of the Germans, the double act began to break down. There was some hint of the trouble to come at the Frankfurt meeting of officials at the beginning of December. It was not until the European Council meeting itself, however, that the rift became general knowledge and the Germans – who still, it seemed, went to Brussels expecting a triumph – found themselves cast in the rather undignified role of go-betweens, running from the French, to the Irish and the Italians in an abortive attempt to save the Grand Design.

The roots of this breakdown are complex and, as the following sections will show, much of the trouble stemmed from developments in the multilateral and bilateral negotiations on the transfer of resources. The most basic explanation, however, is to be found in the differing domestic political fortunes of the two men. Of the German chancellor, relatively little needs to be said. His political base had been strong before the initiative was launched, and the events of the summer and early autumn, and in particular the Aachen meeting, reinforced it still further at both elite and popular levels. Scepticism and hostility towards the project itself were still widespread, but the public statements and private comments of the critics betrayed their awareness that, whatever they said, the scheme would go ahead, while the observations of the chancellor in the private talks that he had with his fellow Community leaders suggested that, although he knew it would be prudent not to act as an entirely free agent, there was no need to pretend to be an unfree one. He used the reservations of the Bundesbank, the financial community, the opposition and some of the more authoritative commentators where it suited him; he was not bound by them when it did not.

The point can be illustrated by events in October when, following a fresh realignment in the Snake, there was a flurry of public discussion about what this implied for the new system. The most prominent contributor to this debate was Dr Emminger, who in a widely publicized address to an employers' meeting in Baden-Baden on 21 October[1] drew the gloomiest conclusions from the experiences of the previous weeks. Those who argued that the realignment set the scene for the EMS were clutching at straws, he argued. The real lessons of the latest troubles inside the Snake were much less reassuring. He himself mentioned four. Firstly, if the defence of existing parities with a few small states could result in an inflow of DM 10 billion within a very short space of time, what would happen if and when there was a crisis of confidence in a system that included three much larger states, Britain, France and Italy? Currency inflows of the dimensions that might be experienced then could undermine the monetary policies of the country on the receiving end, and monetary targets would become totally unrealistic and untenable. Secondly, realignments were difficult enough as matters stood at present, but they were bound to be even harder to achieve when the larger countries joined, because prestige considerations and concern about the possible domestic political consequences of a realignment would play a much more important role than they did with the smaller states. Thirdly, the accession of three countries who between them had gold and dollar reserves amounting to $100 billion would increase both the stakes and the risks in any crisis and, if even a quarter or a third of these funds were mobilized in the defence of one or other of the currencies, the EMS would be brought to a crisis point. Finally, if four realignments within 18 months and enormous interest rate differentials had been necessary to keep the Danes within the same system as the Germans, even though the difference in their inflation rates was 'only' 9%, it was inconceivable that the EMS would escape with less, when the differences in inflation rates between the Germans and some of the new members would be even greater. Similar considerations were advanced by the Advisory Board to the Economic Ministry, composed of experts from the five major economic institutes of the Federal Republic, in their report that was released on 23 October[2]. There was also a rather colourful publicity campaign in the press financed by the leading German banks, which showed a coat stand with a hat on it remarkably like the naval cap favoured by the chancellor. The caption underneath read: 'those who are in favour of stable money need to put their economic system under the same hat'[3]. However, to judge by what the German chancellor said to the president of the Commission when the two men met on 27 October, or to the Italian prime minister at Siena a few days later, Mr Schmidt remained undeterred. He was committed to the success of the initiative, he told Mr

Jenkins, and that, as he indicated to Mr Andreotti, included the participation of all non-Snake countries who were prepared to join. Far from being relieved by the news that Britain would not enter, he made no attempt to conceal his annoyance and contempt.

In other words, he courted his critics but he did not buy their approval with concessions that he knew could not be honoured at Community level or ran counter to the underlying purposes of his plan. The delicate balance between consultation and freedom was illustrated once again in the most striking manner possible at the end of November, a few days before the European Council meeting, when, the first chancellor in the history of the Republic to do so, he travelled to Frankfurt and took part in a meeting of the Central Bank Council of the Bundesbank on 30 November[4]. It was a gesture of conciliation, but it was scarcely a new Canossa. The chancellor had made concessions to his critics in the Bank, but the list of concessions that they and their allies in Bonn had been obliged to make in return – over the inauguration of a system that the majority of them would have preferred to have done completely without, over the Belgian compromise, over the size and distribution of credits, over the membership of the new system and the aid that, as the events of the following days were to show, the chancellor, if not his French colleague, was ready to extend to the Irish and the Italians in order to enable them to participate – was even longer and more impressive. The chancellor, it seemed, even to those who resented the fact, had won, and preparations to mark his triumphant return were already in train before he left for the Brussels Council.

France

For almost the entire period between the beginning of October and the beginning of December, the French president had seemed in an equally strong position, despite some sharp and in certain instances extremely penetrating attacks on the EMS initiative by critics on both the right and the left, by former officials and current ones[5]. The theme of most of the criticisms, whatever their provenance, was essentially the same. M. Giscard d'Estaing, *l'Humanité* declared on 26 October, the day that the president went to Rome, had become 'le courtier des intérêts Ouest-allemands'[6]. Shortly afterwards, *Le Monde Diplomatique* carried an essay by Daniel Biron and Alexander Faire that was probably the most substantial and certainly one of the longest variations on the theme[7]. Entitled, 'Le marc souverain', it was an extremely closely argued essay that set out to explain why the Germans had changed their attitude towards monetary integration, what the implications of the proposal were for Germany's non-Snake partners and in particular for France, and why the French president had identified himself so closely with it. As far as the first of these points was concerned, ignoring it would seem the almost universal misgivings about the

system amongst precisely those Germans who were responsible for economic and financial policies in Bonn and Frankfurt, the authors interpreted the
initiative as an act of national self-interest designed to preserve Germany's
freedom to persist with the deflationary policies that, contrary to the wishes
of the international community, the Federal government had maintained
throughout the recession. This autonomy, it was argued, had been put at
risk by the fall of the dollar and the insistence of the Americans and others
that the Germans and the Japanese should 'help' by reflating their economies. In this situation, the German authorities had concluded that a zone of
monetary stability would provide German exporters with secure markets,
while they themselves would retain their freedom to stimulate or restrain
demand in their own interests as and when it pleased them. This relative
insulation from the ravages that defective American leadership and the
falling dollar threatened would also greatly strengthen the Germans' hand
when applying pressure on the Americans themselves to put their house in
order. For the plan to be successful however, the compliance of the French
was essential. The parliamentary elections of 1978 had therefore been a vital
precondition of its implementation, since they had reinforced the position of
an administration bent on deflationary policies in line with the Germans'
own. Before these elections, the Germans' hopes of imposing their economic policies on the European Community had been limited; after them they
could work through and with a willing, but subordinate partner in the
creation of a system, the net effect of which would be bound to be
deflationary.

This analysis of the Germans' objectives naturally prompted the question
why the French government, and in particular the president, had accepted
partnership on these terms. The reason, the authors suggested, was that the
government saw a chance of reinforcing its authority in the domestic
economy by recourse to the constraints and, in certain circumstances, the
inducements that would be brought into existence through the system. If,
for example, there was a 'hot Spring' in 1979, the government could appeal
to the necessities imposed on it by membership of the system when
negotiating with the dissident social partners. By the same token, if a
pre-election boom seemed necessary in advance of the presidential elections
in 1981, France's good standing with the authorities in the Federal Republic
would enable the government to negotiate credits on generous terms: 'Ainsi
le gouvernement français appelle-t-il à travers le système monétaire européen, une immense accrue de la RFA dans la politique intérieure française.
Pour lui il ne s'agit pas d'un mal, mais d'un bien ...' More generally, the
French government's willingness to accept what the authors described as a
'folding seat beside the command post in the European economy' reflected
the obsession of the present rulers of France with Germany's economic
success, an obsession, they argued, that was absurd and dangerous. By their

own admission the short-term costs of their deflationary policies would be savage. The long-term assumptions on which they were based were, however, illusory. The social and industrial situation in France was radically different from that which obtained in Germany. To imitate the latter's economic success would mean refashioning French society on the German model; 'Et quelle importance pourrait avoir la dépendance ou l'indépendance à l'égard des Etats-Unis si l'Europe était en définitive condamnée au modèle allemand?'

Far from combating criticisms of this nature however, the president seemed almost to invite them. His 'obsession with Germany' was explained and justified in a long interview with M. Servan Schreiber on French television on 16 October[8], which was remarkable for both its candour and its confidence and, as a guide to the ideas and the style of M. Giscard d'Estaing in this most triumphalist phase of his presidential career, it could scarcely be bettered. The subjects covered were numerous, the perspectives broad. The essentials of his argument can however be summarized relatively briefly. In a world in which the risk of a major war involving the use of nuclear weapons had almost disappeared, the principle of competition was still basic in the international system, but it worked itself out principally in the economic sphere. Whereas France was now, in his opinion, the third of the world's military powers (after the USA and the USSR, but ahead of Britain and China), she was only the fifth amongst the major economic powers and was still a long way behind the Big Four – the United States, the Soviet Union, Germany and Japan. To have reached this position was itself a remarkable achievement and had involved passing Britain with whom, in a previous generation, relations had been characterized chiefly by French feelings of inferiority. There was, however, still a long road to travel before France could become the equal of the nearest of the Big Four in size and location, namely Germany. Furthermore, to achieve this goal against the background of a continuing crisis in the world's supply of energy and other essential raw materials, the country would have to submit to economic policies designed to encourage exports, particularly of goods involving high technology and skilled labour, and reduce inflation, and overcome the fundamental impediments to success represented by her political and social instability. Within 15 years, the president claimed, France could, if her people showed the necessary determination and her leaders pursued the right policies, achieve the objective of equality with Germany. The risks of failure were great, not only for France, but for Western Europe as a whole, since the way would be open to the consolidation of German hegemony.

> Why do I talk so much about Germany…? Because it would not be a good idea for Europe to be dominated by one country.… What I want France to achieve is to make sure that there are in Europe at least two countries of comparable influence, … Germany and France.

The changes in French domestic politics that began to undermine the apparently smooth and triumphant progress of the Franco-German initiative, and that go a long way towards explaining the disagreeable surprises of 4 and 5 December and the still more unexpected veto on the inauguration of the system itself on 1 January, derived their force in the first instance from two sources, neither of them directly related to the monetary plan: the initiation of the electoral campaign for the European Parliament and the complaints of French agricultural interests, who made their discontents known in certain areas through well-established forms of direct action. The mobilization of political forces that these two issues caused seems to have prompted the president to try to use the opportunity offered by the European Council to pre-empt the ground that his critics inside the majority were moving towards, and a fortnight later forced him, possibly against his own better judgement, to take an even more determined and damaging stand in defence of the ground that he had claimed as his own.

M. Chirac, the leader of the RPR, had reaffirmed his readiness to honour the political 'truce' within the majority as late as 10 October[9]. Within a very short space of time however, this truce was beginning to look distinctly ragged, as the RPR was pushed rather than led into a series of confrontations with Giscardian elements in the majority by a combination of internal rivalry and confused loyalties to tribal taboos sparked off by the opening of the public debate about the direct elections to the European Parliament. It seems, as so often, to have been M. Debré who made the running. The particular question on which he opened his attack was the decision by the Council of Ministers and the European Parliament to allocate funds from the Community budget to a publicity campaign designed to inform the public, in a non-partisan manner, about the powers and responsibilities of the Parliament to which they were called to elect members for the first time. In a speech in the Assemblée Nationale on 6 October – a few days, that is, before M. Chirac reaffirmed the truce – M. Debré denounced the decision as a financial scandal and an invitation to corruption[10]. His personal campaign to prevent the implementation of this decision was to lead in due course to one of the more spectacular challenges to the president's authority in parliament in December. In October, however, it marked the beginning of a confused and at times extremely emotional debate within the RPR itself about the strategy that they should adopt during the election campaign, which in turn gave rise to a series of challenges to the government to demonstrate its fidelity to the fundamental principles of the Fifth Republic.

Four of these challenges are particularly noteworthy. The first was the call that went out from the RPR Congress on 12 November demanding that the president should extract from his Community partners an explicit promise that the powers of the European Parliament would not in any way be increased following the direct elections[11]. The second was more mundane, but in its way still more damaging to the majority, since it took the form of a parliamentary revolt on 30 November in which RPR deputies joined the Communists and the Socialists to block a proposal designed to bring French VAT legislation into line with the decision of the Council of Ministers in May 1977 to transfer to the Community VAT revenues equivalent to up to 1% of GDP[12]. Several members of the RPR group in the Assembly would seem to have been surprised by the line that the majority of their colleagues took, and some of the most senior amongst them were openly critical. As M. Cointat wrote in *Le Monde* on 7 December apropos the vote: 'comment bâtir l'Europe si la France refuse à ses partenaires du marché commun d'appliquer ses propres lois?'[13] These divisions, which were also apparent on other issues, helped to explain why, a week after the negative vote, the measure was eventually approved in slightly revised form[14]. The revolt was nonetheless a sharp reminder to the president that, however confused the Gaullists might still be about how to conduct the election campaign, 'le débat européen' was once more at the centre of French politics and his opponents could therefore be expected to make the maximum political capital out of any apparent slip on his part. Confirmation of this point was to come while the president was actually in the Brussels Council, when the Law Committee in the Assemblée Nationale approved an RPR motion banning any Community subsidy for the election campaign in France[15]. A week later, this ban was to be upheld in the Assemblée Nationale itself when, led by Michel Debré, the RPR voted with the Communists against the UDF, while the Socialists abstained[16]. In immediate terms, it was to set the scene for the fourth of the challenges: an appeal to the French people, issued by M. Chirac from his hospital bed at Cochin on 6 December, the day after the president returned from Brussels. Strident, emotional, even hysterical, it provides the clearest indication of the electoral atmosphere that had built up in Paris in the days and weeks immediately preceding the European Council and to which the president seemed to many to be pandering, not only within the Council itself, but still more in the statements to the French media with which he punctuated its proceedings[17]:

> L'élection prochaine de l'Assemblée Européenne au suffrage universel direct ne saurait intervenir sans que le peuple français soit exactement éclairé sur la portée de son vote. Elle constituera un piège si les électeurs sont induits à croire qu'ils vont simplement entériner quelques principes généraux, d'ailleurs à peu près incontestés quant à la nécessité de l'organisation européenne, alors que les suffrages ainsi captés vont servir à légitimer tout ensemble les débordements futurs et les carences actuelles, au préjudice des intérêts nationaux.

> 1. le gouvernment français soutient que les attributions de l'Assemblée resteront fixées par le traité de Rome et ne seront pas modifiées en conséquence du nouveau mode d'élection ... Mais la plupart de nos partenaires énoncent l'opinion opposée ...

2. L'approbation de la politique européenne du gouvernement sup-
    poserait que celle-ci fut clairement affirmée à l'égard des errements
    actuels de la Communauté – en dehors d'une politique agricole
    commune, d'ailleurs menacée – tend à n'être aujourd'hui, guère plus
    qu'une zone de libre échange favorable peut-être aux intérêts étran-
    gers les plus puissants ...
3. L'admission de l'Espagne et du Portugal dans la Communauté
    soulève, tant pour nos intérêts agricoles que pour le fonctionnement
    des institutions communes, de très sérieuses difficultés ...
4. La politique européenne du gouvernement ne peut en aucun cas
    dispenser la France d'une politique étrangère qui lui soit propre.
    L'Europe ne peut servir à camoufler l'effacement d'une France qui
    n'aurait plus sur le plan mondial, ni autorité ni idée ni message ni
    visage ...

Comme toujours quand il s'agit de l'abaissement de la France, le parti de
l'étranger est à l'oeuvre avec sa voix paisible et rassurante. Français, ne
l'écoutez pas. C'est l'engourdissement qui précède la paix de la mort.
Mais comme toujours quand il s'agit de l'honneur de la France, partout
des hommes vont se lever pour combattre les partisans du renoncement et
les auxiliaires de la décadence.
Avec gravité et résolution je vous appelle dans un grand rassemblement de
l'espérance à un nouveau combat, celui pour la France de toujours dans
l'Europe de demain.

The other major source of domestic disquiet in the weeks before Brussels
were the problems of French agriculture. During the television interview
that he gave immediately after his return from the Council, the president
went as far as to say that the difficulties of French farmers had, in his view,
been 'at the centre of our discussions'[18]. The connection between agricultural unrest and the new monetary system, which might at first sight appear
improbable, was provided principally by the MCAs, the device that had
been developed by the Community to meet the threat posed to the operation
of the CAP by the breakdown of fixed exchange rates. The question of the
MCAs emerged in several different contexts in the course of the EMS
negotiations. They had been used in August, for example, to challenge the
accuracy of the British case on the UK's contributions to the Community
budget, while the Italian minister of agriculture, Mr Marcora, made several
speeches urging their abolition in the course of the debate about the EMS in
November[19]. French disquiet, however, was conspicuous both for its
intensity and for the anti-German character that it assumed.
The grievances that many French farmers nursed against the Federal
Republic were intelligible and well founded[20]. They stemmed from the
sharp deterioration that had occurred between 1975 and 1978 in France's
surplus in the bilateral trade in agricultural produce, which had traditionally

made a major contribution towards offsetting the massive deficit in the exchange of manufactured goods, and as such had been one of the principal material supports of the Franco-German partnership. In the first half of 1975, the value of French agricultural exports to Germany had been 284% higher than the value of agricultural imports from the Federal Republic. By the first half of 1978, the cover had dropped below 200%. In 1976, the German market had taken 19% of French agricultural exports; in the first half of 1978, the proportion had dropped to 16.6%. At the same time, German agricultural exports to France had increased from a share equivalent to 6.6% during the period 1972–76 as a whole, to 7.9% in 1977 and 8.4% in the first half of 1978. Some sectors had been worse hit than others. French beef exports, for example, had declined between 1977 and 1978 by 26%, while their imports had increased by 21%. Pig farmers had if anything suffered even more. In the course of two years, the number of sows in the Federal Republic had increased by 13% (in Holland the increase was 25%), while in France it had declined by 10%.

It was perhaps going too far to say, as Jacques Grall did, that the future of French agriculture was at risk, but the trends were undoubtedly disquieting from the French point of view. The 'inefficient' German farmer, whom they had not previously minded subsidizing through the CAP because, it was assumed, he could be relied upon to buy a Mercedes rather than increase his exports, might just, it seemed, follow his more fearsome cousins in the manufacturing industries and sweep Europe. Various explanations could be and were given, but the most important and convincing linked the phenomenon with the distortions introduced into the Community market in agricultural produce by the currency movements of the 1970s. Their impact could be seen at at least three levels. Firstly, common prices, which had been from the beginning one of the three fundamental props of the CAP (the others were the common external tariff and Community preference), had become an unattainable ideal, as prices had been renationalized by devaluations and revaluations. Secondly, the MCAs, which had been introduced to combat the ill-effects, had themselves become in some measure at least a subsidy to German, and other strong currency exporters. Thirdly, the increasing sophistication of modern farming meant that farmers had to invest heavily in plant, chemicals and other products of the manufacturing sector and here again strong currency countries were at an obvious advantage.

The perverse effects of exchange rate instability and more particularly of the MCAs had, of course, been evident for a long time, and the Commission and other Community countries had pressed for the dismantling of the system on more than one occasion. Why therefore, one might ask, did the issue suddenly become important enough for the French president to blow first the European Council, then the EMS itself off course? The answer it seems, has to be found in the conjunction of a fresh bout of unrest in the

French farming community and the opening of the debate about Europe to which reference has already been made above. French farmers, *Le Monde* remarked at the beginning of December[21], were disinclined to withdraw to their winter quarters. As always since the inauguration of the CAP, the discontents of pig farmers and milk producers in France had a European dimension, the importance of which was immensely increased on this occasion, however, by the fresh twist that the election campaign had given to French politics. Some indication of the significance that controversies about agriculture had assumed can be found in two developments that occurred in Paris on 5 December while the president himself was in Brussels. The first was the announcement that on the insistence of the RPR the Assemblée Nationale would hold a debate on agriculture on 14 December and the second a decision by the UDF to issue a questionnaire on agriculture problems, the responses to which would serve as the basis for a 'day of reflection' in February, which was itself part of the group's build-up to the European elections[22].

In these circumstances, it was perhaps understandable that the French president should have decided to press the demand for the dismantling of the MCAs as hard as he could in the context of the EMS negotiations in Brussels. It was an obvious occasion for him to do so and, had he been successful, it would have been a major bonus in his struggle to keep the Gaullists in line. His government actually gave advance warning of his intentions through an article by Philip Lemaître that appeared in *Le Monde* on the eve of the Council meeting[23]. Nobody should have been surprised, therefore, by the emphasis that he placed upon this point, or by his insistence that Community rules could not be bent to make concessions under the Regional Fund to Italy and Ireland at a time when the Council was engaged in a conflict with Parliament. What did and still does seem remarkable is that he pushed his electioneering to the point of breakdown. The domestic political situation may explain his behaviour; it scarcely justifies it.

Italy

The Italian negotiating position, both in its original form when hopes still existed of devising a workable ECU-based system, and in the revised version set out by the Banca d'Italia in its 'Blueprint' at the beginning of October, has already been described at length in the previous chapter. In the course of October and November, it was to undergo further changes in response to pressures and setbacks in the bilateral and multilateral negotiations, which will be discussed in the following sections. These shifts in emphasis and detail were not, however, comparable in importance to the change in the atmosphere and context in which the Italian negotiators worked from October onwards in Italy itself. In the period between July and September,

Mr Pandolfi, governor Baffi and their associates and subordinates had been left by and large to their own devices. After October this was no longer the case. The change was signalled and symbolized by Mr Pandolfi's speech to the Camera dei Deputati on 10 October and the consultations with representatives of the majority that preceded and followed it[24], and by governor Baffi's exposition of the Italian government's objectives, first at the Forex Club Congress at Ischia on 15 October and then, in still more detail, before the Senate Committee on Financial and Treasury Affairs on 26 October[25]. Italian strategy and tactics became in other words matters for public, political debate. This development in turn brought about a further change. Whereas before 1 October the technocrats had been the key figures for most of the time, their role was now increasingly overshadowed in importance by that of the prime minister, Mr Andreotti. They were still, it is true, left considerable leeway in the technical discussions and, at his meetings with the French president, the German chancellor, the British prime minister and the Benelux leaders, Mr Andreotti called upon them to present the detailed arguments in favour of the Italian case. But, at both international and national levels, his voice and still more his political judgement became the determinative influence on the development of Italian policy.

In attempting to reconstruct the main features of the prime minister's policy, it is considerably easier to describe the environment in which he operated and to which he responded than to assess his motives. After Aldo Moro, whom Dr Kissinger described as 'the most formidable' of the Italian politicians with whom he had to deal in his years of office[26], Mr Andreotti was almost certainly the most subtle and effective of the Christian Democrat leaders of the 1970s. Indeed in many respects he has been even more effective than Mr Moro because, unlike the latter who was not, as Dr Kissinger remarked, interested in international affairs and who assumed the foreign policy portfolio as a 'power base' and never as a 'vocation', Mr Andreotti was both interested in and skilled at managing his government's external relations. There are obvious dangers in a foreign observer trying to interpret the objectives of a senior Italian politician, and anybody who was privileged to listen to the superb debate between Luigi Spaventa and Giorgio La Malfa on Mr Andreotti's role in the EMS negotiations at Bologna in November 1979 must realize that the risks are greater in this case than in most[27]. When all allowances are made, however, for the inside information to which critics of the Italian prime minister, such as Giorgio La Malfa and Luigi Spaventa, were privy, it does seem on the basis of the evidence that has been available in the preparation of this book that the dominant characteristic of Mr Andreotti's interventions in the episode was precisely the consistency of purpose that his critics are most anxious to deny him. This does not, it need hardly be said, exclude either opportunism or error. Faced with a domestic political situation of enormous and increasing complexity, it was only to be expected that the Italian prime minister should have held his hand when it did not need to be revealed, and exploited any opportunity that arose to discomfort his opponents both inside and outside the Christian Democratic Party. As for errors, the following sections will suggest that the Italians miscalculated on several occasions and in several connections, and although the responsibility for these mistakes may have lain primarily with his advisers Mr Andreotti cannot be spared at least some of the blame. But, whether guilty of miscalculation or clumsiness, the underlying tendency of his policy, which was to take Italy into the system if anything like the right terms could be negotiated, was still evident even when he was at his most taciturn and fallible.

The domestic political background to the negotiations was unusually complicated even by Italian standards. Following many weeks of inter-party talks, in which the dominant forces had been the Christian Democrats and the Communists, Mr Andreotti's mandate as prime minister had been renewed in March 1978 on the basis of a programme subscribed to by five parliamentary parties – the Christian Democrats, the Communists (PCI), the Socialists (PSI), the Social Democrats (PSDI) and the Republicans[28]. The novel feature of the agreement was the position allotted to the Communists, who, after years of electoral advance in the course of which they had far outstripped the two socialist parties, found themselves at last in 'the majority' if not in the government. Italian administrations seem sometimes to exist primarily to fill out the time between crises rather than to weather them, and doubts about the durability of Andreotti Mark III existed from the beginning. It was not surprising. The deal with the Communists had been in large measure the work of the secretary general of the Christian Democrats, Mr Zaccagnini, and Mr Andreotti himself, and was disapproved of by important elements in the party, some of whom, notably Donat Cattin, were included in the government. The Christian Democrats, who had always been more a coalition of factions linked to a medley of greater or lesser chieftains rather than a political party, did not therefore provide the prime minister with a firm home base, and his relations with his party critics became even cooler as the months passed, particularly when, in what they at least chose to see as an unmerited concession to Communist and trade union pressure, he dropped Mr Cattin as minister of industry.

The rest of 'the majority' was scarcely a happy band of pilgrims committed to a common goal. The Republicans, still at this stage led by the enormously impressive and respected figure of Ugo La Malfa, were, as subsequent parts of this chapter will show, a constant reminder to Mr Andreotti of the orthodoxies and verities of an earlier and more optimistic generation of Italian leaders. Further to the left, the PSDI played a not dissimilar role less effectively. The PSI under their new leader Mr Craxi had hazier notions of what they wanted to achieve in Italian society but, for the time being at any rate, greater hope that the years of persistent and demoralizing decline could be forgotten, a mood that encouraged some of them and some of Mr Andreotti's rivals inside the Christian Democrat Party to look ahead to a revival of the centre–left coalition that had dominated Italian politics in the previous decade. This left the Communists, some of whom rejected the whole notion of the historical compromise, still more of whom were concerned that the party had 'peaked' in electoral terms and the vast majority of whom were worried that they might be, or already had been, lured into a position of responsibility without power, in a situation in which the government, with the reluctant agreement of at least some of the most important figures in the party, was pursuing economic policies that were bound to offend and possibly even alienate traditional party supporters. As the summer proceeded and the outlines of government policy became clearer, social and political unrest increased, and the fragile agreement achieved in March appeared ever more vulnerable. In October, there was a serious wave of strikes, including a particularly celebrated one involving hospital workers. Expectations of a crisis increased correspondingly. On this occasion the government survived, partly because most if not all the other members of the majority were not yet ready to chance their arm, but partly too because the prime minister achieved some important successes and made some significant concessions: Mr Cattin was removed, the strikes were settled and the parliamentary debate at the end of the month about the economy, which some had expected to precipitate the crisis, proved in the event to be something of a triumph for the government[29]. But the manoeuvrings continued and, although by the beginning of November most commentators appeared to believe that the government would not fall before the end of the year, few were ready to predict that it would survive long thereafter.

The debate about the EMS was superimposed on this complex and constantly shifting political pattern, both influencing it and being influenced by it. With the exception of the Republicans, none of the majority parties spoke with a clear voice, and even the Republicans were guilty in the first phase of a certain circularity in their arguments. Thus Giorgio La Malfa, in an article published on 25 October[30] entitled 'The real problem is our domestic economic policy', implied that Italy would be capable of facing the rigours of the new system if her domestic economic policies were more appropriate, but, as they were not, the country would not be able to survive within it. His party would not, however, remain associated with the government if the latter decided against entry. Following the economic debate at the end of October and further discussions with Mr Pandolfi, who briefed all the majority parties after the Siena talks with Mr Schmidt at the beginning of November, both La Malfas, father and son, appeared more satisfied that the government was serious about its economic policy objectives, and as a result the initial, rather waspish tone was replaced by a more straightforward insistence on entry and the clear threat that, if entry was deferred or rejected, the Republicans would defect from the majority[31].

It was relatively easy to achieve a consensus within the Republican Party, which was after all small and, in this field at least, not unlike a family business. Elsewhere, however, the position was much more complicated, and good Europeanism was frequently tinged and sometimes overlaid by fears for the social and economic consequences of Italian entry into the system. Eventually, the Christian Democrat directorate decided to endorse Italian membership, but prior to the meeting that took this decision at the beginning of December there was ample evidence to suggest that, despite a great deal of real and rhetorical enthusiasm for the EMS proposal in certain quarters, of whom, apart from Mr Pandolfi, Dr Andreatta was perhaps the most distinguished representative[32], the Christian Democrat leadership reflected the deep divisions on the issue that were constantly apparent to anybody who read the non-socialist press from October 1978 onwards. It is impossible within the scope of this book to attempt anything like a systematic analysis of the debate, which was reported and advanced day after day in *24 Ore, Il Giorno, Il Corriere della Sera, La Repubblica* and several other newspapers, but three contributions at least do merit some consideration, both because of the authority of the persons concerned and because, as far as one can gauge, the views that they expressed were representative of important sections of non-socialist opinion. The contributors in question were Guido Carli, formerly governor of the Banca d'Italia, but by this time president of Confindustria and as such the official spokesman for Italian industry, Rinaldo Ossola, minister for external trade, and Giovanni Marcora, the minister of agriculture.

Dr Carli was on a visit to China when the public debate provoked by Mr Pandolfi's parliamentary statement of 10 October began in earnest, but he lost no time in letting his views be known after his return. Thus on 27 October, he declared: 'you ask whether Italy ought to join the new EMS or not. My answer is no, not so much because I believe Italy is incapable of supporting the constraints that the system will impose, but because I am convinced that this particular system is wrong'[33]. Its faults, which he stressed could still be eradicated in the course of the negotiations, were essentially two: firstly, it was tilted against deficit countries and in favour of surplus countries; secondly, it lacked an adequate dollar policy. Dr Carli himself never indulged in the crude anti-Germanism that emerged fairly frequently in the course of the Italian debate, but he nonetheless stressed that, as matters stood, the proposal was too strongly biased towards the protection of German interests. Even in his early statements, however, there were already hints of two other preoccupations that might, and in the end did, help him to adopt a more positive attitude: the fear that, if Italy did not join, the policy enshrined in the Pandolfi plan, which he strongly supported, might be fatally undermined at a moment when the battle with the unions' 'unrealistic' wage claims was at its most intense; and the concern that by not joining, the Italian economy, which in his own words 'had become and was in the process of becoming still more an integrated part of the European economy', might drift out of the Community orbit with consequences that would be fatal for Italian industry and prosperity[34]. This latter point was made with admirable bluntness in a speech he delivered at Udine towards the end of November[35]: 'If Italy is too weak to participate in the EMS, it is also true that she is too weak not to participate.' Italy, he continued, 'has chosen and is becoming evermore bound by a Community destiny'. Hypothetical alternatives were an illusion, and it was up to the Italians to work towards the improvement of the system from within – in particular to ensure that there was an adequate dollar policy – and to accept the logic of the European commitment in the conduct of their domestic affairs as a whole. This meant among other things the abandonment of policies designed to prop up inefficient and unprofitable concerns with public money. Trade unions and companies, Dr Carli implied, had to learn the rules of the European game: that was the challenge represented by the EMS and it had to be accepted.

The reservations felt by Rinaldo Ossola, minister for external trade, were stated with equal frankness both in public and in the Council of Ministers, when, which was not often, the latter was given an opportunity to discuss the issue. Interviewed on the day following the revaluation of the DM against its Snake partners in October[36] for example, Mr Ossola made it clear that he did not believe that the realignment was adequate in itself, and that the problems of achieving greater order in the European exchanges would be made still more difficult if the EMS came into existence as planned at the beginning of the following year. Life in the Snake was difficult enough even in its present form, but it was at least restricted at the moment to an area that was relatively homogeneous in economic terms. This homogeneity, which was a fundamental precondition of the success of any system remotely like the Snake, simply did not exist amongst the countries that, it was stated, would now join the new system in the New Year. The conclusion was therefore obvious: either the system had to be radically different from the Snake or it would not work, and as all the evidence from the negotiations so far on both monetary questions and the transfer of resources seemed to the minister to suggest that the new system would be broadly similar to the Snake, it was doomed from the start. The general trend of Mr Ossola's arguments, it might be said, did not differ markedly from those that Italian negotiators advanced in Community meetings, but his formulations were more radical and his objections more persistent. On the CAP, for example, he came as near as any Italian public figure to advocating a root and branch attack on its underlying assumptions: the country, he declared, could buy its agricultural imports much more cheaply and increase its overall trade with the countries in question if it turned to Australia, Argentina and certain communist states. As for his persistence, it is enough to refer to the devastating point-by-point analysis of Mr Pandolfi's statement of the case for joining that he made at the Council of Ministers on 28 November[37].

The third figure whose interventions were particularly noteworthy was also a minister, Giovanni Marcora. His anxieties were not as sharply expressed nor indeed as fundamental as Mr Ossola's, but because they touched on the problems of the CAP and more particularly of the MCAs they merit brief discussion here. Mr Marcora himself always stressed that his criticisms were of limited scope: 'I am a peasant [*contadino*]. I only understand a little about the monetary system, but I do know something about cash'[38]. As the detailed arguments that he advanced to support his reservations showed, however, the problems that gave rise to his concern were in many respects more complex than the issues raised by the monetary system itself, and there is no space here to illustrate them with the figures that, for a mere 'peasant', he handled with quite remarkable dexterity. What in effect he argued, however, was that unless the MCAs were dismantled and the existing provisions for negotiated devaluations of the 'green lira' were maintained, Italian agriculture would suffer intolerable burdens. The MCAs, he pointed out, anticipating criticisms that were to become commonplace in France a month later, subsidized German exports, particularly in dairy products, while the green lira devaluations went some way – though not far enough – towards offsetting the consequences of the large differences in national inflation rates when, as happened under the CAP, prices were fixed on a Community basis. If, for example, the Agricultural Council agreed a 2% rise in Community prices in a certain year, but Italian inflation continued at over 10%, Italian farmers would be directly hit unless the green lira could be devalued against the unit of account. The minister always maintained that he was not opposed to the EMS in itself, but he felt sufficiently strongly about the problems that he thought would arise for Italian agriculture unless remedial action was taken to urge his colleagues in the pre-Brussels consultations within the government at the end of November and the beginning of December to postpone Italian entry for at least six months.

In the new political situation created by the March agreement, the arguments of Christian Democrats, bourgeois or non-aligned leaders and experts were of course only part of the picture that the prime minister had to take account of when framing his political strategy. As the leader of a government supported by a five-party majority, he was answerable to, and in large measure dependent on, the three left-wing parties – the PSDI, the PSI and the PCI – and the trade unions with which they were variously linked. The importance that Mr Andreotti attached to securing their support was underlined in the weeks following 10 October by the efforts that Mr Pandolfi, with the prime minister's authority and backing, made to keep them informed of the progress of the negotiations in Brussels and elsewhere and to canvass their support[39]. The prime minister himself remained in the background on these occasions, limiting his public statements on the EMS to more open settings such as television studios and press interviews, but there is ample evidence to show that the impressions of left-wing opinion that he acquired through Mr Pandolfi and more generally through the public statements of the party leaders themselves played a crucial part in determining his approach to both the bilateral meetings with other Community heads of government and the European Council itself on 4 and 5 December.

Of the three parties concerned, the PSDI was the smallest and the least important, a relic of a happier era that survived more on memories than on hope. It was also the most open to what might be described as the Pandolfi line in both external and internal policies. The contrast between its position and that of the PCI and the PSI was evident immediately the debate opened, and was illustrated at length in a speech by Pietro Longo that *l'Umanità* printed in full on 29 October[40]. The PSDI, Longo asserted, rejected the Republicans' argument that Italy should enter on virtually any terms, but was no less opposed to those who believed that membership was impossible in the foreseeable future. Given the openness of the Italian economy, non-membership would indeed pose serious problems but, if the country was to participate, it was essential that certain conditions should be fulfilled. Despite some differences in emphasis, the conditions that Mr Longo listed were not unlike those that Mr Pandolfi had recently rehearsed in public, and for which both he and governor Baffi were pressing in the negotiations. Internally, Mr Longo stressed, it was essential that a serious effort should be made to realize the objectives of the Pandolfi plan, 'which we support and which would seem to have been put into question up until now by the dangerous attitudes of certain trade unionists'. Externally, the government should aim to secure at least five conditions: larger margins of up to 5% or 6%, credit facilities equivalent to $50 billion, an orderly relationship between the EMS and the rest of the international monetary system, particularly the dollar, a reform of the way in which oil prices were expressed in the direction of a basket reference rather than, as at present, the dollar, and a significant transfer of resources, particularly in the direction of the Mezzogiorno, which, Mr Longo hoped, would now at last become a European problem rather than simply an Italian one.

The attitude of the PSI, which was usually stated officially by Fabrizio Cicchitto during the period concerned, was more problematical and more hedged about by reservations[41]. This was particularly true in October when it was at times difficult to distinguish between the Socialists and the Communists. Both stressed Italy's weakness and the threat of German hegemony implicit in what looked likely to be no more than an enlarged Snake. They were also united in their suspicion that the government would 'use' the EMS as an excuse to push through domestic policies that would be deflationary and therefore damaging to the interests that they represented. However, the common ground between the two groups was never complete, and diminished as the weeks passed. Part of the explanation is undoubtedly to be found in the domestic political situation. Like certain elements in the Christian Democratic Party who had profound misgivings about the EMS itself but who saw an opportunity to undermine the working agreement with the PCI if, as seemed increasingly likely, the PCI came out strongly against Italian entry, the PSI, or at least the part of it most closely associated with its new leader, Mr Craxi, could see obvious advantages in distinguishing itself from the Communists at a time when the popularity of the five-party majority system was clearly on the wane within both the Christian Democratic Party and the Republican Party. There were also other factors at work, however. Probably the most important were the links that the PSI had with other socialist parties north of the Alps. These connections could, it might be said, work both ways – the scepticism of the French and the hostility of the British more than cancelling out the enthusiasm of the SPD and the other socialist parties in the Snake countries. At first sight this interpretation would seem to be supported by the extremely strong emphasis that the PSI put on the importance of British entry and its own special relationship with the Labour Party. At the beginning of November, for example, Mr Cicchitto came very close to implying that British membership should be a precondition of Italy's joining, and he and his colleagues indicated the strength of their feelings on the subject by going to London shortly afterwards for talks with the representatives of the Labour government and party[42]. The stress on Italy's interests in having Britain in, and the practical expression that it found in the discussions with Labour colleagues in London, should not, however, be allowed to conceal the fundamental difference that existed between the leaders of the PSI and their colleagues in the Labour Party. In an almost total reversal of the situation that had existed in 1948, when Mr Healey and Mr Morgan Phillips had gone to Rome to urge the Italian Socialists not to identify themselves with the extreme left and to recognize the necessity of western solidarity, the Italians came to London not to learn, but to plead with the British concerned that it was in the interests of both countries that they should move together within the Community on this issue as on many others[43]. Mr Craxi and his colleagues were anyway more disposed to listen to and follow the promptings of the SPD, with whom they were also in touch in the course of November, than the British Labour Party, which had long since forfeited its role as the dominant and model socialist party in Western Europe.

The PSI was therefore open to persuasion, and in the course of November the official statements of policy made by Mr Cicchitto revealed a perceptible shift away from hostility or scepticism towards acceptance. Thus when Mr Pandolfi saw the representatives of the majority parties on 24 November, following his own and Mr Andreotti's talks with Mr Callaghan and Mr Healey in London, and indicated that, despite the near certainty that Britain would not join, the Italian government was disposed to enter the EMS, Mr Cicchitto announced that in his view the progress that Italian negotiators had made since October had been such that it was now possible to contemplate Italian membership, even though the efforts required to remain within the system would be considerable and there were still some outstanding points of detail that needed to be clarified[44]. He took essentially the same line a few days later, at much greater length and with more supporting explanation, in an article that appeared in *Avanti* on 29 November.

The PCI's position, on the other hand, seemed to harden as the weeks passed, and they launched a major and widely noted declaration in favour of delay on the eve of the Council meeting itself. The party's main spokesman throughout the period was Luciano Barca. His tone was sharp from the beginning[45]. He understood the German chancellor's anxiety to create the system, and it was only proper, he added, that Mr Schmidt should seek to defend his country's interests, but it was important to realize that Germany's interests were not identical with Italy's and that entry into the EMS on the terms that the Germans appeared to be insisting on would involve placing the country under German hegemony. It would also reinforce the position of those who were bent on domestic policies that would increase unemployment and lower living standards. Unlike his Socialist counterpart, with whom he attended all the consultation sessions with Mr Pandolfi in October and November, he did not moderate his opposition as the date for the European Council approached. Following the meeting of 24 November, for example, at which the PSI representative had registered his approval of the progress that had been made, Mr Barca made it clear that he did not consider that anything like a sufficient basis for Italian participation had been created[46].

His most celebrated intervention, however, was the article that was published in *l'Unità* on 3 December, the day before the Brussels Council, which many commentators both inside and outside Italy interpreted as a clear attempt to tie the Italian prime minister's hands at the meeting. The arguments were in many respects already familiar and need not be repeated here. What was more significant was the timing and the tone. Mr Barca claimed that the government, led by Mr Andreotti himself, had tried to confuse the issue by representing what was no more than entry into the Snake as a great leap forward towards European unity. It was nothing of the sort. The Italian negotiators, Mr Barca admitted, had achieved some success, but not enough. Almost all the important conditions for Italian entry still needed to be negotiated and, as there was no hope of achieving them all at Brussels itself, the Council meeting should not be seen as the moment for a final decision. Britain's determination to remain outside meant anyway that the alternative that had been posed between membership and isolation was no longer relevant. Italy would be in good company if it avoided a precipitate decision to join a system that could only in its present form result in deflation, unemployment and increasing economic weakness.

The importance of the Barca article was undoubtedly considerable, and it is not particularly surprising that both the French president and Mr Andreotti's critics in the Christian Democratic Party should have challenged Mr Andreotti to demonstrate his independence of the PCI by disowning the arguments advanced by its spokesman. Even in the Communist case however, the party's position was more complex than outsiders feared or opponents chose to depict it. It is quite clear that the PCI leadership did not want Italy to enter the EMS in December 1978, but it seems equally certain that they were embarrassed and perplexed by the position into which they had been forced, and that they were not prepared to precipitate the government crisis over the issue that some commentators anticipated and at least some of their opponents probably wanted. The EMS question put the PCI on the defensive, and Mr Barca's article was less an act of sabotage than an attempt to justify their doubts and save time.

The hesitation and ambivalence of the PCI leadership were apparent in a contribution by one of the party's most senior and respected figures, Giorgio Napolitano, entitled significantly enough: 'Come restare con l'Europa' (how to remain with Europe)[47]. The conference that had recently been held at the new Centre for International Politics demonstrated, he wrote, that 'our decision not only to remain within the EEC but also to play an active part in advancing the process of integration, remains valid for us [Communists] both as an act of political idealism and as a precise, reasoned option in the context of the present international system'. The PCI had, it is true, reservations about the details of the EMS, but these had to be seen against the background of the party's determination to work for a more vigorous and ambitious Community, and its acceptance of the necessity of economic policies designed to reduce inflation and increase productivity. Even if the country were to stay out of the EMS, there would, Napolitano argued, be no escaping the need to persist with these policies and avoid the constant depreciation of the currency. The PCI's objections to the current proposals stemmed therefore not from the principle, but from the details of the scheme and from the motives of certain groups who wished to use it to perpetuate social injustices.

The Italian prime minister's reaction to these and other indications of the views of party and interest group leaders seems to have been characterized chiefly by two features. The first was the conclusion that nothing in the domestic political situation, still less the international negotiations, required him to revise his initial assessment of the Franco-German initiative at Bremen, which was essentially that, whatever the economic disadvantages that might arise from membership, the political costs of non-participation would be still greater. The second was the belief that there was nothing to be gained by isolating the PCI unless it was absolutely inevitable, and that time and additional concessions on the points to which they and other critics attached significance were much to be desired. The first and more important of these points is in many respects totally unsurprising, if the interpretation of the domestic political situation offered above is even approximately correct. The prime minister went to Brussels secure in the knowledge that, although certain members of the Council of Ministers favoured delay or even rejection, the majority did not, that although certain elements in the Christian Democratic Party had had their doubts, most even of them and certainly the majority of the parliamentary party as a whole were favourable by the beginning of December, that the most articulate representatives of Italian industry were also positively disposed, and finally that, however much the PCI rebelled against the additional constraints that the EMS might entail, there was probably no senior figure in the party who wanted a crisis over this particular issue. Even if one accepts the assumption of Mr Andreotti's critics that he acknowledged only the *Primat der Innenpolitik*, which on the evidence available to me seems an unduly cynical interpretation, there was no compelling domestic reason for him to back out of the initial declaration of approval in principle.

The only factor that might have prompted a change of mind, therefore, would have been a development outside Italy, either on detailed negotiating points or on an issue of more general significance. As far as the former are concerned, the discussion in the following sections will suggest that, on the details of the monetary system, the Italians achieved as much as they needed and more than they might have expected. The concurrent studies were another matter but, partly it must be admitted because of his own and still more because of his subordinates' misjudgements, he seems to have gone to the European Council at least in a reasonably optimistic frame of mind, and neither he nor his advisers felt before the dénouement at Brussels that Italy's membership would come to depend upon this issue. The only substantial question in fact that did give rise to serious doubts within the inner groups was the problem posed by the near certainty that the United Kingdom would not join. For governor Baffi, Britain's negative attitude was of decisive importance. To his considerable credit he went on trying until the last moment to persuade the British that many of their doubts were misplaced, but he made no secret of the fact that he did not believe that it would be in Italy's interests to go into the system if Britain was not a member. In the first half of November, at least, Mr Pandolfi would seem to have been inclined towards the same view[48]. What is striking, however, is that the prime minister himself was not. He wanted Italy to enter, as he told one of the inner circle on 2 November, even if Britain did not. He acknowledged the strength of governor Baffi's and others' arguments about the additional inconveniences that Britain's self-exclusion might entail for Italy and the other weaker countries, and he went to London on 22 November armed with a brief that reads more like a lecture on why it pays to be a good European than a negotiating paper. But he does not seem at any point to have accepted the argument that Britain's membership was or could be a *sine qua non* of Italy's. Quite why he should have been so firm on this point remains something of a mystery, but one very strong influence was undoubtedly the meeting with the German chancellor at Siena on 1 November, in which Mr Schmidt spoke of Britain in the most disparaging terms and made it as clear as he could to his Italian colleague that to him the EMS issue had become something of an article *stantis et cadentis ecclesiae* or, as a headline in one of the Italian newspapers put it, a 'test europeo'[49].

The second element in Mr Andreotti's reaction to domestic political developments, namely the calculation that there was nothing to be gained by isolating the PCI unless and until it was absolutely necessary, should become clearer still in the following sections of this chapter. It is, however, obvious that his concern about the PCI's attitude encouraged him to play for high stakes at the Brussels Council meeting and, when the meeting broke down without agreement, to use the 'pause for reflection' to do whatever he could to minimize the political damage and maximize the political advantage that would result from a final, positive decision, which he almost certainly regarded as inevitable all the time. To argue, however, that the Italian prime minister went to Brussels determined to break the meeting up because of his obligations to the PCI is utterly implausible. The contributions that he made to the breakdown of the Council were real enough, but they owed more to the miscalculations of some of his official advisers than to the dictates of the Italian Communists. The latter were important, but ultimately of secondary significance.

The United Kingdom

The British Treasury officials who, according to Frances Cairncross, in the article already referred to in chapter 5[50], wanted a public discussion of the EMS in order to prevent Mr Callaghan from taking the United Kingdom into the new system, cannot have been disappointed by both the volume and, in many cases, the tone of the debate that began in October. They must have been even more gratified by the almost immediate effect that it had on the prime minister, since it quickly became apparent that, whatever his personal preferences might have been, there was simply no way in which he could carry the measure in a Cabinet of which the majority were indifferent or hostile, or in a Parliament where he could not expect the backing of enough of the opposition (which was itself divided on the issue and preoccupied with electioneering) to offset the antipathy of a substantial number, if not the majority, of the Parliamentary Labour Party. British ministers and officials had manoeuvred themselves into a corner: British parliamentary, party and public opinion threatened to shut them in it.

In an article that appeared in the *Guardian* on 23 October, Peter Jenkins stated that the prime minister had arrived at his decision during the weekend of 8 October, following the Labour Party conference at which an attempt by anti-marketeers to secure a vote on an emergency motion denouncing the EMS had been thwarted, but which had nevertheless provided sufficient evidence of the depth of feeling within the party against the scheme to persuade Mr Callaghan that the battle was lost. The prime minister himself had given substantially the same version of events to the German chancellor in their private discussions in Bonn a week earlier, and there seems little reason therefore to doubt the accuracy of the *Guardian* report. In normal circumstances, the prime minister might have chosen to defy his party. The history of the Labour Party is after all littered with examples of conference decisions that have been ignored or disowned by the Labour government of the day. But the circumstances in the autumn of 1978 were not normal, since on 7 September the prime minister had announced that he would not be calling a general election in the near future, as most commentators had expected and many of his supporters had hoped[51]. Far from releasing him from the need to pay heed to his party critics, the decision only increased his dependence upon them. The pre-electoral atmosphere was not dissolved, it was perpetuated, since the law made an election inevitable within a year and Mr Callaghan's lack of an overall majority in Parliament made it possible much sooner.

Ostensibly, of course, matters went on as before. Both Mr Callaghan and Mr Healey continued to claim, not only in public but also in private, that Britain might still enter if the terms were right. When Roy Jenkins expressed sympathy with Mr Callaghan's political problems during a meeting in London at the beginning of November, for example, the prime minister insisted that he had no political difficulties and that if he wanted to join, he would join. Consultations with the Cabinet, the National Executive Committee (NEC), the Trades Union Council (TUC) and the Parliamentary Labour Party (PLP) went on as if no final decision had been taken[52]. When Mr Healey appeared before a subcommittee of the House of Commons' Expenditure Committee on 3 November, he too gave the impression that the question of Britain's membership was still open, distancing himself from the critics of the system of whose comments the chairman of the committee reminded him at the beginning of their session[53]. The government's Green Paper, published as late as 25 November, was even more explicit: 'the government cannot yet reach its own conclusion on whether it would be in the best interests of the United Kingdom to join the exchange rate regime of the EMS as it finally emerges from the negotiations'[54]. In reality, however, there seems little doubt that Peter Jenkins was right: 'it was too big a question for a lame duck government.' From the middle of October onwards, the British government negotiated not to increase the chances of entry, but to reduce the risks of non-entry. The tactics varied from a not altogether convincing attempt by Mr Healey and his officials to convince the world that they rather than the Eight were the true guardians of the 'spirit of Bremen', to diversionary attacks on the inequities of the budget and the negotiation of a 'soft land', preparations for which began before the end of October. But the aim was not membership. That option was closed until after the election.

The fact that the prime minister had ruled out immediate membership before most of those who joined in the discussion of the EMS had had a chance to express their views, must inevitably reduce the interest of the debate. It does not however exhaust it, firstly because it provided a striking illustration of the strength of the forces opposed to British membership, and secondly because it exercised an influence on the tactics pursued by Mr Callaghan and his colleagues and officials, even though the objective of their efforts was now less than most of the parties involved in the debate assumed or feared.

Hostility to the scheme began in the Cabinet and extended throughout all the most important decision-making groups in the Labour Party: the Parliamentary Labour Party, the National Executive Committee and the Trades Union Council. It was a sign perhaps of the difficulties that Mr Callaghan knew he would face at Cabinet level that, despite strong pressure from Mr Peter Shore and others for a thorough discussion of the issue in Cabinet, the prime minister did not give in to these demands until 2 November[55]. Prior to this debate all but a few ministers, handpicked by Mr Callaghan, had had to content themselves with oral reports from Mr Healey or himself, and whatever information they could glean from their more privileged colleagues, their departments or the press. The inner circle, which had originally been restricted to Mr Callaghan, Mr Healey and Harold Lever, was widened a little through the discussions that took place in a special Cabinet committee (GEN 136), which the prime minister himself chaired and the composition of which he determined, but the careful exclusion of those like Mr Rodgers or Mr Shore who could speak on the subject with both passion and authority confirmed the impression that Mr Callaghan's primary concern was to avoid a genuine debate, presumably because he knew that it would be as inconclusive as it was heated[56]. As the prime minister had already decided that British entry was not an immediate prospect or problem, this attempt to minimize the opportunities for internecine strife was perhaps understandable, but, as it proved, hardly successful. The suspicions that many members of the Cabinet, the government and the parliamentary party already nursed about the EMS were compounded by resentment at the way the prime minister was treating them. 'Everyone has always said that Jim is exceedingly secretive,' one left-wing member of the Cabinet observed in October, 'but it is carrying it to ridiculous extremes when a Cabinet minister cannot get access to Cabinet documents'[57].

Even if the Cabinet did not discuss the issue formally, however, the press knew full well that its members were divided over it. In many cases, these divisions fell along predictable lines[58]. Nobody, for example, could have expected Mr Benn, Mr Shore, Mr Silkin, Mr Foot, Mr Orme or Mr Bruce Millan to welcome a plan that, if it succeeded, would tie the United Kingdom still more closely to a Community from which they still hoped the country could escape. Equally, nobody should have been surprised to discover that Harold Lever, Mrs Williams and Mr Rodgers were warmly in favour of entering. What was more remarkable was the indifference bordering on hostility of at least two ministers, Mr Dell, the secretary of trade, and Dr Owen, the foreign secretary, who were normally reckoned to be amongst the 'good Europeans' in the Cabinet. Mr Dell's reservations on the issue, as he subsequently explained[59], were prompted by the differences in inflation rates between Community countries, which, he believed, would burst the system apart within a very short time, while Dr Owen, who had, it is alleged, been amongst those who urged the prime minister to react constructively to the opportunities offered by the Bremen Council decisions, would seem by October to have concluded that these opportunities were more limited than had seemed likely in July. The agnostics also included such important figures as Mr Hattersley, Mr Mason and Mr Varley. Most if not all of these later became warm supporters of the 'half-way house', but in October the outright opponents and the neutrals far outnumbered the supporters of the system in the Cabinet.

Outside the Cabinet in the Parliamentary Labour Party, the National Executive Committee and the TUC, hostility was more apparent than indifference, and those who believed that it would be in the country's interests to join the system were in a tiny minority. As far as the PLP was concerned, the position was made extremely clear in the second week of November, when 120 MPs, constituting over half the non-ministerial membership of the parliamentary party, signed a motion that rejected 'any attempt by the EEC, its institutions or its member states to assume control of domestic policies through a new monetary system for the Community'[60]. The sponsors of the motion claimed, probably not without reason, that many more Labour MPs sympathized with their viewpoint, and that at least half of the members of the government outside the Cabinet were also in accord with them. As for the NEC, which had a meeting with the Cabinet on 23 October, its hostility, given the dominance of the left wing within it, could be virtually taken for granted[61]. The TUC's position, which was expounded both orally in a meeting with the prime minister, Mr Healey and other party members of the TUC and Labour Party Liaison Committee on 30 October, and in writing in a paper submitted to the House of Commons subcommittee set up to report on the EMS, was more cautious, but in the end only a little less negative[62]. Its leaders believed that a return to fixed exchange rates in Europe was desirable as a method of restoring stability in the international monetary system as a whole and for this reason 'the EMS proposals must be welcomed'. But, as there were 'grounds to believe that the EMS would operate in a fashion which would inhibit the growth of some of its members, especially its weaker members', the costs of stability under the system proposed might be too high. The TUC hoped that the 'right terms' could be negotiated, but it was evident both from the text of the document that they submitted and from more informal observations made by their leaders that they did not believe that this was likely.

A higher proportion of the official Conservative opposition favoured the EMS, but even here lukewarmness was more in evidence than enthusiasm. Following the exchanges in the House of Commons after the Bremen Council, the Conservative leadership remained conspicuously silent on the issue, though some individuals made no secret of their views either for or against. On 15 November, however, the Shadow Cabinet discussed the proposal and 'tentatively decided that it must let Britain's European partners know that it supported the principle of the system'[63]. Their meeting was held, ironically enough, only hours before Mr John Biffen rejoined Mrs Thatcher's team, and it is by no means certain they they would have gone as far as they did if he had been involved in their discussions, since in a speech of 30 October he had argued that for Britain to join the EMS would be quite incompatible with the free market economy that the Tories hoped to establish[64]: 'I do not believe it is possible for Tories to argue a liberal economic domestic trade and monetary policy at Westminster and then deny those very tenets by their actions in the European Community.' A politically fixed exchange rate could seriously undermine the money supply targets, reform of the CAP would become virtually impossible if the EMS were set up first, increases in the Regional Fund administered by Brussels could cause damage and embarrassment to a Conservative government and the problems of enlargement would be increased rather than diminished by the attempt to impose monetary uniformity. Mr Biffen was widely admired in the Conservative Party, not least by Mrs Thatcher herself, and it is difficult to believe that the leader of the Opposition was entirely unsympathetic to his position. The Shadow Cabinet may therefore have been more willing to acknowledge the force of the political arguments in favour of a constructive and positive response towards the Franco-German initiative, but they were probably relieved that their political will was not put to the test, since their enthusiasm for the scheme was of a distinctly Laodicean hue. In fact, only the Liberals were prepared to welcome the EMS unequivocally, but in November 1978 they were a small, dispirited group, who had been almost crushed by their liaison with the Labour Party and who were almost certainly more preoccupied by what was about to happen at the Old Bailey than by the debate about Europe over which they could hope to exercise little influence as matters stood, and still less if the Thorpe trial went badly[65].

Outside parliament and the major political parties there was also a substantial body of 'independent' opinion that argued against British entry. It is by definition extremely hard to gauge the strength or significance of these extraparliamentary forces, but even a quick perusal of the pages of evidence submitted by experts and interest groups to the House of Commons' subcommittee on the EMS shows that the great majority of witnesses was sceptical or hostile, and that the critics included some, notably Sir Andrew Shonfield, who could not by any stretch of the imagination be accused of anti-Europeanism[66], and others who rarely if ever agreed on other economic or political questions. As the chairman of the committee noted during the hearings of 7 November, Mr Pepper, Mr Ward, Mr Blackaby of the National Institute of Economic and Social Research and Mr Burns and Dr Budd of the London Business School, 'a most unlikely combination of economists', were all unanimous that Britain should not enter the scheme as it was proposed, though some, including Mr Pepper, Mr Burns and Dr Budd, argued that entry might be possible after a transitional period[67].

Despite this impressive cloud of witnesses against the system, there were some prominent voices that argued in favour of entry. The House of Commons subcommittee itself heard some[68], and most readers of the quality press were aware of others, since, with the exception of *The Times*[69], all the quality newspapers – the *Financial Times*, the *Guardian*, the *Daily Telegraph*, the *Sunday Times*, the *Observer* and the *Sunday Telegraph* – plus *The Economist*, favoured entry.

Of the witnesses heard by the House of Commons committee, the most impressive of those who argued for British entry was Sir Jeremy Morse, chairmen of Lloyds Bank, who before taking up this position had been at the Bank of England and chairman of the Committee of Twenty set up in 1972 to forge agreement on a new international monetary system[70]. He appeared before the committee on 7 November together with two other chairmen of the Big Four London clearing banks, Mr Leigh-Pemberton of the National Westminster and Mr A. F. Tuke of Barclays, both of whom shared his approach and tended in the hearings to defer to his authority. The remaining chairman, Lord Armstrong, who before taking up his position at the Midland Bank had been Head of the Civil Service, was not present and did not agree with his colleagues[71]. The arguments put forward by Sir Jeremy Morse at the meeting were too varied and complex to be discussed at any length here, but what distinguishes them most from other contributions in the same series was the scepticism that they revealed towards the 'theoretic statements' of experts, and the persistent awareness of the importance of the political dimension. Sir Jeremy and his colleagues refused to be drawn into either the 'monetarist' or the 'economist' camp, arguing instead that both approaches should go hand in hand and that what made the present moment peculiarly favourable for a monetary initiative was precisely the fact that, unlike 1972 (when although inflation rates were lower they were beginning to diverge), the European Community appeared to be moving towards a political consensus on the absolute priority of the battle against inflation, which would reinforce and be reinforced by a strong monetary regime. This they felt was much more important than the rather narrow debate about the exchange rate mechanism of which so much had been heard in recent months. In ideal circumstances, they would have favoured waiting a while longer before launching the system, because of the possibility that the dollar storm had not yet played itself out, but it was essential both for the proper functioning of the system itself and in the interests of the United Kingdom that if the French and the Germans pressed ahead the British should not lag behind. It did not matter, Sir Jeremy argued, if the experiment failed: 'I think that we shall have three or four of these experiments. It is to be hoped that on each time the bundle of Europe's monetary position gets bigger and stronger and less easily divided by dollars.' As to the transfer of resources, a term that he deplored, he commented: 'one of my very reasons for wanting us not to be out of the EMS if and when it is launched, is that I think that we need to be in there fighting our corner on the transfer of resources as well as the CAP and the Fund.' In other words, the game was going to go on after the EMS had been established, and the British could only lose by remaining outside.

The approach to the EMS issue apparent in Sir Jeremy Morse's evidence was also characteristic of much of the comment in the quality press. The government, it was repeatedly claimed, had mishandled the negotiations by concentrating on and worrying over details instead of seeing the larger political and historical context in which the proposal had emerged. The scheme would go on even if the British did not join and, by failing to do so, they would be deprived of any influence on its character. It is not possible at this point to quote extensively, but the contributions made by one particular writer, Peter Jenkins of the *Guardian*, do merit some analysis, not simply because they stated the political argument with particular clarity, but still more because, as a senior member of the Callaghan Cabinet observed, Mr Jenkins enjoyed such a privileged relationship with the prime minister and several other senior Labour Party politicians that it seemed on occasions as if he was participating in Cabinet discussions from a distance. An article of 23 October, in which he revealed the prime minister's decision not to enter, has already been referred to above. It was accompanied by another on the inside pages that, while providing further information on why the decision had been arrived at, was intended chiefly to demonstrate why what Mr Jenkins termed the 'consensus of despair' was an improper and inadequate response to the Franco-German initiative, which would go ahead however much the British government might deplore it. The attack was more explicit still two days later. The 'obfuscations of the Treasury' and the ideological objections of 'the old guard anti-European brigade in the Labour party and the Trade Union movement' had combined to precipitate a decision taken 'largely by default'. The consequences of this decision were however grave, since the dollar crisis and the distrust of Mr Carter's leadership had removed one of the fundamental obstacles in the way of the full consummation of the Franco-German marriage, namely their difference of opinion about relations with the United States. By remaining aloof, the British government would ensure the consolidation of the Franco-German axis, less favourable treatment through the Regional Fund and other means than weaker members such as Italy and Ireland would probably enjoy, and '*de facto* relegation to the second division of a two-tier or two-speed Europe'.

Mr Callaghan, who had all along been more sensitive than the majority of his Cabinet colleagues to the political arguments for joining, was not unaffected by these considerations, which were also put with increasing force within the government by Britain's ambassadors in Bonn and Paris, Sir Oliver Wright and Sir Nicholas Henderson. The prospects of obtaining sufficient parliamentary and party support for full membership were still negligible, but the prime minister pressed with growing urgency for the fullest possible commitment short of membership and, as Peter Jenkins reported in the penultimate article in the series that he wrote on the EMS between 23 October and 5 December, he won. Like the piece that appeared on the first day of the Bremen Council, it was based on an exclusive briefing by the prime minister himself and is therefore worth quoting at length[72].

> Mr Callaghan, increasingly fearful of the consequences of British isolation through exclusion from the proposed European monetary system was given the widest possible negotiating brief yesterday by the Cabinet. At the EEC summit … he will be free to embrace any solution save complete and immediate membership of the system … The prime minister's new sense of urgency has to do chiefly with his fear of some future deal between the US$ and the embryonic EMS which could leave Britain standing on the sidelines of the power game. Thus he goes to the summit aware that he is fighting to ensure a role for Britain in the reshaping of the Atlantic relationship threatened as it is by the dollar's decline … The other reasons [for Mr Callaghan's change of mind] are these:
>
> –the change of policy towards the dollar in Washington increases the chances of a general return to an orderly money system in which the EMS could be an important component. Mr Callaghan is a long standing advocate of fixed but flexible rates. He hopes now to see next June's economic summit conference in Tokyo turned into a major endeavour to create a new international monetary order.
>
> –he has been impressed recently both by the political will of president Giscard d'Estaing and chancellor Schmidt and the extent of their willingness to ease Britain's path into the system.
>
> –he has taken note of the more positive approach in Brussels towards restraining farm prices and reviewing the inequitable workings of the

Community budget. These will be important items in the summit compromise.

—he has lost further patience with the ideological knee-jerk response of the Left, and is more prepared than he was a few weeks ago to risk a showdown.

Mr Callaghan was, according to Mr Jenkins, still critical of aspects of the scheme, but it is one of the paradoxes of the EMS episode as a whole that the momentum that fear of a Franco-German axis and criticisms of the government's strategy by some of those whose judgement the prime minister respected most had helped to generate in Downing Street was to be interrupted not by Mr Benn, whose call for the use of the British veto to block the system as a whole at the Cabinet meeting on 30 November was brushed aside[73], but by the French president whose commitment and conciliatory tones had been important factors influencing the development of Mr Callaghan's attitude. M Giscard d'Estaing's transformation of the Brussels summit from a triumphant tryst into a sordid haggle, enabled the British prime minister in the end to shed much of the sense of urgency that, despite the arithmetic of British parliamentary politics and the gloomy prognostications of Whitehall forecasters, he had acquired by the time the Council met on 4 December.

The Republic of Ireland

As in Italy and Britain, the debate about the EMS in Ireland began seriously in October, when the Dail had its first opportunity to discuss the conclusions of the Bremen Council. The outcome of the debate was in many respects predictable once the prime minister and his colleagues had decided in principle in favour of entry, since the main opposition party, Fine Gael, found itself hoisted on the petard of its own oft-asserted Europeanism and its previous attitude towards the sterling connection. Only Labour in fact had any real room for manoeuvre but, as the smallest of the three parties, the prospects of translating its increasingly radical criticisms of the system into a parliamentary majority against Irish entry were non-existent. Despite the near-inevitability of its conclusion, however, the debate is not without interest, partly because it did allow some of the genuine fears of important sections of Irish society about the implications of the EMS to come to the surface, and partly too because, even on the narrow ground on which they were forced by their own predilections to fight, Fine Gael, assisted by a less inhibited Labour Party, succeeded in harrying and embarrassing the government, particularly over the concurrent studies. In doing so, they influenced the Lynch government's approach to the studies.

The Dail had been in recess when Mr Lynch returned from Bremen, and although the conclusions of the Council were duly made available in written form and government ministers referred to the negotiations in speeches and press interviews between July and September, it was not until 17 October, when first Mr Lynch and then Mr Colley, the minister of finance, spoke at the beginning of a parliamentary debate on the Bremen conclusions, that the government gave a formal statement of its hopes and objectives in the EMS negotiations[74]. The speech by Mr Colley, who had been in Brussels at the ECOFIN meeting the day before, was the more detailed and revealing of the two. It was revealing both in what it said and in what it did not stress. Unlike his British and Italian counterparts, the Irish minister of finance clearly attributed rather less than major significance to the controversy about the basket and parity grid, the reason being, as another minister, Professor O'Donoghue, explained later in the debate, that the weighting of the Irish punt in the ECU would be so slight that it stood to gain little and might actually lose from a basket-based system. For Mr Colley, as in their turn for the opposition spokesman, the chief problems facing the Irish were the transfer of resources and the implications of a break with sterling if this should prove necessary. The efforts of the Irish government to secure a transfer of resources will be discussed in more detail in section 6.3, but, in the light of both the criticisms that they attracted from the opposition parties and the terms that they were eventually offered and accepted, Mr Colley's statement of their intentions on 17 October merits quotation. The estimate of £650 million over five years was, he noted, a 'very rough indication' of the investment in infrastructural and industrial development that the government believed Ireland would need.

> This was intended to indicate to our Community partners our desire to participate in the system from the commencement, while at the same time affording them a measure of the problem it represents for us. I should perhaps emphasise that the estimate is confined to the additional investment required in the immediate and narrow context of entry to the system. It might be argued that it should be very much greater, but it is necessary to have regard to and take a view of the balance of political and tactical realities. We anticipate also that there will be a significant expansion of the separate existing grant and loan mechanisms – the regional fund, FEOGA guidance and social fund – as well as the provision of new mechanisms in the pipeline, such as the Ortoli Facility ...

As far as the sterling problem was concerned, the minister of finance was non-committal but explicit, listing five advantages and five disadvantages that might result from a break. The advantages were the link with a currency zone whose member economies were growing more rapidly than the British economy, a boost to the battle against inflation, an increase in investment from non-British firms, who, as experience showed, exported a greater proportion of their output to the continental Community countries, greater scope to pursue an independent monetary policy and additional Community credits and resource transfers. Potential disadvantages stemmed from the fact that Britain was still a much more important trading partner than the other seven combined, that, on the assumption that the punt would rise against sterling, Irish exports to Britain might suffer, that British and Irish investment in Irish industry geared specially to the British market might drop, that Ireland would become more expensive to foreign tourists and that there would be a number of administrative and practical complications, particularly in relation to Northern Ireland.

Opposition reactions to Mr Lynch's and Mr Colley's statements varied between Fine Gael and Labour. The former were trapped by their own record. Part of the Christian Democrat group in the European Parliament, they had constantly claimed that they rather than Fianna Fail, who were linked with the Gaullists, were the 'true Europeans'. Although therefore, like Labour, Fine Gael's spokesman accused the Lynch government of having 'sold the pass' at Bremen, by declaring their agreement in principle before they had had an opportunity to study the detailed implications of the scheme, it was difficult to believe that Fine Gael would have done otherwise had they been in government themselves, and their case suffered therefore from a certain implausibility. Their chief spokesman on economic affairs, Mr Barry, effectively sold the pass himself in his first comment in the Dail on the EMS[75]: 'This is something that should not turn into a Fine Gael–Fianna Fail confrontation. It is something on which we must get as broad a national consensus as possible.' They were in a similar predicament over the possible break with sterling. At least one of their frontbench spokesmen, Mr Kelly, described the issue as 'absolutely crucial'[76], and listed an impressive number of questions that needed to be asked by and of the government. But again there were limits to which the arguments could be pushed since, in office, Fine Gael had been prone to blame the link with sterling for the difficulties that they faced in restraining inflation. As one of their number, Deputy Horgan, observed in the Dail debate in October: 'It seems to me on purely pragmatic grounds that the question of breaking the link with sterling is not so much whether, but when and how often'[77].

Despite these built-in constraints on their criticisms, Fine Gael's spokesmen attacked hard. The principal target was the government's handling of the concurrent studies. As on the other major issues, Fine Gael shared the government's basic assumptions. Where they claimed to differ was in their calculation of how much additional help the country would need and in their choice of negotiating tactics. As far as tactics were concerned, Mr Lynch's critics made exactly the opposite case to the one advanced against the Italian government. Whereas the latter was blamed for being insufficiently specific, the Irish government was accused of having put its cards on the table too early, thereby implying that the £650 million was a maximum that could be scaled down in the course of the negotiations, rather than a minimum that should be increased if the negotiations were successful. Even then, Fine Gael argued, it was not enough. Basing himself on the MacDougall report – a dangerous tactic as it proved, with Professor O'Donoghue sitting on the opposite benches – the leader of Fine Gael, Dr FitzGerald, argued that the country needed £600 million a year, and not, as the government claimed, £650 million spread over five years[78]. The minister for economic planning and development had little difficulty in knocking down this particular argument, since the figures were based on the unwarranted assumption that the EMS was equivalent to a monetary union of the type implied in the report. But, as the weeks passed Dr FitzGerald and his colleagues returned to the attack with a more convincing case, based partly on the increasing likelihood that Britain would not join, which, they argued, would alter the basis on which the original figures had been drawn up, but also on the evidence that had emerged from Mr Lynch's and Mr Colley's conversations in Bonn that the Germans were anxious to restrict most of any transfers approved to subsidized loans rather than grants. In his speech to the Dail on 30 November, following the prime minister's report on his visit to Bonn, Paris and London, the leader of the opposition had something of a field day on both issues[79].

The shift in the argument, linking the transfer of resources and the sterling issue, was not fortuitous. It reflected a growing unease in November amongst important sections of the Irish economy about the consequences of Britain's non-participation, which Fine Gael could not exploit as thoroughly as the Labour Party but which no opposition party could afford to ignore. The break with sterling would be hazardous for the economy as a whole if, as was assumed almost universally, sterling depreciated against the Irish punt. It was particularly menacing, however, to certain older industries such as textiles, clothing, footwear and furniture, which were more heavily dependent on UK markets than the newer industries that the Irish Development Agency (IDA) had attracted. These older industries were by definition less well placed to adapt to the brave new world, and their spokesmen argued with some force that the gulf between old and new, which had already begun to be a problem in the recent high-growth years, would be exacerbated still further by the monetary system. In order to avoid this deterioration, Dr FitzGerald argued, Ireland needed more money and more freedom to administer it according to national interests rather than abstract principles. The government had drawn up a list of infrastructural projects to which funds could be channelled. It was not the infrastructure, however, so much as industry itself and more particularly the older industries that needed help. It was therefore imperative that the money should be made available free of many of the restrictions to which Community grants were normally subject, since a high proportion of the funds would have to go to the current accounts of firms in trouble[80].

The Labour Party, which alone amongst the three parties had opposed Irish membership of the Community in 1972, and which had always been less encumbered by feelings of loyalty or affection towards the European Community, was less inhibited in its attacks on the government. Many of its criticisms were inevitably little more than sharper or shriller versions of those advanced by Fine Gael. As the weeks passed however, it became apparent that the party's objections went beyond the government's tactics or particular aspects of the Bremen proposal to the system itself. In the October debate in the Dail, the party leader, Mr Cluskey, had stressed that the Labour Party was not 'opposed to the regulation of the finances of the EEC' in principle[81]. By the end of November, though still stressing their willingness to approve Irish entry if the terms were right, he and his colleagues had moved far enough towards outright opposition to lay down six conditions for entry. It would probably be true to say that they did not expect these to be fulfilled and that – particularly in the case of the fifth and sixth – these reflected the main themes of their opposition[82]. The six conditions were:

1. that there is adequate transfer of resources in the form of grants to the minimum extent of £650 million over a five-year period, any loans to be in addition to those transfer resources;
2. that the transfer be in the form of grants which are untied, without conditions and capable of being applied as the government sees fit in order to protect employment: for example, they should be capable of being used for either capital or current purposes;
3. that if agreed the grants should be used by the government as expenditure on new projects in addition to current schemes and not as a substitute for them;
4. that there is no alteration in the real value of the CAP income to the Irish economy;
5. that there is a clear commitment given by the government that there will be no statutory incomes policy, that they will not introduce such a policy and then tell us that it is because of our membership of the EMS and that we have no option but to introduce a statutory incomes policy;
6. that the impact of the final scheme be properly evaluated by the government and be presented by them to the Dail showing employment effects in the short run, employment effects in the medium-term, effect on our GNP in 1979, effect on the rate of inflation in 1979 and budgetary changes particularly with regard to foreign borrowing policy.

In the light of pressures and demands of this nature, the energy with which Mr Colley and Mr Lynch threw themselves into their European travels in November is not surprising. Nor is the embarrassment of the Irish prime minister when, as a result of the French president's change of tone, he found himself offered assistance that fell dramatically below the levels that he and his colleagues had insisted would be necessary if the Republic was to enter the system.

6.2   The technical discussions of monetary issues, October–November 1978

Negotiations on the details of the monetary system proceeded throughout October and November 1978, and although they were not unaffected by the domestic political developments described in the previous section, they enjoyed a certain autonomy, which makes it legitimate to consider them separately. As before, a great deal of work was done within the orbit of the Monetary Committee, the Committee of Central Bank Governors and the ECOFIN, but agreements in these multilateral settings were frequently preceded by agreements in bilateral meetings outside the formal Community machinery. In discussing the history of these negotiations therefore, it will be most convenient to take each of the principal issues in turn, rather than to concentrate on the discussions of any particular group or committee. There were essentially four major monetary problems:

(a)   the nature and obligations of the intervention system, including the problem of margins;
(b)   the scope and character of credit facilities under the new system;
(c)   the implications of Britain's non-entry and the negotiation of a special relationship;
(d)   the need to achieve a rational realignment of member currencies at the outset of the system within the context of currency unrest inside the Snake and a new dollar crisis.

The nature and obligations of the intervention system

Eight out of the nine ministers at the September meeting of the ECOFIN had agreed to accept the Belgian compromise as a basis for further study and negotiation. However, as we have seen in section 5.2, the compromise in the form in which it was submitted to the ministers in September was essentially a holding operation. It averted deadlock on the issues that had dominated the expert committees in the first eight weeks of their work and offered ECU supporters time to sort out their problems, but it did not and could not determine the details of an eventual settlement. Its effectiveness for the purposes for which it was designed can be deduced from the relative ease with which at least three of the more contentious and fundamental questions associated with the ECU – namely its inherent bias towards the strong and the large, the problem of arriving at agreed definitions of the so-called divergence threshold and the difficulty of avoiding frequent and potentially dangerous changes in the relative weighting of currencies – were cleared up in the expert committees between September and October, while its limitations were evident in the revival of the basket/parity grid controversy in a different, less virulent but nonetheless troublesome form.

The problems associated with the different and shifting weights of currencies in the ECU have already been explained in some detail in the previous chapter[83]. They were amongst the principal factors prompting the Italians and the French to accept the Belgian compromise in the first place, since it was evident that an ECU-based system might have almost exactly the opposite of the effect that its weak currency advocates had originally intended without some artificial and by definition rather complex arrangement that countered the preponderance that the DM in particular and the Snake in general would inevitably enjoy in such a system. The soundness of their decision, and the utility of the compromise itself, were almost immediately apparent when agreement was reached that, whatever force they might or might not have, ECU margins would be calculated for each currency in such a way as to eliminate the influence of disparities of weight on the probability of reaching them. As *Table 6.1*, setting out the maximum divergence spreads and thresholds eventually agreed, shows, the DM, which under a straightforward, undifferentiated system would have had a wider margin than any other currency, was given the narrowest band, while the 'lightest currency', the Irish punt, had the widest margins other than the lira,

Table 6.1 *Maximum divergence spreads and divergence thresholds*

(1) Currency	(2) Maximum spread (as %)	(3) Divergence threshold 75% of (2)
Belgian/Luxembourg franc	±2.03	±1.52
German mark	±1.51	±1.13
Dutch guilder	±2.01	±1.51
British pound	–[a]	
Danish krone	±2.18	±1.64
French franc	±1.80	±1.35
Italian lira	±5.43[a]	±4.07
Irish punt	±2.22	±1.67

[a] The initial assumption apart, the table gives the effective margin applicable to the lira and does not assign any margin to the pound sterling. It is, however, important to remember that calculation of the margin of each of the other EEC currencies is based on a bilateral movement of 2.25% against all the other currencies, including the lira and the pound sterling

Source: European Economy, July 1979, p. 75

for which, as we shall see, special arrangements were eventually made. It is doubtful, to say the least, whether the Germans would have accepted this discriminatory arrangement if they had not been assured under the Belgian compromise formula of the retention of the parity grid system.

The second of the questions referred to above, namely the points or thresholds at which the divergence indicator would come into operation for each currency, was perhaps not as difficult to settle once agreement had been reached on divergence spreads, but it is significant nonetheless that, by the time that the ECOFIN met on 16 October, experts had agreed that the divergence threshold in ECU could be fixed at 75% of its maximum spread for each currency, which would mean in normal circumstances that a currency would attain this threshold before reaching its bilateral limit. Although this was still some way from the Italian proposal, which will be discussed again in more detail in the following pages, it did ensure the possibility of an independent role for the divergence indicator in the system since, if the spreads had been broader, ECU limits would not have been reached before the bilateral limits. Agreement was also reached in the meetings of late September and early October on arrangements for changes in the weights of currencies in the basket. The preliminary version of this agreement, which went forward to the ECOFIN meeting in October, envisaged a review of currency weights every three to five years. Later it was decided to adopt the five-year alternative, though special arrangements might be made if the weight of any particular currency changed by a significant amount, for example 25%.

Given the difficulties that had arisen over these issues, and more particularly over the first, during the initial period of the negotiations, the achievement of agreements covering them marked an important step forward towards the completion of the EMS. However, the much bigger problem of the obligations involved in the divergence indicator remained, and it was here that the fiercest controversies raged in October. The Belgian compromise in its original form had been distinctly vague. A breach of the divergence threshold would, it said, entail 'certain consequences' for intervention and/or other policies. Now, however, that the problems connected with ECU margins had been settled and agreement had been reached to fix the divergence threshold inside the bilateral limits, it was essential that these 'consequences' should be more precisely defined. But once the discussions of this problem began, the old divisions reappeared. The clash between Dr Emminger and M. Clappier at the Committee of Central Bank Governors on 9 October was perhaps the liveliest example of a conflict that was played out in all the expert committees during these weeks. The president of the Bundesbank opened, explaining why it was impossible for him to accept any 'automatic consequences' as a result of a currency crossing the divergence threshold. He claimed that the indicator was still imprecise, despite the improvements that had been made, and it would encourage rumours and speculation against one currency, even though the currency in question might not be the troublemaker at all. All that the Bundesbank would accept, therefore, was an obligation to consult, which might in certain circumstances result in intra-marginal interventions. To this the governor of the Banque de France replied that he could see no point at all in an indicator that was intended to do no more than trigger off consultations. There was already machinery available for consultations, and talks could take place at any time on the request of any member. He admitted that further study might have to be made of the modalities of intra-marginal interventions, and in particular of the question of which currency or currencies should be used, but he made it quite clear that as far as he was concerned a breach of the divergence threshold should entail an obligation to intervene.

Subsequent contributions to this meeting suggested that the truce that had been arrived at in September had broken down. Dr Zijlstra claimed that the French and their allies were going back on the agreement reached on 18 September, while Gordon Richardson sided with M. Clappier and incidentally scored a palpable hit against the president of the Bundesbank when he observed that as central bankers they were constantly intervening to correct distortions caused by rumours and that he could not therefore see why this particular system should be more vulnerable to rumours than any other. As in the previous month, however, it was the Belgians who came to the rescue in a carefully coordinated move towards a redefined compromise, which Dr de Strycker aired at the bankers' meeting on 9 October and which M. van Ypersele spelled out in more detail on the following day at the meeting of the Monetary Committee. The timing and wording of Dr de Strycker's intervention give perhaps the clearest indication of the spirit and intention that lay behind the compromise, and help to explain why the French accepted it almost immediately. Following directly on from M. Clappier, the Belgian governor declared that he agreed with his French colleagues that the divergence indicator should entail intervention by the central bank concerned in Community currencies in order to prevent the currency in question reaching its bilateral margins. He wondered, however, whether his colleagues could agree to a new version of the compromise under which interventions would follow on the operation of the indicator *unless* the other central banks in the system agreed that they were unnecessary. The nature of the 'obligation in principle', or, as it was later described, the 'presumption', which was at the heart of the Belgian compromise and which distinguished it quite clearly from the kind of cosmetic agreement that the Germans and the Dutch hoped to obtain, was defined at some length in paragraph 16 of the Monetary Committee's report to the October meeting of the ECOFIN. It is worth quoting, partly because it helps to place the rather dramatic exchanges that took place later at the ECOFIN meeting in perspective, but partly too because it provides a useful point of comparison for the agreements that were ultimately arrived at in the ECOFIN of November and the European Council itself in December.

> 16. ... the stabilisation of rates would be preceded, within the margins, by the triggering of consultations and interventions as soon as a certain spread, measured in terms of ECUs, had been exceeded. ...
>
> 16.2 The uses of the ECU set out above are the following:
>
> When a currency exceeded its divergence threshold, the Central Bank concerned would, in principle, be obliged to diversify its intervention practices:
>
> (a) if the bilateral limit had not been reached, it would have to commence intervention, either in Community currencies ... and/ or in dollars, to check the divergent trend;
>
> (b) if the bilateral limit had been reached, the obligation to intervene would be not only in the currency furthest removed from it but also, to alleviate the situation of that currency, in dollars or in other Community currencies close to their bilateral limit in the opposite direction ...;
>
> (c) if it did not take action in the manner indicated under (a) or (b) above, it would have to give reasons for failing to do so in the context of concertation arrangements;
>
> (d) in order to facilitate the diversification of intervention, a Central Bank could not oppose stabilising interventions in its currency up to an agreed ceiling, when its currency was relatively close to a bilateral intervention limit. ...
>
> 16.3 When a currency remained persistently beyond its divergence threshold for a specific length of time, the monetary authorities of the country concerned would be required, in the course of consultations, to give their assessment of the situation and an account of any measures that they intended to adopt.

As the report by the Monetary Committee to the ECOFIN explained, the Belgian compromise in its new form did not secure immediate acceptance by either of the contending groups, though there was a notable defection from the non-Snake group on 10 October when the deputy governor of the Banque de France indicated to his colleagues at the Monetary Committee meeting that his government were satisfied with the blend of the obligation to intervene and the flexibility offered by the possibility of consultations that the Belgian compromise implied. The British and the Italians on the one side, and the Germans, the Dutch and the Danes on the other were less willing to give ground, however. The British and the Italians continued to insist that any movement beyond a currency's divergence threshold should entail an automatic obligation on the central bank in question to intervene, while the Germans and their allies were not prepared to see the divergence indicator as anything more than 'an additional instrument for Central Banks to take account of in their intervention policy, and also as a trigger for consultations on the full range of problems and remedies to be applied in a particular situation'.

These divisions persisted and were exploited ruthlessly by the British chancellor of the exchequer in a speech at the ECOFIN meeting of 16 October that a senior French representative later described as 'dazzling' and ·that another seasoned Community figure considered the most brilliant rhetorical performance that he had ever heard in a Community meeting. Posing as the defender of the 'spirit of Bremen', Mr Healey succeeded in discomforting both the Germans for their obduracy and the French for their craven abandonment of the bold new ideas that their president himself had championed at the European Council. When all allowances are made for Mr Healey's rhetorical skills, however, these would not seem to have had any lasting effect on the proceedings. The delegations arrived divided; they left, if anything, rather nearer agreement. There was, in fact, a striking contrast between British press reports of this meeting and many of the public and private comments on it in Germany, France and Italy. According to the former[84], the meeting had revealed just how deep the divisions between the member states were, and doubts were expressed once again about the feasibility of the self-imposed time limits. To many observers on the Continent by contrast, the predominant impression was that, despite obvious difficulties, most if not all governments concerned were extremely anxious to overcome them. The Italian evidence is particularly impressive in this respect, because there were still good reasons for emphasizing the common ground between Italy and the United Kingdom. Whereas the *Financial Times* described the outcome of the meeting as 'a triumph of sorts for the UK'[85], the Brussels correspondent of *Il Corriere della Sera*, who was not conspicuous for his enthusiasm for the EMS, reported that the ECOFIN meeting had succeeded in dismissing the German approach and perhaps also the Anglo-Italian one, leaving the way open to a genuine compromise on the basis of the Belgian proposal[86]. A similar impression was conveyed by the confidential brief prepared for Mr Andreotti before his talks with the French president on 26 October. The ECOFIN meeting, the document claimed, had shown that a compromise along the lines of the Belgian suggestion was feasible and that, although there might still be some difficulties with the Germans over the issue, there was no serious disagreement between the Italians and the French. If a victor must be found at the October meeting of the ECOFIN therefore, it would probably be more appropriate to settle on M. van Ypersele than Mr Healey.

The impression that, despite the rhetorical flourishes of a chancellor whose prime minister had anyway by this time decided that British entry was impossible, the opposing camps were in fact moving towards agreement was confirmed in the weeks that followed the ECOFIN meeting. The clearest indications of the process are to be found in the final report of the

Monetary Committee, which was ready by 10 November. The most novel features of the section dealing with interventions were contained in two paragraphs, 15.1 and 15.3. The first reported that 'all members' had indicated that the Belgian compromise, set out in a slightly amended form in the previous paragraph, 'could provide a basis for agreement'. There were however still certain qualifications on both sides, which were dealt with in the succeeding paragraphs. The Anglo-Italian reservations, which were described in paragraph 15.2, were concerned principally with the problems of involuntary creditors and debtors and will be discussed shortly. What is more interesting in the immediate context, however, was the description of the German–Dutch position in the paragraph that followed. It needs to be quoted in full, both as an indication of the extent to which the governments concerned had moved since October and as a basis for comparison with the agreement that was finally achieved:

> 15.3. ... other members, who are of the opinion that there should not be intervention obligations as soon as the divergence threshold is crossed, and who are not inclined to consider any necessity to disapprove the presumption to intervene, are prepared to envisage the following procedure:
> –The crossing of the divergence threshold constitutes a presumption to act to correct the situation. The actions to be taken will be discussed in normal concertation procedure among central banks.
> –If, after more than five days, the divergence remains, central banks will consult formally with each other to form a judgement whether one or several of the following measures appropriate to the situation should be taken:
> . further intervention,
> . monetary measures,
> . drawing on the credit facilities,
> . other external and domestic policy measures.

The gap between the counterproposal and the Belgian compromise was still, of course, significant: the latter made no provision for a period of reflection, gave priority in the initial phase to diversified interventions and required the central bank whose currency crossed the threshold to explain why, in exceptional circumstances, it had not intervened. However, if one compares paragraph 15.3 with the corresponding section of the previous Monetary Committee report, the differences in tone and detail are remarkable. Taken together with the statement in paragraph 15.1 that was quoted above, the evidence of the report suggests that agreement on what was by far the most vexatious and serious issue in dispute in the monetary talks was not far off.

The ECOFIN meeting on 20 November was to confirm this impression since, although both the Germans and the Dutch, and the British and the Italians pressed their respective viewpoints and were duly voted down 7 to 2 in each case, the dispute between the seven and the Germans and the Dutch on the intervention mechanism had by the end of the session been narrowed down to one issue. The seven wanted the text of the resolution to emphasize that a central bank could only refrain from intervention 'in special circumstances', which it was obliged to explain to its partners, while the Germans and the Dutch maintained that the exceptional character of non-intervention did not need to be stressed. When the heads of government met in Brussels on 4 December therefore, the words (or word) in question were still bracketed in the draft version of paragraph 3.6 of the Resolution, but the German concession that finally settled the issue came as no great surprise to several and perhaps even the majority of those who had been at the ECOFIN meeting two weeks earlier. As Philippe Lemaître, who was as ever extremely well informed about the views of the French representatives at the meeting, noted in *Le Monde* on 22 November: 'L'écart encore à combler lors du Conseil Européen est, on s'en rend compte, fort limité.' A confidential Italian paper prepared for Mr Andreotti on the eve of his meetings in London with Mr Callaghan and Mr Healey on 22 November was even more explicit and confident. From what the German chancellor had said in the course of the bilateral conversations at Siena on 1 November, the author was convinced that Mr Schmidt would accept the seven's position and, if he did, the British claim, which Mr Healey had advanced on several occasions both before and during the meeting (and which he was to continue to maintain afterwards), that the EMS intervention mechanism was no more than a new version of the Snake could not be sustained. Thanks to the Belgian compromise in its various forms, one might conclude, the ECU had been assured a central role in the system, which if it was not as dominant as its original advocates might have hoped, was certainly more significant than they must have feared in August and September. It remained, of course, to be seen how this new device would work in practice, but whatever second thoughts some of its champions may have subsequently had – when, for example, like the Belgians they found themselves branded as the sole deviants – in the context of the negotiations and against the background of the aims and assumptions of those principally involved, the outcome of the long struggle over the ECU indicator was a genuine compromise, which on balance probably cost the Germans more than it did the non-Snake countries.

The other major problem, which concerned the size of the margins available to non-Snake countries, was important because of the importance the Italians attached to it, both in relation to the construction of the system as a whole and as a means of alleviating some of their own particular difficulties. The main features of the Italian government's strategy have already been indicated in the discussion of Dr Masera's 'Blueprint'. Their hope had always been that the other non-Snake countries, and in particular Britain, would join them in pressing for wider margins, and Banca d'Italia spokesmen never ceased from pressing the case when they met their French or British counterparts either in multilateral groups or in the course of the French president's visit to Rome in October, or the Italian prime minister's visit to London on 22 November. Despite the very considerable skill and eloquence with which they advanced their case however – the speech that Dr Baffi delivered at a dinner in honour of M. Giscard d'Estaing in Rome on 26 October being a conspicuously good example – they received no official encouragement from either country. In fact, the only prominent ally whom Dr Baffi found in London was Samuel Brittan of the *Financial Times*[87], but as the chancellor of the exchequer assumed that any suggestion that the British should accept a wider band must be 'humorous, on the grounds that it implied that the French economy was in better shape than the United Kingdom's (an idea that Mr Healey evidently found outrageous), the governor of the Banca d'Italia and his colleagues must have been aware that Mr Brittan's help, though welcome, was of little practical consequence[88].

In these circumstances, Italian negotiators were forced to change their tactics. They wanted a wider band for their own country at all costs: they hoped that for cosmetic reasons the 'concession' could remain theoretically open to others. The Italians received some encouragement in their campaign on 18 October when, following the ECOFIN meeting, Mr Pandolfi and Dr Baffi visited Germany and spoke with Dr Emminger and the minister of finance. The Bundesbank president, who spoke much more than the minister or indeed anybody else present, was particularly forthcoming, agreeing with his Italian colleague that it would be far more satisfactory, both in the interests of the system as a whole and for their own sake, if the French and the British were to opt for wider margins as well. However, as in the course of the same conversation Dr Emminger suggested that the Italians might delay their entry for 6 to 12 months, it is difficult to avoid the conclusion that the president's 'generosity' was strongly influenced by the feeling, which he had expressed to the German chancellor a month earlier, that life would be a good deal easier if none of the present floating currencies would join the new system in the immediate future. To win their case, therefore, the Italians needed much more than the help of Dr Emminger, and the results elsewhere in October were scarcely encouraging. Their views were duly noted at the Monetary Committee, at the Committe of Central Bank Governors and the ECOFIN, but with the exception of Dr Emminger, who supported the case for a 4% margin at the central bank governors' meeting of 30 October, nobody else seems to have been ready to help, and some, including it would seem Dr Lahnstein, expressed opposition in principle.

The breakthrough came, as so often in the history of the EMS negotiations, following a meeting between Mr Schmidt and M. Giscard d'Estaing, this time at Rambouillet, a few days after the French president's visit to Rome and the German chancellor's conversations with Mr Andreotti in

Siena. From then on matters began to move ahead, though there was a temporary setback on 11 November when Mr Andreotti met Benelux prime ministers at Luxembourg and the latter, largely it would seem because of a genuine misunderstanding of the scope of Dr Baffi's demands, which their experts took to be for margins of 12% on either side, adopted a distinctly negative line. Cordiality was restored a few days later, however, when at the central bank governors' meeting of 14 November it was agreed that the lira could move within margins of 6% either side of the central rate. This decision was subsequently upheld by both the ECOFIN and the European Council and appeared in the Resolution as an option open to all non-Snake countries, and not just Italy. For Dr Baffi and his colleagues the concession was a matter of major significance. Indeed, without it, it seems highly unlikely that the Italian government could have entered, despite the political arguments in favour.

The credit mechanisms

The pattern of the debate about the credit mechanisms in the new system between October and November was largely determined by two factors: the legal constraints by which the majority felt themselves bound at Community level and, some argued, at national level; and the determination of the Germans, supported by the Dutch, to minimize the inflationary risks that they feared would follow from a major increase in the size of credits available. As section 5.2 has shown, legal considerations had already forced the negotiators to base their discussions on the existing Community credit mechanisms, which were the very short-term financing and short-term monetary support (STMS), both of which were under the aegis of the central banks, and medium-term financial assistance (MTFA), which could be granted only by the Council.

As far as the *very short-term financing* was concerned, this referred to the credit facilities that central banks made available to each other through the EMCF in order to permit interventions in Community currencies. Under existing arrangements, the amount of credit available for these purposes was unlimited, but the duration of the financing was only 30 days. Discussion centred on the duration, the problems raised by the introduction of the divergence indicator, which would create an entirely new category of 'involuntary' debtors and creditors, and the use of the ECU as a means of settlement. On the first of these points, opinion polarized between those, like the Germans, who wanted to maintain the existing provision of 30 days and those, notably the British and the Italians, who wanted the period extended to either 60 or better still 90 days, on the grounds that this would create a 'greater probability' of a change in the debtor country's position before settlement became due. At the ECOFIN meeting in November the demandants reduced their target to 60 days, but the difference remained unresolved and it was left to the European Council to decide on a compromise of 45 days.

The complications introduced into the financing of interventions by the use of the ECU, both as a divergence indicator and as a means of settlement between the monetary authorities, were also left unresolved by the expert committees and the ECOFIN, but the issues raised are nonetheless worth examining in the present context. The first was the problem of 'involuntary' debts or credits. When a currency crossed the divergence threshold, it was presumed that the central bank in question would intervene, which, if it was done in a Community currency, would mean the purchase or sale of the currency of another member state. This would create an 'involuntary' credit or debt that would in due course have to be settled. The question was when and on what terms. The aim of the weaker currency countries, and in particular of the British, was to devise rules that would allow a longer term for the settlement of debts incurred in this way and, if the surplus country did not carry out the adjustment measures agreed with its partners, the elimination of interest on at least a portion of the money involved. To be fair, the British also urged that if a deficit country that triggered off the indicator did not carry out the measures decided in consultation with its partners, its access to the short-term credit facility could be limited. The Germans and the Dutch, however, denied that any special rules were necessary. It was not a major issue, as governor Baffi, who supported the British, pointed out, but it provoked a good deal of discussion and remained unsettled not only by the ECOFIN and its related committees, but also in the end by the European Council, which decided that the best action was to shelve the problem, leaving it to the review of the system that the Council Resolution suggested should take place six months after its inauguration[89].

The remaining problem associated with the very short-term financing has already been referred to in the previous chapter during the discussion of the Bundesbank's reservations about the EMS, namely the Bundesbank's fear that if member states were allowed to exchange ECUs for DM when settling their accounts the German authorities would lose control over the availability of DMs. As with their other fears about the implications of 'unlimited' obligations, the Bundesbank authorities were greatly reassured by the chancellor's private promise, which was later made public in a speech by the economics minister, Count Lambsdorff[90], that in practice the Bundesbank would not have to feel bound by an obligation if, in the judgement of its president and his colleagues, doing so would constitute a threat to their commitment to monetary stability. The absence of any specific agreement on this issue before the European Council meeting was therefore not as grave as it might otherwise have been, but it was nonetheless gratifying from the Bundesbank's point of view that the central bank governors eventually decreed that a creditor central bank would not be obliged to accept settlement by means of ECUs of an amount more than 50% of the claim being settled[91].

Important though these skirmishes over very short-term financing were, they did not compare in significance with the debate about the amount and distribution of credits under the *STMS* and *MTFA*. The controversy began, but did not end, with a difference of opinion between the Germans and the Dutch on the one side and the remaining Community states on the other about the precise meaning of the second paragraph of the Bremen Annex, which envisaged the creation of a supply of ECUs for use in credit support operations equivalent to 20% of the gold and dollar reserves of the member states' central banks. In the second half of 1978, this was reckoned to amount to approximately 25 billion ECUs. The French and the majority of their partners argued that the Annex meant that 25 billion represented the maximum amount that could be effectively borrowed from the system, which would be distributed between the STMS and MTFA in proportions still to be negotiated. The Germans and the Dutch, by contrast, maintained that the 25 billion should be understood as equivalent to the sum of all the national currencies made available in the form of creditor quotas *and* extensions, and that the maximum available credits through the STMS and MTFA would therefore amount to no more than 16 billion ECUs (see *Table 6.2*).

This difference about the amount of credits available was complicated by a dispute about the distribution of the credits between the STMS and MTFA. The Germans argued that they could not agree to any additional credit under the MTFA, which allowed for loans of up to five years, without special legislation and, as this might take time, the new credit mechanisms could not become fully operational at the moment at which the system was launched. If and when parliamentary approval was obtained, they suggested that 9.3 of the 16 billion total should be made available under STMS, while 6.7 billion should be allocated to the MTFA. If the constitutional position was as the Germans and Dutch claimed it to be, there was nothing of course that the other countries could do, but the seven did nonetheless produce a formula to avert the delay in the full-scale implementation of the system that the German attitude threatened to entail. They proposed that the full 25 billion should be mobilized immediately, but that in the period before the necessary legislation was passed the whole of the additional credit, which amounted to 20.7 billion ECUs, should be put into the STMS.

The gap between the two sides prior to the November ECOFIN meeting and the extent to which both sets of proposals marked an advance on existing arrangements can be seen in tabular form in *Table 6.2*. Once again however, due almost certainly to direct pressure from the chancellor, the Germans gave ground. At the ECOFIN meeting on 20 November, they abandoned their opposition to the more generous interpretation of the total amount of credits available, agreeing to the 25 billion, and accepted a formula covering their legal difficulties with the MTFA. This obliged them to proceed with the necessary legislation with a view to obtaining parliamentary approval before the end of June 1979, and in the meantime required

Table 6.2 *Possible formulae for extending community credit to an amount of 25 billion ECU (billion ECU)*

	Total financial obligations of member states				Maximum available credit				
	Short-term monetary support (STMS)		Medium-term financial assistance (MTFA)	Total STMS + MTFA	Short-term monetary support (STMS)[a]		Total STMS	Medium-term financial assistance[b] (MTFA)	Total STMS + MTFA
	Quotas	Extensions			Quotas	Extensions			
Present situation	6.5	3.6	5.5	15.6	2.2	3.6	5.8	4.3	10.0
German solution[a]	10.6	5.8	8.6	25.0	3.5	5.8	9.3	6.7[c]	16.0[c]
Other solution	29.4	11.0	5.5	45.9	9.7	11.0	20.7	4.3	25.0

[a] Optimal equilibrium creditors/debtors (= creditors 1 large country + NL or Bel–Lux + DK + Irl and debtors 2 large countries + Italy + Bel–Lux or NL) + complete activation of creditor and debtor extensions
[b] Total commitment ceilings less that of a large country
[c] Only available after increase in MTFA
Source: Monetary Committee Report, November 1978

them to make an interim financing agreement through the central banks covering their extended MTFA quota. There was still some dispute between them and the majority over the exact distribution of the credits between the STMS and the MTFA, the Germans arguing that 12.5 billion should go to each, and the others, 15 billion to the STMS and 10 billion to the MTFA. However, this was a relatively minor matter, which as the European Council showed could be and was quickly dealt with. What was more important was the confirmation that the Germans' shift from their hard-line position gave of the chancellor's determination to achieve an agreement by 5 December despite the political and constitutional obstacles that he faced at home.

The only other respects in which arrangements under the STMS and MTFA in the new regime differed from those that had obtained hitherto lay in the use of the ECU and in an increase in the duration of credits. Under the existing provisions, short-term credit was available for three months, renewable for a similar period at the request of the beneficiary central bank. Representatives of the non-Snake countries pressed for a further prolongation of three months. These requests were resisted in the Monetary and the Central Bank Governors' committees but, as over other issues, the ECO-FIN was able to achieve an agreement at its November meeting. Under the revised instrument relating to the STMS, which was promulgated by the central bank governors in March when the EMS was eventually launched, utilization of the credit was to be for a period of three months, which might be renewed twice for a period of three months. In itself, the concession was not dramatic, but placed in the context of November 1978 it provided yet more evidence of a trend that – despite Aachen, despite the retention of the parity grid and despite the continuing anxieties of the financial community in Germany – was propelling the new system further and further away from the Snake to which so many of its critics likened it. Reference has already been made to the brief that was prepared for Mr Andreotti on 21 November for use during his discussions with Mr Callaghan and Mr Healey on the following day. It was designed to provide the Italian prime minister with ammunition with which to demolish Mr Healey's repeated assertions that the EMS was simply the Snake under another name. Having listed the concessions that the Snake countries, led by Germany, had made, most of which have been touched upon in the preceding pages, the paper concluded with the following words:

The situation which emerges as a result of the meeting on November 20 is a singular one: Britain is bent on staying outside the monetary agreement on the basis of arguments which if the replies to the British objections set out in this paper are valid cannot be substantiated. The system is not as inflexible as the British say it is, nor are obligations asymmetrical, nor are the credit mechanisms inadequate.

The British half-way house

The negotiations for a half-way house, which had been in progress for several weeks, confirm the impression that the arguments advanced against the system by Mr Healey at the November meeting of the ECOFIN and elsewhere were, as the author of the Italian paper himself suspected, 'a smokescreen designed to provide cover for Britain's decision to stay outside'. The negotiations can be covered fairly summarily, but they deserve a brief mention, not least because they throw light on the motives of several of the principal non-British actors in the EMS negotiations, including in particular the French president and the German chancellor.

During their meeting in Bonn on 18 October, Mr Callaghan would appear to have told Mr Schmidt that it would not be possible for his government to take the United Kingdom into the new system before the general election was over. There is nothing to suggest, however, that the two men discussed possible alternative arrangements at any length. On the contrary, the chief short-term result of this meeting was an increase in the chancellor's irritation with the British government. Whether because they were aware of this, or because of a more ancient prejudice inside the Foreign Office in favour of working with and through the French in European Community affairs, the British began their efforts to patch up a compromise in Paris. The three most senior officials concerned with the day-to-day management of the negotiations – Mr Couzens, Mr McMahon and Mr Butler of the Foreign Office – were dispatched to Paris at the end of October. Their visit was followed soon afterwards by a visit by M. Monory to London and the affair was concluded with a meeting between Mr Callaghan and the French president in Paris on 24 November. Doubtless Mr Schmidt knew through Paris of what was going on, but the evidence suggests that in this particular sphere it was the French president rather than the German chancellor who took the lead, and that the latter was reluctant to raise a finger to help Mr Callaghan out of his difficulties[92].

The clearest indication of Mr Schmidt's mood during these weeks is to be found in the reports of conversations that he had with Mr Jenkins on 27 October and Mr Andreotti at the beginning of November. He told the former that there had been no progress in the bilateral consultations with the British a week earlier and that from now on he intended to be 'ruthless'. Dr Schulmann, he said, had been urging him to make concessions to ease British entry, but he had rejected this advice. If the British were more cooperative, he would do all that he could to help in the concurrent studies, but he had had quite enough of the British prime minister's 'poker game' with his Community partners and even more than enough of the 'maverick', Mr Healey. He expressed similar views, if anything more forcefully still, a few days later when he met Mr Andreotti at Siena. The British, he implied, had behaved contemptibly. Indeed, far from wanting to help them, he gave the impression to several of those whom he met in this period that he was anxious to ensure that they did not benefit in any way from a system towards which they had adopted such an ambivalent and unhelpful attitude. In the conversation with Mr Jenkins, for example, he asked several times whether it would be possible to devise credit mechanisms and aid to the less prosperous in such a way as to cut the British out if they did not join. There was therefore little basis for a 'half-way house' or a 'soft-landing' here.

The French, by contrast, were much more cooperative. The official talks went well, as did the Healey–Monory conversations, and the Callaghan –Giscard meeting went better still[93]. Following the latter, the French president declared that, even if the United Kingdom did not participate from the beginning, this would not have any adverse political consequences for the future of Europe, while Mr Callaghan, in his first public admission of the possibility of a half-way house, said that although it was essential that a 'Community scheme' should embrace all nine member countries it was not necessary for all the member states to adhere to every part of the plan. Some might decide that they would be more concerned with certain aspects than others. 'If the scheme is a Community scheme, it clearly embraces all the members of the Community. As to whether all members of the Community take part in particular aspects of such a scheme, that is a different question'[94]. This demonstration of Anglo-French amity was, it need hardly be said, of only limited significance. Maurice Delarue, in a perceptive article on the November meeting between the French president and the British prime minister, which appeared in *Le Monde* on 26 November, remarked on the banter and irony that were such prominent features of the after-dinner speeches and the press conference. This was no Aachen, more a smart deal between business acquaintances who occasionally found it in their mutual interest to cooperate. One point on which they agreed, and which un-doubtedly made it easier for the French to be more accommodating, was their common hostility to any extension of the powers of the European Parliament following the direct elections. It is true that a few days before the summit the British had sided with the Italians and the Parliament over the Regional Fund but, as subsequent events showed, this was a tactical move devoid of any ideological significance, and the communiqué that followed the Anglo-French summit specifically noted the accord of the two leaders on this issue[95]. Against a domestic political background of the kind that has been described earlier in this chapter, any ally who shared the anti-federalist stance that the president had to maintain when dealing with the Gaullists was better than none. Another explanation of their agreement is to be found in the nature of the EMS itself. The effects of weighting had been eliminated in the definition of the ECU spreads, but it was still very much in the interests of France to have the pound in as a further counterweight to the DM in particular, and the Snake currencies in general. Still another factor was that the British were not after all asking a great deal. After some argument, they would seem to have accepted that the short-term credit facilities on which they could draw, though nominally comparable to those available to other large members of the EMS, would in fact remain at their pre-EMS levels until they joined. They also appear to have agreed that although they would continue to press for a fundamental review of the Community budget and for the best possible short-term deal, from which they themselves would hope eventually to profit if they joined, the special concessions of the kind that the Irish and the Italians were demanding were not to be available to them until they became full members. What the British most wanted, in fact, was that they should not be left out of the continuing discussions about the future of the system, in case, as the prime minister in particular feared, it became a going concern and a major force in the international monetary system. Acceptance of this cost the French little, and might eventually profit them greatly since, as the previous chapters have shown, the British were more often than not their allies in the monetary negotiations. As, in addition, Mr Callaghan and his officials indicated that they would do their utmost to keep sterling in line with the EMS currencies on the exchange markets, and would certainly not indulge in competitive devaluations, the French had virtually nothing to lose.

The deal would seem initially at any rate to have been rather more distasteful to the German chancellor, which is doubtless one explanation of the marked change in the tone of British official comment on the EMS in November – witness Mr Healey's evidence to the Expenditure Committee and the government's Green Paper[96] – and the increasingly loud hints that it was only a matter of time before the UK too would join. The Peter Jenkins article of 1 December was one such signal, but there were others, including a letter from Mr Callaghan to his colleagues on the eve of the European Council and more direct and personal assurances to Mr Schmidt[97]. The tactics worked. The chancellor seems to have been persuaded by the evidence and, as a result, in one of several curious twists at the very end of the EMS negotiations, the British enjoyed the Brussels meeting of the European Council more than anybody else.

Developments in the international monetary system, October–November 1978

At the same time as the negotiations for the EMS were proceeding, there were significant developments in the foreign exchange markets involving both the Snake and the dollar. The bare facts of this latest bout of currency unrest can be quickly told[98]. The uneasy truce that had followed on the March agreement between the American and German authorities and President Carter's April speech held for most of the spring and early summer[99], though there were signs of a slippage in June and still more in July. The trouble really began, however, in August. Between the beginning of that month and the end of October, the dollar fell by 18% against the DM, 17% against the Swiss franc, 10% against the French franc, 8% against the pound sterling and 6% against the lira. The United States' authorities responded to this crisis with a series of measures that, though initially unconvincing, were eventually of a totally different order from those that had been adopted during the previous crisis in the winter of 1977–78. Their initial reaction consisted of a mixture of intervention on the foreign exchange markets and the progressive tightening of credit. As far as the former was concerned, the Foreign Exchange Trading Desk of the Federal Reserve Bank of New York intervened increasingly in DM and Swiss francs, drawing on the swap arrangements that existed with both central banks concerned. Between August and October the authorities sold a total of $2204.4 million equivalent of DM and $294.2 million equivalent of Swiss francs. These actions in the foreign exchange markets were matched by increasingly hard credit policies. In August, following a well-publicized meeting between the president and his top economic advisers, the Federal Reserve announced a ½% increase in the discount rate and the elimination of reserve requirements on Euro-dollar borrowings, while the Treasury declared its intention of increasing and extending its regular monthly gold auctions[100]. These measures provided a short respite between late August and September, but speculation began in the second half of September and the authorities were forced to reply with a fresh ¾% rise in the discount rate. Even this was not enough however, and the currency's fall was only halted in the end by a combination of internal and external measures that amounted in effect to a totally new economic policy[101]. It emerged in three stages, of which the first consisted of the long-awaited passage of the administration's energy bill through Congress. This was, however, only relevant to one aspect of the problems of the American economy, since whereas in the winter of 1977/78 commentators, speculators and the authorities themselves had laid particular stress on the size of the United States' oil import bill, attention was by now increasingly concentrated on inflation. This was the target of the second package of measures, a counter-inflation programme announced on 24 October, the main elements of which were:

a. a promise by the federal government to limit spending and to reduce the federal deficit from its 1976 level of 23% of GNP to 21% by 1980.
b. the introduction of a voluntary incomes policy, with a norm of 7%.
c. the setting of a price standard for firms which was half a percentage point below the 1976–1977 average annual rate of price increase, with a ceiling of 9.5%. Both this and the wages policy would be monitored by the Council on Wage and Price Stability.
d. the government itself would encourage the observance of these guidelines through its own regulatory and procurement policies.

Cooperation would also be rewarded by fiscal benefits. Groups of workers who observed the norm would receive a tax rebate if the rate of inflation over the next year were to exceed 7%.

Even these measures were not enough however, and on Saturday evening, 28 October, Mr Carter called his chief economic advisers away from their Washington dinner parties to a late-night discussion of the implementation of a fresh package, which had needless to say been in the making for some time, but which it was now decided would have to be put into effect[102]. The necessary consultations with the United States' principal partners were carried out over the following days, and on 1 November the administration announced the following measures designed to act directly on the dollar's fall:

a. Federal Reserve discount rate was raised yet again from 8.5% to a historic high of 9.5%.

b. 'A supplementary reserve requirement' equivalent to 2% of time deposits of $100,000 or more was to be imposed on banks belonging to the Federal Reserve system. This, it was hoped, would help to moderate the expansion of credit and encourage banks to borrow from abroad.

c. Currency 'swap arrangements' had been increased with the Central Banks of Germany, Japan and Switzerland raising the existing total from $7.4 billion to $15 billion. Of this, the Bundesbank was prepared to provide up to $6 billion, the Swiss bank up to $4 billion and the Bank of Japan up to $5 billion.

d. The United States intended to issue Treasury securities denominated in foreign currencies up to a total of $10 billion. The idea was to sell to private holders rather than other Central Banks.

e. The United States was to draw $3 billion from the IMF out of the total of $4.1 billion which it could draw on automatically.

f. It was intended to sell 2 billion SDRs.

g. Monthly gold sales would be increased from their present levels of 300,000 ounces per month to 1.5 million ounces per month.

The impact of this package was immediate and dramatic. By the end of November 1978 the dollar had advanced 11.75% against the DM, 15.5% against the Swiss franc and 11.5% against the yen. There were to be fresh waves of uncertainty from time to time over the following year, primarily in the summer and early autumn of 1979, but the November support package can be said to have put an end to the protracted dollar crisis that began in the second half of 1977 and continued as a semi-constant counterpoint to the EMS negotiations throughout 1978[103].

Movements of the scale indicated above against the dollar inevitably threatened the stability of the Snake, and from the middle of the summer of

1978 onwards, all Germany's smaller partners, and particularly the Belgians, came under heavy pressure. The extent of their difficulties can be deduced from the size of the interventions that were required to keep their currencies within the permitted margins and the policy measures, including eventually the currency realignment of 15 October, that they undertook. As far as interventions were concerned, the Bundesbank assessed the damage at DM 10 billion in the period between July and the middle of October, while the Belgian authorities calculated that their currency outflows in the same period amounted to approximately a third of that figure[104]. The measures taken to stop the process varied from country to country but the Belgians, who were the most seriously affected, acted on both interest rates and bank lending limits. Interest rates were raised as early as August, but on 11 October the Belgian Banque Nationale introduced a special rate of 8.5% on a quarter of its re-discount facilities and new ceilings on bank lending, which between them, it was hoped, would force companies to repatriate funds that were currently held abroad in the expectation of a devaluation[105]. However, even these measures were insufficient and, following a fortnight in which the Bundesbank had to spend DM 6 billion, culminating on Friday the 13th in an orgy amounting to DM 1.5 billion, the authorities announced a realignment of the Snake's currencies on 15 October, involving a 2% revaluation of the DM against the Belgian franc and the Dutch guilder and a 4% rise against the two Scandinavian currencies. This was the ninth revaluation since the end of 1973 and the fourth within 18 months[106].

In assessing the significance of these developments in the international monetary system for the emergence of the EMS, it is important to distinguish their short-term effects on the political debate about the system and their longer-term impact on the international economic environment in which the EMS was launched and developed during the first two years of its existence. As far as the short-term effects are concerned, reactions were varied, but, as the earlier discussion of contributions made by Dr Emminger, Sir Jeremy Morse and Dr Carli have shown, there was a widespread feeling amongst experts that the crisis made the immediate future a bad time for launching the system and underlined how difficult it was anyway going to be to sustain it. As matters turned out however, these gloomy predictions, which were of considerable importance at the time, were not vindicated by events, and in retrospect one can see – as some indeed saw and argued at the time – that the monetary crises of the autumn of 1978 helped rather than hindered the birth of the system for at least two reasons. Firstly, they provoked an overall realignment of intra-European exchange rates, and secondly they contributed towards and marked a fundamental reorientation of American policy, which, whatever its *economic* merits, was beneficial to the establishment of a monetary system in the medium term.

The first of these problems can be illustrated by reference to the DM rates listed in Appendix 2. In July 1978, following the temporary stabilization of the dollar and, in the French case, the defeat of the left in the parliamentary elections, the DM–lira and DM–French franc rates had sprung back to levels that were well above those that had obtained in March 1978. Taking the end of 1972 as 100, the average rates in March were: DM–French franc 145.9, DM–lira 232.9, while in July the rates were: DM–French franc 136.1, DM–lira 228.4. As on the previous occasion, the autumn dollar crisis affected the major European currencies in different ways. All of them appreciated, but the DM moved up conspicuously faster and, what is more important, stayed up as far as the other major European currencies were concerned, even when, following the 1 November package, the dollar bounced back. The rates as of 1 December, on the eve of the European Council, were: DM–French franc 144.7, DM–lira 244.3. It is, of course, impossible to say what the 'right' rates in each case were, but there seems little doubt that the realignments that the dollar crisis precipitated, not only inside the Snake but still more between the DM and the French franc and the lira, resulted in more 'realistic' levels than those that had obtained earlier in the summer of 1978. These developments, taken in conjunction with the relative stability of the dollar itself in the following 12 months, made for a much more encouraging financial environment during the first phase of the EMS' existence than might have been expected in the light of the history of the international monetary system in 1977 and 1978.

The second factor, which reinforced the relative stability that the markets and the authorities had contrived to produce by the end of 1978, was the fundamental change that occurred in the Carter administration's economic policies during and partly as a result of the dollar crisis. Opinions may differ about whether these changes have been beneficial or harmful, but there can be little doubt about their extent. An administration that had 'embarked on a programme which vastly increased the number of people employed, gave a powerful and sustained lift to international trade and raised the level of welfare and business profits' was forced into reverse[107]. The origins of this about-turn are complex and many, perhaps the majority, were indigenous, but two aspects of it are particularly interesting and important from the point of view of this book. The first was the evidence that it provided of 'the inability of the United States to run its economy in its own way without the accord of the rest of the world'[108], and the second was the confirmation that it gave of the near total victory in the North Atlantic world of habits of mind that may be termed post-Keynesian, Germanic, Friedmanite, even Thatcherite, but that however one likes to label them amounted to a complete break with the assumptions and priorities that had dominated a generation or more of Anglo-Saxon, Scandinavian and even some Continental European leaders. If the launching of the EMS initiative within the European Community itself was only possible because the French, and even the British and the Italians, had begun to 'read the same [German] drill book'[109], its actual emergence as an entity within the international monetary system was made incomparably easier by the fact that the Carter administration had begun to study the same texts in translation, or similar ones in the original. Still later, of course, as monetarism became even more deeply entrenched in Washington and the dollar began to soar rather than merely to recover, a whole new set of problems ensued. But these developments were not and could not be foreseen in November 1978.

6.3   Discussions about the transfer of resources, 1 October–3 December 1978

Unlike the other two technical committees involved in planning the EMS, the Economic Policy Committee never recovered from the deadlock that had marred its proceedings from the first meeting onwards. The committee's final report, which was ready by the second week in November and was extensively leaked to the press in the days that followed, was a testimony to failure rather than a basis for further negotiation[110]. The only hope of fresh progress, the committee itself concluded, lay in a breakthrough at political level. As officials, they had exhausted the limits of their briefs and, in many cases, their patience as well. The political response to this breakdown, including as it did the summoning of a final, pre-Council meeting of the EPC itself, will be discussed later in this section. Before moving on to these belated efforts to achieve understanding, however, it is necessary to look briefly at a constitutional conflict between the European Parliament and the Council of Ministers, which came to a head in October and November, and which exercised a significant influence on both the character and the outcome of the concurrent studies in the final phase of the EMS negotiations.

The conflict centred on the Community budget for 1979, which was drafted by the Commission in the first half of the year, submitted to and amended by the Council of Ministers in June and revised yet again by the Parliament in the weeks and months that followed[111]. Neither ministerial cuts in the Commission's budgetary proposals nor parliamentary protests were of course particularly novel in themselves. Nor were the sums involved enormous. The Commission proposed a budget of approximately 14 billion EUA on the payments side; the Council reduced this by just under 900 million and Parliament more than restored the situation with amendments totalling 993 million. (The contemporary sterling equivalents were approximately £9380 million, £600 million and £670 million respectively. Even the largest sum amounted to less than half the annual budget of a single ministry in Whitehall, the Department of Health and Social Security.) Of themselves, the differences were hardly enough to arouse much excitement outside

Strasburg, Luxembourg and Brussels. What gave the clash a wider significance, however, was not the amount of money in dispute so much as the
timing of the argument and the distribution of the increases that the
Parliament proposed. As far as the timing was concerned, there were three
features of the second half of 1978 that lent more colour and urgency to the
conflict. The first was the proximity of direct elections, which, as the
discussion of French politics in section 6.1 has already shown, began to cast
their shadow over political debate well before the end of 1978. The second
was the imminent change in the basis of Community finances, which were to
be derived henceforth, with the introduction of a common VAT rate, from
its 'own resources'. While the third was the rhetoric as well as the reality of
the EMS proposals, which members of Parliament could and did claim made
a fundamental debate about the Community's public finances desirable and
opportune. As to the question of distribution, the fact that the parliamentary proposals placed such stress on increases in the Regional Fund
highlighted the potential connection between these proceedings and the
EMS negotiations.

These points can be illustrated by the contributions of Mr Bangemann,
the German Liberal who acted as the rapporteur for the Committee on the
Budget and who was therefore the chief exponent of the Parliament's case.
Mr Bangemann linked the dispute with the direct elections at the very
beginning of his speech of 23 October[112]. The closeness of the elections, he
averred, offered an opportunity 'to see the Budget in the context of the
political considerations which must be taken into account in view of direct
elections'. The direct elections were, he claimed, frequently dismissed as
being of little significance because the European Parliament itself had no
function. 'But all of us who are familiar with the progress this Parliament has
made in budgetary powers know that this is by no means true'. For this
reason, he and his colleagues on the Budget Committee and the related
specialist committees had done more than simply 'restore' the funds that the
Council had lopped off the Commission's draft. They had tried to formulate
their own strategy and order of priorities. The proposals that mirrored their
hopes and aspirations cannot be considered in detail here, but the biggest
increases that they envisaged were intended to provide a new boost to the
Social Fund and still more to the Regional Fund. Thus, of the 993 million
EUA that they wanted to restore to the payments side of the budget, 233
million were earmarked for the Regional Fund and 225 million for social
policy, where they would be directed 'towards a resolute attack on
unemployment'. The primacy of the Regional Fund was emphasized even
more strongly in the proposals on the commitment side of the budget.
(Figures for payments referred to money that would actually be spent in the
year in question; those on the commitment side covered funds that would be
engaged but would not be entirely spent during the year.) The parliamentary
counter-proposals covering commitments would have resulted in an overall

increase on the previous years' budget of 29%, and by far the greater part of this was accounted for by the sum added to the Regional Fund, which the ministers, in accordance with the decision of the European Council of December 1977, had fixed at 620 million EUA but which Parliament now proposed should be raised to 1 billion[113]. Speaking as a national of a member state 'which would probably be worse off than at present' if the proposals were accepted, Mr Bangemann justified these proposals, and in particular the move away from the rigid quota system that ensured that every state received something from the Fund regardless of real need, by an appeal to a 'spirit of European solidarity ... which we, the parliament, are most likely to discover. If we do not develop such a sense of European solidarity, if we do not finally move away from thinking in terms of national quotas, then Europe will merely remain a sum of different nations and never gain an identity of its own'[114].

The reply of the Council of Ministers to this attack by the Parliament was made in the debates themselves by Dr Lahnstein, who gave a number of reasons for rejecting the proposed increases, of which three were particularly important. Firstly, at a time when the governments of several member states were having considerable difficulties in funding their own requirements, there was simply not enough money to finance increases in Community spending on this scale. Secondly, whatever the Parliament might wish, the experience of previous years suggested that the extra funds would not in fact be used, and it was not therefore worth entering into disputes about money that the member states, and in particular some of the member states who were believed to need it most, would not actually draw upon. Finally, the European Council had fixed the amounts to be allowed for the Fund for three years at its meeting in December 1977 and it was impossible for Parliament to countermand this Resolution. The second of these points will be taken up again in the discussion of the negotiating tactics of the Italian government. Within the context of the budgetary conflict itself, however, it was the third on which the Germans and the majority of the other member states insisted most strongly.

The issue came to a head in the course of a long and acrimonious meeting of the budget ministers of the Nine in Brussels, following the main ECOFIN meeting on 20 November[116]. It resulted in a 7 to 2 split, with the seven led by Germany refusing to countenance the Parliament's proposal for the Regional Fund and the two, namely Britain and Italy, each of whom had ten votes, withholding their support for the majority position. The failure of the Council to reach agreement created a situation of almost indescribable legal complexity, since without a qualified majority, for which the votes of either Britain or Italy were essential, the Council was not, under a strict legal interpretation, competent to reject the parliamentary amendment, and the latter therefore stood. The money was nonetheless not available, since under a separate vote the Council had also failed to agree a rise in the so-called margin of manoeuvre, a sum that at the time stood at 133 million EUA, which was allowed to meet parliamentary and other amendments. Not only was this sum insufficient in itself to deal with an increase in the Regional Fund of the order indicated by Parliament, it had also been very largely used up in the course of the meeting to cope with other amendments concerned with energy, social policy and staffing.

The dispute was, of course, theoretically distinct from the negotiations for the EMS, but it was in reality closely intertwined with them since the British and the Italians made it clear that they rejected the arguments of their colleagues because, as Mr Joel Barnett, the chief secretary to the UK Treasury, argued, the decision taken by the heads of government on the Regional Fund at their meeting in December 1977 had now to be reviewed in the light of the efforts to create an EMS. Coming as it did from a government that only a few days later declared itself in full agreement with the French over the need to resist any further extension of the powers of the European Parliament, the blocking action taken by the British on 20 November was an act of pure opportunism, which, in the altered circumstances after the meeting of the European Council, they had no scruples about totally reversing, siding with the French and the Danes in a last-ditch struggle to reject the parliamentary proposals[117]. As, however, by this stage it was obvious to most of those involved, and was to be made even clearer at the meeting in Paris a few days later, that the British could not expect to gain anything from the EMS negotiations in the short term, the UK's tactics were not entirely illogical. The behaviour of the Italian government, by contrast, is much more difficult to understand, even though it was consistent with their basic assumptions about the powers of the European Parliament. As a tactical move, however, their action would seem to have run quite counter to their own interests, since they introduced into negotiations on the concurrent studies, which were already difficult enough, the additional complication of a constitutional issue that, as they and everybody else knew, the French government felt strongly about at the best of times, and felt even more strongly about when M. Chirac was attempting to gain as much political capital out of the question as possible. The Irish, who voted with the seven, were shrewd enough to see the trap into which an alliance with Parliament might lead them.

The episode on 20 November is only one of the more striking examples of the widely different approaches of the three less prosperous countries to the discussions of the transfer of resources. Before exploring further the relationship between the Council/Parliament dispute and the EMS negotiations, it is necessary to look more generally at the tactics employed by the three governments in question when it became obvious that the formal negotiations within the context of the EPC were leading nowhere. Of the three governments, the British had in many respects the simplest task. Having decided not to enter the system immediately, their aim was more than ever to secure the maximum number of propaganda points, while safeguarding and improving the terms available if and when entry became feasible at home. As far as their propaganda campaign was concerned, they enjoyed several notable strokes of fortune. One was the parliamentary conflict. Others included the leak of the contents of the EPC report to the press and the publication of a preliminary policy document prepared in Mr Tugendhat's office on how to cope with the problems that would arise when, as was inevitable given the uncontrollable nature of spending under the CAP, the Community exhausted the funds available from its 'own resources', as these latter were currently defined[118]. A central argument in the paper, which Mr Callaghan and his colleagues endorsed for obvious reasons, was that, in future, member states' contributions should be assessed more on the basis of their means than in response to the automatic logic of this or that policy. Amongst the suggestions that it made to give force to the principle was a linkage between contributions and tax potential. It was impartial support that the British government could hardly fail to exploit, and ministerial speeches by the prime minister and several of his senior colleagues rammed home the point frequently and forcefully[119].

This public or semi-public campaign was matched by efforts in multilateral and bilateral meetings to ensure that, even if the British did not enter the system, the concessions available to the less prosperous countries who did and those who like the British themselves might eventually do so, should be substantial. The lack of any real urgency spared them the need to develop detailed proposals comparable to those that the Irish had prepared in July and August, and that, belatedly and somewhat reluctantly, the Italians turned their hands to in the weeks preceding the Brussels Council. Their aim was much more to see that adequate provisions of a general character were written into the system. Thus, at the Frankfurt meeting, the British tabled an amendment, for which they obtained the support of the Italians, to the draft text of the Council Resolution on the parallel measures that would have required the Commission to produce detailed proposals designed to deal with the structural imbalances of the Community by the time the Council next met at Paris in March 1979. 'In the course of these studies, the Commission should examine the possibility of improving all the instruments currently designed to deal with the problems of the less prosperous regions.' As paragraph 4 of the section of the Brussels Council Resolution dealing with the transfer of resources shows, they obtained some of what they wanted in this regard (see Appendix 1B).

The Irish government's tactics were also relatively straightforward. They had stated their targets in private and admitted them in public. Faced by the breakdown of the EPC negotiations, the importance of which Mr Colley, the finance minister, tried to play down[120], they embarked on a round of bilateral diplomacy in the course of which the finance minister himself met all his Community counterparts, either in Dublin or more usually in their own capitals, and the prime minister, Mr Lynch, visited Paris, London and Bonn. If the objectives of these visits were simple, their achievement was not. More even than the Italians, the Irish could count on goodwill everywhere they went and nowhere more so perhaps than in Bonn, where the chancellor, moved it would seem by a mixture of idealism and pique with the British, had virtually committed himself to 'seeing to it' that the Irish came in even if the United Kingdom did not. But, as Mr Colley and his party discovered in Bonn on 8 November, goodwill was tempered and at times almost obscured by preferences and prejudices that the German chancellor held for reasons quite unconnected with the Irish, but that were nonetheless profoundly relevant to their case[121]. The most contentious issue concerned the respective merits of loans and grants. The German chancellor had a pronounced preference for loans, while the Irish, for reasons that have already been explained above and that were needless to say rehearsed both on paper and in the talks themselves, were no less adamant that loans could not solve, and might actually complicate, their problems. There were various reasons for this entrenched German attitude. One was undoubtedly their concern about the current dispute with the Parliament over the Regional Fund; yet another was their absolute determination, which was openly admitted to the Irish and indeed to several other Community leaders in these weeks, that the British should not benefit from any EMS-related aid as long as they remained outside the system. Since help through the Regional Fund or any other existing Community instrument could only be made discriminatory with considerable difficulty, there was an understandable reluctance to try. Better bilateral grants in the last resort, the Irish were told, than multilateral negotiations that might in the end profit the British. Best of all, however, would be loans. The Colley visit, which passed off amicably enough, failed to resolve the differences and, although the finance minister insisted that there was still hope that a package deal would emerge, he admitted that it might be necessary to reinforce the Irish case by prime ministerial visits to Bonn and the other main capitals[122].

Towards the end of November therefore, Mr Lynch set off to Paris, London and Bonn[123]. For obvious reasons, the German capital seemed to hold the key, and from the Irish point of view therefore it was distinctly encouraging to discover that, true to their promise, Dr Lahnstein and his officials had been working hard since the Colley visit to devise methods of helping them. The Germans still insisted that the Irish were setting their targets too high, and that a substantial portion of the sums eventually raised would have to be provided through loans rather than grants. That said, however, they indicated that they were prepared to seek the support of their partners for a package involving a 'third window' on the Regional Fund, which would be specifically related to the EMS, an increase in the credit facilities available through the EIB, amounting to 1 billion EUA, a further extension under the Ortoli Facility and interest subsidies on both types of loan. They were not yet prepared to put a precise figure on the size of the grant through the Regional Fund, and the German chancellor, who had, he said, been on the telephone to the French president about the matter shortly before, admitted that it might be difficult to carry the French with this proposal, but they would continue to work on the problem. Mr Lynch's statement to the Dail on 30 November, in which he claimed that he had come away from the discussions with Mr Schmidt 'much encouraged', was therefore fair comment in the light of the progress that had been made since the beginning of the month, but as he himself admitted the difficulties had not been completely overcome, and Irish entry into the system, which, he insisted, was dependent upon a favourable outcome to the negotiations on the transfer of resources, might still have to be postponed[124].

The special meeting of the EPC at Frankfurt airport a day later, on 1 December, was to give an even clearer indication of both the progress that had been made since the same officials had last met to discuss these problems and the ground that was still to be covered. Before considering it in more detail however, it is necessary to look at the Italian government's tactics, which were a good deal more opaque than those adopted by the Irish. The main objectives of the Italian negotiators during the first phase of the EPC discussions have already been referred to in the previous chapter. They amounted, as we have seen, to a fundamental reform of the Community's public finances, which if carried through would have transformed, though not destroyed, the CAP and opened up new areas and dimensions of Community expenditure. As a definition of what the Community ought to be doing, these aims were admirable. Coming from the Italians, they also sounded authentic. But in the circumstances of October and November 1978 they were simply not feasible. The British and their principal sparring partners in the EPC had between them destroyed whatever slender possibility there might once have been of a systematic discussion of the inadequacies and potentialities of the Community budget. The Irish, who insisted on cash and who were not too bothered with principles, were much better placed to exploit the new situation than the Italians, who admirably but vainly stuck to their principles and were extremely vague about cash. It was not for want of warnings. Mr Ortoli gave Mr Pandolfi some fairly shrewd advice during the Washington meeting of the IMF at the end of September. So too did the French president and the German chancellor in the weeks that followed. So finally did Mr Jenkins, who visited Rome on 28 November and pressed Mr Andreotti to name a figure, taking due account of course of what he described as 'the Franco-German psychological blockage' against action through the Regional Fund and their preference for loans.

Despite these warnings, the Italians remained evasive and vague. Mr Pandolfi, it is true, spoke on several occasions of a project to clean up the bay of Naples. There was also some talk of a major hydraulic scheme in the Apennines, which would cost $3–5 billion over a period of three to five years. But neither of these plans, nor others that were raised and then dropped, would seem to have advanced much beyond the stage of rhetoric, and the evidence suggests that the Italians remained unclear about what they wanted and uncertain of how much it would cost. At the very end of November some of the officials concerned prepared a 'proposal for a special intervention by the EEC in the Mezzogiorno', which drew attention to the problems of the South in general and more particularly to the troubles of the chemical and steel works that had been established there in an earlier period of optimism and generosity, but that were now, like so many other plants in these two industries, in desperate straits. Community help, the paper suggested, would be welcome in the form of direct grants, the reduction or elimination of debts, or assistance with vocational retraining schemes. The cost: 850 billion lira or, at the time, £500 million. It was a sign, however, of how unprepared the Italians still were to come forward with precise proposals that, when Mr Jenkins met Mr Andreotti and Mr Pandolfi a day after this paper was drafted, the prime minister disclosed nothing of the plan, while the minister of the Treasury limited himself to a plea for 'some' Community assistance with Montedison within the context of a much larger (and vaguer) programme of aid for the Mezzogiorno. The Italians, it seemed, were at approximately the stage at which the Irish had been in July.

The Italians' apparent inability or unwillingness to move beyond generalities to details is so striking, and was in the end to play such an important part in the breakdown at the Brussels meeting of the European Council, that it requires explanation. Three reasons seem particularly relevant. The first, which has already been alluded to at an earlier point in this section, was the fact that the Italian government already had more than enough credits with the EEC than it seemed capable of using. The phenomenon of under- or non-utilization of Community funds was cited with considerable effect by Dr Lahnstein in the course of the confrontation with the Parliament in October 1978. It reached its most absurd proportions in the case of the Social Fund, which included within its orbit programmes to reduce youth unemployment, and from which, as even Mr Bangemann had to admit to his regret, less than 1% of the money available had actually been drawn in the first six months of 1978[125]. The problem was not exclusively an Italian one, but Italy was (and still is) the main delinquent. In 1978 alone, for example, Italy did not draw on 51% of the money theoretically available to it under the Regional Fund and by the end of 1979 its unused balances amounted to almost £1.5 billion[126]. There was little point in drawing up yet more pretty schemes on paper, if so many of those that had already been submitted and approved remained unattended to in some dark corner of a Roman office.

The second explanation of the Italians' continuing failure to produce precise projects is to be found in the nature of the arguments that the Italians themselves advanced in these negotiations. However welcome grants might have been under this or that fund, they would not and could not have met the main thrust of the Italians' claim, which was that the present budget was grossly unfair and costly to Italy. The point had been made with his customary clarity and forcefulness by Dr Baffi in the bilateral conversations with the French in September. The Italians, he observed, were paying £300 million per annum more across the exchanges for the privilege of buying agricultural products at prices fixed by a CAP that did virtually nothing for Mediterranean producers than they would have paid if they had had access to world markets. Community grants tied to specific infrastructural projects could be no substitute for a radical reform of the CAP that corrected the overpricing of those products that came within its orbit and brought others, and more particularly those that were the staple output of Mediterranean producers, under its writ. In other words, the Italians wanted the debate to concentrate on the fundamentals, because only if it did would there be a significant improvement in their position.

The third factor explaining the curious, and what proved in the end to be the counterproductive behaviour of the Italians in these negotiations was that, for a variety of reasons, those responsible placed too much reliance on the alliance with the British, and went on doing so long after it had become apparent to almost everybody else that the British would not enter the system. It is arguable that the Italians would not have obtained what they wanted even if the British had not played an ambivalent role in the negotiations. It is certain, however, that once the British had indicated that they could not come in, their partners and more particularly the Germans set their minds against any fundamental reforms or concessions on the basis of the EMS on the grounds that, if they sanctioned these measures, the British would be bound to benefit whether or not they joined. From mid-October onwards, it could be said, it was only a matter of cash. Principles were not on offer. But the Italians continued to hunt with the British, in the Council/Parliament dispute, at Frankfurt and, finally, at the Brussels meeting of the European Community itself. The alliance was not without its uses to the British. However, it is difficult to see how it benefited the Italians at all. As Mr Andreotti remarked ruefully to one of his advisers after the European Council, Mr Callaghan gave him no help at the meeting once he had obtained what he wanted, namely the half-way house.

It was against this background of uncertainty about what the Italians wanted, and of doubts about whether even the Irish claims could be met enough to enable the Dublin government to enter the system, that the Germans made a final attempt to achieve a Community consensus in advance of the Brussels Council, by convening an emergency meeting of senior officials at Frankfurt airport on 1 December. The occasion was slightly melodramatic, despite the conspicuous colourlessness of the surroundings and the unexpected breach of 'top-secrecy' by an Italian journalist, who managed to get a telephone call to Renato Ruggiero put through to Dr Lahnstein, who was chairman for the occasion. The atmosphere notwithstanding, the main conclusions arrived at at the meeting seem relatively clear. The first, which was subsequently reflected in the first and second paragraphs of the section in the Council Resolution of 5 December dealing with the transfer of resources, was that the heads of government should issue a declaration affirming the need for the Community to strengthen and develop policies designed to hasten the convergence of the member states' economies. The British attempt, already referred to above, to insert a request to the Commission for precise proposals by the following meeting of the Council in Paris in March 1979 was also accepted, if not exactly in the form desired[127]. The second conclusion was that, whatever specific measures were adopted by the Council, they should be limited to the states that participated in the EMS. The British representative, Mr Butler, apparently argued that the United Kingdom should benefit as long as the government made it clear that it intended to participate as soon as possible. But, although his claim was not dismissed out of hand, there was an obvious preference on the part of the more prosperous countries' representatives for an approach along the lines of the one that was later incorporated in paragraph 3 of the Resolution. As far as the measures themselves were concerned, the spokesmen for the prospective donors continued to place the main emphasis on loans at subsidized interest rates through the EIB and possibly the Ortoli Facility. Disagreements arose, however, on the level of subsidy and the types of project that might qualify. On the former, the French urged that the subsidy should be limited to 2%, while the majority were apparently prepared to agree to 4%. In the end, Dr Lahnstein, invoking the authority of the chancellor himself, managed to persuade his partners to split the difference. The dispute about the types of project that might qualify affected the Italians most of all, since they had come to the meeting armed with a request for help with the chemical and steel industries in the South. This request was strongly and in the end successfully opposed by the French and the Luxembourgers, who claimed not surprisingly that it would be impossible for their governments to justify subsidies to the Italians at a time when their own chemical and steel industries were in such grave trouble. As a general rule, therefore, it was agreed that neither loans nor grants advanced under the scheme should distort competition. Both the Italians and the Irish would appear to have accepted the limitations placed on the type of project and the level of interest rate subsidy.

Agreement was not reached, however, over the question of how much money was needed overall, or the problem of the form or forms in which the aid would be given. Since his meeting with the Irish a few days earlier, Dr Lahnstein and his colleagues had worked on a draft embodying their proposal for a 'third window' on the Regional Fund, linked with the EMS and confined to the less prosperous countries. The money granted through this instrument, they proposed, would be advanced in the following proportions: 50% to the Italians, 30% to the Irish, and 20% to the British, which, given the size of the United Kingdom's contribution, would ensure that it neither benefited nor gained from the exercise. The French, however, resisted even this concession, citing the difficulties that would be bound to arise in the dispute with Parliament if the Council took unilateral steps to increase the Regional Fund at the same time as they were denying parliamentary efforts to do the same. The chief French representative at the meeting, Jean-Claude Payet, promised to take the matter up in Paris once again, but the threat of a breakdown on this issue was evident. What was also obvious, however, was that the French, no less than the other representatives of the more prosperous countries, were already prepared to make an exception of the Irish. M. Payet himself was alleged to have made this point personally to Mr Horgan of the Irish ministry of finance, but it was sufficiently widely known for the representative of at least one other country to report to his government that even if French objections to an extension of the Regional Fund were upheld, they and the other governments concerned were prepared to create a special fund for the Irish, whose difficulties in taking more loans were recognized by everybody.

The uncertainty about the Regional Fund was compounded by a failure to arrive at any precise estimates of the amount of money that could or should be allocated, either through it or in the form of loans. Part of the trouble stemmed from the figures advanced by Mr Horgan, which were regarded as too high, but still more arose from the continuing failure of the Italians to declare a price. Far from apologizing for their lack of precision, they still apparently maintained that it would be much more sensible to achieve agreement on the financial instruments that were to be employed before entering into detailed discussions about figures. The figures, they claimed, could be brought up in the course of the European Council debate itself, as the general principles were clarified. Under pressure, Mr Ruggiero and Dr Ciampi of the Banca d'Italia would seem to have volunteered some approximate estimates, quoting, as a rough idea of what they might need, the increase to the Regional Fund that the European Parliament claimed was necessary and that they together with the British had recently supported in the ECOFIN. This estimate, which was anyway only presented as an approximate one, and which, as the following section will show, bore only slight relation to the demand that Mr Andreotti advanced at the European Council, was still not supported, it need hardly be said, by any detailed indication of how it would be spent. It was not, therefore, entirely convincing in itself nor, given French sensibilities on this score, was it particularly tactful to quote as a starting point a claim that the majority of Italy's partners, but more particularly the French, had rejected on principle.

The Frankfurt meeting therefore dispersed without agreement on two of the central questions – the overall size of the aid that was required and the channels through which it should be dispensed. In the days that remained before the Brussels Council, the Germans, who held the presidency, did their best to formulate draft proposals covering the contentious issues, but the gap between the French and the Italians was a large one and, although some, and perhaps most, of those who attended the meeting preferred to believe that all would work out 'on the night', this hastily convened gathering provided an ominous and as it proved accurate portent of what was to happen in the following week.

6.4   The European Council and its immediate aftermath, 4–15 December 1978

Although the Frankfurt meeting provoked a certain uneasiness in Rome and Bonn and prompted Mr Lynch to make a remarkably cautious prediction about the chances of success at the European Council before he left Dublin[128], the evidence suggests that most if not all the heads of government who assembled in Brussels on 4 December began the meeting on the assumption that, however hard the bargaining might prove to be, the political will that had created and maintained the momentum so far and removed so many of the potential obstacles would prevail, and that the Council would in the end agree to establish a European Monetary System composed of eight members, with the British in a half-way house, neither completely in nor completely out. Much of the discussion on the first afternoon appeared to justify this assumption. The Council almost romped through the first five sections of the draft resolution establishing an EMS that the German presidency, drawing on the results of the technical discussions and the ECOFIN of 20 November, had circulated before the meeting. The contentious issues that the experts had already settled were laid finally to rest, and solutions were found to those – like the lingering dispute about the meaning of the Belgian compromise, the size and distribution of credits and the unresolved problem of the involuntary debts – that the ECOFIN had come near to but had finally failed to resolve. Each provoked some discussion; none precipitated or even threatened a crisis. If any country or group of countries gave way, it was, as I have already suggested above, the Germans and the Dutch rather than the non-Snake countries. A small example will suffice to supplement the larger ones that have already been referred to in section 6.2. The original German version of paragraph 3.6 in section A of the Council resolution, which specified the measures that crossing the threshold of divergence would entail, included under (b) 'measures on monetary policy'. This was now strengthened to 'measures on domestic monetary policy', and a third phrase (c), which had not figured at all in the original draft, was added dealing with 'changes in central rates'. A comparable spirit of compromise prevailed in the discussion of the British problem. Mr Callaghan, who had circulated a letter to all the heads of government shortly before the meeting, explained his difficulties and the United Kingdom was duly granted by common consent a half-way house.

The harmonious note that was struck during the early hours of the Council was not, however, sustained. The trouble arose, as those who had read the French press or, alternatively, had attended the Frankfurt meeting must have feared it would, over two issues: the monetary compensatory accounts and the concurrent studies. The dispute about the latter was subsequently more widely publicized than the controversy over the former, for the obvious reason that it was the problem that finally put paid to the hopes of the German chancellor and most of the other heads of government that the Italians and the Irish would see their way to joining, but the clash over the MCAs is in some respects even more interesting for the light that it throws on the French president's approach to the meeting. The original, presidential draft of paragraph 6.1 of the Resolution made no explicit reference to MCAs. It simply listed three Council Regulations that, it was proposed, the ECOFIN should consider at its meeting on 18 December. The principal issue dealt with in the Council Regulation covering the CAP was the situation that would arise if, as the Commission believed was both inevitable and right, the ECU replaced the unit of account that was currently in use for the calculation of 'green' exchange rates. As the Commission had already explained at the meeting of the ministers of agriculture in November[129], if the change-over was effected without any corrective action the result would be a fall in farm prices of up to 21% and a corresponding change in the MCAs that would leave only the UK with a negative MCA. The Commission therefore proposed the application of a corrective factor ('coefficient correcteur') of 1.21, which would cancel this effect and leave prices and MCAs as they were. Much to the relief of the other heads of government present, neither Mr Callaghan nor his officials vetoed this procedure, which effectively prevented a rather drastic reform of the CAP. Their agreement was incorporated in an additional sentence tacked on to paragraph 6.1(c), in which the Council affirmed 'that the introduction of the EMS should not of itself result in any change in the situation obtaining prior to 1 January 1979 regarding the expression in national currencies of agricultural prices, monetary compensatory amounts and all other amounts fixed for the purposes of the common agricultural policy'.

For the French president, however, this was not enough. Even if the British prime minister was ready to agree not to exploit the opportunity that he undoubtedly had to damage the CAP, he for his part was not disposed to be so magnanimous where French interests were concerned. He therefore insisted that the Council should use the occasion offered by the inauguration of the EMS to make a serious start on the dismantling of the whole MCA regime. The argument that his amendment provoked went on to the very end of the meeting. Indeed, it was still going on when Mr Callaghan left to return to London. As he told journalists[130]: 'The thing we're stuck on at the moment is the CAP.' There was, he noted, 'a very natural and understandable desire to get rid of MCAs ... but ... that problem isn't going to be resolved this afternoon'. Mr Callaghan's prediction proved correct: the problem was not solved at the Council, even though an additional sentence was eventually grafted on to the Resolution as a result of the French president's intervention. The exchanges that took place over it were nonetheless important for the outcome of the meeting as a whole, not simply because the French were to go on insisting that the settlement of the MCA issue was a precondition of the inauguration of the system, but also because the bitterness that was generated during the discussion of this issue contributed towards the progressive poisoning of the atmosphere as a whole – which was scarcely improved by the impromptu press conferences that M. Giscard d'Estaing gave to French journalists and television reporters between and even during sessions. They only strengthened the impression that he had decided to use the Council as an occasion to hit back at his Gaullist critics and to show, as he himself proudly claimed during an interview that he gave immediately after his return to France on 6 December, that thanks to him French farmers had been at the centre of the Council's deliberations[131].

It is difficult to believe that the French president actually wanted a breakdown, even though understandably enough his behaviour prompted several commentators to speculate afterwards that this had been his intention all along[132]. It was nonetheless a high risk strategy, and when the Council turned to the concurrent studies the crisis that his approach had threatened to provoke during the initial and inconclusive exchanges on the MCAs became a reality. The discussion of the transfer of resources centred on four major issues:

(1) The possibility or desirability of opening a 'third window' on the Regional Fund, or of devising some alternative arrangement that would provide aid in the form of grants.

(2) The possibility of using the Ortoli Facility as well as the EIB, which the German presidential text suggested should be the sole source of loans. (The advantage of the Ortoli Facility over the EIB was that its terms of reference were more flexible.)

(3) The possible threat that assistance to certain industries or projects in the less prosperous countries might pose to established concerns in the richer states.

(4) The total amount and distribution of the funds that were to be made available, whether in the form of loans or grants.

The debate was dominated by the French president, who disputed almost every point made by the representatives of the less prosperous countries and their friends and protectors with a bluntness that bordered on rudeness. He concentrated his initial fire on the proposal to use the Regional Fund, arguing that the Council's position in the continuing dispute with Parliament over the budget would be seriously weakened if the heads of government were to make fresh sums available on their own initiative and that, even if some means were found of overcoming this obstacle, he could not contemplate discriminatory arrangements of the kind suggested in the presidential draft. If the United Kingdom and Italy were to benefit, so too must France. However, even these detailed attacks on the Regional Fund were in the end overshadowed by a more general demand for parsimony and responsibility. 'France', he declared, in a statement that filtered through to journalists of several countries, 'cannot upset her own financial arrangements in order to ensure the adhesion of those for whom membership ought to be an act of political will rather than a question of cash'[133].

There can be no doubt that both the tone and much of the substance of the president's remarks surprised and embarrassed his colleagues. But the efforts of Mr Schmidt and others to find a way out of the impasse that M. Giscard d'Estaing's intransigence had created were made considerably harder by the position adopted by the Italian prime minister. Mr Andreotti had declared his hand at the very beginning of the meeting. The Italian government, he said, welcomed the EMS as a major step forward in the construction of Europe, but if they were to participate effectively they would need help, particularly in the Mezzogiorno. If, for example, they were to reduce inflation, they would have to cut their public sector borrowing requirement, but this in turn would inevitably have serious consequences for the South, where public investment would be essential. His government would therefore like Community aid in the form of both grants and loans to improve the infrastructure, to develop tourism and services and assist certain industries that were in serious difficulties. Accounts vary as to the precise figure that Mr Andreotti put on Italy's requests in his opening statement, but the estimates circulated by the French during the meeting, which spoke of 1800 million EUA (£1.2 billion) in grants over three years, plus subsidized loans from the EIB, the Ortoli Facility and EURATOM, are confirmed by other sources and may even understate the case[134]. It was in any event a substantial sum and even those, like Mr Schmidt, who were disposed to help were somewhat incredulous. It could be argued, of course, that when adjustments were made for the differences in the population and size of the two countries, the Italian claim was proportionately lower than the Irish demand for £650 million over five years. But the Irish had made their requests known months in advance, and had furthermore already been told by the Germans and the others with whom they had negotiated over the previous weeks that there was no hope of their obtaining all that they wanted. The Italians, by contrast, had remained evasive when pressed for details and seemed now to have taken no account whatsoever of the pruning that had been carried out on the Irish proposals.

The German chancellor and his colleagues nonetheless went to considerable lengths to salvage the negotiations. When it became clear, for example, that the proposal for a third window on the Regional Fund would never be acceptable to M. Giscard d'Estaing, Dr Lahnstein was dispatched to discuss a fresh package with the Irish that would have involved raising the loan ceiling to 2 billion EUA per year over three years at subsidized interest rates, 60% of the loan and interest going to the Italians and 20% to the Irish, with the remaining 20% kept in reserve in case the British joined[135]. The Irish agreed to this suggestion, so long as the additional loans could be used for a wider variety of projects than those contained in the original list. Dr Lahnstein duly departed with this information, but returned an hour later with the news that the French regarded even this claim as excessive. And so it went on. As the chancellor said repeatedly in the days that followed, he had been quite prepared to raise the offer to the Irish and the Italians, but he had not been able to persuade all those who would have been required to finance the aid to follow his lead[136]. The negotiations came to a halt therefore. The most generous offer that Mr Schmidt could persuade the French president to agree to consisted of the following elements:

(1)   Loans of up to 1 billion EUA (£670 million) per annum for five years to be issued through both the EIB and the Ortoli Facility, two-thirds going to Italy and one-third to Ireland.
(2)   The loans were to be for 15 years, with a moratorium on principal repayment of 3 or 5 years.
(3)   Interest rate subsidies at a level of 3% totalling no more in any one year than 200 million EUA or £130 million per annum.
(4)   The total subsidy to be drawn immediately the loan was agreed.

The Irish government later calculated that the capital benefits available to them under these arrangements amounted to £45 million per annum for five years or £225 million for the whole period, compared with the £650 million that they had originally declared as their target[137]. Adopting the same bases of calculation, the Italians would presumably have drawn twice this amount, or, in other words, £450 million over five years. As one element in a package that included in addition a 'third window' on the Regional Fund, these interest rate subsidies might have been appealing. As the sum of what they could expect, however, they were clearly not. The Irish stood to receive slightly more than a third of what they had asked for in a form that was at best inconvenient and at worst might be harmful to their economic interest. The Italians, who very belatedly had asked for over £1200 million in grants and a further £1000 million in interest rate subsidies, were offered instead a mere £450 million in interest rate subsidies and other, hidden benefits arising from the terms of the loans themselves. When every allowance is made for the Italians' miscalculations and the Irish government's excessive optimism, therefore, the gap between claim and offer was in each case very considerable and it is hardly surprising in the circumstances that both governments asked for a 'pause for reflection'.

So ended the European Council of 4–5 December 1978. The EMS had been launched, but with only six members. As Mr Jenkins observed:

> I would not be frank if I did not say that there have been times in the past few weeks when I expected that we might have got even further so far as a full Community is concerned.

Mr Schmidt, who had staked the most and therefore lost the most, agreed. It was not a 'major setback', but neither was it more than a 'limited success'[138]. Back in Bonn, the chancellor's disappointment was by all accounts more obvious still, and even those who had nursed the most serious doubts about the wisdom of his initiative found it hard not to sympathize with him[139]. The *Frankfurter Allgemeine Zeitung*, though conscious that it had not been quite the 'major historical event' that its sponsors had hoped it would be, observed that the chancellor had performed a considerable service over the previous months by bringing the Community governments to a position where they were obliged to take a major decision of the kind that they had avoided for many years[140]. Even the CDU spokesman in the Bundestag debate of 6 December, Mr Häfele, paid tribute to Mr Schmidt's efforts to achieve a greater degree of unity and financial stability in Europe, though inevitably perhaps he also pointed out the risks implicit in the scheme[141]. The French president, as was only to be expected, minimized the problems that had arisen at the last minute[142], while the British prime minister, who found himself unexpectedly and happily free from the pressure to which he had been subject before the Council, could scarcely conceal his satisfaction at being able to bask in the approval of his left wing as a result of a European fiasco for which his government had no immediate responsibility[143]. There were others in Britain who took a less sanguine view of the threat of a two-tier Europe that emerged from the unforeseen complications that had arisen for the Irish and the Italians[144], while in Ireland and Italy this fear was probably more widespread still. The *Irish Times* commented with unusual bitterness on 6 December that 'the suspicion that the Community is a rich man's club is bound to grow'[145]. On the same day a leading Irish trade unionist described the Six as a group of 'avaricious, conservative states'[146].

Despite the setback, however, and the sense of disappointment that it caused in most of the European Community, the game was still not over. The Italians and the Irish had asked for and obtained a 'pause for reflection'. In fact, far from putting an end to the negotiations, the Brussels Council inaugurated a new phase that was in some respects even more agitated and complicated than the one that had preceded the meeting. Of the two governments whose attitudes remained uncertain, the Irish had undoubtedly the easier task. Unlike Mr Andreotti, Mr Lynch did not run the risk of a major political crisis over the issue at home. He knew furthermore that he could still call on a body of goodwill in the Community that might well be sufficient to carry his country into the system. At the Frankfurt airport meeting, for example, at which signs of the impending crisis had been so clearly foreshadowed, even the French had stressed that they regarded the Irish as a special case and that they were willing to contribute towards a bilateral package if this proved necessary. There were therefore solid grounds for hope. Even so, the week that followed the Brussels conference was not without its problems and mishaps. The first occurred at Brussels itself during the post-Council press conference when Mr Lynch was supposed by all the leading Irish newspapers to have said that the total package of loans *and* interest rate subsidies over five years amounted to no more than £225 million[147]. The officials who were present during this briefing session deny as strongly as Mr Lynch did at the time that this is what he actually said, but although one must presume that they would, as they claim, have spotted such a major error, the misleading reports of what had been agreed provided grist to the opposition's mill and an extra burden to the prime minister's back. Even without this additional complication, the task of defending his government's performance in the negotiations was difficult and time-consuming, and the exchanges in the Dail following Mr Lynch's statement of 7 December and in the interim debate on the EMS that was held on 13 December, not to mention the comments of much of the Irish press, give a good indication of the vulnerability of his government to taunts that they had aroused great expectations on the basis of inadequate evidence, at the end of poorly conducted negotiations[148].

Mr Lynch's problems at home were, however, only part of the picture. At the same time that he and his ministers were defending their record in the Dail, he received fresh evidence of the willingness of the German chancellor and some of his colleagues in the European Council to help Ireland in. In his report to the Bundestag on 6 December, Mr Schmidt went out of his way to stress his 'special understanding' for the position of the Irish government[149], and the same message was given by letter or by telephone by at least two other prime ministers, Mr Jørgensen of Denmark and Mr van Agt of the Netherlands[150]. It was therefore only natural that the Dublin government should test the ground once again in order to see whether special terms of the kind that had already been spoken of as a possibility on several occasions prior to the European Council meeting might not in fact be available[151]. As before, Bonn was the principal focus of action and on 7 December the prime minister telephoned the German chancellor to find out his views. The upshot was a secret meeting in Luxembourg on 11 December where three Irish officials, Dermot Nalley of the prime minister's office, Maurice Horgan of the ministry of finance and Brendan MacDonald of the ministry of economic planning and development, met a small number of German officials led by Dr Lahnstein. In the course of the talks, Dr Lahnstein disclosed the details of a special package that the Germans and four other Community governments – the Belgians, the Danes, the Dutch and the French (the Luxembourgers were to join in at their own request shortly afterwards) – were ready to finance. The grant element in the offer totalled approximately £50 million over two years. It was furthermore open to review and extension at the end of the two-year period. The Luxembourg meeting was followed by one other meeting between officials on 14 December in Brussels and by several other bilateral contacts, including a telephone conversation between Mr Lynch and the French president on 12 December. By the end of 14 December, the details had been fully worked out, including *inter alia* a special clause inserted by the French that required the Irish to use the money provided by the French government exclusively for purchases in France. However, as the bulk of the money was being provided by the Federal Republic and neither the Germans nor indeed any of the other goverments made similar demands, this curious piece of special pleading caused no difficulties. On 15 December, therefore, Mr Lynch announced that Ireland would join the EMS[152].

At £50 million over two years, the new offer did not amount to a great deal, even though ministers were quick to point out that the sum was equivalent to a 100% increase in Ireland's receipts under the Regional Fund and that it was also open to review and extension after two years. The total package still fell well short of the £650 million that the Irish government had originally asked for and the £400 million or so that they had been offered by Dr Lahnstein on 5 December. Why then did they accept it? The answer, it seems, is that they concluded that they had little choice. They had asserted their independence of the United Kingdom before Brussels and they had to accept the consequences of it now. If they went in, they obtained some extra cash in the short term and kept the goodwill of the governments with which they and the official opposition felt their future increasingly lay. If they stayed out, they ran the risk of forfeiting this goodwill and, still more important, of tying themselves even more strongly than before to the United Kingdom. To understand this last point, it ought to be recalled that at this stage several if not all Mr Callaghan's colleagues, not least Mr Schmidt, believed from what the British prime minister had told them that it was only a matter of time before the UK entered. If this actually happened, the Irish government knew that it would have no alternative but to enter itself. Better therefore to enter immediately while there was cash and kudos on offer, than to creep in on the coat-tails of the British government at a moment of their choosing. Despite the disappointing shortfall in the funds available, therefore, Mr Lynch and his colleagues had no real alternative.

The government's decision to enter the EMS left two items of business outstanding: the introduction of exchange controls and a parliamentary debate. The threat of disorderly capital movements between Ireland and the United Kingdom in the event of a break with sterling had been evident in the weeks immediately preceding the Brussels Council when, it was reckoned, up to £400 million had flowed into the Republic, on the assumption presumably that, if the break came, sterling would fall and the punt would rise, an assumption that was soon to be proved false, and that must have cost some at least of the speculators who marched their pounds westward as dearly as it benefited Irish house buyers who found their building societies unusually well off and generous for a few weeks at the end of 1978 and the beginning of 1979[153]. Although, however, the threat of speculation against sterling via Dublin receded, the possibility of sudden capital movements remained, and to provide some protection against them the government drew on its powers under the Exchange Control Act, which had been renewed and amended at the end of November, to introduce a series of regulations governing the movement of capital between the Republic and the United Kingdom[154]. Given the amount of trade between the two countries and the number of Irishmen who either lived in Britain or visited it regularly, it was no easy task, and there was inevitably a long list of exceptions, including for example payments related to trade and normal commercial operations, small payments of up to £100, and legacies and gifts to members of the family living in Britain or elsewhere. But the restrictions placed on the export of currency, the holding of bank accounts abroad and investment in British or other foreign securities were severe, and they provided a further stimulus to the development of indigenous financial institutions capable of handling transactions that had hitherto been carried out almost exclusively through London.

As far as parliamentary approval was concerned, Mr Lynch made the formal announcement of his government's decision in the Dail on 15 December. Apart from the few, relatively short but sharp observations by members of both opposition parties immediately after the statement, debate about the issue was held over until a special one-day session on 21 December. There is no need to quote from the exchanges that took place, and followed the pattern established in previous debates. Both opposition parties predictably attacked the government for its handling of the negotiations but, whereas the Labour Party carried its opposition as far as tabling an amendment rejecting membership on the terms that the government had obtained, the main opposition party, Fine Gael, limited itself to a long motion deploring 'the government's action in relation to our entry into the EMS' and abstention in the lobbies. In the end, therefore, the government's decision was approved by a majority of 77 to 13[155].

The circumstances surrounding the Italian government's decision to enter the system, which Mr Andreotti announced in the Camera dei Deputati on 12 December at the end of the week of 'reflection'[156], are much more mysterious and controversial than those that preceded Mr Lynch's statement to the Dail. They were also, however, much more parochial. There were contacts between Italian leaders and their Community partners. For example, the prime minister's chief diplomatic adviser, Mr La Rocca, visited Germany[157]. So too did the Social Democrat leader, Mr Longo, who saw Mr Schmidt on 9 December[158]. M. Ortoli went to Rome on the same day[159] and Mr Andreotti, like Mr Lynch, received letters and telephone calls from his colleagues on the European Council, including Mr Schmidt, M. Giscard d'Estaing and Mr Jørgensen[160]. But one is left with the impression that these developments were in the final analysis marginal. His colleagues were reassuring; some, like M. Giscard d'Estaing, were slightly menacing as well. If Italy did not enter, it was implied, it would be taken as a sign that Mr Andreotti's experiment of cooperating with the Communists was carrying the country out of the western orbit. But there were no renegotiations. Unlike the Irish, the Italians were not offered, and almost certainly did not ask for, more money. The German chancellor apparently repeated promises that he had already made before Brussels that, if Italy joined, he would do his best to encourage German firms to invest in the South, and both he and the French president are supposed to have reassured Mr Andreotti that the system would not be so inflexible that the government would be obliged to defend the lira rate regardless of the damage that this might do to the reserves. But neither the promise nor the assurance broke new ground. Italy simply entered.

Who then took the decision and why the delay? The answer to the first of these questions is clear: it was Mr Andreotti himself. He consulted his ministerial colleagues, his official advisers, his party and the parties of the majority, but he kept his own counsel. At least some of those who might have been expected to know what the official line was were left to define or justify the government's policy without having any clear notion of what it consisted of. Mr Pandolfi, for example, hurriedly prepared a comment on the Brussels summit for inclusion in a speech that he had to make to the Camera dei Deputati on 6 December, and was apparently only prevented from taking an even gloomier line than he did by some friendly advice from Ugo La Malfa, whose political instinct convinced him that in the end Mr Andreotti would decide to enter[161]. Others were less fortunate. Mr Forlani, the foreign minister, who had stayed on in Brussels for a NATO meeting, gave such a forthright defence of the government's decision not to enter immediately that those who read it must have concluded that, without some major concession from her partners, Italy might not enter for some time[162]. Others who were close to Mr Andreotti, or whom Mr Andreotti saw, felt encouraged to think of alternatives – half-way houses Italian style[163]. Mr Andreotti did not guide; he merely decided.

Why then the delay? Given the personal character of the decision, not to mention the character of the person, any attempt to reconstruct the motives that prompted the prime minister to wait a week and then take Italy in on terms that had been available at the Council itself must be somewhat hypothetical. The chief explanation, however, is almost certainly to be found in Italian domestic politics, though a secondary consideration may have been the desire to allow time for the moral effect of his decision not to decide at Brussels to elicit from his Community colleagues the gestures of solidarity and goodwill that they duly made. As far as the Italian political situation is concerned, enough has already been said in section 6.1 to indicate the main alignments on the EMS issue and their relevance to the gathering political crisis. Manoeuvring began immediately the news of the Brussels breakdown arrived in Rome, and certain tendencies were already clear before Mr Andreotti briefed his own party leadership on 7 December and the other parties in the majority on 8 December. The first, which was important even though it was also predictable, was that the Republicans were not disposed to accept any prolonged postponement of Italy's entry. They were prepared to hear the prime minister's explanation of why he had not taken a decision to enter immediately, but as a sign of their dwindling confidence they announced on 6 December their intention to abstain in the vote on the Budget and Finance Bill before seeing Mr Andreotti[164]. The second, and still more important, development was the immediate evidence of the determination of Mr Andreotti's opponents within his own party to exploit to the maximum the suggestion – touted already by the French in Brussels[165] – that the prime minister had adopted the line he did because he was unwilling or unable to offend the Communists. The most conspicuous exponent of this line was Donat Cattin, who had been removed from his post as minister of industry as a gesture towards the left, and consoled with the deputy secretaryship of the Christian Democratic Party[166]. But the anxieties and prejudices to which Mr Cattin gave expression were by no means peculiar to him and, although the most dramatic rumour of anti-Andreotti action by his rivals within the party (according to which Mr Piccoli had called on the president of the Republic during the Brussels Council itself to express his own and his colleagues' dissatisfaction with the way in which the EMS negotiations had been led by Mr Andreotti) was later shown to have been false, the fact that it emerged at all was an indication of the character and strength of the currents building up inside Mr Andreotti's own party[167]. Of the remaining parties in the majority, the Social Democrats were nearest to the Republicans in their criticisms of the prime minister[168], while the Socialists, whose leader, Mr Craxi, established immediate contact with colleagues in Germany, France and Britain[169], and still more the Communists were inclined to welcome the postponement of Italy's entry[170].

These tendencies became even clearer after the consultations that Mr Andreotti had with the various party leaders on 7 and 8 December[171]. What remained totally unclear, however, was what Mr Andreotti himself thought. Several of those who met him, including the Communist delegation and Ugo la Malfa, were convinced that he had already made up his mind to enter without further negotiations by 8 December if not earlier. Others, notably the Socialists, were not so sure. Indeed, the Socialists felt that they had been encouraged to launch an initiative of their own, designed to find a compromise solution. They may well have been. Although it is virtually certain that Mr Andreotti had already made up his mind, it is equally obvious that he intended to extract the maximum political benefit from the opportunity that the period of reflection offered him. The isolation and embarrassment of the Socialist Party, whose right wing was a target of interest to his own opponents inside the Christian Democratic Party, was a consummation devoutly to be wished.

Like so much else that Mr Andreotti wanted in these days, it actually happened. The prime minister's announcement that Italy would enter the EMS, which European Community leaders praised as an act of states-manship and political courage[172], was also the culmination of a masterly political manoeuvre. Those who like the Republicans and the majority of the Christian Democratic Party had for whatever reasons come out strongly in favour of immediate entry could only express their gratification at the decision, while the Socialists, who had been hoping to exploit what they took to be a fluid situation and who had not therefore decided for or against the system, could only abstain[173]. The crowning touch, however, was the clarification of the relationship with the Communists. Their opposition to the EMS, which had been confirmed after the meeting with Mr Andreotti on 8 December and which was explained yet again in the parliamentary debate itself[174], left them isolated within the majority. However, their no less obvious desire to avoid a crisis, which was also reaffirmed before and during the debate, left them tied to Mr Andreotti, who was more clearly than ever the only guarantee they had against those within his own party who wanted to precipitate the break. Mr Andreotti was therefore able to pose at one and the same time as their opponent and their understanding ally. He could make his party points and, particularly in press interviews and statements abroad, emphasize his belief that the Communists' European convictions were genuine[175]. The EMS episode left him therefore obliged to almost nobody and in command of almost everybody. As Francesco Damatto noted in *Il Giornale* on the day after the debate: 'anybody who was working away in the shadows of the Christian Democratic party to replace Mr Andreotti will have to do their sums again'[176].

No victory ever lasts for long in Italian politics, but this was nonetheless a famous one.

6.5   Third countries and international organizations

The fifth paragraph of the Brussels Resolution covered relations between the EMS and 'third countries and international organizations'. Of the former, the United States was for obvious reasons the most important. Enough has already been said in previous sections however to show how, through a combination of auto-persuasion and diplomacy, the fears that some senior American officials had originally harboured about the plan were gradually worn down. Amongst the European founders of the system too, the note of anti-Americanism that had undoubtedly been present in early stages of the negotiations became less marked as the months passed. The administration and the Federal Reserve were briefed on several occasions before the Brussels Council and, immediately it was over, the Treasury secretary, Mr Blumenthal, and Anthony Solomon were able to discuss the details of the final text with German officials during a short visit to Bonn on 7 December on their way back from Moscow[177]. When therefore Mr Jenkins travelled to Washington a week later he found little of the suspicion and hostility that had still been apparent in administration circles in September. Mr Carter himself congratulated him and through him the other architects of the scheme, and assured him of the American government's full support. The same message was repeated more publicly by senior administration officials both at home and abroad. In January for example, Anthony Solomon was positive and encouraging in a speech that he made on the international monetary system at Chatham House[178], while in Rome, Ambassador Gardner, whose qualifications to speak on the subject were second to none, gave an address to the Italian Bankers' Association on 12 February entitled 'From Bretton Woods to EMS' in which he spoke of the benefits for the 'entire world economy' if the EMS developed as it was intended to[179].

The IMF's anxieties were rather less easily assuaged, as the Commission president found when he called at the Fund at the request of the director, following his meeting with Mr Carter on 14 December. M. de Larosière and two of his most senior officials, Mr Polak, who had been with the Fund since 1947, and Mr Wittome, who had special responsibilities for Europe and had played the key role in negotiations between the Fund and the United Kingdom and Italy in 1976 and 1977, submitted their guest to a searching cross-examination. The questions that they asked covered a wide range of problems, including the potential threat to international liquidity that might arise from the creation of ECUs, relations between the latter and the SDRs, and the continuing effectiveness of IMF surveillance. If, for example, the IMF felt that a particular currency within the system was overvalued, was it not possible that those responsible for the management of the EMS would interpose themselves between the Fund and the country concerned? Were the rules governing the conditions under which credit might be advanced sufficiently strong? Would the central banks in the EMS be more dutiful about consulting the IMF in advance of realignments than the Snake countries had been? And so on. Mr Jenkins answered as best he could, but the doubts persisted. A week after this meeting for example, the IMF staff initiated yet another investigation of the system, and Mr Polak in particular was to go on raising questions throughout 1979[180]. Community spokesmen always denied the dangers that he saw, but the debate continued.

Other than the United States, the countries that those who drafted the Resolution had principally in mind were the four small industrialized democracies that bordered the Community and had or had had special relations with the Snake or the DM: Norway, Sweden, Austria and Switzerland. Norway had belonged to the Community currency grouping since 1972, first on the assumption that the country would join the EEC itself and then, following the referendum in the autumn of 1972, as an associate. For the first four years, the Norwegian krone remained one of the stronger members of the system[181]. From the latter half of 1976 onwards, however, there was a series of devaluations: 1% in October 1976, 3% in April 1977, 5% in August of the same year and 8% in February 1978. The first two adjustments, which were anyway very slight, caused little debate. The same was not true of the third, which coincided with the Swedish government's decision to leave the Snake altogether, or the fourth, which was the biggest. However, despite the growing reservations of several senior officials and public figures outside government, the minister of finance, Per Kleppe, and the governor of the central bank, Knut Getz Wold, remained convinced that membership was in the country's best interests, and their opinion was endorsed and defended by the prime minister, Odvar Nordli. When therefore the Franco-German proposal was announced at Bremen, the Norwegian authorities indicated that, although they could not commit themselves before the details had been worked out, they were disposed to take up the option of associate status that the Bremen Annex itself mentioned as a possibility[182]. Their attitude was particularly welcome to the Danes and the Germans, both of whom kept them informed of progress in the negotiations. By 23 November, matters had advanced sufficiently far for Mr Nordli and Mr Kleppe to tell the German chancellor, in the course of a meeting in Hamburg, which was largely devoted to the EMS, that they were satisfied with the details of the scheme that had emerged so far and that they would almost certainly recommend Norwegian participation after the Brussels Council[183].

They had clearly not reckoned however with the opposition that they were to meet on their return to Oslo. For the following two weeks the Norwegian media gave the EMS issue the prominence once given to the question of EEC membership itself[184]. Organizations like the People's Movement, which had played a major role in the 1972 campaign, threatened to revive, and the Christian People's Party, the left wing of the Labour Party, and the extreme left joined in protests against what they represented as an attempt to take Norway into the Community by a back door. This noisy, populist campaign naturally attracted a great deal of public attention, but it seems clear that the most damaging attacks on the system came not from the anti-Common Market groups as such, but from leading economists both inside and outside government and the representatives of major economic interests. The anti-Marketeers could be and were met with the argument that Norway was not being offered and was certainly not seeking a degree of involvement in the system that would entail any greater 'loss of sovereignty' than was currently at risk in the Snake and that had been tolerated by the Christian People's Party itself when their leader, Mr Korvald, had been prime minister[185]. The economic arguments against membership were, by contrast, much more difficult to demolish; so, still more, were the groups that advanced them. In the central bank itself, for example, the governor, Mr Wold, who presided over a five-man board, found himself outvoted in a widely reported 'revolt' led by his deputy, while in the ministry of finance, Per Kleppe was surrounded by a multitude of sceptics. Outside, the Shipowners' Association and spokesmen for the pulp and paper industries, for fisheries and by no means least for Norway's off-shore oil interests expressed their hostility[186].

Their attack was not concentrated against the EMS as such, so much as against any special association with a small group of European states in which the British and the Swedes were not represented. The attack could have been, and indeed had been, made against the Snake. The EMS therefore focused rather than provoked discontents that had been growing for some time. There were three arguments that were constantly repeated[187]. Firstly, the countries that made up the EMS accounted for only one-third of Norway's foreign trade. Britain and Sweden alone accounted for a further third. If these latter two countries had been prepared to join, the position would have been very different but, given the importance of non-EMS trade and the likelihood that the EMS, like the Snake, would be a strong currency zone by comparison with the rest of Norway's trading partners, the krone would tend to become increasingly overvalued in relation to the currencies of the country's principal commercial partners if it were to form part of the system. The second argument emphasized the importance of the dollar for both the oil industry and shipping, most of whose business was denominated in the American currency. The third argument was the existence of a viable alternative, namely an arrangement comparable to the one that had been adopted by the Swedes when they had left the Snake in 1977. Of the three arguments, this last was in many respects the most persuasive. Sweden had not only not suffered, but had it seemed actually prospered as a result of switching from the Snake to a more flexible arrangement in which the krone was kept in line with movements in a basket of currencies, weighted according to their importance in the country's external trade. Were Norway to do the same, the DM would be the heaviest element in the basket, but its influence would be counterbalanced by the inclusion of the dollar, the pound and the Swedish krone.

In the light of these arguments and of the political forces that built up towards the end of November, the Norwegian government's decision not to join the new system for the time being, which was announced by Mr Nordli on 11 December and explained by Mr Kleppe in the Storting on 14 December, is not difficult to understand[188]. Nor is the decision of the Swedish government, which was announced on 14 December, following consultations between the Riksbank and the government[189]. There were still some elements in both countries who hankered after the 'discipline' of the German connection[190], but in a period in which they were having to come to terms with the abandonment of Keynesianism or Myrdalism, an association that would make an unpleasant situation still less pleasant had few attractions to many.

The Austrians and the Swiss were in a quite different position. Neither was or ever had been formally connected with the Snake. Austria had not even tried to become a member, while the Swiss, who had, had failed because the French, who were still members when the application was made in 1975, had insisted that they should impose controls over foreign account holders, which would doubtless have aided the work of the French tax inspectorate but which were inconsistent with Swiss traditions and laws. Despite their formal autonomy, however, the authorities in both countries were, with the Dutch, Germany's closest allies in monetary affairs, and there was a well-established tradition of consultation and cooperation, not only at central bank level, but also between the three finance ministers, who met regularly to discuss matters of common concern. One such meeting was held in Salzburg in June 1978[191], shortly before the Bremen summit. It ended, as so often before, with what the *Neue Zürcher Zeitung* described as a 'confession to the priority of stability'. The Swiss minister, Bundesrat Chevallaz, was particularly outspoken, rejecting the OECD's demand that the Swiss authorities should run higher budgetary deficits to encourage international growth, and insisting that the country, with its high proportion of immigrant labour, price stability, low interest rates and import surpluses, was already contributing more than its share to the common good. All three ministers affirmed the need for a speedy return to orderly monetary relationships.

There was therefore a large measure of common interest and sentiment between the Swiss and the Austrians on currency questions and a general disposition to welcome the Franco-German initiative. The EMS issue nonetheless provoked important divisions of opinion both within the two countries and between them. In Austria, for example, the views of the vice-chancellor and minister of finance, Dr Androsch, differed markedly from those of the governor of the central bank, Dr Koren. The latter wanted essentially to maintain the current policy, which was aimed at keeping the Austrian schilling on a par with the DM. Adjustments could and did take place, but the Austrians fixed their new rates according to their own calculations and without any of the obligations to join multilateral consultations of the kind that preceded realignments in the Snake. The realignment of October 1978 was a case in point[192]. The authorities decided that some adjustment was opportune, but limited the devaluation against the DM to 1% rather than the 2% change that occurred between the Benelux countries and the DM. It was evident from early on in the EMS negotiations, however, that Dr Androsch was inclined to press for a closer relationship than had existed hitherto. He even spoke of full membership as one of the options that might be considered[193]. In due course, it became apparent that this particular possibility did not exist, since neither the French nor the Germans were ready to countenance non-Community states as full members of the EMS. This did not deter Dr Androsch unduly, and following the Brussels Council he reaffirmed his interest in a 'closer link, in order to emphasize the fact that we believe that this is a move in the right direction'[194]. The arrangement that by this time he had in mind was not association of the kind specified in the Resolution, which would have involved Austria in the responsibilities of membership without its benefits, in the form of stand-by credit facilities, but a privileged observer status under which the Austrian authorities would be allowed to sit in on the consultations of the EMS central bankers and would be kept informed on the same basis as full members of any changes that were planned. He spoke of this possibility both in public and in the context of bilateral and trilateral discussions with Mr Matthöfer and his Swiss colleague in February and March 1979[195], but no decision was arrived at, and when the EMS eventually came into force in the middle of March the Austrians reaffirmed the policy that they had pursued towards the Snake[196].

The Swiss federal government appointed a special working party under the chairmanship of Dr Languetin of the central bank to consider the problems raised by the EMS proposal in August 1978[197]. It was only one of several moves, however, in the second half of 1978 to review Swiss exchange rate policy in the wake of the dollar crisis, which had forced the Swiss franc up further even than the DM, and it was not given such immediate priority as the effort that began in October to talk the franc down against the DM. Full membership of the EMS was never seriously considered, partly because, having tried unsuccessfully in 1975 to join the Snake, the Swiss authorities considered it unlikely that any new effort would succeed, but partly too because, despite their intense preoccupation with overvaluation, they remained even more concerned about the possible destabilizing consequences that might ensue from a link with a currency zone that included such a heterogeneous group of economies. Some kind of public policy towards the EMS was nonetheless essential in order to guide the markets and prevent new speculation. In the end, therefore, following the advice set out in the working party's report, the Swiss authorities declared their approval of the system and their intention to cooperate with those responsible for managing it. They would, however, continue to pursue their own independent policies as before[198].

6.6 The dispute over the MCAs, December 1978–March 1979

The French president's behaviour at the European Council at the beginning of December had come as a disagreeable surprise to most if not all his colleagues. By 15 December, however, the damage had been largely undone and the spectre of a two-tier Europe had been banished once again with the decisions of Italy and Ireland to join. When the ECOFIN met on 18 and 19 December, therefore, its principal business was seemingly to put the final touches to a system that would begin to operate on 1 January. It was evident that the technical problems of accommodating the CAP to the new monetary regime would be amongst the harder subjects on the agenda, and negotiations to find solutions went on throughout the fortnight between the European Council and the ECOFIN meeting[199]. But it did not seem remotely probable that these problems would prevent the inauguration of the monetary system as a whole. In the event, however, that was exactly what happened. At the ECOFIN itself, M. Monory put a reserve on the implementation of the detailed arrangements for the EMS that the Council had worked out. This reserve, it was declared, would only be lifted when the nine governments had given proof of their readiness to enforce the decisions on agriculture taken at the European Council[200]. Meanwhile, in an adjoining room in the same building, M. Monory's colleague, M. Méhaignerie, was engaged in a stormy meeting of the agriculture ministers, at which he endeavoured, not altogether successfully, to explain what the European Council's undertakings amounted to in French eyes. The inability of the Agricultural Council to agree on almost any aspect of the problems involved, in a meeting that lasted until the early hours of 20 December, and the non-occurrence of the Schmidt–Giscard 'intervention' that, it was widely believed in Brussels, would salvage the situation at the last moment, meant that M. Monory's reserve remained in force and that the EMS could not begin to function on 1 January[201]. It was not to do so for another ten weeks.

The details of this dispute need not be analysed at any depth in the context of this book. As they are virtually unintelligible anyway to all but those directly involved (a latter-day equivalent of the Schleswig–Holstein question, which reputedly drove those who could grasp its intricacies to madness, amnesia or death), this is perhaps a mercy. It does, however, belong to the story of the launching of the EMS and a brief discussion of why it was considered of sufficient importance to delay the inauguration of the system and how it was eventually resolved is therefore necessary.

The answer to the first of these questions is to be found partly in the complexity of the issues the EMS raised for the agricultural regime, but still more in the domestic political situation in France. The technical issues would have been difficult enough to resolve even had there been goodwill.

The most important of them – the application of the ECU in agro-monetary transactions – had already emerged at the European Council, where, it will be recalled, agreements were reached that the drastic effect that this could have on agricultural price levels was too severe and that a corrective factor should therefore be introduced[202]. However, this proposal went only part of the way towards solving the problems that an ECU-based system would create. Amongst these were discrepancies between the MCAs, since not all currencies would be at their central rate against the ECU at the same time and on the day of the change-over, therefore, there could be variations of 1% or more in either direction. The system could also lead to the introduction of MCAs between Belgium and the Netherlands, which would have been incompatible with their longstanding customs union. In fact, far from helping to dismantle the MCA system, the introduction of the ECU threatened to extend it and make it still more complex. There were other problems too. France and Italy, with floating currencies, were at the time allowed 1.5% fluctuation margins, and the French made it clear that they were not prepared to sacrifice the benefits of this arrangement in the new system. There was also a move by the Italians to have the green lira devalued by 5% for reasons frequently rehearsed during the EMS debate by Mr Marcora, and by the French to devalue the green franc by 3.6%.

It was predictable, therefore, that the Agricultural Council meeting of 18/19 December would be a difficult one. And so it proved. Tempers rose so high that at one point Dr Ertl, who as German minister of agriculture was both the chairman and a principal combatant, had to hand over to his deputy in order to allow himself time to cool down[203]. Almost every government was involved in the imbroglio at one point or another, and such was the complexity of the issues that alignments changed according to the subject under discussion. The dispute that finally broke the meeting, however, was the disagreement between France and Germany over the interpretation of the last part of paragraph 6.1 of the Council Resolution of 5 December. The sentence in question stressed the importance of 'henceforth avoiding the creation of permanent MCAs'. Taking this as his starting point, the French minister insisted that from now on any new MCAs that might be created as a result of the revaluation of the currency should be subject to an automatic time limit of 12 months. Unless this was agreed, he argued, the French government would not accept the Commission's proposal on the corrective factor and the new ECU link system would not therefore come into operation. If accepted, this French attempt to impose an automatic rule would almost certainly have resulted in a fall in farm incomes in Germany, an outcome that Dr Ertl pronounced totally unacceptable.

Given the difficulties that the MCAs had undoubtedly caused French farmers, the minister's attempt to spell out the implications of the Council decision and thereby hasten the end of the whole MCA regime was understandable. The French were furthermore by no means alone: the

Italians and the Irish, for example, supported them strongly. What is surprising, however, is that the minister of agriculture and the government as a whole pursued their efforts to the point at which they placed the EMS in jeopardy. The European Council had after all managed to reach a comprom- ise on this point. The commitment to avoid the creation of permanent MCAs had been inserted into the text to satisfy the French, but there had been no reference to a time limit and the concession was anyway carefully balanced by a promise that existing prices would be unaffected. Why then did a precise timetable become a matter of such fundamental importance only two weeks later? Why could it not be left for further negotiation and discussion as the problem itself became more real and within the context of the implementation of the other part of the Resolution, which pledged the progressive dismantling of the MCA system in general? Why, finally, did the German chancellor and the French president not manage to sort it out, as they were widely expected to, through one of their famous personal meetings or telephone conversations?

The answer to these questions is to be found principally in the further escalation of the conflict within the majority in France that occurred after the Council meeting. Once back in Paris, where he gave a lively account of his achievements on television, M. Giscard d'Estaing was confronted by fresh attacks of still greater vehemence than before from the Gaullists and the left. On 6 December, M. Chirac launched his appeal to the nation and indicated that the Gaullists would not accept the president's call for a common, majority approach to the European elections, but would form their own list[204]. Both the president and the prime minister engaged in counter-propaganda of their own: the latter by ostentatiously refusing to enter into any controversy with M. Chirac, the former by indirectly denouncing him[205]. They had solid grounds for concern. The RPR was still the largest party in parliament and, as it showed yet again on 11 December, when Gaullist deputies joined with the Communists in supporting a motion to forbid the use of Community funds in the European elections, it could if it so wished precipitate a major political crisis[206]. M. Chirac denied that this was his intention; furthermore, there was strong evidence to suggest that he was not the complete master in his own house[207]. But the threat remained. So too did the disquiet of French farmers. The president's hard line at the European Council had been warmly greeted by M. Debatisse, the president of FNSEA, the principal farmers' organization[208], but, in the days that followed, demands grew for still further action to break the MCA system. The formal debate in the Chamber of Deputies on 14 December, which had been arranged at the request of the RPR, provided a convenient opportunity for election-minded deputies to express them to the full though, as Jacques Grall pointed out in his report on it, attendance in general was not good[209]. Answering to the debate, the minister of agriculture reaffirmed the government's intention to go on working for the dismantling of the MCA regime. His inclination to pursue this line still more vigorously was reinforced by extraparliamentary developments, including a major demonstration at Vassy (Calvados) that, according to one report, so disturbed him that his presentation of the French government's case at the Agricultural Council on 18/19 December suffered[210]. Whatever French obduracy may have done for the credibility of the European Community therefore, it was certainly good politics at home, and when the announcement was eventually made that the government would not lift the reserve on the EMS until their demands had been met, the president and his ministers received warm praise from leaders of the agricultural lobby and their political allies[211].

Once the decision to postpone the inauguration of the system beyond the symbolic date of 1 January had been taken, the urgency seemed to go out of the search for a solution. It was hoped that the president and the chancellor would be able to reach agreement during the summit at Guadeloupe with President Carter and Mr Callaghan at the beginning of January. They did not[212]. Nor did the agricultural ministers a few days later, nor the French and German foreign and agricultural ministers who held a special, secret meeting immediately afterwards[213], nor numerous other bilateral and multilateral meetings in the weeks that followed. The atmosphere was progressively poisoned. The Franco-German summit for example, which was held in the middle of February, was a far cry from the marriage of minds and hearts that had been celebrated at Aachen only five months earlier[214]. German newspapers that had waxed lyrical then about the depths of the connection were by January and February singing quite another tune[215]. As for the EMS, there was a growing feeling that it might never begin, an eventuality that Dr Emminger for one, reflecting both the general atmosphere and his own continuing prejudices, found distinctly unalarming[216]. It was an absurd state of affairs and a rather sordid conclusion to a negotiation that until almost the very end had reflected considerable credit on both the German chancellor and the French president. Perhaps the most appropriate comment was one made by Jonathan Carr of the *Financial Times* in an article on 5 January:

> What does it matter, it is asked, if the system were to start operation, let us say, one month later when the farm ministers have sorted out matters to their satisfaction?
>
> The answer is that it matters very much when the heads of state or government of the nine Community countries take a unanimous decision on what they say is of historic importance on December 5th and then permit discord among farm ministers to undermine it on December 19th. Even to those whose minds are dulled by excessive consumption of alcohol over Christmas and New Year (or by stultifying discussion of the history of monetary compensatory accounts in EEC farm trade), it must be clear that this topsy turvy procedure undermines the credibility of

Europe's leaders and is the worst possible psychological preparation for the eventual introduction of the EMS. If the Europeans want to be taken seriously by the Americans they will surely have to do better than this.

The dispute ended as unexpectedly as it began however. At the meeting of the agricultural ministers on 5/6 March, the French gave in[217]. There was a partial sop to their feelings in the form of a gentleman's agreement to reduce the newly created MCAs in two stages, but no time limit was imposed and, still more important from the German point of view, the agreement (to which the British for this reason did not subscribe) specifically excluded any reduction of agricultural prices in the currency of the country concerned as a result of the phased elimination of the MCAs. Quite why the French chose to give up the fight at this point and in this manner remains mysterious, but as a result of the 'agreement' the president himself announced in Paris on 7 March that France would lift its reserve on the EMS, which could therefore begin to operate[218]. This it did on 13 March 1979.

1 See *The Times*, 25 October 1978

2 *Neue Zürcher Zeitung*, 25 October 1978

3 *Le Monde*, 27 October 1978, has a useful survey of opposition to the EMS inside Germany

4 *Frankfurter Allgemeine Zeitung*, 1 December 1978

5 *Le Figaro*, 2 December 1978, carried an article by Olivier Wormser, a former governor of the Banque de France, expressing 'understanding' for the British position

6 *L'Humanité*, 26 October 1978

7 *Le Monde Diplomatique*, 18 November 1978

8 *Le Monde*, 18 October 1978. See also the interview with M. Monory, the minister of finance, in *Der Spiegel*, 30 October 1978

9 *Le Monde*, 12 October 1978

10 See *Le Monde*, 17 October 1978

11 ibid.

12 *Journal Officiel*, Débats parlementaires, Assemblée Nationale, 1978/79, 75ᵉ Séance, 30 November 1978, pp. 8567–75

13 *Le Monde*, 7 December 1978

14 *Le Monde*, 8 December 1978

15 *Le Monde*, 7 December 1978

16 *Journal Officiel*, op. cit. (note 12), 88ᵉ Séance, 11 December 1978, pp. 9174–91

17 *Le Monde*, 8 December 1978

18 Transcript of interview reprinted in *Europa-Archiv*, **34**(5), 10 March 1979, pp. 129ff

19 See below p. 264

20 *Le Monde*, 3 December 1978 and 1 January 1979

21 *Le Monde*, 7 December 1978

22 ibid.

23 *Le Monde*, 3/4 December 1978

24 Text in Italian Senate, *Rassegna della Stampa, Il sistema monetario europeo*, vol. 1, 26 October 1978, pp. 9ff

25 ibid., pp. 15ff. and 25ff

26 H. Kissinger, *The White House Years*, Boston, 1979, p. 101

27 Luigi Spaventa, *Italy and the EMS*, Johns Hopkins Center, Bologna, Occasional Papers No. 32, pp. 67–91

28 See *Il Corriere della Sera*, 17 March 1978

29 See article by Pietro Armani in *Il Corriere della Sera*, 3 November 1978, for a useful discussion of the recovery of Andreotti and its significance for the EMS debate

30 *24 Ore*, 25 October 1978

31 See *La Voce Repubblicana*, 3 November 1978

32 For Nina Andreatta's views, see, *inter alia, La Lira e lo Scudo: la scommessa europea*, Bologna, 1978, pp. 7–31, and *24 Ore*, 25 October 1978

33 See *24 Ore*, 27 October 1978 and *La Repubblica*, 29 October 1978

34 *24 Ore*, 10 November 1978

35 ibid., 25 November 1978

36 *La Repubblica*, 17 October 1978

37 ibid., 29 November 1978

38 *La Nazione*, 24 November 1978. See also *Il Tempo*, 16 November 1978, and *La Gazzetta del Popolo*, 28 November 1978

39 See, *inter alia, La Repubblica* and *L'Unità* of 8 November 1978 for different views of the consultations on 7 November 1978

40 For the PSDI, see also the views of Vizzini in *Il Tempo*, 18 November 1978

41 See the useful, if not entirely disinterested, discussion in *La Voce Repubblicana*, 25 October 1978

42 *La Repubblica*, 8 November 1978

43 I am grateful to Dr Antonio Varsori of the European University Institute for drawing my attention to the Healey–Phillips visit to Rome in 1948, which will be discussed in his EUI thesis on Anglo-Italian relations between 1947 and 1950

44 *La Repubblica*, 25 November 1978

45 See, for example, *L'Unità*, 5 November 1978

46 *La Repubblica*, 25 November 1978

47 *Rinascita*, 17 November 1978

48 *La Repubblica*, 8 November 1978

49 *24 Ore*, 17 November 1978

50 *The Guardian*, 23 September 1978

51 *The Times*, 8 September 1978

52 See, for example, *The Guardian*, 23 October 1978 (on the meeting with the NEC) and *The Times*, 31 October 1978 (on the TUC–Labour Party meeting)

53 First Report from the Expenditure Committee, Session 1978–79, *The European Monetary System*, HMSO, pp. 60–76

54 Reprinted in full in *Financial Times*, 25 November 1978

55 On Mr Callaghan's tactics see, *inter alia*, *The Observer*, 22 October 1978

56 *Financial Times*, 23 October 1978 and 1 December 1978

57 *The Observer*, 22 October 1978

58 See, for example, *Financial Times*, 18 October 1978

59 *Financial Times*, 27 November 1978

60 *The Guardian*, 10 November 1978

61 ibid., 23 and 24 October 1978

62 Expenditure Committee, op. cit. (note 53), pp. 138–43

63 *The Times*, 16 November 1978. See also 30 November 1978

64 *Financial Times*, 31 October 1978

65 For the trial of Mr Jeremy Thorpe, the former leader of the party, on a charge of conspiring to murder Mr Norman Scott, see the British (and a good deal of the foreign) press throughout late November

and December 1978. For Liberal Party views on the EMS, see reports in *The Times*, etc., on the debate in the House of Commons on 29 November 1978

66 Expenditure Committee, op. cit. (note 53), pp. 57–60

67 For example, ibid., pp. 86ff., 120ff., 133ff

68 ibid., p. 92

69 For example, *The Times*, 13 October 1978, 'This EMU has no clothes'

70 On Sir Jeremy Morse's role in the Committee of Twenty see R. Solomon, *The International Monetary System, 1945–76*, New York, 1977, pp. 236ff. For his evidence, see Expenditure Committee, op. cit. (note 53), pp. 89–101

71 See *The Guardian*, 25 October 1978

72 ibid., 1 December 1978

73 ibid.

74 Dail Eireann, *Parliamentary Debates/Official Report*, vol. 308, cols 404ff

75 ibid., col. 88

76 ibid., col. 575

77 ibid., col. 559

78 ibid., col. 891

79 ibid., vol. 310, cols 420ff

80 ibid., col. 424

81 ibid., vol. 308, col. 455

82 ibid., vol. 310, col. 438

83 See above p. 163

84 An exception was the *Sunday Telegraph* on 22 October 1978, which reported that the gap between the opposing groups had narrowed

85 *Financial Times*, 17 October 1978

86 *Il Corriere della Sera*, 17 October 1978

87 See, especially, *Financial Times*, 16 November 1978

88 Expenditure Committee, op. cit. (note 53), p. 69

89 See Resolution (reproduced in Appendix 1B) paragraph 3.6

90 Deutscher Bundestag, *Stenographischer Bericht*, 122 Sitzung, 6 December 1978 pp. 9485ff

91 European Commission Monetary Committee, *Compendium of Monetary Texts*, Brussels, 1979, pp. 55ff. *Agreement of 13 March 1979 between the Central Banks … laying down the operating procedures for the EMS*

92 See *Financial Times*, 3 November 1978, which suggests that the chancellor agreed to the half-way house in principle at the Rambouillet meeting of 2 November 1978

93 See *The Times*, 7 and 25 November 1978
94 *International Herald Tribune*, 25 November 1978
95 *The Times*, 25 November 1978
96 Expenditure Committee, op. cit. (note 53), esp. p. 61 and *Financial Times*, 25 November 1978
97 See, for example, *Financial Times*, 4 December 1978
98 See, especially, *Federal Reserve Bulletin*, December 1978, pp. 939ff
99 *Federal Reserve Bulletin*, June 1978, pp. 448ff
100 US Treasury Press Releases, B. 1126, 22 August 1978
101 For the following, see OECD, *Economic Outlook*, No. 24, December 1978, pp. 70ff
102 *Wall Street Journal*, 6 November 1978, contains a well-informed article on the immediate background by Richard F. Janssen and Richard Levine
103 In addition to the factual report cited in note 98 above, see the Statement to Congress by G. William Miller, chairman of the Board of Governors of the Federal Reserve, on 16 November 1978, in *Federal Reserve Bulletin*, November 1978, pp. 843ff
104 See *The Times*, 17 October 1978 and *Neue Zürcher Zeitung*, 18 October 1978
105 *The Times*, 13 October 1978
106 See, *inter alia*, *Financial Times*, October 1978
107 Andrew Shonfield, 'The Politics of the Mixed Economy in the International System of the 1970s', *International Affairs*, January 1980, p. 13
108 ibid.
109 ibid., p. 11
110 See, for example, *Irish Times*, 7 November 1978, and *The Times*, 8 November 1978
111 *Official Journal of the European Communities*, Debates of the European Parliament, Session 1978/79, 12 September 1978, pp. 30ff., contains essential background information
112 ibid., 23 October 1978, p. 6
113 For the decision of December 1977, see *European Report*, 7 December 1977
114 European Parliament, op. cit. (note 111) 23 October 1978, p. 11
115 ibid., pp. 16ff. and p. 77ff
116 See *International Herald Tribune*, 22 November 1978, and *European Report*, 22 November 1978
117 For Britain's subsequent behaviour, see *European Report*, 7 February 1979, etc.

118 See, for example, *The Times*, 13 November 1978
119 See, especially, *The Times*, 14 November 1978
120 *Irish Times*, 7 November 1978
121 ibid., 9 November 1978
122 ibid.
123 See Dail, op. cit. (note 74), vol. 310, cols 412ff
124 ibid., especially cols 414–15, and *Irish Times*, 30 November 1978
125 European Parliament, op. cit. (note 111), 23 October 1978, p. 8
126 *Corriere della Sera*, 22 April 1980
127 Council Resolutions (reprinted in Appendix 1B), paragraph 4 of section B. In his speech to the Italian Chamber of Deputies on 12 December 1978 Mr Andreotti declared that he (and one must assume the British) would have liked an even more explicit undertaking. See Italian Senate, op. cit. (note 24), vol. 1, p. 101
128 *Irish Times*, 4 December 1978
129 See *European Report*, 25 November 1978
130 Transcript of press conference given by Mr Callaghan on 5 December 1978
131 *Europa-Archiv*, 34(5), 10 March 1979, p. 130
132 See, for example, *The Observer*, 10 December 1978, in which William Keegan and Robert Stephens expounded the thesis that the breakdown had been engineered by the French president and the British prime minister. Although Mr Callaghan was (for a week) happy about what had happened and M. Giscard d'Estaing did not betray any sign of contrition, the story seems extremely far-fetched
133 For example, *Corriere della Sera*, 6 December 1978
134 See, *Il Tempo*, 6 December 1978
135 *The European Monetary System*, Paper laid before both Houses of the Oreachtas, Stationery Office, Dublin, December 1978, p. 17
136 For example, Deutscher Bundestag, op. cit. (note 90)
137 White paper, op. cit. (note 135), pp. 17–18
138 Transcript of presidential press conference held by Mr Schmidt and Mr Jenkins, 5 December 1978
139 See, for example, *Der Spiegel*, 11 December 1978, p. 23
140 *Frankfurter Allgemeine Zeitung*, 6 December 1978, leader headed 'Schmidts Verdienst'

141 Deutscher Bundestag, op. cit. (note 90)
142 *Europa-Archiv*, **34**(5), 10 March 1979, p. 129ff
143 See, for example, *Financial Times*, 6 December 1978
144 For example, ibid. and *The Guardian* and other quality newspapers on 6 December 1978 and following days
145 *Irish Times*, 6 December 1978
146 ibid., 7 December 1978
147 For the controversy over Mr Lynch's press conference, see, especially, Dail, op. cit. (note 74), vol. 310, cols 989ff
148 ibid. and cols 1322ff
149 Deutscher Bundestag, op. cit. (note 90)
150 Dail, op. cit. (note 74), vol. 310, cols 1336–7
151 ibid., cols 2047ff. contain a report by Mr Lynch on the negotiations after the European Council
152 ibid., cols 1987ff
153 *The Guardian*, 27 January 1979
154 Dail, op. cit. (note 74), vol. 310, cols 2159ff
155 ibid., cols 2043–174, for the debate of 21 December 1978
156 Italian Senate, op. cit. (note 24), vol. 1, pp. 97ff. Spaventa, op. cit. (note 27), contains a great deal of information on events between 5 and 12 December
157 See *Frankfurter Allgemeine Zeitung*, 13 December 1978
158 *L'Umanità*, 9 December 1978
159 *Le Monde*, 9 December 1978
160 Italian Senate, op. cit. (note 24), vol. 1, p. 103. See also Spaventa, op. cit. (note 27)
161 Spaventa, op. cit. (note 27)
162 *Il Corriere della Sera*, 8 December 1978
163 For example, Dr Andreatta, *La Discussione*, 11 December 1978
164 *La Repubblica*, 7 December 1978
165 See *Le Monde*, 5, 6, 7 and 9 December 1978
166 *La Repubblica*, 7 December 1978
167 ibid., but see denial in *Il Popolo*, 8 December 1978
168 For example, *L'Umanità*, 8 December 1978
169 *Il Popolo*, 8 December 1978
170 *24 Ore*, 7 December 1978, contains an anthology of statements by representatives of all the majority parties, including Barca
171 For the consultations, see, *inter alia, Il Corriere della Sera*, 8 and 9 December 1978
172 For quotations from various sources see *Frankfurter Allgemeine Zeitung*, 13 December 1978

173 On the Socialists' dilemma, see especially Spaventa, op. cit. (note 27)
174 *L'Unità*, 9, 10 and 13 December 1978
175 See *Le Monde*, interview with Mr Andreotti, 9 January 1979
176 *Il Giornale*, 13 December 1978
177 *New York Times*, 7 December 1978
178 US Treasury Press Releases, B 1342, 12 January 1979
179 US Embassy, Rome, transcripts of speeches by Ambassador Gardner
180 For example, J. J. Polak, unpublished paper on the European Monetary Fund read at conference in Geneva, 7/8 December 1978
181 *Stortings forhandlinger*, 1978/79, 14 December 1978, pp. 1783ff. Statement by Per Kleppe contains a useful survey of Norway's relations with the Snake
182 *Le Monde*, 11 July 1978
183 *Financial Times*, 24 November 1978
184 The best sources are obviously the Norwegian newspapers themselves from approximately 24 November to 12 December 1978, but for those who cannot read Norwegian there are useful summaries in the *Financial Times*, 7, 8 and 12 December 1978, *Neue Zürcher Zeitung*, 8 and 14 December 1978, and *Frankfurter Allgemeine Zeitung*, 13 December 1978
185 See *Stortings forhandlinger*, op. cit. (note 181), p. 1840, speech by Kare Willoch of Høyrepartiet, 18 December 1978. For Mr Korvald's own views, see pp. 1843–45
186 See *Neue Zürcher Zeitung*, 8 December 1978
187 The best summary is to be found in the speech by Per Kleppe of 14 December 1978 justifying the decision, see note 181 above
188 ibid. and *Neue Zürcher Zeitung*, 12 December 1978
189 *Frankfurter Allgemeine Zeitung*, 15 December 1978
190 See, for example, Kare Willoch, speech quoted in note 185 above
191 *Frankfurter Allgemeine Zeitung*, 12 June 1978, and *Neue Zürcher Zeitung*, 13 June 1978
192 *Frankfurter Allgemeine Zeitung*, 17 October 1978
193 *Neue Zürcher Zeitung*, 14 October 1978
194 ibid., 9 December 1978
195 *Süddeutsche Zeitung*, 16 February 1979, and *Neue Zürcher Zeitung*, 21 March 1979
196 *Süddeutsche Zeitung*, 12 March 1979

197 See, especially *Neue Zürcher Zeitung*, 24 December 1978
198 *Neue Zürcher Zeitung*, 27 March 1979
199 See *European Report*, Nos 556ff
200 *Frankfurter Allegemeine Zeitung* and *Le Monde*, 21 December 1978
201 *Le Monde*, 29 December 1978, contains a very good survey of the dispute
202 See above p. 263
203 *Frankfurter Allgemeine Zeitung*, 21 December 1978; *Le Monde*, 21 and 29 December 1979
204 *Le Monde*, 8 December 1978
205 ibid., 11 December 1978
206 *Journal Officiel*, op. cit. (note 12), 88ᵉ Séance, 11 December 1978, pp. 9174–91
207 See *Le Monde*, 14, 19 and 20 December 1978
208 ibid., 8 December 1978
209 ibid., 15 December 1978
210 ibid., 29 December 1978
211 ibid., 30 December 1978
212 See conflicting reports in *Le Monde*, *Frankfurter Allgemeine Zeitung*, etc., between 9 and 12 January 1979, which proved eventually that nothing had been settled
213 *Frankfurter Allgemeine Zeitung*, 17 January 1979
214 ibid., 23 February 1979
215 See, for example, *Frankfurter Allgemeine Zeitung*, 29 January and 22 February 1979
216 *Süddeutsche Zeitung*, 15 February 1979. For the feeling that the EMS might never begin, see, for example, *Die Zeit*, 9 February 1979
217 *European Report*, 7 and 10 March 1979
218 *Financial Times*, 8 March 1979

Conclusions

The protracted negotiations over technical details of greater or lesser significance, and, still more, the unexpected delay caused by French hostility to the MCAs, undoubtedly deprived the launching of the EMS in March 1979 of some of the glamour and excitement that it might otherwise have had. This may have been no bad thing. Almost every Community initiative, from the Schuman Plan onwards, has suffered from a surfeit of rhetoric, which has only been dissipated slowly or painfully through years of sober and sobering experience. Starting from a more modest base, without the fanfares that accompanied the first proclamation of a new European monetary initiative in 1978, the EMS has functioned much better than its critics expected and some of its advocates feared.

During the first three years of its existence[1], the system has helped to provide the countries who have participated in it with a greater degree of protection against currency unrest than, given what has happened in the world since 1979, they would have had, and the British have had, without it. It has also shown, in October 1981 and February 1982, that it can accommodate major realignments, which the divergence in the economic performance of member states made inevitable, while at the same time preventing unacceptable dashes for freedom through competitive devaluations. The realignment of February 1982 is a particularly instructive episode in this respect. The Belgians, to whom it is reported the IMF, whose strictness had been so strongly stressed by its supporters in 1978, was quite prepared to concede a 12% and perhaps even a 15% devaluation, found themselves forced by their European partners to accept 8.5%, while the Danes, who made what seemed to the representatives of several of the other governments involved in the weekend negotiations, a singularly inelegant attempt to exploit the opportunity offered by the Belgian request to achieve a 7% devaluation of the krone, were obliged to limit themselves to 3%[2]. The EMS, it may be said, has done enough in three years to justify its existence and to confirm its utility as an element in a learning process that, given the constraints built into the global and regional economic system, the states of Western Europe could scarcely avoid and which they will have to go through by other means even if this particular experiment collapses. As Christopher McMahon of the Bank of England observed: 'If the EMS did not exist, it – or something similar – would have to be invented'[3]. His counterpart in the Central Bank of the Netherlands, Dr Szasz, who was, and indeed is, even more sceptical about the durability of this particular experiment, made a similar observation: 'In the end, stabilization of exchange rates with all its constraints on domestic policies is . . . inevitable, though the learning process of this reality may outlast the present EMS.[4]'

However satisfactory the performance of the EMS may have been in the first three years of its existence and however inevitable the learning process that it has encouraged may be, there are nevertheless several grounds for fearing that its future, at least in the short term, may not be as peaceful as its past. Three are particularly important. Firstly, part at least of the explanation of its 'success' is to be found in external developments that may well not persist. Secondly, despite the opportunity and the incentives that the system has provided to member states to coordinate their economic policies, the economic performance of the countries concerned has continued to diverge since 1979 at a rate that is incompatible with long term monetary stability. Thirdly, the peculiar political constellation that gave rise to its birth has begun to wane and there seems little hope, at the moment at any rate, that it will be replaced by another, equally favourable to progress towards economic and monetary union.

There is neither space nor need at this juncture to enter into a lengthy discussion of international economic history since March 1979. It is enough to point out that, partly as a result of the second oil shock and partly because of the dramatic shift in the economic policies of the United States, which began under President Carter, but which has been carried to new extremes since President Reagan took office, the international monetary system has not behaved in anything like the way in which critics of the Schmidt–Giscard proposals envisaged in 1978. The inexorable decline of the dollar has been sharply reversed, and the American currency which seemed in 1978 to be heading for a 1:1.50 DM rate was, in April 1982, worth over 2.40 DM. The implications of this strange reversal for the development of the EMS need hardly be emphasized. With a weak 'key' currency, the system has been the opposite of the strong currency zone that many commentators anticipated in 1978, and life with the DM, which was so widely feared in Italy and France three years ago, has proved to be a great deal less demanding than it was expected to be, and indeed, in the light of the economic performance of the countries concerned, should have been.

This leads on to the second point. The DM's weakness and the Federal Republic's current account deficit notwithstanding the German economy has continued to perform significantly better in almost every important respect that those of most of its partners in the monetary system[5]. Whether one looks at inflation rates, or public sector borrowing requirements, or economic growth, or trade in manufactured goods, the gap between the German economy and the economies of the weaker member states is still too large for monetary stability to persist over the medium or even the short term. In 1980, for example, consumer prices in Germany rose by 5.8%, while in Italy the increase was of the order of 20%, in Ireland of 18% and in France of 13%. The situation did not change greatly in 1981, and despite some improvement in the early part of 1982, as the recession has become more intense, the difference between rates in the Federal Republic and Italy is still over 10%. Although, therefore, it is possible to argue, as Niels Thygesen has recently done with considerable force[6], that the EMS has helped Western Europe to survive the second oil shock without such a wide divergence in inflation rates and other key indicators as occurred in the period 1973–76, it is difficult to see how the system can ride roughshod over the differences that have persisted despite its beneficial consequences.

The likelihood of increasing instability within the system, if not of its complete collapse, seems all the stronger in the light of the third factor referred to above, namely the decline of the political constellation that presided over the birth of the EMS in 1977–79. If it is legitimate to argue, as Christopher McMahon and Dr Szasz among others have done, that the EMS is in certain perspectives 'necessary', it would be wrong to conclude that it was somehow inevitable. On the contrary, as this book should have shown, the system was the product of a very special political constellation that has weakened in several important respects since 1978, and which may not return in anything approaching the same strength in the near future. Four aspects of the political history outlined in this book require particular emphasis in this connection. The first is the crucial role played by the German chancellor; the second, the closeness and effectiveness of Mr Schmidt's partnership with M. Giscard d'Estaing; the third, the efficacy of the European Council; the fourth, the emergence of a broadly based Western European consensus about the priorities of economic policy.

The EMS was arguably the first major act of German leadership in the history of the European Community. The point was made many times in Italy, France and the United Kingdom by critics of the system who hoped that by stressing Germany's hegemonial role, they could undermine support for the initiative. What they overlooked, however, was that this act of leadership was only possible because the chancellor of the day possessed sufficient political authority to brush aside the collective strength and wisdom of the guardians of the German economy in Frankfurt and Bonn. It may be true that Mr Schmidt himself was primarily concerned with defending German interests, but the fact was that his perception of German interests was seriously at variance with the majority of informed opinion in the Federal Republic. The system depended for its birth therefore not simply nor even mainly on the strength of Germany, but on the strength of the chancellor within Germany. A decline in his political fortunes of the kind that has occurred since the Federal elections of 1980 must therefore be of considerable significance for any evaluation of the short term prospects of the European monetary system.

The second and third points referred to above can be taken together. Mr Schmidt, no less than his predecessors in the Bundeskanzleramt, was acutely aware of the psychological and political dangers that might arise from any overt act of German leadership in Western Europe. Like them, he did not want his country to seem to be taking the initiative alone. Hence the significance of the special relationship with France and in a broader sense of the European Council. As the discussion in Chapter 4 has suggested, there is evidence to suggest that the German chancellor would have liked to have built up a directorate of three, consisting of the French president, the British prime minister and himself. In the event, the episode confirmed a tendency towards a directorate of two, which from the beginning of 1978 until the fall of Giscard d'Estaing in May 1981 became the principal motor of European action on or statements about the international scene. As the curious postscript to the EMS negotiations between December 1978 and March 1979 showed, there were occasions even at the height of the Schmidt–Giscard partnership, when the two principals misunderstood each other or were unable to act together to overcome domestic political difficulties, but viewed as a whole the partnership that developed between the two men was remarkably harmonious and effective, not only at the summit level at which they both operated in their own right, but also at lower levels, through the sense of direction and purpose which they conveyed to their subordinates.

The close relationship with the French president did not however prevent Mr Schmidt from making effective use of the European Council. Rather the reverse. The Council, which for a brief season managed to combine the best features of a political dining club with the effectiveness of a good council of ministers or cabinet, was essential as an instrument for neutralizing any resentments that high handed action by the 'big' might provoke, and for broadening the circle of those responsible for imposing an initiative, which to the German chancellor and the French president was an act of high politics, rather than an exercise in monetary manipulation. There are of course limits to the extent to which heads of government and state can change the course of events. The boldest action outside normal channels tends in the end to be turned back by bureaucratic operators and vested interests into the familiar conduits of every day, and a monetary system that was intended to defy the preferences and prejudices of central bankers all the time, would be bound in the end to fail or be adulterated by compromise. Prime ministers can initiate; they can only partially implement. They can communicate a vision of things as they would like them to be; they cannot completely ignore things as they are. They can indicate how and where the bridges ought to be built; they cannot walk on the waters. The expert committees and the ministerial councils had to be allowed in on the plan, if the latter was not to remain little more than a rhetorical gesture. But the fact that they worked so effecively, and, contrary to the expectations of sceptics, kept to the timetable laid down at Bremen in July 1978, was due in large measure to the clarity of the instructions that the Council gave and the sense of urgency which its members conveyed to the national administrations.

If personalities and institutions were important in 1977–1978, so too were ideas. The EMS was at one and the same time an act of political imagination, and an expression of a growing consensus in Western Europe about the priorities of economic policy. There were still, it need hardly be said, special emphases from country to country, but the Schmidt government in Bonn, the Giscard–Barre administration in Paris, the Andreotti–Pandolfi regime in Italy and the Callaghan–Healey partnership in London spoke essentially the same language and shared the same objectives in economic matters. It was not, it should be stressed, the more strident language that the Thatcher administration was to introduce in Britain a year later, and which prompted the Bundesbank to issue a gentle reminder of the virtues of pragmatism in its submission to the House of Commons' Treasury and Civil Service Committee study of monetary policy[7]. It was less dogmatic and more common sensical, an acknowledgement by most if not all the leaders of Western Europe that the Germans had weathered the economic storms of the decade much more effectively than any other country, and that the methods that they had used to do so were therefore worth studying and emulating. The French President was most open in admitting that this was what he was trying to do, but to a greater or lesser extent his objectives were shared by most if not all of his colleagues.

In the years that have elapsed since March 1979, these political foundations of the system have weakened, and the resolve to move on to a second phase, which was publicly affirmed by the European Council at its meeting in December 1978, has slackened if not died altogether. The ideological consensus, for example, has begun to be called into question, and although it is still not clear whether the French administration will persist with policies which their partners, and in particular the Federal Republic, regard as inflationary and therefore as incompatible with continuing membership of the EMS, it is already obvious that economic policy-makers in West Germany are even warier than they were in 1978 about linking their country's fortunes too closely with those of a potentially unstable partner. The European Council and the Franco–German partnership have also suffered in the last two years, the former from the deep disharmony created by the dispute over the British contributions to the Community budget, the latter from the change of regime in France. It would be rash to predict that neither the Council nor the special relationship will revive, but for the time being at any rate neither is exactly in its heyday. Finally, and perhaps most important of all in the light of the emergence of the monetary system, the political fortunes of the German chancellor have declined sharply since those days in 1978 when he seemed able to cajole and convince even the most sceptical opponents of his initiative into accepting its inevitability. The significance of this fact was illustrated rather strikingly in the first three months of 1982, when there was a serious attempt by senior officials in the Commission and some member governments to take advantage of the opportunity offered by a pro-EMS Belgian presidency to press for a number of sensible, if undramatic improvements to the system[8]. The initiative quickly foundered, however, partly because the Bundesbank made it quite clear that it was not at all interested in the proposals, and partly because the German chancellor, who was preoccupied with many other problems, refused to take the side of the proponents of the scheme. It would be misleading to suggest that the survival of the monetary system is dependent upon the political survival of the German chancellor, but in the light of both this episode and the negotiations of 1978, the chances of developing it beyond the present stage would seem to be much slighter without a strong impulse from the chancellor's office in Bonn.

What conclusion, it might be asked, should be drawn from this rather gloomy assessment of the present position? It is not, it need hardly be said, that the governments involved would be well advised to abandon the experiment. Events may yet force some of them to do so, even temporarily, but a high degree of interdependence within the European Community and a no less high degree of vulnerability without, make orderly monetary arrangements in Western Europe no less desirable or necessary in 1982 than they were in 1977 or 1978. There is no automatic escalator that will transport the member governments from the present EMS to a full blown EMU, but a lesser degree of cooperation between the monetary authorities in face of the problems posed by American interest rates, global recession and sundry other internal and external threats and problems would be much worse than the present, admittedly inadequate state of affairs. Even the Bundesbank, which in 1978 was so sceptical about any extension of European currency arrangements beyond the confines of the Snake, seems ready now to concede this point. In a remarkable speech in London in October 1981, which would appear to have taken his British hosts as much by surprise as anybody else, the President of the Bundesbank, Dr Poehl, affirmed, firstly that 'Central Banks will be called upon ever more urgently to do something about the volatility of exchange rates, the longer it continues', and secondly that the EMS would not be complete unless Britain participated fully in the scheme[9]. A retreat from the ground that has already been won would therefore be as unnecessary as it would be absurd.

The problem however is to discover how and where to advance. It is relatively easy to identify the questions that require further study. They are the 'fundamental' problems that policy-makers in 1978 skated over because, to use the terms of the times, they belonged to phase II rather than phase I. They are both economic and political. Of the former, probably the most important is the question of how the ECU, if its use were to be developed, could fit in to the international currency system without causing more problems than it solved. Advocates of the EMS in 1978 spoke freely of an international monetary system based on three currency zones, but at least some of those who indulged in these thoughts when the dollar was weak admit now to a much greater awareness of the difficulties involved in an orderly transition from the present regime to a three-block system. Internal problems are however scarcely less pressing, since if there is to be a system which provides the Western European economies with some measure of protection against the damaging consequencies of United States monetary and budgetary policies, much more serious attention will have to be given than hitherto to the practical and theoretical implications of coordinating EEC exchange rate and monetary policies. In the light of the growing threat to the consensus about the priorities of economic policy which was of such importance in the launching phase of the EMS, discussion about how the latter might develop cannot be separated from the still more fundamental question of how to achieve recovery from the recession without a relapse into runaway inflation. Of political and institutional questions that need to be looked at, those associated with the Fund, which were scarcely touched upon in the original negotiations and have been almost entirely ignored since, are the most obvious. They are not however the only ones, and perhaps not even the most important. The experience of the last two or three years has underlined again and again the need for a radical review of decision-making processes, not simply inside Western Europe, but within the Western alliance as a whole, with a view to overcoming the dislocation between economic affairs and foreign policy and security matters which in the luxurious days of American hegemony and western prosperity, the nations of the Atlantic alliance could live with, but which in these more troubled times stands revealed as a dangerous nonsense. It is understandable that the Western Europeans should deplore the likely consequences of American budgetary deficits, but as these are to some extent at any rate accounted for by increased American spending on western security, the United States administration can respond to these criticisms by pointing out that a greater Western European contribution to the defence of the North Atlantic could make a major contribution to the reduction of interest rates and the recovery of the western economy. The present machinery of the alliance, however, militates against any serious consideration of the linkage between such problems.

There is therefore a formidable agenda of work still to be done. Whether or not any of its bears fruit in policies will however, depend very largely on developments beyond the control of the experts who take part in the discussions, and the central bankers and officials who are eventually called upon to implement the ideas. The political forces that moulded the system in the first place have already been discussed. Those that might carry it forward still further can only be guessed at. As in 1978 they will need to combine the general and the personal. The external threat or the internal crisis will have to be matched by political leadership. Two developments that might possibly act as catalysts are worth mentioning. The first would be a radical overhaul of the United Kingdom's policies towards and within the European Community. The second would be if the debate about western security, which has gathered pace over the last two years for reasons that are obvious enough, were to develop real momentum and provoke concrete proposals and action about the organization of the western alliance in the light of the new era in East–West relations that began at the end of the 1970s, and the growing divergence of interests between the United States and Europe that the history of the last 10 to 15 years has so frequently illustrated. The two developments are not – or at least ought not to be – unrelated.

To take the British question first. Previous chapters have, it is hoped, suggested that there is no simple explanation for the United Kingdom's decision not to enter the system. The Labour Party conference of October 1978 may to all intents and purposes have settled the issue, but it had been preceded and it was followed by a series of incidents that suggest that the decision was due to much more than the ability of the left to hold a minority Labour Government to ransom in a pre-electoral period. Amongst these additional factors, one might mention the indecision of the prime minister; the luke-warmness of the Conservative opposition; the failure of the Foreign Office to insist with sufficient strength and perhaps with sufficient conviction, that however finely balanced the economic arguments were, the political case for membership should be decisive; and the singular inability of the senior Treasury personnel involved, from the Chancellor downwards, to temper their professional doubts or certainties by political insight. Treasury officials buttressed their hostility to the system with impressive looking appeals to hard economic 'facts', but on close inspection their antipathy to the Franco–German proposal would seem to have had its roots in a want of imagination and a surfeit of prejudice, of the same kind that prompted the French Government in May 1940 to ask Keynes to intervene with Churchill to bring the Treasury to heel in the interest of the alliance and of the war effort[10]. The impression that their hostility had less to do with the 'facts' that they cited, than with the necessities of tribal politics, is confirmed by what happened once the EMS was inaugurated. As sterling rose to heights that threatened to hasten the deindustrialization about which they had professed such anxiety during the EMS negotiations, the same officials who had argued so vigorously in 1978 that notthing *should* to be done to prevent sterling from falling to its proper levels, were apparently to be found arguing in the new situation that nothing *could* be done to prevent it from rising.

The hostility of the Treasury has been reinforced from another angle by the Conservative government which came into office in May 1979. Committed to tight monetarist policies, Sir Geoffrey Howe and his acolytes argued that an exchange rate target was incompatible with policies geared to internal monetary targets. This case was in theoretical terms both plausible and respectable. Once again however, subsequent events make it legitimate to ask whether the good theoretical case was not a cover for more fundamental prejudices, since after more than two years of miserable experience with the £M3 etc., the British government would seem to have adopted an exchange rate policy. The chancellor was, it is true, still unwilling to concede the point in his Budget statement in March 1982, but even he admitted that 'while the government has no target for the exchange rate, its effect on the economy and therefore its behaviour cannot be ignored'[11]. Along at the Bank of England, where the governor and Mr McMahon have always been credited with a more positive attitude towards the EMS than the Treasury or Mrs Thatcher's ministers, there seems little inclination to conceal the fact that the British authorities have since the latter part of 1981 tried to keep sterling somewhere between 89 and 92 on the Bank of England's trade-weighted index[12]. The theoretical objections to an exchange rate target would appear, therefore, to have been abandoned, and the only serious economic argument that is now advanced against reinforcing the new policy by membership of the EMS is that the United Kingdom would be obliged to enter at an excessively high sterling–DM rate. Even this argument is, however, chiefly significant for the light that it throws on the British government's lack of confidence in the political processes, since they are by no means alone in Western Europe in believing that the DM is seriously undervalued and it should not be beyond the wit of skilled negotiators, who are not locked in compartmentalized negotiations, but who are ready to exploit links between different questions and to place the whole negotiation in a broad political perspective, to bring about a realignment at the moment of British entry which would meet most if not all of the British Government's requirements vis-à-vis the DM.

Whatever economic arguments this or that group of ministers or officials may have advanced, therefore, the key to the United Kingdom's reactions to the Schmidt–Giscard proposals and to the government's policies towards the EMS, once the system was established, is political and psychological. The EMS episode is in fact only one, significant but by no means exceptional, in an increasingly tedious story of misunderstanding and non-cooperation between London and the rest of the EEC. The origins of this 'comedy of errors' are, it need hardly be said, complex and the British are by no means alone responsible for the 'British problem'. But whoever is to blame, it is difficult to see who stands to gain from the impasse. It is certainly not the British. The Europeanization of their economy and of their external interests has continued, however much those engaged in the wearisome and unreal debate about Community membership may try to ignore the facts. When Mr Jenkins took up office as President of the Commission at the beginning of 1977, 36% of UK exports and 32% of her imports went to or came from the Community. (The comparable figures in 1958 were 20% in each case.) By 1980, the Community's share of UK exports had risen to 43%

and of imports to 39%. Taking the other three large European economies as points of comparison, it can be seen that the United Kingdom's case is no longer significantly different from that of Germany, France or Italy and that if present trends continue, it will soon be on a par with them. Thus in 1980, 49% of German exports went to the Community and 48% of her imports came from it. For the French the Community's share of exports was 52%, while imports from the rest of the Community accounted for 46% of the total. In Italy the Community took 49% of exports and provided Italy with 44% of her imports[13]. The non-economic evidence is equally persuasive. The United Kingdom's interests in East–West relations, in the Middle-East, in Africa and sundry other areas or issues, has seemed increasingly to coincide with those of her Community partners still more than with those of the United States. The United Kingdom is in other words inextricably bound up with the rest of Western Europe, however hard some of its political leaders may try to pretend otherwise, and instead therefore of battering the present, lopsided, feeble and demoralized Community into a grouping that costs less but almost certainly also achieves even less, the British have as much if not more interest than any other member state in devising imaginative proposals that would exploit the advantages of scale that European-wide policies could still bring internally, and allow Europeans to play a role on the world stage commensurate with their present wealth and past history. And in addition to these general gains for the common good, a constructive approach that fastened on the broader issues at stake would make concessions on the United Kingdom's contributions to the Community budget both more likely and more palatable. As it is, it is quite possible that single-minded concentration on this issue will, given the material advantages with which the United Kingdom starts, result in a succession of British 'victories', but although these may bring short-term political advantages to whichever government happens to be in charge at a particular moment, they can only, like the victory of May 1980, make the Community that much nastier and more brutish. Trench warfare tactics may win battles, but they are not suitable for winning wars, and still less for paving the way for postwar reconstruction.

In the light of the events of 1977 and 1978, it seems likely that an imaginative British counter offensive in the Community could only succeed if it were led from the very top, not simply because foreign offices, even when they are presided over by a Lord Carrington, are no longer powerful enough in domestic politics to act as catalysts across a broad front, nor because imagination is much more easily lost than acquired by those who are involved in the day-to-day conduct of the Community affairs, but because it is only at the very top that the Western alliance possesses institutional arrangements appropriate to the mounting of a multi-dimensional initiative of the kind that is needed. It is of course asking a great deal of a government and a prime minister who have never concealed their belief that domestic

regeneration is the pre-requisite of external strength, and who have therefore, with the exception of Lord Carrington, been almost totally immersed
in internal politics. In the context of the European Community, however,
the relationship between domestic and external policies is so complex that
domestic recovery at the expense of European cooperation is a contradiction
in terms. A bold European policy, far from undermining domestic policies,
could reinforce them.

The most promising point of departure for any really serious attempt to
extend the scope and scale of European cooperation at the present juncture is
almost certainly in the defence and foreign policy fields. Acting in a situation
in which the inability of the countries of Western Europe to provide for
their own security out of their own resources seemed both tolerable and
inevitable, Mr Jenkins hoped that progress on the monetary front would of
itself be a sufficient catalyst, taking the Community over 'a political
threshold'[14]. Historically, however, international monetary regimes have
usually reflected the balance of military power, and although it may have
seemed realistic in the mid 1970s, when power appeared to have been diluted
by interdependence, to think that the European Community, as 'the purest
expression in the international system of . . . "civilian power"'[15], could
defy normal experience, it is not as easy to be so optimistic in the 1980s. If
there is to be any significant extension of the European Community's
internal cohesion and international role, therefore, it is hard to believe that
progress on monetary and trade questions can proceed very far unless and
until these latter are linked with a systematic attempt to improve Western
Europe's capacity to defend itself and uphold its interests in the world
beyond. Such an advance is no longer as inconceivable as it was only four or
five years ago, however, since in the context of a new era in East–West
relations, awareness of the need for a more definite and influential Western
European voice in the North Atlantic alliance has begun to take root. It
would be rash to predict that anything like a full scale European defence
community will emerge within the next few years, but unless there is an
advance in this direction, the impetus towards and therefore the likelihood
of gains in other spheres, including the monetary system, will be much less
strong. A reappraisal by the United Kingdom of its decision to purchase the
Trident missile, which seems less improbable in the wake of the Falklands'
crisis than it did before, might just, it it were carefully linked with the ideas
that Mr Genscher and Mr Colombo have recently been working on, and
with other indications that the British government was serious about its
Community membership, such as entry into the EMS, trigger off a broadly
based advance across several fronts. Such an initiative need not and indeed
should not be construed on either side of the Atlantic as anti-American,
since a European attempt to become entirely independent in security matters
would be foolish and impracticable. The same could be said of a parallel
effort to build up the EMS as a rival to the dollar. Far from undermining the

Atlantic relationship, indeed, a stronger Western Europe capable of acting forcefully on both security and economic questions would be a much more useful partner to the Americans.

These are of course only possibilities, and in an atmosphere which is in many respects even gloomier than it was when Mr Jenkins became president of the Commission at the beginning of 1977, it is difficult to be optimistic. But whatever happens to the Community in the short term, the realities of interdependence within, and the common vulnerability without, are hardly likely to vanish, and the tasks that the Community of nation states ought to be doing, even through lack of political will it does not yet do them, will increase rather than diminish. For most of the present century, Western European integration has had much in common with the central figure in the following lines:

> As I was going up the stair,
> I met a man who wasn't there,
> He wasn't there again today,
> I do so wish he'd go away.

Like the man on the stair, European union has proved elusive and insubstantial. It has also, however, continued to haunt us, and it seems unlikely that it will cease to do so until it has achieved more tangible form. Hard though it may be therefore, to keep the longer term perspective in view in the midst of a process in which the majority of those involved have resigned themselves to accepting the short-term struggle for survival as the only cause worth fighting for, and who view more radical ideas, such as those that the president of the Commission threw at a dispirited Community in 1977, as 'politically absurd', the advocates of 'adventurous ideas' will almost certainly in the long term prove to have been the true realists[16].

1 Although the rest of the book was finished in the winter of 1980/81, the publishers agreed to accept a new version of the conclusions, at the very last moment possible before publication, in order to take account of the important events that have occurred in the second half of 1981 and the first three months of 1982. The EMS has already spawned a large literature, some of it extremely technical and much of it manifestly ephemeral. The following are some of the more important individual and collective contributions to the debate:

P. H. Tresize (ed.), *The European Monetary System: its promise and prospects*, Washington, 1979; R. Triffin (ed.), 'The emerging European Monetary System', papers and proceedings of the First International Seminar on the EMS held at Louvain-la-Neuve, 24–25 March 1979, published in *Bulletin de la Banque Nationale de Belgique*, 54th year, 1(4), April 1979; Robert Triffin (ed.), 'European Monetary Fund: Internal planning and external relations', *Banca Nazionale del Lavoro Quarterly Review*, Rome, September 1980; Robert Triffin and A. L. Swings (eds), *The Private Use of the ECU*, Kredietbank, Brussels, 1980; R. Triffin and N. Thygesen (eds), 'The European Monetary System: The First Two Years', *Banca Nazionale del Lavoro Quarterly Review*, September 1981. Tom de Vries, *On the Meaning and Future of the European Monetary System*, Princeton Essays in International Finance No. 138, September 1980; see also the publications of Rainer Masera cited in note 57 to Chapter 5

2 For a general account of the negotiations in February 1982, see the *Financial Times*, 22 and 23 February 1982. On the Belgian case specifically, the Flemish newspaper *De Standaard* contained a number of extremely interesting and apparently very well informed reports in the week beginning 22 February.

3 Christopher McMahon, 'The Long-Run Implications of the European Monetary System'. In Tresize (ed.), op. cit. (note 1), p. 92

4 A. Szasz, 'EMS: Controlled exchange rates in a world of uncontrolled capital flows', lecture to the 1980 Euromarkets Conference, London, 22 January 1980

5 The information contained in this paragraph is culled from the admirable journal, *European Economy*, which is edited by the Directorate-General for Economic and Financial Affairs of the European Commission. See especially November 1981

6 See R. Triffin and N. Thygesen, op. cit. (note 1), pp. 297–322

7 House of Commons, Treasury and Civil Service Committee, Sessions 1979/80, *Memoranda on Monetary Policy*, vols 1 and 2, London, 1980

8 See *inter alia*, *The Times*, 4 January 1982

9 *Financial Times*, 21 October 1981

10 Paris, Ministère des Finances, B10887, Monick (Financial Attaché in London) to Bouthillier, Secretary General of the Ministère des Finances, 31 May 1940

11 *Financial Times*, 10 March 1982

12 Ibid., 1 February 1982

13 See *European Economy*, op. cit. (note 5), November 1981

14 R. Jenkins, First Monnet Lecture, Florence, 1977, p. 24

15 A. Shonfield, *Europe: Journey to an unknown destination*, London, 1974, p. 62

16 For the conflict between Mr Jenkins and the gradualists, see Chapter 2 *passim*

Extract from the conclusions of the Presidency of the European Council of 6 and 7 July 1978 in Bremen and Annex

2. Monetary Policy

Following the discussion at Copenhagen on 7 April the European Council has discussed the attached scheme for the creation of a closer monetary cooperation (European Monetary System) leading to a zone of monetary stability in Europe, which has been introduced by members of the European Council. The European Council regards such a zone as a highly desirable objective. The European Council envisages a durable and effective scheme. It agreed to instruct the Finance Ministers at their meeting on 24 July to formulate the necessary guidelines for the competent Community bodies to elaborate by 31 October the provisions necessary for the functioning of such a scheme – if necessary by amendment. There will be concurrent studies of the action needed to be taken to strengthen the economies of the less prosperous member countries in the context of such a scheme; such measures will be essential if the zone of monetary stability is to succeed. Decisions can then be taken and commitments made at the European Council meeting on 4 and 5 December.

The Heads of Government of Belgium, Denmark, the Federal Republic of Germany, Luxembourg and the Netherlands state that the 'Snake' has not been and is not under discussion. They confirm that it will remain fully intact.

Annex

1. In terms of exchange rate management the European Monetary System (EMS) will be at least as strict as the 'Snake'. In the initial stages of its operation and for a limited period of time member countries currently not participating in the snake may opt for somewhat wider margins around central rates. In principle, interventions will be in the currencies of participating countries. Changes in central rates will be subject to mutual consent. Non-member countries with particularly strong economic and financial ties with the Community may become associate members of the

system. The European Currency Unit (ECU)[1] will be at the centre of the system; in particular, it will be used as a means of settlement between EEC monetary authorities.

2. An initial supply of ECUs (for use among Community central banks) will be created against deposit of US dollars and gold on the one hand (e.g. 20% of the stock currently held by member central banks) and member currencies on the other hand in an amount of a comparable order of magnitude.

The use of ECUs created against member currencies will be subject to conditions varying with the amount and the maturity; due account will be given to the need for substantial short-term facilities (up to one year).

3. Participating countries will coordinate their exchange rate policies *vis-à-vis* third countries. To this end they will intensify the consultations in the appropriate bodies and between central banks participating in the scheme. Ways to coordinate dollar interventions should be sought which avoid simultaneous reverse interventions. Central banks buying dollars will deposit a fraction (say 20%) and receive ECUs in return; likewise, central banks selling dollars will receive a fraction (say 20%) against ECUs.

4. Not later than two years after the start of the scheme, the existing arrangements and institutions will be consolidated in a European Monetary Fund.[2]

5. A system of closer monetary cooperation will only be successful if participating countries pursue policies conducive to greater stability at home and abroad; this applies to the deficit and surplus countries alike.

6.* The competent Community bodies are requested to elaborate the provisions necessary for the functioning of the scheme and to conclude their work not later than 31 October 1978.

---

[1] The ECU has the same definition as the European Unit of Account
[2] The EMF will take the place of the EMCF.

*The sixth paragraph, which formed part of the original Clappier–Schulmann draft, was omitted from the final text of the Bremen Annex, because its contents were covered in the preface.

Resolution of the European Council of 5 December 1978 on the establishment of the European Monetary System (EMS) and related matters

A.   The European Monetary System

1.   Introduction

1.1 In Bremen we discussed a 'scheme for the creation of closer monetary cooperation leading to a zone of monetary stability in Europe'. We regarded such a zone 'as a highly desirable objective' and envisaged 'a durable and effective scheme'.

1.2 Today, after careful examination of the preparatory work done by the Council and other Community bodies, we are agreed as follows:

A European Monetary System (EMS) will be set up on 1 January 1979.

1.3 We are firmly resolved to ensure the lasting success of the EMS by policies conducive to greater stability at home and abroad for both deficit and surplus countries.

1.4 The following chapters deal primarily with the initial phase of the EMS.

We remain firmly resolved to consolidate, not later than two years after the start of the scheme, into a final system the provisions and procedures thus created. This system will entail the creation of the European Monetary Fund as announced in the conclusions of the European Council meeting at Bremen on 6 and 7 July 1978, as well as the full utilization of the ECU as a reserve asset and a means of settlement. It will be based on adequate legislation at the Community as well as the national level.

2.   The ECU and its functions

2.1 A European Currency Unit (ECU) will be at the centre of the EMS. The value and the composition of the ECU will be identical with the value of the EUA at the outset of the system.

2.2 The ECU will be used:

(a) as the denominator (numeraire) for the exchange rate mechanism;
(b) as the basis for a divergence indicator;
(c) as the denominator for operations in both the intervention and the credit mechanisms;
(d) as a means of settlement between monetary authorities of the European Community.

2.3 The weights of currencies in the ECU will be re-examined and if necessary revised within six months of the entry into force of the system and thereafter every five years or on request, if the weight of any currency has changed by 25%.

Revisions have to be mutually accepted; they will, by themselves, not modify the external value of the ECU. They will be made in line with underlying economic criteria.

3.   *The exchange rate and intervention mechanisms*

3.1 Each currency will have an ECU-related central rate. These central rates will be used to establish a grid of bilateral exchange rates.

Around these exchange rates fluctuation margins of ±2.25% will be established. EEC countries with presently floating currencies may opt for wider margins up to ±6% at the outset of EMS; these margins should be gradually reduced as soon as economic conditions permit.

A Member State which does not participate in the exchange rate mechanism at the outset may participate at a later date.

3.2 Adjustments of central rates will be subject to mutual agreement by a common procedure which will comprise all countries participating in the exchange rate mechanism and the Commission. There will be reciprocal consultation in the Community framework about important decisions concerning exchange rate policy between countries participating and any country not participating in the system.

3.3 In principle, interventions will be made in participating currencies.

3.4 Intervention in participating currencies is compulsory when the intervention points defined by the fluctuation margins are reached.

3.5 An ECU basket formula will be used as an indicator to detect divergences between Community currencies. A 'threshold of divergence' will be fixed at 75% of the maximum spread of divergence for each currency.

It will be calculated in such a way as to eliminate the influence of weight on the probability of reaching the threshold.

3.6 When a currency crosses its 'threshold of divergence', this results in a presumption that the authorities concerned will correct this situation by adequate measures namely:

(a) diversified intervention;
(b) measures of domestic monetary policy;
(c) changes in central rates;
(d) other measures of economic policy.

In case such measures, on account of special circumstances, are not taken, the reasons for this shall be given to the other authorities, especially in the 'concertation between central banks'.

Consultations will, if necessary, then take place in the appropriate Community bodies, including the Council of Ministers.

After six months these provisions shall be reviewed in the light of experience. At that date the questions regarding imbalances accumulated by divergent creditor or debtor countries will be studied as well.

3.7 A Very Short-Term Facility of an unlimited amount will be established. Settlements will be made 45 days after the end of the month of intervention with the possibility of prolongation for another three months for amounts limited to the size of debtor quotas in the Short-Term Monetary Support.

3.8 To serve as a means of settlement, an initial supply of ECUs will be provided by the EMCF against the deposit of 20% of gold and 20% of dollar reserves currently held by central banks.

This operation will take the form of specified, revolving swap arrangements. By periodical review and by an appropriate procedure it will be ensured that each central bank will maintain a deposit of at least 20% of these reserves with the EMCF. A Member State not participating in the exchange rate mechanism may participate in this initial operation on the basis described above.

4. The credit mechanisms

4.1 The existing credit mechanisms with their present rules of application will be maintained for the initial phase of the EMS. They will be consolidated into a single fund in the final phase of the EMS.

4.2 The credit mechanisms will be extended to an amount of ECU 25 000 million of effectively available credit. The distribution of this amount will be as follows:

Short-Term Monetary Support = ECU 14 000 million;
Medium-Term Financial Assistance = ECU 11 000 million.

4.3 The duration of the Short-Term Monetary Support will be extended for another three months on the same conditions as the first extension.

4.4 The increase of the Medium-Term Financial Assistance will be completed by 30 June 1979. In the meantime, countries which still need national legislation are expected to make their extended medium-term quotas available by an interim financing agreement of the central banks concerned.

5. Third countries and international organizations

5.1 The durability of the EMS and its international implications require coordination of exchange rate policies *vis-à-vis* third countries and, as far as possible, a concertation with the monetary authorities of those countries.

5.2 European countries with particularly close economic and financial ties with the European Communities may participate in the exchange rate and intervention mechanisms.

Participation will be based upon agreements between central banks; these agreements will be communicated to the Council and the Commission of the European Communities.

5.3 The EMS is and will remain fully compatible with the relevant articles of the IMF Agreement.

6. Further procedure

6.1 To implement the decisions taken under A., the European Council requests the Council to consider and to take a decision on 18 December 1978 on the following proposals of the Commission;

(a) Council Regulation modifying the unit of account used by the EMCF, which introduces the ECU in the operations of the EMCF and defines its composition;

(b) Council Regulation permitting the EMCF to receive monetary reserves and to issue ECUs to the monetary authorities of the Member States which may use them as a means of settlement;

(c) Council Regulation on the impact of the European Monetary System on the common agricultural policy. The European Council considers that the introduction of the EMS should not of itself result in any change in the situation obtaining prior to 1 January 1979 regarding the expression in national currencies of agricultural prices, monetary compensatory amounts and all other amounts fixed for the purposes of the common agricultural policy.

The European Council stresses the importance of henceforth avoiding the creation of permanent MCAs and progressively reducing present MCAs in order to reestablish the unity of prices of the common agricultural policy, giving also due consideration to price policy.

6.2 It requests the Commission to submit in good time a proposal to amend the Council Decision of 22 March 1971 on setting up machinery for medium-term financial assistance to enable the Council (Economics and Finance Ministers) to take a decision on such a proposal at their session of 18 December 1978.

6.3 It requests the central banks of Member States to modify their Agreement of 10 April 1972 on the narrowing of margins of fluctuation between the currencies of Member States in accordance with the rules set forth above (see Section 3).

6.4 It requests the central banks of Member States to modify as follows the rules on Short-Term Monetary Support by 1 January 1979 at the latest:

(a) The total of debtor quotas available for drawings by the central banks of Member States shall be increased to an aggregate amount of ECU 7 900 million.
(b) The total of creditor quotas made available by the central banks of Member States for financing the debtor quotas shall be increased to an aggregate amount of ECU 15 800 million.
(c) The total of the additional creditor amounts as well as the total of the additional debtor amounts may not exceed ECU 8 800 million.
(d) The duration of credit under the extended Short-Term Monetary Support may be prolonged *twice* for a period of three months.

B. Measures designed to strengthen the economies of the less prosperous Member States of the European Monetary System

1. We stress that, within the context of a broadly based strategy aimed at improving the prospects of economic development and based on symmetrical rights and obligations of all participants, the most important concern should be to enhance the convergence of economic policies towards greater stability. We request the Council (Economics and Finance Ministers) to

strengthen its procedures for cooperation in order to improve that convergence.

2. We are aware that the convergence of economic policies and of economic performance will not be easy to achieve. Therefore, steps must be taken to strengthen the economic potential of the less prosperous countries of the Community. This is primarily the responsibility of the Member States concerned. Community measures can and should serve a supporting role.

3. The European Council agrees that in the context of the European Monetary System, the following measures in favour of less prosperous Member States effectively and fully participating in the exchange rate and intervention mechanisms will be taken.

3.1 The European Council requests the Community Institutions by the utilization of the new financial instrument and the European Investment Bank to make available for a period of five years loans of up to EUA 1 000 million per year to these countries on special conditions.

3.2 The European Council requests the Commission to submit a proposal to provide interest rate subsidies of 3% for these loans, with the following element: the total cost of this measure, divided into annual tranches of EUA 200 million each over a period of five years, shall not exceed EUA 1 000 million.

3.3 Any less prosperous member country which subsequently effectively and fully participates in the mechanisms would have the right of access to this facility within the financial limits mentioned above. Member States not participating effectively and fully in the mechanisms will not contribute to the financing of the scheme.

3.4 The funds thus provided are to be concentrated on the financing of selected infrastructure projects and programmes, on the understanding that any direct or indirect distortion of the competitive position of specific industries within Member States will have to be avoided.

3.5 The European Council requests the Council (Economics and Finance Ministers) to take a decision on the above mentioned proposals in time so that the relevant measures can become effective on 1 April 1979 at the latest. There should be a review at the end of the initial phase of the EMS.

4. The European Council requests the Commission to study the relationship between greater convergence in economic performance of the Member States and the utilization of Community instruments, in particular the funds which aim at reducing structural imbalances. The results of these studies will be discussed at the next European Council meeting.

External value of the Deutsche Mark*, March 1973–December 1979

External value of the Deutsche Mark* March 1973–December 1979

End-1972 = 100 1

Average during month	External value of the Deutsche Mark	against the currencies of the countries participating in the European Monetary System (EMS)						against the currencies of other countries								
	against the U.S. dollar	French franc	Netherlands guilder	Italian lira	Belgian franc	Danish krone	Pound sterling 2	Japanese yen	Norwegian krone	Austrian Schilling	Swedish krona	Swiss franc	against the currencies of the countries participating in the EMS 3	against the currencies of the EEC member countries	against the 17 currencies officially quoted in Frankfurt	Total (23 of Germany's major trading partners)
1973 March	114.0	100.8	101.9	112.1	100.9	100.7	107.9	97.5	101.2	100.7	106.1	95.7	101.5	103.7	104.0	104.3
June	125.0	103.9	105.1	127.8	104.4	104.3	113.8	106.9	103.2	101.8	109.2	99.3	104.8	109.1	109.7	109.9
Aug.	132.9	110.4	108.8	130.9	109.6	108.6	125.9	114.2	110.1	101.8	114.6	102.8	109.9	114.6	115.0	115.4
Sep.	133.0	110.7	106.4	129.0	109.5	108.8	128.9	114.4	110.8	102.5	116.0	104.4	109.4	114.1	114.9	115.2
Oct.	133.6	110.0	102.8	129.9	109.0	108.0	129.0	115.4	109.8	102.5	115.8	105.2	107.8	112.9	114.3	114.5
Nov.	124.9	107.6	103.2	126.8	107.5	106.7	122.6	112.6	105.4	101.7	112.6	102.9	106.4	111.0	111.5	111.6
Dec.	121.4	108.8	104.9	126.7	109.2	107.9	122.7	110.3	103.3	101.7	114.2	101.2	107.8	112.1	111.7	111.6
1974 Jan.	114.7	112.4	103.6	127.1	109.4	109.2	120.9	110.5	102.9	101.7	114.1	100.4	4 108.6	112.7	111.2	111.0
Feb.	118.7	115.0	103.4	133.5	108.6	109.3	122.4	112.0	103.1	101.7	115.4	98.2	106.7	114.3	112.7	112.5
March	122.9	115.9	104.3	134.6	109.5	109.9	123.3	112.4	104.5	102.1	116.7	98.6	107.7	115.2	114.0	113.9
April	127.7	121.2	105.1	139.4	110.8	110.7	125.3	114.9	105.5	102.6	116.6	100.5	108.5	117.9	116.5	116.5
May	131.1	124.5	104.8	142.3	110.0	110.3	127.3	118.5	105.0	100.8	116.3	99.3	108.1	119.1	117.6	117.5
June	127.6	122.2	104.1	142.5	108.0	109.2	125.3	117.0	104.2	99.3	115.8	99.4	107.0	117.8	116.1	116.0
July	126.2	117.5	102.4	139.5	106.7	107.1	123.9	118.7	102.4	98.3	114.6	97.4	105.4	115.2	114.0	114.0
Aug.	123.1	114.9	101.3	138.6	106.3	106.5	123.1	120.7	101.5	98.0	113.1	95.6	104.5	113.9	112.6	112.7
Sep.	121.1	113.6	101.2	137.8	106.5	107.5	122.6	117.5	101.2	98.0	112.6	94.5	104.5	113.5	111.9	112.1
Oct.	124.2	114.9	101.7	142.4	106.9	107.2	124.9	120.7	102.9	98.5	113.4	93.8	105.0	114.9	113.4	113.7
Nov.	128.1	117.0	102.8	146.7	107.8	107.9	129.0	124.6	104.8	98.8	114.9	92.0	106.1	116.9	115.3	115.7
Dec.	131.1	116.2	102.8	148.7	107.9	108.5	132.1	127.7	104.8	98.4	114.3	89.2	106.1	117.3	115.7	116.4
1975 Jan.	136.3	116.3	103.1	151.0	107.8	109.5	135.3	132.5	104.7	98.2	114.3	89.6	106.3	118.1	116.9	117.7
Feb.	138.4	115.8	102.7	151.8	107.4	109.6	135.6	130.9	104.2	98.2	114.3	89.2	106.0	117.9	116.9	117.8
March	139.1	114.1	101.6	150.9	106.6	108.2	134.9	129.7	102.7	98.2	113.3	89.7	105.0	116.8	116.2	117.1
April	135.7	111.3	101.3	147.8	106.4	107.2	134.3	128.6	101.8	98.0	112.0	90.3	104.5	115.4	114.9	115.8
May	137.2	108.5	101.6	147.9	106.8	107.2	138.7	129.7	102.0	97.9	112.0	89.4	104.8	115.2	114.9	115.9
June	137.7	107.8	102.2	148.1	107.4	107.2	141.6	131.1	101.5	97.8	112.0	89.4	105.2	115.5	115.2	116.2
July	130.7	107.8	102.7	145.8	107.3	106.9	140.4	125.6	102.0	97.6	111.9	88.8	4 106.1	115.2	114.1	115.1
Aug.	125.1	107.0	101.9	143.7	106.9	106.8	138.8	121.0	102.9	97.5	112.2	87.4	105.6	114.3	112.7	113.7
Sep.	123.2	107.6	101.9	143.5	107.7	107.1	138.6	119.8	103.8	97.7	113.6	86.8	106.1	114.6	112.7	113.8
Oct.	124.8	107.5	102.2	145.6	108.5	107.6	142.4	122.5	103.7	98.0	113.9	86.6	106.4	115.4	113.6	114.8
Nov.	124.6	107.2	101.9	145.4	108.4	107.6	142.5	122.3	103.4	97.9	113.5	86.0	106.2	115.2	113.3	114.6
Dec.	122.8	107.1	101.7	144.3	108.3	108.2	142.5	121.8	102.7	97.6	112.5	84.3	106.0	115.0	112.7	114.1
1976 Jan.	123.8	108.3	101.9	149.1	108.5	109.2	143.2	122.4	103.5	97.7	112.6	83.9	106.5	116.2	113.6	114.9
Feb.	125.9	110.0	103.3	165.9	109.9	110.7	145.7	123.2	104.6	98.8	114.4	84.2	108.0	119.7	116.6	117.8
March	125.9	113.7	104.4	178.4	110.2	110.8	151.8	122.8	105.0	99.3	115.2	84.1	4 109.7	123.2	119.0	120.1
April	127.1	116.0	105.2	191.8	110.4	109.9	161.4	123.3	105.0	99.1	116.2	83.6	108.3	126.4	121.2	122.3
May	125.8	115.6	105.3	185.1	110.0	109.2	163.2	122.1	104.0	99.0	115.3	81.5	108.1	125.6	120.3	121.5
June	125.1	115.8	105.5	182.4	110.6	109.8	166.2	121.4	104.4	99.0	115.6	80.4	108.4	125.8	120.3	121.4
July	125.2	118.4	105.2	180.2	110.9	110.5	164.4	119.7	105.2	98.4	116.2	80.9	108.5	126.2	120.5	121.7
Aug.	127.5	123.7	105.1	183.5	110.9	110.9	167.7	120.2	105.6	98.2	116.8	82.3	108.6	128.2	122.3	123.4
Sep.	129.3	124.3	103.9	187.7	110.8	111.0	175.2	120.6	105.6	98.1	116.9	83.3	108.0	129.1	123.2	124.4
Oct.	132.6	129.1	104.1	194.9	110.4	112.0	189.6	125.2	106.1	98.2	117.2	84.5	108.1	132.4	126.0	127.2
Nov.	133.7	130.3	103.7	198.7	110.2	113.0	191.6	128.0	105.9	98.2	117.1	84.9	107.9	133.2	126.7	126.1
Dec.	135.1	131.7	103.5	201.5	109.7	113.0	188.9	129.3	106.0	98.2	116.8	06.2	107.7	133.5	127.3	128.8
1977 Jan.	134.8	130.9	103.9	203.7	110.3	113.7	184.6	127.3	106.9	98.2	117.9	87.4	108.2	133.5	127.4	128.8
Feb.	134.0	130.4	103.7	203.4	110.3	113.6	183.9	123.9	106.6	98.3	118.2	87.9	108.2	133.2	127.1	128.6
March	134.8	131.2	103.6	205.4	110.3	113.2	184.1	122.6	106.5	98.2	118.0	89.5	108.0	133.6	127.7	129.2
April	135.8	131.8	103.4	207.2	110.1	116.3	185.3	121.4	108.0	98.2	122.5	89.3	108.7	134.1	128.4	129.9
May	136.7	132.3	103.4	208.3	110.0	117.6	186.5	123.1	108.4	98.4	123.6	89.6	108.9	134.5	129.0	130.5
June	136.9	132.2	104.5	208.3	110.2	118.5	186.8	121.2	108.9	98.4	125.6	88.7	109.7	134.9	129.2	130.8
July	141.1	133.8	106.1	214.1	111.7	120.5	192.2	121.2	111.6	98.1	127.5	88.6	111.4	137.3	131.8	133.3
Aug.	139.2	133.2	105.0	211.1	110.5	120.1	187.6	120.4	111.0	98.2	128.6	87.2	5 110.5	135.8	130.8	132.4
Sep.	138.7	133.4	105.2	210.6	110.8	122.7	186.6	120.1	114.4	98.5	139.8	85.8	109.1	136.0	131.3	132.9
Oct.	141.5	134.3	106.2	214.2	111.8	123.8	187.5	117.0	116.7	98.6	141.0	83.9	110.1	137.3	132.3	134.0
Nov.	143.8	136.3	107.2	217.0	112.9	126.1	185.3	114.2	118.0	98.6	143.2	82.3	111.3	138.6	133.4	135.1
Dec.	149.7	140.2	107.5	225.4	112.9	127.5	189.2	117.1	118.2	99.2	147.7	80.9	111.5	141.0	135.8	137.7
1978 Jan.	152.1	140.3	106.4	228.1	111.5	125.8	184.6	119.0	117.9	99.3	147.6	78.8	110.4	140.2	135.4	137.5
Feb.	155.3	146.8	106.5	229.5	111.9	126.2	187.7	121.0	122.9	99.4	149.7	77.0	110.8	142.4	137.3	139.4
March	158.4	145.9	106.2	232.9	111.9	127.1	194.7	119.1	126.9	99.6	151.6	78.3	111.0	143.0	138.4	141.1
April	157.9	141.5	106.1	233.2	112.1	126.9	200.2	113.6	127.5	99.5	150.9	78.2	111.0	142.4	137.7	140.5
May	153.0	139.0	106.2	228.9	112.2	124.9	197.5	112.3	125.4	99.5	147.9	78.2	110.8	141.0	136.2	138.9
June	154.6	138.4	106.5	228.4	112.8	124.9	197.5	107.4	125.7	99.4	148.0	75.9	111.2	141.1	136.0	138.8
July	156.9	136.1	107.2	228.4	113.3	125.9	194.2	101.6	127.3	99.7	148.0	73.6	111.9	140.6	135.5	138.4
Aug.	161.4	137.2	107.6	232.1	113.2	127.1	195.1	98.7	127.7	99.7	148.8	70.0	112.2	141.5	136.1	139.2
Sep.	163.5	139.4	107.9	233.4	113.3	127.2	195.9	100.8	128.2	100.1	150.3	66.8	112.4	142.4	136.7	139.9
Oct.	174.8	144.0	108.0	243.9	113.4	128.2	204.4	104.3	129.7	100.9	155.8	70.0	112.7	145.4	140.6	144.1
Nov.	169.8	144.1	107.5	245.7	112.9	127.6	202.8	105.4	129.0	101.2	154.0	73.6	112.1	145.2	140.3	143.9
Dec.	171.2	144.6	107.6	248.0	113.8	128.7	202.5	109.0	131.3	101.3	155.9	74.8	6 112.7	145.9	141.2	144.8
1979 Jan.	174.4	144.5	107.2	250.7	113.4	128.1	204.1	111.3	132.9	101.3	157.4	75.8	111.2	145.9	141.9	145.6
Feb.	173.6	145.0	107.3	250.7	113.3	128.0	203.2	112.9	133.1	101.3	157.5	75.7	111.2	146.0	141.9	145.6
March	173.2	145.2	107.2	250.5	113.7	128.8	199.4	116.0	132.9	101.4	157.1	75.8	7 140.8	145.8	141.8	145.5
April	170.2	144.7	107.4	246.9	114.0	128.5	192.5	119.4	131.6	101.5	155.2	76.0	140.4	144.9	140.8	144.5
May	168.9	145.6	108.2	247.3	115.1	130.5	192.6	119.5	131.9	101.8	154.2	76.0	141.3	145.8	141.2	144.9
June	171.2	145.9	109.0	248.6	115.5	133.1	190.1	121.5	132.7	101.8	154.3	75.7	142.1	146.3	141.8	146.0
July	176.7	146.7	109.3	249.2	115.1	132.7	183.4	124.0	134.1	101.6	154.9	75.8	142.3	146.0	142.3	147.1
Aug.	176.2	146.6	109.0	247.9	115.1	133.1	184.6	124.5	133.4	101.1	154.5	76.0	142.1	145.9	142.2	147.0
Sep.	179.5	147.4	109.3	250.4	115.5	133.5	191.4	129.4	134.6	99.9	156.3	75.4	142.8	147.1	143.4	148.3
Oct.	180.1	147.8	110.2	255.8	116.0	135.1	196.9	134.5	134.6	99.6	157.5	76.3	144.0	148.7	144.7	149.6
Nov.	181.6	147.8	110.6	257.9	116.5	136.9	200.2	143.9	137.2	99.5	159.4	77.9	144.6	149.5	146.0	150.9
Dec.	185.8	147.7	109.8	259.3	117.0	143.1	198.2	144.8	139.1	99.6	161.3	77.4	144.9	149.5	146.6	151.7

* For the method of calculation see the Statistical Supplements to the Monthly Reports of the Deutsche Bundesbank, Series 5, The currencies of the world. – **1** The figures for end-1972 are in principle based on the central rates at the time, but in the case of the pound sterling, the Irish pound and the Canadian dollar, whose exchange rates were floating, the market rates of end-1972 were taken as a basis. The indices for the groups of countries are weighted geometrical means. – **2** At present the United Kingdom is not participating in the exchange rate mechanism of the European Monetary System. – **3** Excluding the United Kingdom. Up to February 1979 against the currencies of the countries participating in the joint float at the time. From March 19, 1973 the countries participating in the joint float were: Belgium/Luxembourg, Denmark, the Federal Republic of Germany, France (up to January 18, 1974 and from July 10, 1975 to March 12, 1976), the Netherlands, Norway (up to December 11, 1978) and Sweden (up to August 26, 1977). The transition from the joint float to the EMS took place on March 13, 1979. – **4** Including France; excluding France: January 1974 = 106.9, July 1975 = 105.4, March 1976 = 107.9. – **5** Including Sweden; excluding Sweden: 108.5. – **6** Including Norway; excluding Norway: 111.7. – **7** Against the currencies of the countries latterly participating in the joint float: 111.4.

Source: Monthly Reports of the Deutsche Bundesbank, Frankfurt. (Reproduced by permission)

External value of the Deutsche Mark (weekends), 16 September 1977 – 29 December 1978

External value of the Deutsche Mark*
Weekends: 16 September 1977–29 December 1978

Period	against the U.S. dollar	Belgian franc	Danish krone	Netherlands guilder	Norwegian krone	French franc [2]	Italian lira	Japanese Yen	Austrian Schilling	Pound sterling	Swedish krona [3]	Swiss franc	against the joint float [2,3]	against the EEC member countries	against the 16 currencies officially quoted in Frankfurt	Total (22 of Germany's major trading partners)
1977 Sep. 16	138.6	110.9	122.7	105.2	114.4	133.6	210.6	120.1	98.3	186.5	139.7	85.9	109.7	140.8	136.1	137.5
23	138.4	110.8	122.6	105.3	114.8	133.4	210.4	120.0	98.6	185.2	139.6	85.2	109.1	140.7	135.9	137.5
30	139.7	111.4	123.1	105.7	115.6	133.9	211.8	119.3	99.0	187.6	139.9	85.0	109.6	141.4	136.7	138.2
Oct. 7	140.5	111.4	123.2	105.7	116.2	133.8	213.1	117.8	98.7	187.4	140.3	84.7	109.7	141.6	136.9	138.5
14	141.7	111.9	123.7	106.1	116.7	134.1	214.4	116.4	98.6	187.9	140.9	84.3	110.1	142.2	137.4	139.0
21	141.9	111.9	123.9	106.6	117.0	134.8	214.6	117.2	98.7	188.0	141.2	83.3	110.4	142.6	137.7	139.3
28	142.3	112.0	124.6	106.5	117.1	134.7	215.3	115.6	98.6	187.9	141.7	83.1	110.4	142.7	137.8	139.4
Nov. 4	142.7	112.4	125.0	106.8	117.9	135.3	215.6	115.2	98.6	185.3	142.6	82.5	110.8	142.8	137.9	139.6
11	143.2	113.1	126.1	107.4	118.3	136.5	216.5	114.5	98.6	184.7	142.8	82.5	111.5	143.5	138.5	140.1
18	143.6	113.1	126.2	107.1	118.3	136.2	216.9	114.0	98.6	185.1	143.4	82.6	111.4	143.5	138.6	140.2
25	145.4	113.3	127.8	107.4	118.3	137.7	219.0	113.2	98.7	187.4	144.8	81.9	111.7	144.6	139.6	141.2
Dec. 2	146.2	113.1	128.1	107.4	118.1	138.2	220.5	114.9	98.9	188.3	145.6	81.3	111.6	145.1	140.1	141.8
9	147.2	113.4	128.1	107.3	118.4	139.4	222.2	115.9	99.1	188.8	146.9	81.8	111.7	145.8	140.8	142.7
16	150.5	113.2	127.9	107.6	118.4	141.1	226.3	117.5	99.3	190.7	149.0	81.0	111.7	147.2	142.3	144.1
23	149.7	112.0	126.4	107.0	118.4	140.1	225.7	117.2	99.4	188.4	147.5	79.7	110.9	146.2	141.3	143.3
30	153.1	112.1	126.5	107.4	118.4	140.3	229.4	119.0	99.4	188.5	148.5	79.9	111.1	147.0	142.5	144.5
1978 Jan. 6	150.6	111.6	126.3	106.8	118.3	139.6	226.7	117.9	99.3	185.6	147.1	79.4	110.7	145.8	141.2	143.2
13	151.2	111.2	125.6	106.2	117.9	139.5	229.2	118.9	99.2	184.3	147.2	78.4	110.1	145.9	141.3	143.4
20	151.7	111.6	125.4	106.3	117.9	140.3	227.6	119.1	99.2	184.0	147.2	79.3	110.3	145.9	141.4	143.4
27	152.6	111.2	125.4	106.4	118.1	141.1	228.1	119.6	99.3	183.5	147.5	78.5	110.2	146.1	141.7	143.8
Feb. 3	153.2	111.5	125.5	106.3	118.1	145.8	228.7	120.2	99.3	185.3	148.0	78.6	110.3	147.6	142.8	144.8
10	152.8	111.7	125.4	106.3	118.2	146.4	227.0	119.9	99.2	185.3	147.9	77.9	110.4	147.5	142.7	144.7
17	156.6	112.3	126.6	107.0	126.7	147.4	230.0	121.5	99.4	189.1	150.7	77.0	111.5	148.9	144.6	146.6
24	159.7	111.8	127.9	106.6	127.2	148.8	233.9	123.3	99.6	192.1	152.5	74.2	111.2	150.2	145.9	148.0
March 3	160.2	112.2	127.7	106.2	127.5	148.9	234.2	123.5	99.8	193.8	152.6	77.2	111.2	150.4	146.3	149.1
10	156.6	111.7	126.9	106.0	126.2	149.5	231.3	119.7	99.7	191.7	151.0	80.1	110.8	149.6	145.2	148.1
17	158.4	111.9	127.1	106.1	126.4	144.3	232.6	118.2	99.6	194.1	151.5	77.3	110.9	148.8	144.8	147.6
23	158.2	111.8	127.7	106.3	127.3	143.4	232.5	117.8	99.6	196.2	151.7	78.3	111.1	148.8	144.8	147.7
31	159.3	111.9	127.0	106.3	127.9	142.8	235.5	115.4	99.7	201.3	151.7	77.6	111.1	149.3	145.3	148.2
April 7	159.6	112.3	127.6	106.1	128.4	142.0	233.6	113.8	99.6	199.8	152.2	77.6	111.1	149.0	145.2	148.1
14	156.6	112.0	127.1	105.9	127.5	141.7	233.2	113.1	99.6	200.1	151.1	77.8	110.9	148.8	144.8	147.8
21	155.3	111.9	126.2	106.0	127.0	140.8	231.6	113.7	99.5	199.6	149.7	79.2	110.8	148.2	144.0	146.8
28	155.8	112.0	126.0	106.1	126.6	140.5	232.5	113.3	99.6	199.8	149.6	78.6	110.8	148.3	144.1	146.9
May 5	155.5	112.0	126.0	106.1	126.3	139.9	231.7	113.3	99.5	199.2	149.2	78.7	110.8	148.0	143.8	146.6
12	152.8	112.3	125.0	106.3	125.1	139.1	228.8	111.8	99.5	196.8	147.6	78.7	110.9	147.1	142.7	145.7
19	152.3	112.3	124.9	106.3	125.1	138.9	228.4	112.7	99.4	197.6	147.5	78.4	110.9	147.0	142.7	145.5
26	151.7	112.1	124.0	106.2	124.9	138.2	227.4	111.6	99.4	196.6	147.4	77.3	110.7	146.5	142.1	144.9
June 2	154.5	112.7	124.5	106.5	125.3	138.6	229.3	111.0	99.4	198.7	148.4	75.9	111.1	147.3	143.0	145.9
9	154.1	112.6	125.2	106.4	126.0	138.7	228.3	110.7	99.4	198.0	148.3	76.5	111.1	147.1	142.8	145.8
16	153.6	112.9	124.9	106.5	125.3	138.4	227.6	108.0	99.3	197.0	147.6	76.0	111.2	146.9	142.6	145.4
23	154.9	113.0	124.5	106.7	126.0	138.8	228.4	104.5	99.6	196.9	147.7	75.3	111.4	147.1	142.7	145.3
30	155.3	113.3	125.3	106.8	126.3	136.8	228.1	103.1	99.6	195.6	147.5	75.0	111.6	146.6	142.3	145.3
July 7	156.1	113.3	126.1	107.2	127.5	136.5	228.4	102.8	99.7	195.9	148.0	74.2	112.0	146.7	142.5	145.6
14	156.8	113.3	125.9	107.2	127.5	136.1	228.3	102.9	99.7	195.0	148.1	73.9	111.9	146.5	142.4	145.5
21	156.9	113.3	125.8	107.4	127.3	136.1	228.2	102.3	99.6	192.5	148.1	73.2	112.0	146.3	142.2	145.3
28	157.1	113.3	125.5	107.5	127.4	135.0	228.4	97.4	99.7	192.8	147.9	73.2	112.0	146.1	142.0	145.1
Aug. 4	158.9	113.4	125.8	107.4	127.4	136.0	229.6	97.3	99.7	193.1	148.1	70.5	112.1	146.6	142.5	145.6
11	163.6	113.4	127.3	107.8	128.2	137.3	233.0	96.8	99.7	195.6	149.6	70.8	112.4	148.1	144.1	147.4
18	164.0	113.1	128.1	107.6	128.1	137.9	233.4	99.4	99.7	196.0	149.4	69.0	112.2	148.1	144.2	147.5
25	159.8	112.9	127.3	107.7	127.2	137.5	231.6	99.7	99.8	195.1	148.1	70.1	112.1	147.6	143.2	146.6
Sep. 1	162.2	113.2	127.9	107.8	128.2	137.9	232.8	100.9	99.9	195.8	149.6	68.6	112.4	148.1	143.9	147.3
8	161.5	113.2	128.6	107.8	128.0	137.8	231.8	100.3	99.9	195.2	149.5	68.0	112.3	147.8	143.6	147.1
15	162.8	113.3	127.0	107.9	128.6	138.6	232.9	100.4	100.1	194.8	149.6	67.4	112.5	148.2	144.1	147.5
22	164.6	113.4	127.4	108.0	128.6	141.3	234.3	100.9	100.2	196.7	151.2	65.7	112.5	149.4	145.1	148.6
29	166.2	113.3	127.6	108.0	128.3	140.8	235.3	102.1	100.3	197.9	152.2	67.0	112.5	149.5	145.6	149.1
Oct. 6	169.2	113.4	128.1	108.0	128.6	142.5	239.3	103.4	100.4	200.4	153.9	70.2	112.6	150.9	147.2	150.9
13	173.1	113.4	128.1	107.9	128.6	143.9	242.3	104.5	100.6	204.1	155.4	68.7	112.6	152.2	148.6	152.3
20	176.8	113.9	128.6	108.5	128.9	145.5	246.8	104.6	100.8	207.6	156.6	70.0	113.1	153.9	150.5	154.3
27	183.0	113.0	128.3	108.3	129.2	144.6	250.8	106.3	101.3	207.8	158.7	71.9	112.7	154.2	151.8	155.9
Nov. 3	170.6	112.4	127.4	107.1	128.9	143.0	245.0	104.0	101.2	202.1	153.6	71.8	111.7	151.8	148.1	152.1
10	170.7	112.7	127.4	107.3	128.9	143.6	246.3	104.4	101.2	203.4	154.0	72.3	112.0	152.4	148.6	152.6
17	168.6	113.0	127.7	107.5	129.0	144.7	245.2	106.3	101.1	202.5	153.4	74.5	112.2	152.6	148.5	152.5
24	167.7	113.1	127.6	107.7	129.5	144.6	244.9	105.6	101.2	202.8	153.7	75.2	112.4	152.6	148.5	152.4
Dec. 1	166.5	113.9	128.5	107.9	130.6	144.7	244.3	109.5	101.3	201.7	154.2	75.5	112.8	152.6	148.5	152.3
8	168.3	113.8	128.4	108.0	130.8	145.3	245.3	108.3	101.3	202.1	155.8	74.6	112.7	152.8	148.8	152.7
15	170.1	113.8	128.3	107.6	130.9	144.8	247.4	108.1	101.3	201.4	155.8	74.6	111.7	153.1	149.4	153.2
22	173.9	113.8	128.5	107.5	131.0	144.6	250.3	109.7	101.2	203.2	156.7	74.4	111.6	153.7	150.4	154.4
29	176.3	113.6	128.4	107.4	131.1	144.6	252.0	111.4	101.4	203.6	157.3	74.5	111.5	154.0	151.1	155.1

* For the method of calculation see the Statistical Supplements to the Monthly Reports of the Deutsche Bundesbank, Series 5. The currencies of the world, November 1977, page 55.

Source: Monthly Reports of the Deutsche Bundesbank, Frankfurt (Reproduced by permission)

Index

7